Advance praise for

Branded!

Branded! is a must read for everyone who ever wondered how to use their purchasing power to transform the behavior of giant corporations. Drawing on a wealth of insider knowledge, Conroy weaves a riveting tale of the people and strategies that have brought us fair trade coffee, certified wood, sweatshop free apparel, eco-tourism and more. His cogent analysis suggests the "certification revolution" has only just begun.

— Fran Korten, Publisher, *YES! Magazine*

Branded! illuminates through the knowledgeable lens of practice and applied analysis the emerging force of collaboratively-developed standards and certification initiatives as the 21st century's grass-roots driven approach to global governance.

— Simon Zadek, Chief Executive of AccountAbility, Senior Fellow at
J F Kennedy School for Government at Harvard University, and
author of the award-winning book, *The Civil Corporation*

Michael Conroy leads us on a remarkable tour de force of the development of certification systems and their impact on business sectors from forest products to retailers. His book is instructive reading for business leaders and civil activists alike.

— Travis Engen, former President & CEO, Alcan Inc.

Branded! is a must read for everyone interested in shaping more accountable corporate social responsibility standards and practices—ensuring that the economic metrics tell the whole truth about producing commodities, goods and services—and for those in the global justice and sustainability movement.

— J. Gabriel Lopez, Director of Global Strategies,
The World Conservation Union

An intriguing set of stories that depict the growing "age of corporate accountability." *Branded!* is required reading for every global business and NGO senior manager. Conroy surveys the past, exposes the present — and forecasts the "collaborative standards" on which corporations will be certified and ultimately valued by investors, employees, consumers and civil society."

— Barbara Fiorito, Board Chair, Oxfam America Advocacy Fund, and
Board Chair, Fair Trade Labelling Organizations International,
Board Chair, Forest Stewardship Council - US

As *Branded!* goes to print, a global network of NGOs is living the story told by Dr. Conroy and trying to bring accountability to the mining sector. The net result should be a guilt-free wedding ring, new incentives to mine right, and more accountability where it matters—in communities.

— Stephen D'Esposito,
president and executive director, Earthworks

I highly recommend *Branded!* as the best analysis I have ever seen of how and why sustainability certification is helping to transform the global marketplace. Michael Conroy looks at the warts as well as the successes, and gives a fair assessment of the prospects for certification over the long haul.

— Barbara Bramble, Senior Advisor for International Affairs,
National Wildlife Federation, and Board Chair, Forest Stewardship Council

Is it in global corporations' self-interest to act as environmental and social stewards? Conroy's book provides an insider's account of the answer to this question by assessing NGO efforts to 'certify' companies who agree to behave according to a set of "on the ground" standards, to target and shame non-compliers. *Branded!* will be indispensable to scholars and practitioners alike who care about understanding how market incentives can transform corporate behavior, and will be required reading for my class on corporate social responsibility.

— Benjamin Cashore, Professor,
Environmental Governance and Political Science, Yale University

BRANDED!

HOW THE 'CERTIFICATION REVOLUTION' IS TRANSFORMING GLOBAL CORPORATIONS

MICHAEL E. CONROY

NEW SOCIETY PUBLISHERS

CATALOGING IN PUBLICATION DATA

A catalog record for this publication is available from the National Library of Canada.

Cover design by Diane McIntosh.
Cover image © and courtesy of NoSweatShop.com.
Sneaker is a Hemp Hightop made with 100% organically-grown hemp uppers,
vegan and sweatshop-free, produced by the pioneers of the anti-sweatshop brand,
www.NoSweatShop.com, based in Massachusetts, USA.

Printed in Canada. First printing July 2007.
Paperback ISBN: 978-0-86571-579-0
Inquiries regarding requests to reprint all or part of *Branded!*
should be addressed to New Society Publishers at the address below.
To order directly from the publishers, please call toll-free
(North America) 1-800-567-6772, or order online at
www.newsociety.com

Any other inquiries can be directed by mail to:
New Society Publishers
P.O. Box 189,
Gabriola Island, BC V0R 1X0, Canada
(250) 247-9737

New Society Publishers' mission is to publish books that contribute in fundamental ways to building an ecologically sustainable and just society, and to do so with the least possible impact on the environment, in a manner that models this vision. We are committed to doing this not just through education, but through action. This book is one step toward ending global deforestation and climate change. It is printed on acid-free paper that is 100% post-consumer recycled (100% old growth forest-free), processed chlorine free, and printed with vegetable-based, low-VOC inks, with covers produced using Forest Stewardship Council-certified stock. Additionally, New Society purchases carbon offsets annually, operating with a carbon-neutral footprint. For further information, or to browse our full list of books and purchase securely, visit our website at: www.newsociety.com

NEW SOCIETY PUBLISHERS   www.newsociety.com

I dedicate this book
to my life partner and wife, Lucy Atkin,
whose help with conceptualization and tone was critical,
whose early reading of the whole book improved it immeasurably,
and without whom the dozen years of work behind its conceptualization
and completion would have been far less fulfilling…and much less fun.

And to my brother Ger Conroy, taken from us at the peak of his power,
in 2004, who continues to be my strongest inspiration
for the righteous pursuit of a fairer, saner, racism-free world.

And to Lucy's kids and mine, each inspiring in his or her own way,
while forging their own ethical futures in this increasingly complicated world.

And finally to the thousands of dedicated staff
of the scores of nonprofit organizations who labor for NGO salaries,
far less than they could earn in the corporations they seek to transform,
while moving this certification revolution forward.
You are the "salt of the earth," struggling for global social
and environmental accountability, and the hope of the future!

Contents

Acknowledgments

I want to acknowledge, with special *cariño,* the support of my colleagues at the Ford Foundation, who listened patiently — over nearly ten years — to my arguments on the importance of this evolving movement, and who approved, however reluctantly, significant amounts of financial support for the early development and later maturation of many of the certification systems discussed in this book. I am especially grateful for the strikingly generous research support of the Ford Foundation over the past three years, which permitted me to test my ideas in front of colleagues and students at Yale University's School of Forestry and Environmental Studies, to use its extraordinary library resources, and to engage a number of the students in the research process for this book. The Foundation's support also permitted me to lecture widely on the evolving global transformation of corporations and to participate in technical advisory and board capacities with a number of the key groups discussed here. Without that support, there would be no book. Without the Foundation's support to the dozens of organizations that have contributed extensively to this corporate transformation, there might be significantly less transformation.

My colleagues at the Rockefeller Brothers Fund (RBF) have been supremely patient with my extracurricular attention to the continuing development of the modern certification movement over the last three years of my work with them in philanthropy. It was not, they all recognize, a direct part of my job responsibilities, but their patience was kindled, I hope, by their appreciation of the importance of what was occurring. RBF did, in fact, contribute significantly to the development of sustainable forestry certification in terms of both financial resources and the leadership resources of its staff. The insightful work of RBF's Michael Northrop has been inspirational.

At Yale I had the privilege of teaching seminars, together with my colleague Ben Cashore, on certification of sustainable forest management and on broader certification systems and their relationship to corporate accountability. Students from those seminars will find many of my ideas, raw at the time of my presentations to them, now somewhat better defined because of their comments and critiques. I am indebted to all of them and grateful. The broader support of students and staff of the Yale Program on Forest Certification convinced me, time and again, that Yale was the best place for working on these topics, and it will continue to be, well into the future.

I am especially pleased to have this book appear among the excellent publications of New Society Publishers, where positive stories on critical issues of social change inspire readers around the world. Their publishing ethic incorporates the best accountability in their field, a good reflection of the leading practices of the Canadian publishing industry: FSC-certified, 100% post-consumer recycled paper, processed chlorine free, and printed with vegetable-based inks low in volatile organic compounds. And their entire operation is now "carbon neutral." I appreciate both the commitment and the patience of Chris Plant and Ingrid Witvoet as the book came together less quickly than any of us preferred. Audrey McClellan, the editor they assigned to the task of transforming my Byzantine academic prose into something much more readable, has been both brilliant and patient in gently improving every paragraph.

Preface

There is a movement afoot that has the potential to transform the way global corporations do their work. It is also capable of affecting producers positively at all levels, from artisanal fishers, farmers, miners, and loggers to larger, but not global, companies producing myriad products all around the world. Glimpses of the movement are popping up with increasing frequency in many places, from the *Financial Times* and the *Wall Street Journal* to Oprah Winfrey's *O, The Oprah Magazine* and industry journals in every field affected.

Whispers about the efficacy and reach of this movement are heard in corporate boardrooms as well as in union halls and in church, temple, and synagogue sanctuaries. Many people, on both the political right and the political left, are skeptical, partly because this movement creates unusual — and some would say unholy — alliances between hard-hitting advocacy nongovernmental organizations (NGOs), other nonprofit organizations trying to facilitate the effectiveness of the movement without taking harsh positions, and the very corporations they are trying to influence.

I will refer to this movement as the "certification movement." It produces what I call the "certification revolution," which occurs in three stages:

- Nonprofit civil society organizations create new standards for corporate social and environmental accountability, often in stakeholder negotiations with companies themselves.
- Companies are moved to adopt those standards, either because of internal corporate culture and the new business opportunities they offer or due to NGO pressure in the form of tough market campaigns.
- Newly created, nonprofit, standard-setting organizations implement a credible and efficient method for certifying corporate compliance with the new standards.

What the certification revolution has achieved, contrary to most expectations prior to about 15 years ago, is nothing less than a profound transformation of the social and environmental practices of global corporations representing significant portions of the industries on which they focus. In *Branded!* we will be looking at case studies describing specific attempts to bring greater social and environmental accountability to major sectors of the economy. We will also be analyzing a large body of information, with many concrete examples, in order to evaluate the effectiveness of the three central phenomena on which the book focuses: the changing expectations of accountability, powerful market campaigns, and the creation of certification systems as new solutions for the accountability challenges.

MY BACKGROUND

I confess to being a lifelong economist, with nearly 35 years of teaching economics courses and writing about economic problems behind me. In that time, the professional field of economics has narrowed to focus on mathematical modeling of greatly simplified theoretical economic systems, which may or may not reflect the reality of economic life for the majority of the world's population. As a result, my colleagues would classify me as a political economist. I find no fault with that label, since it gives me the right to draw upon several hundred years of economic thinking, economic history, and economic theory to analyze phenomena with straightforward statistics, logic, and observation. It also saves me from the ultimate curse of economists: the notion that we see something happening in the real world and spend our careers attempting to find out whether it can happen in theory!

I have taught and published in a variety of economics fields, but have concentrated mostly on the theory and practice of economic development (with special emphasis on Latin America and the Caribbean), urban and regional economics, the economics of sustainable development, and economic demography. The work behind this book taps much of that background, as well as theories of the firm and international economics.

After 23 years of teaching at the University of Texas at Austin, I was offered an opportunity to work, on sabbatical leave, for the Ford Foundation. To the delight of some of my Texas colleagues and, I hope, the disappointment of others, I never looked back. The opportunity provided to foundation program officers, which I enjoyed for nearly 12 years, has astounding reach and potential. Foundation staff are in the position to help nascent movements blossom and grow, sitting in the catbird seat while others do the truly hard work of building the movement. Foundation staff can connect, encourage, scold, or punish, while dedicating much of their own time to understanding how the bigger picture, the broader scenario, is evolving. And the ultimate satisfaction from that work is the thrill of seeing something new and powerful, built through the efforts of hundreds of hardworking NGOs, expanding more rapidly than anyone can trace, and developing self-sufficiency and an innate ability to adapt and grow. One of the purposes of this book is to share that thrill with you.

METHODOLOGY

The material in this book is drawn from over a decade of work with certification systems on several levels: as a funder, an analyst, a board member of some of the certifying organizations, a strategist working with some of the market campaign organizations, and an academic focused on studying, and teaching about, the political and economic significance of what we were seeing on the ground.

Most of the information presented here is closely footnoted. Yet there is a large body of information to which I had access that consists of the unpublished, and often confidential, internal documents of the designers and organizers of the market campaigns that I will describe. Their work is generally available only to those with whom they work closely, for it often contains important strategic considerations and other confidential information. The authors and owners of those documents have encouraged me to draw freely from them, on the condition that I not reveal tactical information that might compromise future campaigns and that I keep the existence of the documents, details of the conversations, or, in several cases, the names of the authors confidential.

A couple of caveats: The book is far too short and the material far too complex to allow me to include adequate reference to all the individuals and groups who should be mentioned in each chapter. Most of the chapters could easily be expanded into books of their own, which would allow historical completeness. As well, the book is hopelessly biased toward experiences in and around the United States, despite its pretense of covering the transformation of global corporations. That's an inevitable result of the historical experience behind my own analysis and my relative lack of experience on these issues outside the US.

TRANSPARENCY ANNOUNCEMENTS

It is important that I make even clearer the relationships that I have had with some of the organizations mentioned in this book. The portfolio that I managed for the Ford Foundation included, over the years, a broad initiative to support the development of certification systems for natural resource management and poverty alleviation. The Foundation provided extensive support for the Forest Stewardship Council, several of its country-specific national organizations, and other FSC-supporting organizations. It also supported the Rainforest Alliance's programs on forest certification, especially Smartwood and TREES, as well as its rapidly developing work on sustainable tourism. Support for sustainable tourism certification went to the International Ecotourism Society, the Center for Ecotourism and Sustainable Development, and the United Nations Environment Program. The Ford Foundation was an early *padrino* for TransFair USA, from its inception and into its present period of meteoric growth, while also providing support for advocacy organizations, such as Oxfam America, Lutheran World Relief, and Co-op America, that stimulated the growth of the Fair Trade movement in the US.

The Ford Foundation provided support, on my watch, for market campaign organizations such as ForestEthics and Rainforest Action Network. It supported early efforts toward mining certification through Earthworks (initially under its previous name, Mineral Policy Center), as well as explorations of community-based mining standards in the Andean region of Latin America through funding provided to the Environmental Law Institute. During the years I worked for the Rockefeller Brothers Fund, I managed grants that supported the incipient development of a common set of stakeholder-based standards for big-box stores, such as Wal-Mart.

I should also make it clear that while I was completing this book, I served on a number of NGO boards related to the certification revolution. They include the international board of the Forest Stewardship Council, where I was a nonvoting technical advisor, and the board of the FSC Global Fund, a small fundraising organization dedicated to strengthening the FSC. I served on the board of directors of Earthworks, the NGO advocating standard setting for the mining industry. I was elected in 2003 to the board of directors of TransFair USA, and in 2006 to the governing board of FLO Cert, the wholly owned auditing and accreditation arm of Fairtrade Labeling Organizations International, the global governing body for Fair Trade certification. One of my struggles in writing this book has been to ensure that I don't draw on information I have accessed confidentially as a member of one of these boards. I trust, however, that these background experiences enrich the material you will read, and that this transparency will allow you to recognize, and appreciate, the biases that these experiences necessarily carry.

— Michael E. Conroy
May 2007

Branded!
The Unexpected Consequences
of Successful Global Branding

"Branding" is the name of the global corporate game in the 21st century. But what a risky game it is! Brands may be the most important assets of many global corporations. Brands may also be their most vulnerable assets. Corporations can spend millions of dollars strengthening public awareness of their brands, but a small mistake in production, a thoughtless policy, or an attempt to cut corners to eke out a little extra profit may turn all their investment in building brand awareness into a scathing critique. That could lead to a global rejection of products associated with that brand, both by consumers and, more importantly, by other businesses to whom they sell. The world is now full of organizations that are more than delighted to bring those shortsighted production practices, or those errors, to global attention.

In this book I analyze the transformation of global branding, the most powerful tool for expanding sales worldwide, into a strategy that gives both businesses and consumers around the world more power than they have ever had to encourage and reward the responsible practices of producers everywhere. They can also discourage and punish irresponsible practices in ways that were inconceivable just 20 years ago.

In this opening chapter, I will show how branding has become both a corporate marketing department's dream…and its nightmare. We will see how the *No Logo* movement, inspired by Naomi Klein's book of the same name, which encouraged consumer advocates to avoid major global corporate brands in order to change global corporate practices, can be modified, just slightly, so that pressure on those brands might transform corporate practices much more effectively.

We begin by exploring a series of seemingly improbable events in which corporations turned away from what appeared to be their most profitable short-term courses of action and moved toward potentially more responsible social and environmental practices, encouraged by both business partners and consumers. We will revisit the age-old concept of "certification" and see how contemporary certification systems just might be producing a "revolutionary" transformation of corporate behavior.

SEEMINGLY IMPROBABLE CORPORATE EVENTS

There has been a revolution in the ability of advocacy organizations to affect corporate markets directly. If you doubt this, examine with me the following changes in corporate practices that have emerged in recent years.[1]

- In June 1998, **MacMillan Bloedel (MacBlo)**, a giant Vancouver-based timber and paper company, announced that it would dramatically change its logging practices throughout British Columbia by eliminating clearcutting, moving to variable retention in logging, increasing the number of trees it left standing on the banks of streams, and, in general, adhering to the sustainable forest management practices of an international nongovernmental organization (NGO) called the **Forest Stewardship Council (FSC)**. Though an announcement of that sort was not unprecedented — many forest management companies in Europe had made the same commitment between 1995 and 1998 — MacBlo was the first Canadian company to publicly endorse the FSC. Greenpeace, the Natural Resources Defense Council, the Sierra Club, and several other environmental groups were present at the press conference to encourage businesses and consumers around the world to give preference to the products of MacBlo, even though they had been excoriating the company for years in the harshest of terms. How did the environmental groups convince this company to change its logging practices, even though it was apparent that logging costs would be higher?

- Just months later, in October 1999, the **Rainforest Action Network (RAN)** published a full-page advertisement in the *New York Times,* urging consumers nationwide to shop at **Home Depot,** the largest do-it-yourself chain in the United States. The ad was unlikely for many reasons. RAN had actively campaigned against Home Depot for more than two years, orchestrating over 700 demonstrations in stores and at shareholder meetings to criticize the company's lumber-purchasing policies. The *Times* ad followed Home Depot's decision, announced on August 26, 1999, to end all purchases of wood products from "old-growth" forests and to give preference in its purchases to products certified as coming from forests managed more sustainably using the principles and criteria of the same Forest Stewardship Council. Why would Home Depot make that commitment, pay a price premium for FSC-certified products, and not increase the price of the sustainably harvested wood products in its stores?

- In April 2000, **Starbucks** announced that it would offer **Fair Trade Certified** coffee in every one of the 2,700 outlets that it owned in the United States, even though that coffee was going to cost considerably more than the uncertified coffees the company was currently selling. Since then, Starbucks has continued to expand its purchases of Fair Trade coffee, reporting in 2005 that it was buying more than 10 million pounds a year. In response to the Starbucks decision, Global Exchange, a social activist organization based in Oakland, California, turned threatened demonstrations against Starbucks in 30 US cities into celebrations at the company's stores, encouraging consumers to patronize those shops over cafés that did not offer Fair Trade Certified coffee.

- In June 2003, **Citigroup,** the world's largest financial institution, led a consortium of ten banks that announced they would be embracing strict new voluntary standards "to prevent massive construction efforts [which they financed in whole or in part] from poisoning the air and water, denuding forests, and destroying the livelihoods of locals who get in the way."[2] The principles to which they agreed to abide, created in collaboration with the World Bank's International Finance Corporation, were called the **Equator Principles.** Why would these banks, and more than 30 others that have agreed to adopt the principles through mid-2006, create a new mechanism that effectively legitimates the criticism they had been receiving for years from the unintended victims of the projects to which they were lending money? Why would Citigroup take the lead in organizing its most avid competitors to sign a set of principles that meant increased social and environmental scrutiny of all their project lending, after arguing for years that there was no need to do so?

- In October 2004, the simple announcement of a new campaign by another advocacy organization, **ForestEthics,** to encourage **Victoria's Secret,** the lingerie and clothing company, to reduce the use of virgin wood fiber in its catalogs generated articles in the *Wall Street Journal* and the *Globe and Mail,* Canada's leading business newspaper. ForestEthics, a small NGO based in Portland, Oregon, criticized Victoria's Secret because the 395 million catalogs that it mailed each year (more than a million a day) were manufactured almost exclusively from pulp drawn from Canadian forests where stands of old-growth trees, herds of caribou, and grizzly bear populations were endangered. ForestEthics called for a gradual shift to 50 percent recycled paper in the catalogs. Within two weeks of the launch of the campaign, the share price of Limited Brands, Inc., Victoria's Secret's parent company, began to fall from its historic high. Over the next year, punctuated by expanding protests in front of Victoria's Secret shops and by advertisements placed in major national newspapers (see page 4), the stock price fell by 32 percent. How is it that the business press and financial markets have become so sensitive to environmental challenges affecting major brands that a campaign by a small NGO is immediate news and leads to severe loss in share value if the company refuses to deal quickly with the problem?

- In April 2005, a large and coordinated campaign to transform many of the social and environmental practices of **Wal-Mart,** the world's largest private-sector employer, was launched by a coalition of nearly 80 American grassroots and advocacy NGOs and two major US labor unions. For more than 15 years, advocates in the "socially responsible investment community," such as the Interfaith Coalition for Corporate Responsibility, had been attempting to persuade Wal-Mart to change the labor and environmental practices at its suppliers' factories, as well as at its burgeoning number of retail stores, with little or no impact. In the 20 months that followed the launch of the concerted campaign, Wal-Mart made no fewer than 35 major, concrete commitments to change its practices. These addressed a wide range of energy and

VICTORIA'S DIRTY SECRET

Some companies get a tree for the holidays.
Victoria's Secret is taking a whole forest.

Every day, Victoria's Secret mails more than a million catalogs—most of which are printed on paper that comes from Endangered Forests, not recycled fiber.

To you, all those catalogs are probably annoying. To the environment, they've been devastating.

For example, 25% of that paper comes from North America's Great Boreal Forest. The Boreal is a vital line of defense against climate change—and it's being logged at a rate of two acres per minute, 24 hours a day.

The worst part is this: the destruction is completely unnecessary. Major catalog companies like Williams-Sonoma, Dell and Norm Thompson Outfitters have proven that. They've found that it's possible— and economically feasible—to make significant improvements to the environmental quality of their paper.

Even Victoria's Secret knows it's possible. Because of our campaign, they've switched to recycled paper for all of their clearance catalogs. Unfortunately, that's less than 10% of their catalog production—leaving 900,000 catalogs a day still printed on paper that's destroying our forests.

So we'll keep exposing Victoria's Dirty Secret—and you can help.
Go to **www.VictoriasDirtySecret.net** and send Victoria's Secret CEO Leslie Wexner a fax.
Tell him that taking down an entire forest for the holidays just isn't very merry.

FORESTETHICS

Because protecting forests is everyone's business · ONE HAIGHT STREET · SAN FRANCISCO, CALIFORNIA 94102 · 1.800.725.0087 · www.ForestEthics.org

environmental issues, health benefits for its workers, and improvements in its scrutiny of the labor practices in the factories of its suppliers. What set off this cascade of transforming changes in Wal-Mart's corporate behavior after so many years of resisting change?

- In June 2006, representatives of some of the world's largest mining companies (including Newmont and BHP Billiton), representatives of some of the world's largest and most distinguished jewelry companies (including Tiffany and, yes, Wal-Mart), and representatives of advocacy NGOs attempting to transform mining practices (such as Earthworks and Mining Watch Canada) agreed to the **Initiative for Responsible Mining Assurance.** Driven by pressures from both the retail jewelry industry and the NGOs, the initiative should lead to the first comprehensive set of standards for more equitable, sustainable, and responsible mining practices worldwide. The industry committed itself to this new initiative after more than five years of attempting to create alternative standard-setting mechanisms through industry-led organizations such as the International Council for Mining and Minerals and the Council for Responsible Jewelry Practices, which never managed to gain much traction among consumers. But why would companies that had belittled advocacy efforts in the past decide the time was right for reaching an agreement and setting up a system to reassure consumers and business partners?

The number of companies involved in significant social and environmental change is far greater than this short list illustrates. According to the Business Ethics Network, advocacy campaigns in the United States have also led to the following transformations in major corporations:

- **Dell Computer** announced it would stop using prison labor to disassemble its recycled computers and, following industry leader HP, recently signed contracts with eco-recycling firms. This is just the first step toward motivating computer manufacturers to take responsibility for the entire life cycle of their products and shift toward continuous recycling of materials.
- **McDonald's** is now requiring its suppliers to treat animals more humanely and to reduce use of antibiotics. As a consequence, McDonald's is transforming not just fast food but factory farming as well.
- **Kaiser Permanente** and **Catholic Health Care West** — two of North America's largest hospital chains — have virtually stopped incinerating medical waste, and major retailers have phased out their sales of mercury thermometers. Former opponents in the hospital industry have allied themselves with public health advocates working to phase out the production and use of toxic chemicals.
- Grassroots pressure on tobacco giant **Philip Morris/Altria,** including a boycott targeting its Kraft Foods subsidiary, contributed to the company's adoption of the Framework Convention on Tobacco Control (FCTC) — the first global health and corporate accountability treaty.[3]

Lester Brown of *World Watch* commented on the MacBlo decision in terms that seem appropriate to all the events described here: "Among giant corporations that could once be counted on to mount a monolithic opposition to serious environmental reform, a growing number of high-profile CEOs have begun to sound more like spokespersons for Greenpeace than for the bastions of global capitalism of which they are a part. . . . What in the world is going on?"[4]

This book will lead you from questions about these seemingly improbable events, which occurred over the first 15 years of what I call the "certification revolution," to an understanding of the motivations of NGOs, corporations, and consumers for supporting it. We will examine the decision-making processes in some of the leading firms practicing a new corporate accountability. And we will reflect on the efforts of many companies to ignore the revolution, often at their own peril.

The answers begin with *branding* and its links to new forms of 21st century corporate accountability. They lead, in the most effective cases, to the creation of global "certification systems" that help companies transform their corporate practices and grant them credit in the marketplace for that transformation...but only if the certification has credible independent verification. This combination of forces and actors constitutes a revolutionary new form of global governance with power that transcends national boundaries in the same way that multinational corporations transcend those boundaries. It gives civil society, worldwide, new power to demand, and to reward, corporate practices that raise the bar on environmental protection and social responsibility. It is a very positive and encouraging new world!

FROM BRANDING TO *BRANDED!*

Most of us first encounter the concept of "branding" in tales of the American West or the Australian Outback, or in simple experiences on farms and ranches, where a brand is the iron stamp, often heated in a fire, that is used to leave an indelible mark on horses or other livestock. Current use of the term is not far removed from that original meaning.

> *A product's brand, if successful, leaves an indelible mark in what some have called "the most valuable real estate in the world: the corner of a consumer's mind."* [5]

The word "brand" conveys more specific meanings today:
- "Simply put, a brand is a promise. By identifying and authenticating a product or service it delivers a pledge of satisfaction and quality." Walter Landor, advertising genius.
- A brand is "a set of assets (or liabilities) linked to a brand's name and symbol that adds to (or subtracts from) the value provided by a product or service." David Aaker, *Building Strong Brands*.
- More succinctly, "a brand is a collection of perceptions in the mind of the consumer." [6]

The brand tells us first about the standard qualities of a product: how well it will work and how long it will last. For services, the brand tells us how efficiently and pleasantly the service will be rendered. In both cases, for products as well as services, it also conveys some sense of the satisfaction that we will receive from purchasing them. And satisfaction will be associated with stylishness and other aesthetics, as well as the standard qualities of the product or service itself.

In business, the purpose of branding is to create a name or a symbol that consumers associate positively with products and services. But branding can have negative connotations as well as positive ones. Brand management is the science of creating positive associations with the name and symbol. Brand risk management is the set of strategies protecting the brand from acquiring negative connotations that drive away consumers and business partners.

Branding is ancient. Potter's marks on Greek and Roman clay pots identified those made by individual potters, using symbols such as a star, a cross, a fish, or a thumbprint.[7] The creation of the brand, however, did little to protect the potter. The British Museum has examples of imitation Roman pottery, which analysts have determined were manufactured in Belgium and exported to Britain two thousand years ago, with imitation Roman potter's marks.[8]

It wasn't until the 19th and 20th centuries that branding became synonymous with the products of major global companies: Singer sewing machines, Coca Cola beverages, Quaker oat products, Kodak film, and American Express travelers checks are some of the best-known examples. What are some of the elements that each of these brands carry?

- They are "intrinsically striking." That is, they developed a visual distinctiveness based on a name, a symbol, a signature, a shape, a slogan, or a recognizable typeface.
- They create an "indelible impression." They permit consumers to "shop with confidence" in the midst of an often bewildering array of competing products from producers whose reputations may be unknown.
- They carry "underlying appeals." They imply lifestyles, suggest values, and link buyers to others whose judgment or choices or purchasing patterns they may want to emulate.[9]

Brands become business assets as quickly as they become recognized. But they also become business liabilities when they are associated with negative characteristics of products, such as low quality, bad reputation, or unpleasant experiences. The value of brands, as assets, can greatly exceed the value of the tangible wealth of companies. The Coca-Cola Company was valued at about $136 billion in 2002, but the total value of all its tangible assets (buildings, factories, delivery vehicles, vending machines, and inventories of product) was little more than $10.5 billion. Most of its market value lay in the value of its brand, the highest valued brand in the world.[10]

Corporate missteps can have a huge impact on shareholder value when they affect the brand. In 1999, 30 Belgian schoolchildren became ill after handling, and drinking from, Coca-Cola cans. The government banned the sale of Coca-Cola for ten days, until the problem was resolved. This cost Coca-Cola hundreds of millions of dollars in direct sales losses, but its shareholder value plunged by billions of dollars because of the damage to the brand. In March 2004, Coca-Cola launched its Dasani-brand bottled water in the United Kingdom, only to recall all 500,000 bottles because a manufacturing error left excessive levels of bromate in the water, giving it a foul taste. Critics also called attention to the potential carcinogenic properties of bromate. The recall, which took only 24 hours, had far less impact on profitability than the damage to the Dasani and Coca-Cola brands in European markets.[11]

The importance of branding to the share value of corporations can be seen in Figure 1.2, taken from a report by Interbrand published in *Business Week* magazine. For 12 of the 100 companies with the most valuable brands, brand value accounts for more than 50 percent of the company's market capitalization. The same figure shows how the value of the brand can change rapidly. Eight of the companies suffered losses in their brand value between 2004 and 2005. Interbrand also reported that 18 of the 100 most valuable brands in the world declined in value between 2004 and 2005. The largest decline took place at Morgan Stanley, where brand value dropped 15 percent, losing nearly $1.5 billion in shareholder value, following a troubling shake-up in the company's senior management that drew much attention in the financial press.

The enormous value of brands and the efforts of companies to maximize the value of their brands so as to raise share value has also generated an "antibranding" movement that peaked with the publication of Naomi Klein's powerful book *No Logo*.[12] Klein chastises corporations for seeking to raise brand value, which she sees as having no useful social purpose, rather than providing more products and services at lower prices or providing responsible engagement with communities and workers. She lambastes the biggest and baddest of the companies for driving down wages, pillaging the environment, abusing human rights, giving in to repressive regimes, and undercutting their home-country labor force by "outsourcing" work to labor markets where wages are more exploitative. Hers is a proudly "anti-globalization" tract, cast as a series of battles on production fronts around the world. And it sold more than 40,000 copies in its first year on the market. One review of the book argued, while disagreeing with its fundamental premises, that "this is a book that should be read by all age groups to understand why rioters trash McDonald's and Starbucks," because the "immediate target" is "a corporate culture that substitutes image (brand) for substance (decent jobs and conditions)."[13]

I do not disagree with the basic premises laid out by Klein, but in *Branded!* we will see that the brands themselves give civil society new leverage for solving some of the corporate problems she addressed. We will explore and analyze a series of mechanisms for transforming corporate behavior that have evolved and become successful in the years since the publication of *No Logo*. These new mechanisms actually tap into and use fundamental characteristics of global-

Figure 1.2. Brand Value as Percent of Market Capitalization for Top 25 of the 100 Most Valuable Brands in 2005

Rank by % of Market Cap	Company	Brand Value as % of Market Capitalization	2005 Brand Value ($ million)	2004–05 % Change in Brand Value	Rank by Brand Value
1	Bulgari	80%	2,715	*	94
2	Tiffany & Co.	77%	3,618	-1%	81
3	McDonald's	71%	26,014	4%	8
4	Ford	71%	13,159	-9%	22
5	Kodak	66%	4,979	-5%	62
6	Coca-Cola	64%	67,525	0%	1
7	BMW	61%	17,126	8%	16
8	Porsche	58%	3,777	4%	76
9	Heinz	55%	6,932	-1%	47
10	Gucci	55%	6,619	**	49
11	Harley-Davidson	53%	7,346	4%	46
12	Adidas	53%	4,033	8%	71
13	Mercedes	49%	20,006	-6%	11
14	Hermes	48%	3,540	5%	82
15	Disney	46%	26,441	-2%	7
16	Nintendo	46%	6,470	0%	50
17	Nike	45%	10,114	9%	30
18	Kellogg's	44%	8,306	3%	39
19	Louis Vuitton	44%	16,077	**	18
20	IBM	44%	53,376	-1%	3
21	Xerox	43%	5,705	0%	54
22	Wrigley's	43%	5,543	2%	57
23	Gap	43%	8,195	4%	40
24	Volkswagen	39%	5,617	-12%	56
25	Reuters	37%	3,866	5%	74

* New to the top 100 this year
** Restatement
Source: Interbrand, Inc. Published in *Business Week,* July 2006.

ization, especially the enormous increase in Internet-based communications among NGOs, to turn the tables on the corporations that are associated with many of those practices. The certification revolution offers a new solution to the problems identified by Klein, and the new solution is based directly on the importance and value of branding to corporations themselves.

Brands have become the point of leverage for a rapidly increasing number of NGO efforts to change corporate practices through "market campaigns." As we will see in much more detail in Chapter 3, a market campaign is a set of strategies designed to influence business and consumer purchases by informing buyers of some characteristics of the supply chain that might make them avoid a particular product. It is a direct attack on the brand of a company, or a product line, based on information about that company's practices, and it is designed to push some of the company's production or supply-chain activities toward more socially and environmentally responsible practices. It seeks to do that by reducing both sales of those products *and* the shareholder value embodied in the brand (see Profile 1.1). From the point of view of one of the leading analysts of market campaigns, the attacks on products and brands seek to inspire a "race to the top" in social and environmental practices, replacing the race to the bottom that fundamental forces of globalization seem to be promoting.[14]

The techniques developed by the market campaigners in recent years have become extraordinarily sophisticated. We will discuss them in greater detail in Chapter 3, but for now, in order to complete the introductory picture I am sketching here, we need a preliminary knowledge of "certification systems" so that we understand the combined strategies that persuade companies to engage with the creation of new standards in order to reduce the risk of attacks on their brands and improve their ability to market to a rapidly expanding "ethical marketplace."

THE BASICS OF CERTIFICATION SYSTEMS

"Certification" is a process that enters our lives in many ways every day. We hear radio advertisements for "certified pre-owned cars." Many readers may be certified public accountants, and hundreds of other professions include systems for certifying that their practitioners meet certain standards of knowledge and skill. Software is often certified as compatible with certain operating systems. We purchase certified organic and Fair Trade Certified products. All these systems have several characteristics in common:

- There is a set of standards that must be met in order to achieve the certification.
- There is a process for verifying that a product, a service, or a person has met those standards.
- There is a "certification mark," logo, or seal that identifies the standards and the verification that have been fulfilled.
- There is a system for auditing to ensure that the certification mark is being used properly and that the product or service or individual continues to meet the standards over time.

One of the oldest certification systems that is still in use today is that provided by Underwriters Laboratories Inc. Underwriters Laboratories (UL) was founded in 1894 by the insurance industry as a not-for-profit testing facility for "electric" products that were then emerging. It developed voluntary standards for public safety that companies were encouraged to use, both to avoid the financial risk associated with consumer injuries arising from faulty products and, critically, to meet the expectations (and ultimately the requirements) of insurers. Some of us are old enough to remember when a new electric appliance, say a toaster, was just as likely to splutter and spark, when first plugged in, as it was to function properly.

A Corporate Cautionary Tale

The Story of Nike

A new English-language verb has appeared in recent years that describes both the phenomenon of market campaigns and the worst corporate nightmares that arise from them. The verb is "to be niked," and it refers to the classic case of the impact of social practices in the Nike supply chain, which were analyzed, and pilloried, in the mid-1990s. It is what no company wants to experience in the future.

Nike is the legendary company that grew and prospered by outsourcing the production of footwear, and then apparel, to those countries where labor costs were as low as possible and labor practices were generally not scrutinized.[15] Founded in 1964 by Phil Knight and Bill Bowerman, the company established the Nike brand in 1972. Although initially producing in Japan and New England, by 1982 Nike had moved 86 percent of its production to Korea and Taiwan. As economic development began to increase labor costs there, Nike created a network of footwear factories throughout Southeast Asia. By 1991 its share of the global footwear market reached 22.5 percent; spectacular growth then took it to 35.3 percent by 1997. During that growth period, Nike stock rose from $8 per share to $70 per share.

Then the troubles began to hit. Criticism of labor practices in the factories of Nike suppliers began early in this period of enormous growth. *Harper's Magazine* featured a two-page "Annotation" by Jeffrey Ballinger, a labor rights activist in Indonesia, who showed that women workers in a Nike supplier plant were making about one dollar per day in wages for 10.5 hours of work, including forced overtime, and that the cost of labor to produce a single $80 pair of Nike shoes was approximately 12 cents. A number of advocacy groups began to coordinate a campaign for social change in Nike's supplier factories. They included Vietnam Labor Watch (New York), Community Aid Abroad (Sydney), Hong Kong Christian Industrial Committee (Hong Kong), Global Exchange (Oakland), and Transnational Resource & Action Center (San Francisco). Nike's response was that it was not responsible for those conditions because it did not own the factories where the shoes were made.

A CBS News *48 Hours* report in October 1996, narrated by Dan Rather, began a virtual flood of negative news on conditions in Nike's supplier factories around the world. CBS interviewed workers in Vietnam, who complained of physical abuse and sexual assault on the production line, at the same time as Nike headquarters was celebrating record high profit levels. A month later the *Washington Post* published a feature-length story on conditions in a factory in China that produced for both Nike and Reebok. The reporter documented "harshly regimented labor conditions," corporal punishment of workers, forced 12-hour shifts, and "prison-like" conditions, with workers not allowed out of the compound except on weekends.[16] A Harvard Business School case study of this period analyzed media mentions that linked Nike with "exploitation," "sweatshops," and "child labor." From virtually no links in 1995, the campaign against Nike led to nearly 300 articles linking Nike to those conditions in 1997.[17] Nike's problems even became a story line in the popular *Doonesbury* cartoon strip. Mike Doonesbury takes his Vietnamese orphan girlfriend back to Vietnam, where she finds that her only living relative is working on the production line in a Nike supplier factory (see Figure 1.3).

Nike responded by commissioning Andrew Young, the African American civil rights icon and former US ambassador to the United Nations, to investigate conditions in 12 of its suppliers' plants. Young returned and produced a 75-page full-color report in which he claimed that he had found "no evidence or pattern of widespread abuse or mistreatment of workers." The report was ridiculed by *The New Republic* as "a classic sham, marred not just by shoddy methodology but by frequent misrepresentations."[18] The magazine noted that Young had relied solely on translators provided by Nike's suppliers, listed consultants who were never consulted, and included photos of "union representatives" who were not, in fact, representatives of any union. Then an Ernst and Young report, commissioned by Nike, was leaked to the *New York Times*. The front-page *Times* article, based on Nike's own report, indicated that workers, mostly women, in Nike supplier plants in Vietnam were exposed to environmental carcinogens at 177 times the limit allowed by Vietnamese standards, and most had no protective gear. They labored 10.5 hours a day for six days a week and earned slightly more than $10 a week at a time when Nike posted $800 million in profits on $9.6 billion in sales.[19]

The financial consequences of the campaign began to show. Revenues fell by 16 percent in the last quarter of Nike's 1997–98 fiscal year, and profits per share plunged 49 percent. The stock, which peaked at $73.09 on February 18, 1997, fell by 57 percent to $31.15 on September 2, 1998, during the period of heaviest media criticism. The *New York Times* reported on "the swoon of the swoosh," noting that "having plastered the world with a corporate icon rivaled perhaps only by Coca-Cola's cursive, Nike is trying to tone it down, hide it, possibly even lose it." Nike's "brand soul" had been especially hurt by "the spate of negative stories about its overseas labor practices and its defensive posture."[20]

Nike has rebounded since then, partly due to the creation of a stronger set of labor standards and the adoption of some of the better mechanisms for factory monitoring, which we will discuss in Chapter 10. However, as we will see in that chapter, even in 2007 there are no widely credible, enforceable labor standards and no widely applicable labor certification system in the footwear and apparel industries. Nike has reduced its vulnerability, and in doing so it has countered some of the worst criticism. But it remains vulnerable to continued well-documented criticism and further reputational damage to its brand and its financial performance.

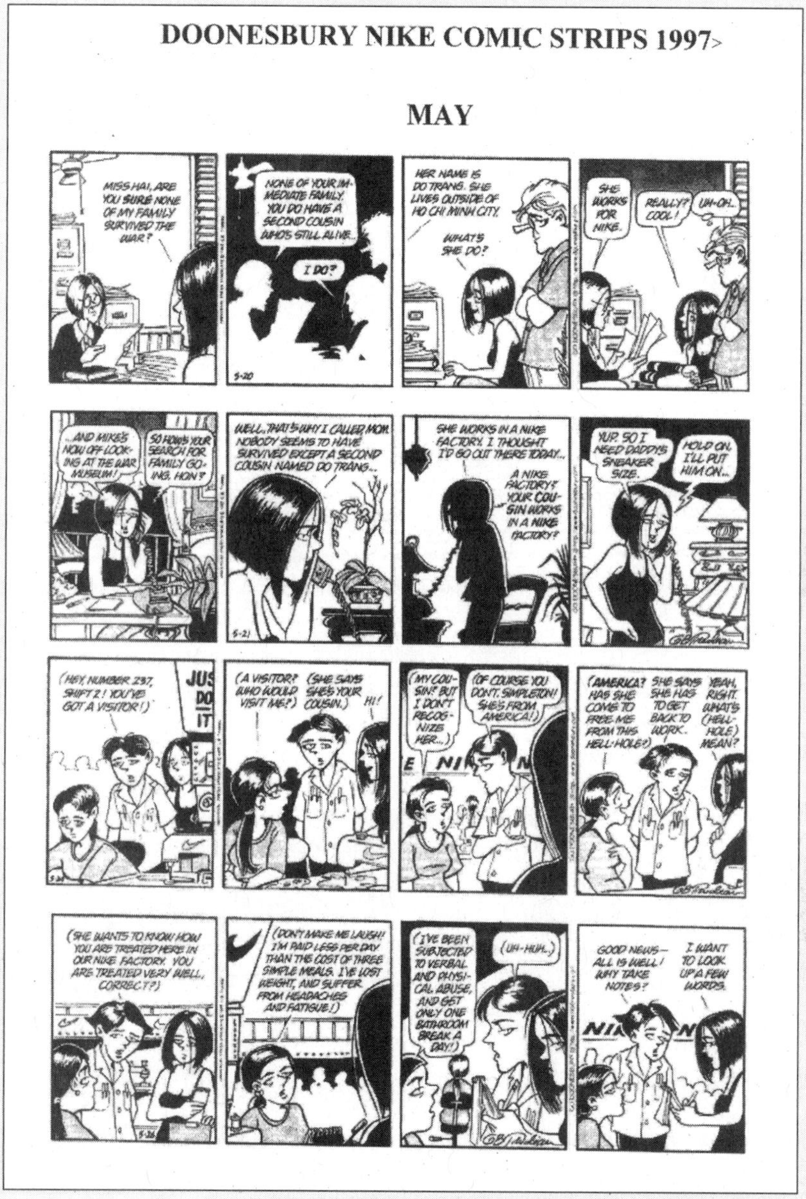

Figure 1.3. Doonesbury Cartoons.

Our parents actually looked for the "UL Listed" logo on products as an assurance that electrical safety standards were being met. Our children are completely oblivious to this certification because there are no electrical appliances in the market, large or small, that don't carry it.

This is relevant to the certification revolution because it shows how "UL Listed" evolved. Originally a product characteristic that consumers had to check, it became a minimum condition for doing business in the electrical appliance field. That is, it moved from being consumer driven to being business driven; it changed from being an exceptional "extra" quality of a product, sought by careful consumers, to a minimum element of quality assurance required by retailers and others in the product's supply chain. Underwriters Laboratory now offers standards for testing a wide range of public safety dimensions of products, and it offers its "listing" as a sign of compliance with those standards in some 35 countries.[21]

Certification systems such as the UL seal of approval created, in effect, a new level of accountability for manufacturers of electric equipment. As it became ubiquitous, we stopped paying attention to it; instead, we rely on the insurance and re-insurance industry to ensure that products that don't meet UL standards never make it to the market. We will see in Chapter 2 that 21st-century corporate accountability now requires that products, services, and individuals be certified with respect to most of the characteristics they claim. More importantly, many consumers are now searching for quality that goes well beyond the efficiency, durability, stylishness of the product, and the pleasantness of the purchase and delivery process. For hundreds of millions of consumers in the United States and around the world, quality now means that the social and environmental characteristics of the production process meet high standards. And as global sales become increasingly concentrated in retail chains that order a huge diversity of products, the reputation of that chain (and the value of its brand) depends on the social and environmental characteristics of the production processes throughout the whole supply chain.

There are major differences, however, between certification systems and their relationship to corporate social responsibility and corporate accountability. In Chapter 2, we will see the differences between 19th- and 20th-century corporate social responsibility (the "CSR" that many still debate) and 21st-century corporate accountability. The most important difference rests in who verifies that a company has met the standards to which it has committed itself.

- **First-party certification** means that the company itself is the sole judge of how well it has fulfilled its own public commitments. Despite all the paper and ink invested in "corporate responsibility reports," they carry very little credibility these days unless they report on commitments that have been audited by an independent agency.
- **Second-party certification** exists when an industry has an association that creates some standards for its members and then verifies in its own way whether the members meet those standards. Second-party certification has

somewhat more credibility than first-party, but not a whole lot. Most observers outside industry (and many within) doubt whether industry associations, reliant on membership dues, are capable of policing the application of standards without independent verification by an organization without a conflict of interest.

- **Third-party certification** is the highest level of certification available to date. It usually involves standards created jointly by the full set of stakeholders. This generally means that the standards are negotiated by industry representatives and representatives of social, environmental, and community organizations, then audited annually by a totally independent outside organization.

We must also make an important distinction between certification of management systems and certification of actual performance. The International Organization for Standardization (ISO) offers hundreds of standards for everything from the width and depth of threads on screws to environmental management for corporations. ISO charges for copies of its standards, and other "compliance assessment" firms certify, for a fee, whether they have been met. Most of its standards, however, are specifications for management systems. In the environmental field, for example, the ISO 14000 series of standards certifies that companies have put in place the management systems needed to produce better environmental impacts. But it doesn't certify whether companies have actually put these systems into practice or achieved improved environmental results. For many observers, this is a major shortcoming of ISO approaches.

What has emerged more recently is certification to sets of standards related to actual performance. This "performance-based" mode of certification requires that companies demonstrate they have changed their practices, not just put a management system in place. In forestry, for example, the performance certification standards of the Forest Stewardship Council require that auditors visit logging operations and verify that companies are actually leaving the quantity of trees along streams and shores required by the standards and that they are not taking more logs out of a forest than their certificate allows. This is why performance-based standards and performance-based certification give far more assurance to businesses down the supply chain, and to consumers, that a company's forest management meets the standard.

WHY DO BUSINESSES ENGAGE?

What we will see in the following chapters is that corporate decisions are rapidly becoming part of a five-pronged process that is at the heart of the certification revolution. These, in brief, are the critical components:

1. Branding, as we noted above, is the name of the game in globalization. The more effectively a corporation can get its name and its logo recognized by hundreds of millions of consumers around the world, the more its sales, profits, and share value will grow. Successful branding makes the purchasing decision easier, quicker, and more likely at *every* stage of the supply chain.

And brand value can grow well beyond the value of the products and services actually sold, because a successful brand is closely associated with long-term growth and profitability.

2. However, every dollar, or euro, or peso successfully invested in expanding brand recognition *also* increases the vulnerability of the brand to well-organized, well-documented civil society challenges to all aspects of the supply chain, from worker safety to wages, from human rights to environmental practices. Yes, there are "unbranded" firms in many supply chains, companies that manufacture for others and whose name and logo never appear on the product. But global information flows are now so rich and abundant that final sellers of products are being held accountable for every stage of production, whether it takes place in their own factories or not.

3. The most effective way to reduce the risk to reputation (and brand) is to participate in a certification system that verifies that established standards for social and environmental practices have been met. In the 21st century, the only credible and effective form of certification is a third-party system with independent verification of standards that have strong support from engaged NGOs. This technique for risk reduction is technically equivalent to purchasing insurance against fire, accident, and theft; investing in forward-exchange markets to reduce the financial risk from currency devaluation; or purchasing director and officer insurance to protect shareholders from malfeasance.

4. Major additional benefits that may accrue from participation in a social and environmental certification system include reduced insurance rates, improved employee morale leading to lower staff turnover, and access to new, lower-cost financing from socially responsible investors. In other words, if avoiding the risk of brand damage isn't enough, businesses may realize other important financial benefits that can help to cover any costs incurred in meeting the higher social and environmental standards.

5. Finally, successful participation in a social or environmental certification system offers a market differentiation for the products and services of the participating firms, lessening the market threat from uncertified firms and often making it easier to charge a higher price for the final product. In many of the cases that we will discuss, the market campaigners who encourage participation in a certification system then turn around and praise the complying firms publicly, encourage consumers to purchase the products of those firms, and turn their attention to the laggards in the industry. The speed with which other companies agree to comply has been truly amazing in several sectors.

So the title of this book applies on three different levels. *Branded!* refers, first, to the global process of branding that expands a company's opportunity to sell in increasingly global markets. Second, it refers to the negative consequences that well-branded firms face if there are serious social or environmental problems in their supply chains. And it refers, finally, to the opportunity to associate a company brand with systems of third-party independent certification to show — in ways that are credible to a skeptical public — that the company is complying with the highest standards for social and environmental practices.

THE CRITICAL THREE-WAY COMBINATION

In the long history of social and environmental activists trying to change corporate behavior (which we, mercifully, will not attempt to summarize here), there is emerging an understanding of what is needed to move corporations toward more responsible and more ethical practices. To begin with, there is growing evidence that simply "launching a campaign" against a company — accusing it of doing something dastardly and demanding that it change its practices — may have a few short-term impacts, but there's little evidence that it leads to lasting change or, more importantly, systemic change beyond that company. For example, in the mid-1990s, a Chicago-based advocacy group demanded that Starbucks improve the prices it was paying for coffee from poor farmers in Guatemala. After months of media attacks and demonstrations in front of the company's stores, Starbucks agreed to change its practices, and the campaigners declared victory. But when it came time to verify that Starbucks was discharging its commitment, the company claimed that it couldn't distinguish which Guatemalan coffee came from poor farmers and which from wealthier farms. So there was still no basis for moving beyond Starbucks' own claims about its coffee-purchasing practices.

More generally, however, I will argue that the most successful and long-lasting transformation of industries requires at least three interrelated actions:

- The creation of a **market campaign** to pressure the industry to change its practices. The campaign may begin (and often does) with the largest or the meanest or the most egregiously irresponsible firm in the industry (which is not always the same firm). Once that firm commits to change, the rest of the industry usually follows suit relatively quickly.
- The creation of a **stakeholder-based set of standards** for improving corporate practices. This doesn't mean that the social and environmental advocacy groups go off and set the standards; in fact, the participation of industry is critical to ensure that the negotiated standards are fundamentally feasible, as they raise the bar for the companies. It is similarly critical to have the advocacy organizations buy in to the system if it is to have legitimacy and credibility in the marketplace.
- The creation of a **credible independent mechanism for certifying companies,** initially, and then continuously monitoring and auditing certified companies' compliance with the negotiated standards.

Without a market campaign or some comparable form of pressure on the industry, companies initially have little incentive to participate in the certification system, and certification provides little value for the companies, especially when it increases their costs. (Profile 1.2 illustrates one such case.) Yet an important lesson of the past 15 years is that credible certification of ethical practices can become, on its own, a source of strategic value and market access, even when the pressures from civil society diminish. On the other hand, as noted above, the absence of independent (third-party) assessment, monitoring, and transparent auditing lessens the credibility of a certification system and, hence, its market value. Finally, though many consumer organizations refuse to give credibility to standards when corporations have played a role in their development,[22] the evidence accumulated in recent years suggests that corporate participation (at some level) is critical for defining standards that can be successful. Does corporate participation mean that standards may be set lower than social and environmental advocacy groups might set them if they had their druthers? Undoubtedly. Does it mean that companies have to change their practices in order to meet the final standards? If the process is to make any sense, yes! The standards that result may be the best set of feasible standards at that moment, acceptable to all parties as an important step in the direction of further corporate transformation and accountability. They are also subject to further review as corporations and advocacy organizations continue to engage over time.

The most successful social and environmental certification systems share two other traits in common. Both focus on corporate characteristics and the corporate response to advocacy-led, stakeholder-based standard setting:

- The final result of the transformation created by the certification system must make financial sense to the firms involved. The costs of certification cannot destroy the fundamental competitive position of the firm. This means that if there are significant increases in the costs of production, there will have to be offsetting increases in the prices of the products (price premiums) or other financial benefits. Lower financing costs, lower insurance costs, lower labor turnover costs, and the reduction of reputational risk are also real, tangible financial benefits that can be counted against the increased costs of meeting higher standards without necessarily requiring price premiums for the final products.
- In almost every successful case of companies taking the lead on meeting the demands of advocacy groups and adopting higher standards, there has been a highly placed internal corporate champion for the process. Sometimes it is a person at the CEO level, sometimes someone in senior management who convinces the CEO. I know of no cases, however, of successful initial transformation (among companies that are the first to commit) where that feature has not been present. We will meet some of these impressive internal champions in future chapters.

DEVELOPMENT STAGES FOR CERTIFICATION SYSTEMS

Those who study certification systems have begun to discuss evidence of "stages" in their development, implementation, and acceptance in global markets. Noting the conclusions of some of these analyses will help us understand how the certification revolution is creating legitimate, credible, and effective systems for

An NGO Cautionary Tale
The Story of Green Seal

When Green Seal was set up in the early 1990s, there were huge expectations that it would drive corporate environmental transformation.[23] Its seal would distinguish products that represented the best environmental practices of the time, and it was expected to be a significant moneymaker for the environmental community, with companies from many industries competing to use its logo on their products and paying for the privilege. That expectation was so strong that the leaders of many of the major US environmental groups in Washington were on Green Seal's start-up board.[24] It was created and originally headed by Dennis Hayes, the coordinator in 1970 of the first Earth Day celebration and international chairman of the 20th Earth Day in 1990.

The basic notion was simple — a "no-brainer, win-win" situation according to the current CEO, Arthur Weissman. In the late 1980s, more and more manufacturers were making undocumented environmental claims about their products. Green Seal's founders cited polls of that time indicating that from 75 to 94 percent of the public wanted to buy environmentally sound products and were even willing to pay a price premium of 5 to 10 percent for the products. But they didn't trust the unverified claims made by the manufacturers.

Green Seal was set up to create an independent "seal of approval" for those products, in any given line, which met the highest environmental standards. Product by product, Green Seal created standards, verified in many cases by outside experts, that identified the environmentally best 15 to 20 percent of products in a specific product line, such as air conditioners or cleaning fluids, based on technology of that moment and products in the market at that time. The Green Seal on the product gave consumers a clear indication of the best environmental choices. The governments of Germany and the Nordic countries had created similar programs and labels, which garnered very high levels of consumer recognition and strong consumer preference. In the absence of a government label in the US, Green Seal appeared to have an open field.

At the launch of Green Seal, Dennis Hayes indicated that consumers would eventually be able to find and buy a Green Seal item for all environmentally sensitive products in the grocery store. Companies and product lines without the seal would find their market share dropping dramatically and would seek to get into the program.[25]

Rather than rapid industry uptake, however, Green Seal encountered significant opposition. When it released its standards for household cleaners in 1992, the national Soap and Detergent Association in the US claimed that the standards were "inconsistent and scientifically invalid." [26] Proctor and Gamble (P&G) took a lead role in opposing Green Seal, belittling its potential environmental impact.[27] P&G then joined the Grocery Manufacturers Association of America to create a Coalition for Truth in Environmental Marketing and Information, designed specifically to fight third-party standards, both nationally, within the Clinton administration, and in international trade fora. In response, the advocacy community created the Consumers Choice Council.[28] The two groups dueled to a draw: neither Clinton's nor Bush's administration pursued the policies demanded by industry, and voluntary systems of eco-labeling were accepted by the World Trade Organization, but with certain limitations.

Green Seal's first product certifications appeared in 1993. By the end of the decade it had developed standards for several hundred products. But although its 1993 business plan forecast income of some $3 million per year from fees, which was to fund extensive media work to raise awareness of the label, Green Seal never earned enough money to create an effective marketing campaign. It did develop public service advertising, to be run without charge by television stations and in environmental magazines, but few ads appeared. And market recognition never developed.

The Energy Star program of the US Environmental Protection Agency proved to be tough competition in many product lines. By 2003, Energy Star had certified some 7,000 products from 1,200 manufacturers in the appliance market, while Green Seal had certified only about 50 to 75 products in that market, from a total of seven manufacturers.[29] Other competitors, especially Green Cross, an environmental label created by Scientific Certification Systems, a small for-profit certification company, entered the market and generated considerable competition and, some argue, consumer and industry confusion.[30]

Of the three major components for successful certification systems discussed in this chapter, Green Seal missed all or part of two.

- There have been no major campaigns demanding better environmental performance from companies manufacturing appliances, household cleaning products, or most of the other products for which Green Seal developed standards. So there has been little incentive for industry uptake, other than a vague sense of consumer desire for environmentally preferable products.
- Green Seal's standard-setting process has excluded corporations (earning high praise from Consumers Union), but it has been rejected by many of the industries it was designed to transform.

Green Seal has returned to prominence in a role that couldn't have been anticipated when it was created. Having gained extraordinary skill in evaluating the environmental characteristics of a broad range of products, it has now been invited by Wal-Mart to help develop standards for measuring the relative environmental qualities of a host of products that Wal-Mart sources and sells (see Chapter 12 for more on the campaign to transform Wal-Mart). According to Arthur Weissman, Green Seal's president, when Wal-Mart's buyers are evaluating what products to stock, they will include data on environmental characteristics of production and performance, as well as price and quality.[31]

Green Seal continues to be a pioneer in setting environmental standards, especially, now, for institutional purchasers. The City of Santa Monica, California, contracted with Green Seal to develop further standards under its Sustainable City Program. Following a Clinton administration executive order to "green the government" through procurement policies, Green Seal has helped reduce the environmental impact of some US federal government agencies. And it has had some success with an initiative focused on greening the hotel and lodging industry. But it has not met the, admittedly high, early expectations of transforming major industries.

transforming corporate behavior without, in most cases, active involvement of national governments or international agencies. Benjamin Cashore, my former colleague at Yale's School of Forestry and Environmental Studies, has arguably written more than any other analyst on the processes through which certification systems pass. He describes these systems as "non-state, market-driven" (NSMD) forms of governance.[32]

According to Cashore and his co-authors, the critical stages in the development of certification systems involve the quest for "political legitimacy."[33] How do the communities (both the companies and the social and environmental advocacy groups) engaged in developing such a system come to accept it as an appropriate and justified shared set of rules for behavior?

Cashore and his colleagues have reviewed both inductive theory and recent empirical evidence and developed the following three-stage model. Although the perceptions of firms and NGOs are initially very different, they become close to synonymous in the final stage.

In the **Initiation Phase:**
- A relatively small community of both firms and NGOs are driven by strategic calculations of the benefits of improved practices, generally before targeted market campaigns begin. This process may be led by NGOs that do not engage in market campaigning, such as the World Wildlife Fund.
- The firms whose processes are closest to the proposed standards are the first to join because the cost of changing their practices may be least, and the perceived benefits of independent validation of their practices may be high.
- The result is likely to be a segmented or niche market for the products of the firms that adopt the standards most quickly.

In the **Building Support Phase:**
- Supporters of the system must find ways to incorporate firms that will incur higher costs if they comply with the new standards, so this is the phase where more widespread market campaigns are invoked, boycotting or shaming companies whose practices don't meet the standards.
- Some firms respond by pushing back, defending their practices, criticizing the standards proposed, building their own industry-based standards that are less demanding, and attempting to create legitimacy for those lower

standards. Some companies that first resisted begin to feel market pressures
and flip from opposition to support.
- NGOs are bolstered by the fact that they have learned, in the first phase, that
firms can live with the standards as proposed. This emboldens them to demand the same of all firms in the sector, picking first on industry leaders and
then on those who compete with the leaders.

In the **Political Legitimacy Phase:**
- The full set of stakeholders recognize the legitimacy, and the usefulness, of
the system within which they are working.
- Power struggles may continue, but they continue within the rule-making
framework of the certification system. Both firms and advocacy NGOs commit to improving the functioning of the system, though each reserves the
right to leave the system as one of the most important points of leverage.
- The possibilities increase for regulatory implementation of standards similar
to those of the voluntary system. Ironically, companies' willingness to commit to private voluntary standards that are higher than previously existing
regulatory standards makes it easier for advocates to pursue a legislative implementation that further strengthens the competitive position of the leading-edge companies that have complied with the standards. These leading-
edge companies often support the legislation that forces other companies to
rise to their level of ethical practice.

Each of the certification systems we analyze in the following chapters can be
viewed, in part, in these terms. Every industry considers itself unique, vastly different from any other. Each company believes that it is pursuing a unique course,
unlike that of any of its predecessors. And many NGOs believe they have to create and pursue new strategies, distinct from those of other groups, though the
pace of sharing learning is perceptibly more rapid among NGOs than it is among
firms and industry groups. But the patterns identified above are proving very
common and powerful, especially in the more nuanced forms discussed by
Cashore and his colleagues.

Turning to the empirical side, Hank Cauley, until recently the CEO of ECOS
Consulting, a corporate sustainability consulting firm with operations in the US
and Australia, has offered an assessment of the relative progress in the development of corporate sustainability systems based on a detailed analysis of market
campaigns in the US through mid-2006. Cauley proposes both an alternative
characterization of the stages in developing certification systems and a chart that
illustrates where he thinks most of the key sectors we will analyze tend to fall in
his spectrum. The four stages are almost self-evident, but Cauley links them to
market indicators that will be helpful to our analysis.
1. **Nascent Stage.** There is little to no broad industrial impact and no coordinated effort on the part of advocacy NGOs, who rely on regulatory strategies.
The issues don't get traction in the media. Campaigners begin to understand

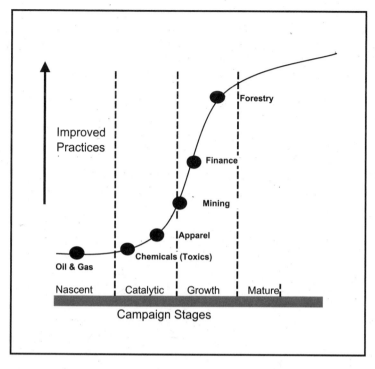

Figure 1.4. Campaign Stages and Progress. Source: Hank Cauley, Business Ethics Network conference call.

what the issues should be. There is little value at stake for companies. Illustrative sector: Oil and gas.

2. **Catalytic Stage.** Individual companies become aware of the issues and respond to pressure that sends key market signals. The industry association responds with a defensive strategy and develops counter strategies. The profile of issues rises in the media. Industry leaders acknowledge that there is value at stake. Local or state legislative efforts create a threat to companies operating under the status quo, and standards begin to develop. Illustrative sectors: Chemicals/toxics and apparel.

3. **Growth Stage.** A broadly consistent resolution begins to emerge. The industry association upgrades its standards, and continuous improvement and education efforts are evident. Companies engage with market campaigners. There is widespread adoption of practices as leaders are joined by second-tier companies. They see that "business as usual" is clearly not tenable. Implementation groups figure prominently in the rapid spread and development of options for change. Illustrative sectors: Project finance and sustainable forestry.

4. **Mature Stage.** Several stakeholders collaborate to advocate and drive the

need for government policy. Legislation indoctrinates new practices, and new societal expectations are set. On the ground, quantitative changes are evident and widespread. Illustrative sectors: None yet.

THE VOICES OF FUNDAMENTAL OPPOSITION

The transformation of global corporations described in this book, and the processes that drive that transformation, face fundamental opposition from both ends of the political spectrum. On the political right, there are people and organizations that find the empowerment of global civil society, through the growing strength of national and international advocacy organizations, almost as frightening — and as damnable — as the growth of governmental and inter-governmental regulation. We will run into those voices throughout the book. Their argument is that if consumer choice, under present conditions of consumer attitudes and information, is not producing optimal market solutions, why should we expect liberal advocacy organizations to come up with a better solution? Who gives these advocacy groups the right to pick the companies they will attack, to drive the creation of standards beyond those that have been created by law, and to ask of corporations anything other than maximizing shareholder value? Why should we believe that these so-called market-driven processes add anything to the current functioning of global, national, and local markets?

These voices from the right are balanced, perhaps ironically, by voices on the left that condemn as "reformist" the effective transformation of global corporations through advocacy-driven standard setting. Does this not legitimize the corporate form, they ask, empowering corporations that embrace minimal reforms, and providing blatant opportunities for "greenwashing" or "fairwashing"? Can the nascent certification systems, chronically underfunded and learning on the fly as they create themselves, possibly withstand the huge financial and political influence of transnational corporations? Can the certification systems become financially self-sufficient without becoming beholden to the very corporations they seek to transform? Can they embrace and contribute to broader global goals, such as the alleviation of poverty, the protection of human rights, and the reduction of global climate change? If not, shouldn't we be looking for far more fundamental, more revolutionary, less reformist courses of action?

It is difficult for both sides to understand the phenomenon represented by the certification revolution. Environmental advocacy groups want to take credit for forcing companies to enact policies that they would not have undertaken without NGO pressure. Social advocacy groups similarly want to convince themselves, and the rest of the world, that the changes they have produced in corporate behavior would not, and could not, continue if it weren't for their continuous watchdog roles. Neither of these groups wants to focus on the need to make these changes work for business as a basis for their strategies. Corporations, on the other hand, prefer to insist that they are changing their practices "because it is good for business," and definitely not because they have been coerced into making the changes.

Yet they are all right. As we will see by the end of the book, significant meaningful social and environmental transformation in corporate practices is underway precisely because social and environmental advocacy groups have succeeded in "raising the bar" for acceptable corporate practice, creating new products and services that are qualitatively different from those that are uncertified, and giving businesses an opportunity to enter those new markets and make good profits. Making it work for business has been essential, even if the advocacy groups don't like to acknowledge that this is the mechanism that is working.

There are still many questions and doubts, for both the right and the left, about the value of certification. In the chapters that follow, we will probe, with brutal honesty, the strengths and the weaknesses of the evolving certification systems for transforming corporations. I will present the evidence, to date, of the impacts that they are having. And I will leave it to the reader to determine whether there is adequate evidence of progress toward our broadest common goals to warrant further development of this approach toward global transformation.

THE REST OF THE BOOK

Each of the chapters that follow analyzes a distinct aspect or implementation of the certification revolution. In Chapter 2 we will see how 19th- and 20th-century corporate social responsibility has evolved into 21st-century corporate accountability, which I call "corporate social responsibility with teeth." In Chapter 3 we will analyze the strategies and tactics of market campaigns or "ethical business campaigns" as some would prefer to call them. Chapter 4 will cover one of the first, and to date the most successful, social and environmental certification systems, the Forest Stewardship Council. Its origins and evolution have paved the way for many other systems, even as it continues to struggle with its increasing success in transforming the forest management practices deployed in a rapidly growing proportion of the world's working forests.

What does it mean to bring "fairness" to markets of agriculture commodities and other products imported from less-developed countries? Chapter 5 will chronicle the rapid surge in Fair Trade Certified products, the campaigns that have brought them to the attention of the public in developed countries, and the successful integration of Fair Trade into a number of important companies, large and small.

Do the world's largest banks have any responsibility for the projects they fund? Or is their responsibility limited to efficient and transparent lending? Chapter 6 describes the dramatic new standards guiding the social and environmental characteristics of bank project lending that have emerged and been adopted by *most* of the world's largest financial institutions in a process that has taken less than five years.

The world's largest service industry is travel and tourism, and mass-market tourism is moving millions of travelers to environmentally endangered beach resorts. Chapter 7 shows the work presently underway to create a Sustainable

Tourism Stewardship Council in a manner quite distinct from other social and environmental certification systems.

Mining is an industry that I once wrote was incapable of creating an effective certification system. Chapter 8 shows how, and why, I was wrong.

Chapter 9 takes a step back from the interaction of companies and NGOs and asks the more profound developmental question: Can certification systems reduce poverty? The answers are complicated but fundamentally encouraging.

Chapter 10 provides brief overviews of several other market campaigns and certification systems that are presently less well-developed or have run into major obstacles, but continue to struggle to transform the practices of important corporations in the computer hardware, cosmetics, health care, seafood, and footware and apparel industries.

In Chapter 11 we take a break from describing new and emerging certification systems and focus on the "push back" from industry when it finds that the standards being asked of it are too high, or when it decides that it can certify for itself without the sometimes painful and frustrating engagement with NGOs. It is a chronicle of huge sums of wasted funding, with virtually no positive market impacts, but it is repeated, sector after sector, as companies attempt to avoid the implementation of credible standards and certification techniques.

Then we turn, in Chapter 12, to the "mother of all market campaigns," the attempt to bring social and environmental accountability to big-box retail stores, particularly Wal-Mart, the largest private employer in the world. Here, again, the results are little short of astounding.

Finally, Chapter 13 explores the conceptual and practical limitations of the certification revolution that once again distinguish between old-fashioned corporate social responsibility and contemporary corporate accountability. Our tale comes to a sobering, but fundamentally optimistic, conclusion.

2

Redefining Corporate Social and
Environmental Accountability for the 21st Century

Societal demands for independent third-party certification of the social and environmental practices of corporations is a relatively new phenomenon. However, the demand that businesses be socially responsible is as old as the organization of business. It took on new importance with the invention of the corporate form — in which businesses are granted the privilege of limited liability by government — yet the fundamental notion of corporate social responsibility (CSR) has been under considerable attack in recent years. That is ironic, because there is ample evidence that global civil society is now expecting more responsible social and environmental practices from firms at every level, not less.

In this chapter we explore the transformation of old-style CSR into corporate social and environmental accountability (CSEA) and the relationship of that change to the creation of mechanisms for enforcing accountability. When seen in this light, the certification revolution becomes a logical outgrowth of the transformation of worldwide expectations for corporations of all sizes, with their full range of stakeholders expecting improved practices in all areas, including the social and environmental fronts.

A BRIEF HISTORY OF CORPORATE SOCIAL RESPONSIBILITY

Demands that business be socially responsible have existed for thousands of years, according to prominent historians of CSR.[1] Laws to protect forests from commercial operations can be traced back some 5,000 years. King Hammurabi introduced a legal code in ancient Mesopotamia (around 1700 BC) under which builders, innkeepers, and farmers could be put to death if their negligence caused the deaths of others "or major inconvenience to local citizens."

During the period of European colonization of "new worlds," the emergent public-private companies (the Spanish colonial monopolies and the crown companies, such as the British East India Company and the Dutch East India Company) were bound by detailed rules on the treatment of locals, the conservation of resources, and the proper management of their enterprises. Libraries of the colonial period are full of reports from company managers to the respective royal patrons, as well as reports by other observers, especially representatives of the church, on the ways in which the company has or, in many cases, has not fulfilled its responsibilities.

In the industrial era of the 19th and early 20th century, it became common for the wealthiest industrialists — especially in the United States — to dedicate some of their wealth to support paternalistic and religiously motivated philanthropic ventures, partly, one assumes, to counter the rampant attacks by journalists (and by competitors) on their corporate practices. The philanthropy of Andrew Carnegie and John D. Rockefeller, for example, left significant legacies, not the least of which are the enduring foundations which they endowed. The "corporate paternalists" of the late 19th and early 20th centuries discussed their social responsibilities openly, but they tended to set the terms of the discussion as they wished, using church tithing and corporate philanthropy as the mark of their responsibility, rather than standards for practices within their businesses.

In 1929 the Dean of the Harvard Business School, Wallace Donham, argued, in an address at Northwestern University, that "business started long centuries before the dawn of history, but business as we now know it is new — new in its broadening scope, new in its social significance. Business has not learned how to handle these changes, nor does it recognize the magnitude of its responsibilities for the future of civilization."[2]

CRITIQUE OF CORPORATE SOCIAL RESPONSIBILITY

Michael Hopkins, an expert in CSR and sustainable development, has provided one of the clearest definitions of conventional corporate social responsibility:

> CSR is concerned with treating the stakeholders of the firm ethically or in a responsible manner. "Ethically or responsible" means treating key stakeholders in a manner deemed acceptable in civilized societies. Social includes economic and environmental responsibility. Stakeholders exist both within a firm and outside. The wider aim of social responsibility is to create higher and higher standards of living, while preserving the profitability of the corporation, for people both within and outside the corporation.[3]

Conventional CSR has been criticized by many, under widely varying definitions. For some observers, such as Nobel laureate (and self-declared libertarian) Milton Friedman, there is "only one social responsibility of business," which is "to use its resources and engage in activities designed to increase profits so long as it stays within the rules of the game."[4] He showed no patience for capitalists who claim that "business is not concerned 'merely' with profit but also with promoting desirable 'social' ends; that business has a 'social conscience' and takes seriously its responsibilities for providing employment, eliminating discrimination, avoiding pollution," etc. For Friedman, that kind of thinking involves "preaching pure and unadulterated socialism." Business people who talk this way "are unwitting puppets of the intellectual forces that have been undermining the basis of a free society these past decades."[5]

Criticism of conventional CSR also comes from contemporary sources on the progressive end of the political spectrum. For example, David Vogel, a professor of business ethics, sees CSR as "business virtue" and defines it as "practices that improve the workplace and benefit society in ways that go above and beyond what companies are legally required to do."[6] Vogel believes there are important limits to the market for virtue and, therefore, to the business case for CSR. In his view it is a niche strategy rather than a generic strategy, making business sense only for some firms, in some areas, and under some circumstances. The only alternative for pursuing broader social goals is statutory regulation by government.

Vogel also comments that the principal locus of activity around CSR has shifted from the United States to the United Kingdom. A recent reflection of that shift can be seen in the UK government's passage of the *Companies Act of 2006,* which stipulated that most publicly listed companies in the UK *must* report on their social and environmental impacts at home and abroad, as well as on all material employee and supply-chain issues.[7] The law emerged after broadly based pressure from civil society, including social development organizations, environmental activists, faith-based groups, trade unions, and human rights organizations. One of the key organizations supporting it was the Corporate Responsibility (CORE) Coalition, which is linked to Amnesty International, Friends of the Earth, and some 125 other groups.

For the CORE Coalition, CSR is "the friendly face of capitalism," despite the fact that there is "often a wide chasm between what's good for a company and what's good for society as a whole." In a widely distributed article, Deborah Doane, chairperson of the CORE Coalition, described the "four key myths" of CSR:[8]

- It's a myth that the market can deliver both short-term financial returns and long-term social benefits. Doane argues that it would be difficult to prove that financial markets, in particular, give firms the time they need to reap the benefits of protecting natural assets, ensuring an educated labor force for the future, or contributing to community organizations.
- It's a myth that the ethical consumer will drive the change. She notes that consumer surveys frequently indicate a willingness to pay extra for ethically superior products, but analyses of consumer purchases suggest it's a very small proportion of consumers who actually "walk the talk" by seeking, and paying more for, socially and environmentally preferable products.
- It's a myth that there will be a competitive "race to the top" over ethics and sustainability among businesses (of the sort that we will analyze in Chapter 3), reflected in competition for listing on "most ethical" and "most sustainable" or "socially responsible" lists. Though some companies compete, there doesn't seem to be anything in this "race" that excludes egregiously irresponsible companies (like tobacco companies), and very little that is consistent or systematic in the criteria used to identify ethical or sustainable businesses.
- It's a myth that countries will compete to have the best ethical practices. The global market system puts too much pressure on developing countries to undercut one another on social and environmental grounds in order to attract investment, Doane argues, and there are too many incentives for corporations to accept, and work under, falling national standards.

Michael Porter and his colleagues at the Institute for Strategy and Competitiveness at Harvard Business School have categorized and critiqued conventional CSR as well. Historically, they note, there have been four prevailing justifications for CSR:

- **Moral obligation** is the basic argument that companies have a duty to be "good citizens" and "to do the right thing," but the nature of corporate social choices involves "balancing competing values, interests, and costs."
- **Sustainability** is the argument that environmental and community concerns must be a part of every business decision, leading to analyses of the "triple bottom line" of economic, social, and environmental performance. This approach works best when it coincides with economic and regulatory interests, such as when changes in environmental practices save the companies significant money.
- **License to operate** is a fundamentally pragmatic approach, especially prevalent among companies that need the forbearance of their neighbors because their operations are unavoidably noxious or environmentally hazardous, and among companies that need governmental consent to operate (for example, mining or logging companies that operate on public lands). It offers a clear rationale for maintaining good relations with local communities, but it also requires that companies cede significant control of their CSR agendas to outside stakeholders.
- **Reputation** as a motivation for CSR focuses on satisfying external audiences as a form of insurance against public criticism in the event of a crisis. This approach runs the risk, Porter argues, of "confusing public relations with social and business results."[9]

All four of these approaches, Porter and his colleagues argue, have the same weakness: "They focus on the tension between business and society rather than on their interdependencies."[10]

At the core of these critiques is the implicit assumption that, "ultimately, trade-offs must be made between the financial health of the company and ethical outcomes."[11] One of the most important goals of this book is to demonstrate that this assumption is not necessarily valid for a constantly widening range of companies functioning in a world where stakeholders have far more information than ever before, where ethical consumers are a rapidly growing element in final markets, and where new business models are emerging that value and reward the highest levels of corporate accountability.

RE-SPECIFICATION OF CSR FOR THE 21ST CENTURY

These days, concerns about social and environmental responsibility are a politically critical dimension of the corporate search for profits. In a now-classic dissent among libertarians, John Mackey (founder and CEO of Whole Foods, Inc., the largest chain of natural and organic food stores in the US) expressed a dramatically different perspective, disagreeing strongly with Friedman's basic premise:

From an investor's perspective, the purpose of the business is to maximize profits. But that's not the purpose for other stakeholders — for customers, employees, suppliers, and the community. Each of those groups will define the purpose of the business in terms of its own needs and desires, and each perspective is valid and legitimate....

The most successful businesses put the customer first, ahead of the investors.... In the customer-centered business, customer happiness is an end in itself, and will be pursued with greater interest, passion, and empathy than the profit-centered business is capable of....

At Whole Foods, we measure our success by how much value we can create for all six of our most important stakeholders: customers, team members (employees), investors, vendors, communities, and the environment.

The business model that Whole Foods has embraced could represent a new form of capitalism, one that more consciously works for the common good instead of depending solely on the "invisible hand" to generate positive results for society.[12]

Corporate standards for responsibility are constantly changing as citizens become more aware of the scale and content of corporate impact around the world and as institutions and technology demonstrate that higher standards are possible. By the early years of the 21st century, society's expectations with respect to corporate behavior had increased dramatically. Reflecting growing corporate awareness of this phenomenon, the *Financial Times* reported in 2005 that "more than half of the world's biggest companies reveal details of their environmental and social performance."[13] A KPMG study found that 52 percent of the 250 largest corporations published CSR reports and that they covered a much wider range of issues in 2005 than they had covered in 2002. Socially responsible investment firms, such as Calvert Financial Services, now issue regular assessments of the social, environmental, and governance performance of many companies, covering the full range of activities from workplace and business practices, human rights behavior, environmental responsibility, and community relations.[14] And, as shown in Profile 2.1, the Internet has created new mechanisms for virtually instant global awareness of charges of social irresponsibility, such as human rights violations.[15]

The difference between "responsibility" and "accountability" plays a large role in the recent evolution of societal expectations. To be "responsible," according to the *Oxford English Dictionary,* means to be "morally accountable for one's actions" and "capable of fulfilling an obligation or trust." To be "accountable," on the other hand, means "liable to be called to account or to answer for responsibilities or conduct," or "able to be accounted for or explained."[22] Corporate responsibility has typically been defined by the corporation, on its own terms, and reported by it without external audits. Corporate accountability means the corporation is held to account for commitments made, with consequences if the commitments are not met. Civil society — the community of investors, shareholders, and other stakeholders — has begun to demand not only better

Internet Instruments
for Corporate Accountability
The Business and Human Rights Resource Centre

The field of human rights accountability has often been seen as "squishy," without much impact on corporate practices. This is especially true in the United States, where most of the fundamental human rights conventions of the United Nations have never been ratified. What need was there for corporate attention to codes of conduct that carried only the weight of United Nations consensus?[16] However, the Internet's globalization of communications has given the UN conventions more weight, and corporate social risk management must now include much closer attention to the possibility that corporate practices around the world will be challenged on fundamental human rights grounds.

A small, smart organization was created in 2004 and launched at the 2005 World Economic Forum in Davos, Switzerland. The Business and Human Rights Resource Centre (B&HRC) was designed by a small group of former Amnesty International staffers, and its purpose is to provide new incentives to encourage companies worldwide to respect human rights. It does this by

- providing one-stop access to a broad range of information on the application of human rights in the corporate context,
- accumulating company-specific information on complaints of human rights violations, and
- documenting company responses to those complaints.

The mechanisms B&HRC uses are simple, straightforward, and powerful. The organization gathers complaints on possible human rights violations from around the world, relying on regional reporters and civil society organizations in more than 160 countries. After minimal screening, most complaints received are forwarded directly to the companies involved with a request for a formal public response and a clear indication that the complaint will be published on the organization's website (business-humanrights.org) whether or not there is a response.

Every week, B&HRC distributes a free electronic newsletter to a rapidly growing list of opinion leaders, companies, NGOs, academics, and individuals worldwide. The newsletter contains the week's "top stories," follow-ups on earlier stories, lists of new reports on human rights relevant to the business community, and actions taken by companies based on human rights considerations. The website and the weekly updates are available in English, French, and Spanish. Topics include discrimination, the environment, poverty and development, labor, access to medicines, health and safety, security, and trade.[17]

One early example illustrates the direct impact that B&HRC can have. It involves Tiffany & Co., a jewelry company that plays a critical role in the story of emerging certification systems in mining (see Chapter 8). When US law was changed in 2003 to ban imports of products from Myanmar (Burma), Tiffany stopped buying rubies, spinel, and jadeite from Burma. However, it also sought a formal ruling from US Customs on whether gems mined in Burma that received significant processing outside Burma should also be excluded. The jeweler was notified, a year later, that those processed gems would not be covered by the law. In the February 16, 2005, issue of *Professional Jeweler,* a small announcement stated that Tiffany & Co. would resume imports of stones mined in Burma but processed extensively elsewhere.

Advocates for Burmese democracy brought the announcement to the attention of B&HCR, which passed it to Tiffany & Co. for a response. A brief formal response from Tiffany's public relations department, received and posted on March 1, indicated that the announcement was both correct and within the law.[18] A US representative of B&HCR contacted Michael Kowalski, Tiffany's CEO, and asked him for further explanation. On March 4, Kowalski issued a press release that said Tiffany & Co. would stop purchasing gems from Burma because "despite the Customs ruling, mining of these gems supports the existing Burmese regime. We support democratic reforms and an end to human rights abuses in that country. We believe that our customers would agree with our position."[19]

The Business and Human Rights Resource Centre has become the world's leading independent resource on human rights related to business. Its website is updated hourly with news and reports about companies' human rights impacts worldwide — both positive and negative. The site tracks over 3,000 companies in more than 160 countries. It receives over 1.5 million hits per month. Mary Robinson, who chairs the B&HRC advisory panel of 80 international human rights experts, wrote of the group: "No debate can move forward, no positive change can be made, without facts. The Resource Centre is the only website to provide such a broad range of balanced information on business and human rights — company by company, country by country, issue by issue."[20]

Christopher Avery, B&HCR's founding director, wrote recently that "companies that fail to respect human rights expose themselves to a wide range of risks, including legal action, negative media coverage, protests, shareholder action and boycotts, with all the reputational and financial costs that these can bring."[21] The techniques that he and his colleagues have designed for bringing charges of company-specific human rights violations to a global audience — and for creating potential solutions to the problems — is proof positive of his statement.

practices on the part of corporations, but also independent external validation of corporate claims to better practices. Corporate accountability, in these terms, is *CSR with teeth*!

In the 19th century, companies set their own standards for corporate responsibility, and the company itself verified its claims that it was meeting these standards (as we saw in Chapter 1, this is known as first-party certification or "self-certification").

By the end of the 20th century, corporate disasters, such as the explosion
of the Union Carbide chemical plant in Bhopal, India, led to industry-wide
standard setting, such as the Responsible Care system of the chemical industry,
which was designed to assure regulators, insurers, financiers, clients in the supply
chain, and final consumers that industry standards were high enough to avoid a
repeat of those disasters.[23] But the only verification was provided by company
reports to an industry association or reports from an industry-controlled watchdog group, followed by the industry group's assertion that the standards were being met (second-party certification). Any credibility accorded this type of verification comes from the reputation of the industry group. A number of
industry-led systems of this sort have been created to provide the illusion of true
corporate accountability. They, and their limited usefulness for full corporate accountability, are discussed in Chapter 11.

Over the past 15 years, a new model of corporate accountability has emerged
in which the standards are negotiated and set by a wide range of stakeholders,
there is fully independent and transparent monitoring and auditing of a company's compliance, and the company is rewarded with "certification" of its practices, often accompanied by the use of a third-party "seal of approval" or "trust-
mark" that informs the world that the standards are being met. This has now
become the most effective and most credible mechanism for imposing and auditing full corporate accountability.

Why would companies choose to engage in these more rigorous processes?
Michael Porter and his colleagues at the Harvard Business School argue that
"CSR has emerged as an inescapable priority for business leaders in every country,"[24] and they add a new conceptual category to the four traditional bases for
CSR discussed above (moral obligation, sustainability, license to operate, and
reputation). They call it "strategic CSR." Strategic CSR provides "an affirmative
corporate social agenda" that moves from "mitigating harm to reinforcing corporate strategy through social progress." Strategic CSR requires attention to both
the impacts of company practices on society and the external social conditions
that influence corporations. More importantly, strategic CSR "moves beyond
good corporate citizenship and mitigating harmful value chain impacts to
mount a small number of initiatives whose social and business benefits are large
and distinctive." Companies implementing these initiatives often seek independent external validation, so it becomes, in effect, new-style corporate accountability. The recent history of transformation at the British retail giant, Marks &
Spencer, illustrates several aspects of this approach (see Profile 2.2).

Both the arguments of John Mackey and the strategies of Michael Porter are
found in an ever-expanding number of US corporations, despite the fact that
regulatory tendencies in the early years of this century moved in the opposite direction. A *Washington Post* article in the early days of George W. Bush's second
term as president questioned why "compassionate capitalism" would be on the
rise at the same time that "America is supposedly turning conservative on social
values."[32] Citing the example of Hewlett-Packard, Dell, and IBM agreeing on

Rebuilding a Company Around Corporate Social Accountability...and Winning!

The Marks & Spencer Story

Marks & Spencer is one of the most famous and venerable names in British retailing, comparable in its traditions and reputation to Sears, Roebuck & Co. in the US. Founded in the 1880s by a Russian Jewish immigrant in a market stall in Leeds, by 2006 it had grown to more than 400 stores across the UK, with total sales (turnover) of US$7.5 billion.[25] One of its distinguishing characteristics is that it offers only private-label products produced to its specifications in some 650 factories around the world.

Celebrated in 1990 as the first British retailer to earn £1 billion in profits, by the start of the 21st century it was best known as a floundering old-style company that had lost its way, was losing its customer base, and had profits barely one-quarter those of its peak year. It was forced to lay off more than 4,000 staff in 2001, about 10 percent of its total direct employee base, in the face of falling sales.[26] By 2004, with its share value at the lowest level in decades, it was constantly in the news as British entrepreneur Philip Green made several offers at 20 and 30 percent over the market value to buy the firm and take it private. He was rebuffed by the Marks & Spencer board, which hired a new chief executive who set out to make M&S the most ethically branded retailer in the business.

Corporate social responsibility was already deeply ingrained in the business. Ed Williams, head of CSR for the firm, laid out its corporate perspective in an impressive speech given at a "Business in the Community" conference in Hong Kong in early 2004. He first articulated the notion that "the marketplace in the 21st century is more than transactions between buyers and sellers"; it is, rather, "increasingly about relationships between businesses and their consumers."[27] He then pointed out that, in his experience at M&S, "consumers increasingly want to be sure that the companies they deal with reflect their values, can be trusted to behave responsibly, are who they say they are and are the kind of organisation they like to be associated with." That is all summed up, he argued, in a company's brand. "For most consumer businesses, it's the most valuable resource we've got," he said, adding:

> Until just a few years ago, our customers and other stakeholders would trust us simply because we were Marks & Spencer. We can no longer automatically assume that trust. The world has been moving from a "trust me" to a "show me" to a "prove to me" world — and increasingly we are entering an "involve me" world in which all our stakeholders expect to be heard and their views taken into account.

Marks & Spencer took the older and more traditional CSR, which Ed Williams admitted meant little more than "handing out cheques to worthy causes," and converted it into forms of CSR that would make the business as a whole more sustainable. Certified Fairtrade (as Fair Trade is written in the UK) has become an important component of those efforts. The following are some of the newer dimensions of the M&S CSR program:

- In 2004, M&S launched a new "flagship community program" that offered work experience to people normally excluded from the workplace, including the homeless, people with disabilities, unemployed youth, parents returning to work after raising their children, and students who are the first in their families to aim for higher education. The program benefits at least 2,500 people each year. It extends financial assistance to students preparing for college and university, provides mentoring and buddying with present employees, and gives brief work experience and training to those with special difficulties in finding work. The program aims to expand M&S's own sources of recruitment and diversity in the workforce and also create beneficial external communications and customer awareness of its community programs.
- Also in 2004, M&S created a "Look Behind the Label" program, which calls attention to the sources of the products it sells. The company has focused on more responsible sourcing of seafood, coffee, fresh produce, dairy and eggs, and foodstuffs for its large takeout meal business.
- In response to challenges from animal protection advocates, M&S was the first major UK food retailer to sell only free-range eggs. It also uses only free-range eggs in its bakery and restaurant products.
- It banned the use of growth-enhancing hormones and antibiotics in dairy and meat products, even before the European Union ban became effective.
- It is the only major UK food retailer to guarantee that no genetically modified ingredients are used in the manufacture of any of the food products it sells, including its precooked takeout meals.
- It has stopped selling all 35 fish species identified by the British Marine Conservation Society as endangered. As a result, M&S was listed as a leading global retailer for sustainable fishing by the Seafood Choices Alliance. It remains the only UK organization and retailer to be listed by that group.
- In June 2005, M&S, which is the third-largest coffee chain in the UK on the basis of total sales, converted all of the coffee and tea offerings in its Café Revive coffee shops to certified Fairtrade. It also greatly expanded sales of certified Fairtrade fresh produce, including avocados, bananas, mangos, and pineapples.[28]
- In January 2006, M&S responded to survey research indicating that "a third of its shoppers had put clothes back on the rails amid concerns about their origins" by launching a line of clothing made from certified Fairtrade cotton from India.
- In October 2006, M&S announced the conversion of all the coffee and tea sold in its stores, including 38 lines of packaged products in the grocery section, to certified Fairtrade.[29]

This focus on corporate accountability has been rewarded by customers and the financial markets. From its low point at 270 pence in December 2003, share value has increased to 705 pence in December 2006, a 160 percent rise.[30] Both total sales and profits have risen dramatically, including a 32 percent increase in profits in the first half of 2006. During this same period, most competitors in retailing in the UK have been floundering.[31]

Is this financial success solely a result of engaging with its full range of stakeholders, building CSR into every level of management, and transforming traditional CSR into corporate social and environmental accountability? Probably not. But Marks & Spencer's financial success does indicate that some of the highest standards of corporate accountability need not occur at the expense of shareholders and the bottom line.

new and far-reaching codes of conduct to protect the health, safety, labor rights, and human rights of people working for their suppliers in developing countries, which no law requires them to undertake, the reporter concluded that corporate CEOs define "values" more broadly than politicians to mean the beliefs and principles that govern their business practices — in essence, how they do what they do. While the federal government was becoming more secretive, leading companies were becoming more open and transparent about their supply chains. The reporter noted that not only are many of America's biggest companies "becoming more socially responsible, more green, more diverse, more transparent and more committed to serving the common good," but they have come to believe that "moral values, broadly and liberally defined, can help drive shareholder values."

The potential risks associated with not recognizing those changing societal expectations were reflected in a *Fortune* magazine article about the steep price companies might pay for ignoring their "moral liability." Moral liability is the notion that companies have a responsibility to behave ethically. Often the price paid for violating this expectation is damage to a brand or a reputation. At other times the cost is more concrete and takes the form of lawsuits, damage awards, or lost sales.[33] The scope of this expanding and sobering risk was reflected in a major report, "The Changing Landscape of Liability," issued by the London-based international NGO SustainAbility, in collaboration with Swiss Re, Insight Investments, and the major international law firm Foley Hoag LLP.[34]

The SustainAbility report recognizes that "there is an accelerating shift in societal values and expectations, and a corresponding mistrust of industry, which feeds a demand for greater corporate accountability." Further, it argues that trends in legal liability now include "a progressive 'internalization' of social and environmental costs [that] is bringing business into the firing line of liability for its past and future impacts. This will not only bring huge costs to business for its on-going trading, but might also render companies vulnerable to legal action for past and future impacts resulting from corporate actions which are perceived to be 'irresponsible.'"[35]

Legal liability on social and environmental issues — i.e., the obligations under local, national, and international regulation — is deepening, and the report's authors argue that the notion of moral liability is hardening and has increased potential to adversely impact any businesses that are still focusing exclusively on strict legal compliance.

The SustainAbility report contains several recommendations for boards and senior management of companies that wish to address this increase in social, environmental, and economic liability, including the following:

- Shift from passive to active corporate responsibility, assuming in risk-management reviews that boundaries of accountability will progressively expand through the value chain and through the whole life cycle of a product's development, production, use and disposal.
- Make stakeholder engagement an essential and integral part of risk management, using this engagement to alert the company to shifting expectations.
- Ensure alignments of standards and behaviors, including all key codes, charters, voluntary agreements, and public social/environmental commitments, and test them for consistency and alignment with current and emerging societal expectations.[36]

A *Boston Globe* op-ed argued similarly that:

> Corporations are now expected to play leading roles in promoting diversity, eradicating poverty, protecting public health, eliminating child labor, developing communities, ensuring privacy, and upholding human rights. And they must govern not just themselves, but also take responsibility for the behavior of companies up and down their supply chains.
>
> Call it the age of accountability. Corporations must step up their performance on environmental and social measures along with financial ones — posting results according to the so-called "Triple Bottom Line." Today's smartest companies are embracing these expectations and turning them to their advantage.[37]

COLLABORATIVE GOVERNANCE AND CAPITALISM 3.0

There are two further concepts that can help us understand this changing landscape of liability and the emergence of the certification revolution. The first is the notion of collaborative governance. Simon Zadek is the chief executive of AccountAbility, another London-based nonprofit international organization exploring the leading edges of accountability for organizations of all sorts (governments, nonprofits, and for-profit organizations). In another recent paper, published by the Center for Business and Government at Harvard's Kennedy School of Government, Zadek argues that in a globalized world, where the rule of law as imposed by any single nation is inadequate to establish controls over increasingly transnational business, new forms of governance are emerging.[38] Building on some of his earlier award-winning writing about "civil corporations,"[39]

Zadek sees corporate responsibility as part of a dynamic process in which corporations "absorb societal expectations and lessons regarding risks and opportunities" and embody them in the design and practice of business. Some of their responses will be tactical, responding to new knowledge that extends corporate boundaries of accountability. They must now face a full range of stakeholders, increasingly well-informed final consumers, global civil society organizations, as well as national governments at each location in their supply chains. Some will be strategic, perhaps shifting the incentives of fund managers so they extend their time horizons beyond quarterly performance reports to align more clearly with societal expectations. And some will be transformative, requiring that investors recognize they will be held liable for social and environmental aspects of their business.

Collaborative governance, in Zadek's interpretation, involves "deliberative multi-stakeholder collaboration in establishing rules of behavior governing [a] broader community of actors." When corporations sit down with advocacy groups to discuss appropriate responses to the concerns expressed by the advocates, they are sharing the process of rule setting and allowing the advocates to participate in that process. When a wide range of stakeholders comes together with corporate representatives to develop standards for social and environmental behavior by corporations, both the outside stakeholders and the corporations are participating in collaborative rule setting, which is collaborative governance. Note that the rule setting may, or may not, involve formal governmental regulation setting. Engagement by all stakeholders in this collaborative governance requires that each sees a way to pursue his or her specific interest. If there are no points of agreement where the interests of all overlap, then there may be no standards developed.

Stakeholder-based standard setting is at the heart of the certification revolution. The results are new collaborative governance mechanisms that address the moral liability faced by corporations as societal expectations for social and environmental responsibility continue to rise. In many ways, the process of setting standards offers corporations the best of all worlds for facing that liability: they directly participate in negotiating the standards to which they will be held; they clarify the changes in practice that will be expected of them; and they receive external validation of the appropriateness of their practices, which can become a competitive business edge. At the same time, this process offers powerful incentives for the social and environmental advocacy groups. They participate in reshaping corporate standards in the directions that they have been demanding; when companies agree to the changes, the advocates receive public validation of their demands for change; and they obtain continuing leverage to monitor the fulfillment of the commitments made by the companies.

The second concept that helps explain the changing corporate landscape is the notion of the "commons." Traditionally, the commons was public space shared by everyone. For Peter Barnes, co-founder of Working Assets, the socially responsible financial services firm, the commons consists of all the gifts we collectively inherit and all those we create together. Examples of the commons include the air, water, biodiversity and ecosystems, music, languages, mathematics, public parks and protected areas, the Internet, and public health. Just as we all inherit these commons, Barnes writes, we all have a joint obligation to preserve them.

One of the reasons why corporations have difficulty conceptualizing their responsibility to protect the environment is that neither markets nor governments have been especially successful in establishing the rules required to protect the commons. On the contrary, to the extent that corporations can take advantage of the natural commons to dilute their effluents in the air and in rivers, lakes, and oceans, they reduce their direct costs and pass the costs to others in society. Similarly, corporations have difficulty conceptualizing their responsibilities to their workers because the social problems created by extremely low wages, lack of health benefits, dangerous working conditions, and job uncertainty are not part of their direct costs and are passed on to others in society.

In his stunning book *Capitalism 3.0,* Barnes explains how many of the debates over social and environmental responsibility pertain to the global, national, and local "commons."[40] According to Barnes, Capitalism 1.0 was the "shortage" capitalism prior to 1950, when the demand for goods exceeded the supply, workers worldwide struggled to meet their basic needs, production was more localized than global, financial capital was scarce worldwide, and production's visible impacts on nature were relatively limited.

From the 1950s to the end of the 20th century, Capitalism 2.0 prevailed. This was the era of the "affluent society," in the words of John Kenneth Galbraith. Most people in the United States, Europe, and other wealthy countries had more than enough food, housing, clothing, and other goods. This "surplus" capitalism was reflected in increasingly abundant financial capital; corporations with difficulty finding enough customers for all they could produce; and the cumulative destruction of nature apparent in the form of global warming, deforestation, rampant pollution of rivers and lakes, and the exhaustion of fish stocks in what have come to be called the "empty oceans."

Governmental solutions, such as regulation, taxation, and public ownership, have been decreasing in effectiveness precisely as corporate wealth and political clout increased. Although there was an ideological swing away from governmental activity to protect the commons, starting with the radical conservatism of Margaret Thatcher and Ronald Reagan in the early 1980s, there may be a return swing of the political pendulum in the early years of the 21st century as mass movements arise to battle the consequences of corporate-led globalization around the world, especially in Latin America.

Privatization of the need to protect the commons — i.e., leaving it to corporations — also failed during the last quarter of the 20th century, according to Barnes. Corporations are driven by an algorithm, a set of computational rules, that requires they maximize return to investors, distribute their income on a per-share basis, and leave the price of nature (or more broadly, the cost of taking advantage of the commons) at zero. "Nothing in the algorithms requires or encourages corporations, either individually or collectively, to preserve anything," writes Barnes.[41] He recognizes that there is a remote possibility that socially responsible corporations, responding to socially responsible investment funds (like the one he founded) and socially responsible shareholders, might create conditions where a triple bottom line is an acceptable pursuit. But he is, sadly, skeptical about the long-term prospects for CSR on these levels because even socially responsible investors must seek the same level of returns, which means they tend to limit the areas of responsibility that they demand of companies (lest they damage returns too much) and inevitably loosen their "responsibility screens" as they successfully draw huge increases in funds that they must place effectively.

Barnes argues that what is needed is a Capitalism 3.0, characterized by the creation of a powerful new "commons sector." This sector would consist of a new set of institutions, separate from government and corporations, designed to preserve the commons and financed by selling the rights to sustainable use, rather than "giving them away" to corporations. There are examples of this kind of institution already in place. The Alaska Permanent Fund Corporation was created in 1976 to capture and redistribute to present and future generations of Alaskans the royalty revenues received by the State of Alaska from the extraction of oil and gas within the state; it presently distributes an annual dividend to each and every resident of the state. The Permanent Fund of the State of Texas, created in the 1930s to channel oil and gas royalty revenue into public higher education, currently accounts for significant shares of the total revenues of the University of Texas, Texas A&M University, and a group of related institutions.

Barnes's vision is much more ambitious. He pictures a wide range of common property trusts derived from a much wider range of revenue sources and dedicated to preserving the commons and solving persistent social problems. But that's a distraction from our tasks here.

For our purposes, the key fact is that neither governments nor corporations acting alone are likely to protect, much less build, our global commons. There is a critical need for additional actors. The certification revolution incorporates one of the most powerful sets of alternative tools created in recent years to pursue that goal. Global civil society, responding to the destruction of the natural commons, especially in extractive industries, has begun to create new mechanisms of collaborative governance that encourage and reward higher levels of environmental accountability on the part of corporations, transforming the ways in which they interact with nature and delivering benefits to present and future generations. Similarly, civil society pressure on corporations to alter their negative impacts on all the people participating in their value chains — all of their real stakeholders — has led to the creation of new forms of accountability for the social consequences of corporate practices. The remainder of this book illustrates both the successes of this movement and its continuing challenges.

3

Leveraging the Brand:
The Essence of Ethical Business Campaigns

How does civil society change the nature of the expectations for social and environmental accountability that we effectively place on corporations? In coming chapters we will see the histories of a dozen or more civil society campaigns organized to transform individual companies and also whole industries in sectors that range from forestry and fisheries to finance, toxics, and international commodity trade. They will illustrate the approaches and techniques developed in recent years and practiced, increasingly, by scores of NGOs around the world. In this chapter we will synthesize some of the lessons that have been learned in practice and shared across groups. Understanding the specific strategies being developed and applied is critical for seeing the remarkable effectiveness of these campaigns and for comprehending how corporate transformation is taking place.[1]

FACTORS BEHIND THE EMERGENCE OF MARKET CAMPAIGNS

There are a number of questions we need to address before summarizing the techniques used in these campaigns. Why, for example, do civil society organizations feel they have to persuade corporations to change through voluntary processes rather than forcing change through national and local legislation? To what extent does globalization require that efforts go beyond national boundaries? Why is it that certain critiques of corporate behavior have been more effective in recent years than they were in past decades? And is it possible that corporate market campaigns might feed into broader legislative and regulatory processes?

Many of these questions can be answered by looking at political and economic developments over the past few decades, particularly the creation of the World Trade Organization, the increasing corporate influence over governments, and the rise in globalization.

The World Trade Organization

As a start, you can blame the World Trade Organization for the ascendancy of corporate market campaigns over governmental regulation. The Uruguay Round of global trade negotiations, launched in 1986 in Punta del Este, Uruguay, culminated in the *Marrakesh Agreement*, which established the World Trade Organization (WTO) in April 1994. One of the many elements included in the *Marrakesh Agreement* was a prohibition on the use of "production and process methods" (PPMs) as a basis for banning imports of a product. That is, WTO members are not allowed to block the importation of products solely on the basis of how they are produced. Timber imports cannot be blocked, even if it can be shown that they were logged in devastatingly unsustainable and even illegal fashion. Cocoa imports cannot be banned even when cultivation involves child labor or child-slave labor. Apparel imports cannot be banned even when they are sewn by coerced prison labor. And mineral imports cannot be banned even when the mining that produced them has been explicitly associated with human rights violations, the forced relocation of communities, and the poisoning of rivers and water systems. The WTO rationale for the ban on PPMs is the fear that countries will set up "production and process screens" that favor their own manufacturers or processors over producers from other countries, or that some countries will attempt to impose their environmental, health, and safety rules on others.

One of the classic PPM cases involved dolphins and tuna. It was adjudicated even before the WTO was created, under the rules of the WTO's predecessor, the General Agreement on Tariffs and Trade (GATT). The United States banned the importation of tuna caught with purse seine nets that tended to kill a large number of dolphins who swam among, and above, schools of yellowfin tuna. This ban extended elements of the US *Marine Mammal Protection Act* to other countries. At the request of Mexico (and with the support of several other tuna-exporting countries), an international trade-dispute panel ruled in 1991 that the US "could not embargo imports of tuna products from Mexico simply because Mexican regulations on *the way tuna was produced* did not satisfy US regulations" [2] (emphasis in the original). The GATT decision meant that the US government could no longer protect dolphins from yellowfin tuna fishing, and it could no longer block the importation of tuna from countries that ignored the fishery's impact on dolphins.

The panel's reasoning was that if the US policy was accepted, "any country could ban imports of a product from another country merely because the exporting country has different environmental, health and social policies from its own." For many of us, that would seem to be a valid reason for limiting imports. However, for the GATT's multilateral trading system, focused primarily on expanding trade at all costs, bans of that sort constitute unreasonable and unacceptable "technical barriers to trade."

Before the trade panel's ruling came down, a relatively early market campaign was set up to convince the largest importers of tuna to voluntarily stop buying tuna caught in dolphin-endangering ways, independent of the challenged US regulations. The H. J. Heinz Company, which sold the market-leading Star-Kist tuna, had refused to exclude tuna caught in purse seines and by other fishing techniques that inadvertently killed many dolphins, so Earth Island Institute and its allies developed a set of full-page ads, which ran in the *New York*

Times and the *Wall Street Journal* and urged consumers to help stop the "dolphin massacre" by boycotting Star-Kist tuna. This message was supported by a film made by an Earth Island Institute biologist in 1988, when he posed as a deckhand on a Panama-registered fishing boat. The biologist documented as many as 200 dolphins drowning in the tuna nets over four months of fishing on one vessel.

The campaign was characterized by a boycott involving a growing number of schoolchildren and their parents, which Heinz began to feel. It also produced what Heinz's CEO called an "epic debate" inside the company, "almost theological in tone," which reflected the troubling moral liability of association with unnecessary killing of dolphins.[3] In the end, the damage to Heinz's socially conscious reputation became too much, as consumer tracking surveys showed a jump in awareness of the dolphin issues.

Heinz announced that its Star-Kist brand would no longer use tuna caught in dolphin-endangering nets, and it agreed to a monitoring procedure, for which it would pay, to assure consumers that dolphins were not killed in the process of catching tuna.[4] Two other leading canned-tuna vendors, Van Camp Seafood Company (a Thai company, marketer of Chicken of the Sea tuna) and Bumble Bee Seafoods (an Indonesian company, marketer of Bumble Bee canned tuna), agreed to the same procedures within hours of the announcement of the Heinz decision.[5] The code of conduct the companies agreed to is reproduced in Figure 3.1.

A "Dolphin Safe" label began to appear on cans of tuna from the companies that agreed to the standards and the monitoring procedure. Eventually 90 percent of all tuna canners worldwide agreed to Earth Island Institute's standards and procedures. Constant scrutiny was required because there was some evidence of backsliding a few years later.[6] By 2006, Earth Island Institute had monitors around the world to ensure the tuna fishery did not harm dolphins, and the slaughter of dolphins linked to tuna fishing was reduced some 97 percent, from 90,000 per year to numbers in the low hundreds.[7]

Corporate Influence over Governments

Another factor that led to the emergence of market campaigns was the inability of social and environmental advocacy organizations to persuade governments to draft or enforce laws and regulations that effectively implemented standards civil society considered reasonable for the protection of social, economic, and cultural rights and the preservation of common property natural resources such as the oceans, the atmosphere, rivers, lakes, and biodiversity.

Why were advocacy groups unsuccessful in those political spheres? Partly, some would argue, because of weak and corrupt governments in many parts of the world. Partly because the corporations the advocacy groups sought to transform had so much financial and political influence over government that regulatory and legislative routes were fundamentally ineffective. With government often a captive of the giant corporations, legislation came too slowly, at best, and was often severely compromised by the time it emerged. Enforcement was

INTERNATIONAL "DOLPHIN SAFE" STANDARDS FOR TUNA

These standards form the basis of policies utilized by the largest tuna producers in the world. It is required for approval and monitoring by Earth Island Institute.

In order for tuna to be considered "Dolphin Safe", it must meet the following standards:

1. No intentional chasing, netting or encirclement of dolphins during an entire tuna fishing trip;
2. No use of drift gill nets to catch tuna;
3. No accidental killing or serious injury to any dolphins during net sets;
4. No mixing of dolphin-safe and dolphin-deadly tuna in individual boat wells (for accidental kill of dolphins), or in processing or storage facilities; and
5. Each trip in the Eastern Tropical Pacific Ocean (ETP) by vessels 400 gross tons and above must have an independent observer on board attesting to the compliance with points (1) through (4) above.

By agreement between Earth Island Institute and the participants in "Dolphin Safe" fishing operations:

- All processing, storage, and transshipment facilities and procurement records related to the purchase, processing, storage, transport, and sale of tuna must be made available for independent monitoring.
- Companies listed as "Dolphin Safe" must maintain "Dolphin Safe" policies approved by Earth Island Institute and apply them to all international aspects of their operations and related subsidiaries.

Further, Earth Island Institute and the 85-member Dolphin Safe/Fair Trade Campaign strongly encourage tuna fishermen and tuna companies to work to reduce bycatch of non-target species and to release alive, to the maximum extent feasible, any non-target species caught in purse seine nets.

These "Dolphin Safe" standards were developed in 1990 by Earth Island Institute and the H. J. Heinz Corporation (Star-Kist Tuna); endorsed by the U.S. Tuna Foundation, Chicken of the Sea, and Bumble Bee Tuna; and have been adopted by approximately 300 tuna companies, canneries, brokers, import associations, retail store, and restaurant chains around the globe.

By way of background, in 1997, only 2.9% of the world's tuna supply was caught by chasing and setting nets on dolphins. More than 90% of the world's canned tuna market has pledged to buy and sell only "Dolphin Safe" tuna in accordance with Earth Island's "Dolphin Safe" standards.

As a result of the "Dolphin Safe" commitment by tuna companies, dolphin mortality has dropped by more than 97% in the past ten years.

For further information: Mark Berman, Assistant Director, International Marine Mammal Project, Earth Island Institute, 300 Broadway, Suite 28, San Francisco, CA 94133; (415) 788-3666; (415) 788-7324 (fax); marinemammal@earthisland.org.

Source: earthisland.org/immp/

subject to political whim, which meant the advocacy organizations that had pressed for new laws and regulations had to take legal action to ensure they were enforced.

In this case, market campaigns can be seen as a strategy of appealing to the business community and consumers in order to achieve preferred transformation. Is this a question of overriding more broadly democratic processes? Probably not, for a market campaign will go nowhere if it doesn't appeal to deeply held business and consumer values. It will have little or no effect if it doesn't provide valid and defensible information to the public. Market campaigns are comparable to business and consumer "plebiscites," giving business clients and final consumers a chance to vote their preferences with their purchasing expenditures.

Globalization

A third, and even more important, motivation for market campaigns is the fact that so much of commerce is now globalized, transcending the ability of any single nation or government to regulate it. With no major international agency or organization setting enforceable standards, the ethical constraints of civil society are the only countervailing force limiting the exercise of corporate power. Market campaigns are a powerful tool for creating, expressing, and enforcing those ethical constraints. In the words of one research team that studied the phenomenon, advocacy-led market campaigns and certification processes "have arisen to govern firm behavior in a global space that has eluded the control of states and international organizations."[8]

PROMOTING A RACE TO THE TOP

The intent of most market campaigns, which some would prefer to call "ethical business campaigns," is to promote a "race to the top" for corporate social and environmental practices. That phrase, of course, plays off the frequently discussed "race to the bottom," in which environmental protection and social justice are overridden by cutthroat competition among companies for profits or among countries for investment. A report called *Race to the Top*, prepared by the Business Ethics Network, provides considerable insight into the thinking behind these market campaigns, as well as recognizing their shortcomings.[9] Drawing from that report and from conversations with dozens of representatives of market campaigns over the past ten years, I've identified a number of key steps that underlie the most successful campaigns.

- **Campaign organizers have the strategic opportunity to frame the debate** by selecting the language that begets clear and powerful mental images and structures the discussion in a way that is disadvantageous to the companies. We will see effective framing in almost every campaign, but it has been especially powerful in the No Dirty Gold campaign (see Chapter 8), which seized the moral high ground by framing the debate around the social and environmental "dirtiness" of common and undeniable practices in the gold mining industry. To change forestry practices in British Columbia, the Mid-Coast

Speaking Truth to Power

Michael Marx and the Evolution of Corporate Market Campaigns

If there is a single "elder statesman" in the young and entrepreneurial field of market campaigns, it is 56-year-old Michael Marx.

A slender, bespectacled, and crisply articulate speaker, Michael Marx specialized in his early career in developing personality and skill profiles of employees at major firms, building assessment systems, and helping human resources staff select the people most likely to succeed in a given job. He also used his skills to help lawyers question, vet, and select juries in multimillion-dollar civil lawsuits. A life-threatening medical scare motivated him to change his career in the late 1980s, and he became an active advisor, campaign director, and executive in more of the forest-oriented market campaigns than virtually anyone else to date.

Michael was born in Spokane, Washington, and studied organizational communications and social psychology at Gonzaga University, the University of Oregon, and the University of Wisconsin, where he earned his PhD in 1980. In 1988, when Randy Hayes was starting Rainforest Action Network, Michael helped set up its early management processes before joining the board of directors two years later.

By 1992, wishing to be more engaged, he stepped down from RAN's board and became director of its international Boycott Mitsubishi campaign. Mitsubishi was, at that time, the largest corporation in the world and the largest importer of wood in Japan. RAN focused on Mitsubishi because the World Rainforest Movement had reported that its logging practices in Sarawak, Brazil, Chile, Canada, and Alaska were environmentally unsound. But Mitsubishi's pulp and paper division was primarily a trading company, rather than a production company, and it had few branded forest products in global markets. RAN felt that a campaign focused on Mitsubishi Motors and Mitsubishi Electric, which did sell branded products in the US, might ultimately pressure the trading company to change. It would also keep the issue of rainforest destruction in the media spotlight and help turn hundreds of young activists into corporate campaigners.

This campaign preceded by several years the creation of consensus-based sustainable forest management practices by the Forest Stewardship Council (which we will discuss in Chapter 4), so RAN's demands were a bit obscure and tough to verify. Although the company sold several of its logging operations and reduced its log imports, the ultimate value of the campaign wasn't felt until 2003, when the grand chairman of the Mitsubishi Companies, Minuro Makiharo, announced that all of Mitsubishi's forest holdings around the world would become certified to FSC standards. Then, in 2006, the Alberta Pacific Company in Canada, partially owned by Mitsubishi, brought its 5.6 million hectares of forests into FSC certification, the largest single FSC certification in the world to that date.

In 1998 Michael became the first executive director of the Coastal Rainforest Coalition (CRC), which brought together Greenpeace, Rainforest Action Network, the Natural Resources Defense Council, and American Lands Alliance for their combined work in British Columbia and the Pacific Northwest. The market campaigns that evolved there achieved major breakthroughs in strategy. Using a variety of ingenious techniques (some still under wraps), CRC activists identified the principal buyers of products from Interfor, West Fraser, and Western Forest Products, the three major logging companies whose practices they wished to transform. The activists learned that paper products produced using pulp from logs cut by these companies were being sold to major branded companies in the US, Europe, and Japan. They also learned that Home Depot was a major buyer of wood products from these companies, and RAN took charge of organizing the campaign specifically focused on Home Depot (also discussed in Chapter 4).

Employing a then-bold campaign move, CRC members sent letters to many of the companies in the US that were sourcing timber and pulp from British Columbia, calling on them to stop using products that contributed to the destruction of the last remaining old-growth forests and to shift toward ecologically sustainable alternatives. They gave the companies 90 days to respond, politely adding that they would then run a full-page ad in the *New York Times* that would list those willing to sign a commitment to save North America's last great ancient rainforest and those who refused. The publication of the ad in December 1998, linked to a CBS News report that aired the day before the ad appeared, shook the government of British Columbia and the timber industry to their respective roots.

In 2000, Michael presided over CRC's transformation into ForestEthics, a stand-alone NGO with the same commitments to market campaigns, but without the complexity of a coalition of four larger NGOs. ForestEthics retained its role as leader of the BC campaign and soon launched a "paper campaign" targeting office supply stores, beginning with Staples. The paper campaign was an important complement to campaigns involving wood products. Increased use of recycled paper, especially post-consumer recycled paper, was viewed as another major contribution to reducing pressure on forests.

Michael left ForestEthics in 2003 to set up Corporate Ethics International (CEI), a think tank and training center focused on corporate transformation. This move gave Michael two new roles: teaching much larger cohorts of young market campaigners how to organize their own campaigns, and conceptualizing corporate transformation at even broader and deeper levels. CEI created the Business Ethics Network, which produced *Race to the Top*, a study of market campaigns. The network also organizes annual conferences on market campaigning, issues the BENNY Awards for the best corporate market campaigns each year, and coordinates major projects for the Big-Box Collaborative, the principal coalition of NGOs focused on transforming Wal-Mart and other big-box stores.

When asked about the most important lesson he has learned in his first 15 years of work around market campaigns, Michael responds quickly: "I never cease to be amazed by how the most powerful corporations in the world, despite billions of dollars in revenue, tens of thousands of employees, and immense political influence in the halls of government, remain extraordinarily vulnerable to well-organized, well-informed, grassroots campaigns that speak truth about their practices to their customers, their shareholders, and the general public."

How leading U.S. companies are saving ancient rainforests without ever chaining themselves to a tree.

AALTANHASH VALLEY, BRITISH COLUMBIA, intact unprotected river valley scheduled for logging by Western Forest Products. *photo by Ian McAllIster, 1998*

These companies are leading the way in the protection of ancient forests.

- 3M
- Advanced Micro Devices
- Bristol-Myers Squibb Co.
- Dell Computer Corporation
- Estée Lauder Companies
- Hallmark Cards, Inc.
- Hewlett-Packard Company

- IBM
- Johnson & Johnson
- Kinko's, Inc.
- Levi Strauss & Co
- Liz Claiborne Inc
- Lockheed Martin Corporation
- The McGraw-Hill Companies

- Mitsubishi Electric of America, Inc.
- Mitsubishi Motor Sales of America, Inc.
- Mother Jones
- Mutual of Omaha Companies
- National Geographic Society
- NIKE, Inc.
- Pacific Gas & Electric Company

- Patagonia
- Quantum Corporation
- Seventh Generation
- Starbucks Coffee Company
- United Stationers Supply Co.
- Utne Reader

Many of America's leading companies realize that saving the earth's last ancient forests is an essential part of doing business. And for good reason. The buying public is making it clear that it doesn't want wood products that destroy old-growth forests. These forests provide a home for 90 percent of all plant and animal species, and are a source for the life-saving medicines of tomorrow.

Sadly, less than a quarter of the world's original ancient forests remain intact. One of the most threatened old growth forests is the coastal rainforest of British Columbia in Canada. Of the original 353 valleys on B.C. coast, only 69 still remain pristine. The vast majority of these valleys are slated for clearcut logging, or to be split open by damaging roads – largely to feed U.S. consumption. The major offending logging companies are Interfor, Doman and West Fraser.

The good news is influential U.S. industry leaders are committing to sound business practices that will help preserve the world's last old-growth stands. They have committed to survey their wood and paper suppliers, shift away from old growth to independently certified or alternative materials, and to reduce overall virgin wood fiber use. We don't always agree with these companies on other issues, but today we roundly applaud them for their leadership in helping to save the world's ancient forests.

There's a long way to go. Some companies are resisting making a commitment to save what cannot be replaced. There's still time for other companies to join the effort. You can help. Call the Coastal Rainforest Coalition at 510-540-8730 to learn how your company can join those leading the way, or how you can encourage those companies lagging behind to catch up. *Visit our website at www.coalition-tbc.org*

These companies are lagging behind.

- AT & T - C. Michael Armstrong, CEO
- BellSouth Corp - F. Duane Ackerman, CEO
- Home Depot - Arthur Blank, CEO
- Hercules - R. Keah Elliot, CEO
- HomeBase, Inc. - Allan Sherman, CEO
- Los Angeles Times - Kathryn Downing, CEO
- Wal-Mart Stores - David D. Glass, CEO

Timber Supply Area was reframed and renamed "The Great Bear Rainforest," with the rare white "Spirit Bear" as its most recognizable icon. That reframing was especially powerful when campaigners asked European publishers to announce that they would not purchase paper products that came from British Columbia until conservation of critical areas, including Spirit Bear habitat, was achieved and logging practices were made more sustainable.

- **Successful campaigns involve extraordinary efforts to gather intelligence about the companies and industries targeted,** including their business strategies, products, supply chains, and financial situations. In the age of the Internet, these tasks are considerably easier than they were when corporate information was less available. Some of the most important market campaign breakthroughs, as we will see in several chapters, have come from successfully tracking supply chains, approaching companies that buy from a targeted firm, and getting those buyers to make their suppliers accountable for their practices. Some of that information comes from inside sources, but much more comes from clever techniques for tracing products bought by key customers. The largest, most branded, and most visible companies are often the targets of choice, but sometimes financial vulnerability, management approachability, or other industry factors suggest starting with smaller or less visible firms.

- **Crafting an appropriate set of demands can be one of the most complicated parts of market campaigning.** In some cases it's easy. For example, given the well-demonstrated health risks of mercury, it was easy for Health Care Without Harm to demand that the health-care industry eliminate mercury thermometers and replace them with digital electronic temperature gauges. Simply demanding that companies discontinue practices that have long been part of their business may be less effective than encouraging them to adopt alternative practices, even if the alternatives are more expensive. It is not always easy to determine what those alternatives should be, and retrofitting them into existing production units may be even more difficult. The cost of transforming practices may leave targeted companies with no alternative but to resist change if they are to remain competitive.

- As a result, **campaigners frequently discuss the need to give companies an "exit strategy" and to work through back channels and third-party negotiators** to find cost-effective ways to make products and services more socially and environmentally responsible. I believe that one of the self-limiting characteristics of market campaigns of the 1980s and 1990s was that they focused too much on "stop doing this" or "stop doing that" and not enough on "here's what you should be doing." One of the most effective "exit strategies" is to move companies toward the adoption of third-party certification processes that provide assurance of more responsible practices and offer the highest level of risk reduction to protect the company's reputation and brand value.

- Therefore, **one of the key breakthroughs in corporate campaigning over the last 15 years has been the creation and successful implementation of** certification systems that whole industries can adopt. The existence of a certification system reduces the difficulty of crafting the set of demands. If advocacy groups join with companies to design stakeholder-based, negotiated standards, the system that emerges will be at least minimally feasible for the companies and may lead to significant improvement in corporate practices. Smart and effective market campaigns, combined with the creation of certification systems to monitor and assess corporate compliance for as long as necessary, have led to some of the biggest transformations.

- **Campaigners have come to recognize the importance of the business-to-business dimension of corporate accountability.** Rather than attempting to exert influence directly on companies associated with inappropriate production practices, campaigners have begun to focus on highly branded retail companies. Home Depot was more vulnerable than Georgia Pacific Lumber Company; major jewelers are more responsive to criticisms of mining practices than major mining companies; computer manufacturers are more sensitive to criticism of recycling issues for their products than the little-known recycling companies that create human and environmental damage from the toxics in the electronics. However, the focus on retail is not based on an assumption that consumers will ultimately drive the transformation. Consumer education is a lengthy and expensive process. It is far simpler to inform retail firms, the financial community, shareholders, insurers, and other stakeholders of potential problems or questionable practices in the supply chains of products.

- **Most of the successful campaigns we will see have both an "outside strategy" and an "inside strategy."** That is, they apply strong pressure on companies to change, and then they negotiate a good agreement while the heat is on.

- **Another important lesson of this past decade is the realization that total victory need not be achieved at the very start.** Negotiating timetables for change, processes for reaching preferred levels of accountability, and commitments to achieve goals within reasonable periods of time may be more effective than demanding total and immediate fulfillment of a set of demands.

- **Campaigners have come to see they are in for the long haul.** It may be hard to believe, in view of the harshness of some of the campaigns we will feature, but most market campaigns have led to ongoing relationships between the target companies and the campaigning organization as they work together to develop solutions. Home Depot, the target of one of the toughest campaigns (described in Chapter 4), still meets quietly but regularly with the groups that began campaigning against it nearly ten years ago. The advocacy groups ask for, and receive, information on improvements in sourcing of wood products sold in Home Depot. Many targeted companies will need to have, and will seek, the continuing support (or at least the acquiescence) of the market campaigners as they craft their responses over time.

Michael Brune, executive director of Rainforest Action Network (RAN), added a number of refinements to these ideas when he addressed my seminar at Yale during the fall of 2005. He suggested five "rules" for effective campaigns.

- **Rule 1: Don't be shy.** Reviewing the language and imagery of some of the campaigns RAN had organized, Brune noted that it didn't hurt to make bold claims about the practices of the companies on which campaigns focused. The headline of one RAN's attack ads against Home Depot said, "How can two guys in pinstripe suits [the board chair and CEO of Home Depot] cut down more rainforest than anyone in flannel shirts?" In the text of the ad they continued, "They currently fuel the chainsaws by selling dozens of products made from trees ripped out of pristine, old growth forests."
- **Rule 2: Frame your issues morally and symbolically.** A striking image from the 1999 demonstrations against the WTO in Seattle was a huge banner, suspended from the arm of a tall construction crane, which showed a huge arrow with the word "Democracy" pointing in one direction, and a second arrow with the initials "WTO" pointing in the opposite direction. Another morally powerful image was an anti-tobacco advertisement showing two cowboys riding their horses out of a corral, into the sunset, with one looking at the other and saying, "I miss my lung, Bob."
- **Rule 3: Make activism fun.** Many of the market campaign organizations generate participation in their actions against specific companies by making the work fun, whether with outrageous costumes, through drumming and singing, or by arranging social events where groups of like-minded people, often youth of similar ages, gather, work, and then play together.
- **Rule 4: Keep the heat on.** Plan a diversity of strategies and tactics, keep the target companies off-balance, and orchestrate relentless pressure once a campaign begins. "Piling on," Brune suggests, "is fair play." In Chapter 6 we will look at how this strategy successfully transformed the global project finance industry in a relatively short period of time.
- **Rule 5: Play fair.** Recognizing the importance of the steps taken by corporations that change their policies is an important element of market campaigns. We will see "Attaboy!" ads, congratulating the companies that have agreed to change their practices (and naming the competitors who refuse to change theirs), in several of the campaigns reviewed in the coming chapters.

A sixth rule, based on RAN experience, should perhaps be "Get ready for backlash!" The Boise Cascade lumber company (now simply called Boise), when confronted with a RAN campaign to force it to stop logging in old-growth forests, launched a countercampaign to undermine RAN itself. It called for the IRS to revoke RAN's tax-deductible status, claiming that RAN's campaign to get Boise to stop logging in old-growth forests was a violation of its tax-exempt charter. Boise apparently contracted with a right-wing NGO to send letters to major foundations throughout the US, including many that had never funded RAN,

The Making of a Market Campaigner
Michael Brune of Rainforest Action Network

The saga of the conversion of Michael Brune, from an accounting and economics major who thought he would work on Wall Street to the head of one of the world's most effective market campaign organizations, may be a prototype for much of the current generation of youth who are seeking a more ethical and more powerful opportunity to change the world. Soft-spoken, articulate, and intense, Brune moves easily from stirring condemnations of corporate environmental practices in front of large audiences to boardroom discussions with senior staff at Home Depot, Citigroup, and Goldman Sachs.[10]

Born and raised in Chadwick Beach, New Jersey, Brune went to college close to home at West Chester University of Pennsylvania. After he graduated in 1993, he took off several months to travel before looking for the job he had planned to seek in the financial district in New York City. When he returned from his travels, he was convinced that he should work more directly on environmental issues and took a job as a neighborhood canvasser for the Greenpeace office in Philadelphia. As his skills grew, he was promoted within Greenpeace to run the sustainable forestry canvassing campaigns out of its San Francisco office from 1995 to 1997, and then moved to what became the Coastal Rainforest Coalition in 1997. This was just as CRC was organizing some of its high-profile campaigns to convince major companies — including the *New York Times,* Nike, Pacific Gas and Electric, AT&T, Esteé Lauder, and Levi Strauss — to stop buying wood and paper products from old-growth forests, particularly those in the Pacific Northwest of the US and British Columbia. CRC's goal was to have the companies switch to alternative sources, including products certified by the Forest Stewardship Council. The companies CRC targeted were not directly part of the paper and wood products industry, but most of them used paper from suppliers logging in the areas on which the campaign was focused.

In those days in the late 90s, Brune recalls, purchasing managers had "no awareness whatsoever" about the origins of their paper, fiberboard, or wood products. His "cold calls" to these managers were always a bit tense because they weren't accustomed to being contacted directly by the representative of an environmental group. What often followed was an opportunity for Brune and other CRC staff to make a presentation to the company's purchasing staff. The CRCers would explain the problems caused by conventional logging practices, describe the environmentalists' campaigns to change those practices, and then show the company's staff the political risks they faced if they weren't aware of the problems, as well as the opportunities they might have to become industry leaders in sourcing more carefully.

In August 1998, Rainforest Action Network hired Brune to run its emerging campaign to transform Home Depot purchasing practices (see Chapter 4). Building on previous work, they raised the tempo of the campaign and intensified their focus, and by August 1999, Home Depot announced a completely new set of policies, committed to eliminating old-growth forest products from its supply chain, strengthened its public preference for wood certified under FSC standards...and shook up the US do-it-yourself retail industry. Within a week, the second-largest DIY chain, Lowe's, committed to meet or beat Home Depot's sustainable forest products sourcing policies. By the summer of 2000, eight of the ten largest DIY chains had made similar commitments.

Brune subsequently led RAN's campaign to encourage Citigroup to improve the social and environmental characteristics of the major global projects it was financing (see Chapter 6). The campaign began in spring 2000, and it took until spring 2003 for Citigroup to agree to negotiate with RAN. By June 2003, Citigroup had convinced nine more banks to commit to the Equator Principles, a major step in the direction of greater social and environmental accountability and sustainability.

Brune became executive director of RAN in 2003, shortly after the Citigroup success. He sees the marketplace as "arguably the most powerful basis for change in corporate practices at this time," and he believes that, "in the future, if we can find ourselves with a government that is less dysfunctional, and not necessarily less or more conservative, we would have some hope of building social and environmental accountability into business-supported legislation."

In March 2004, *Fortune* magazine dedicated a lengthy story to RAN.[11] The writer, with grudging admiration, noted that the group, with an annual budget of barely $2.4 million and a staff of 25, mostly in their 20s and 30s, used "street theater, Internet organizing, celebrity endorsements, and an understanding of brand vulnerability...to push corporate executives' buttons."

Reflecting on the *San Francisco Chronicle*'s view that RAN is a "fighting machine" that "hits corporations where it hurts for the good of the environment,"[12] Brune notes that conflict is sometimes required in conversations with companies, but not always. "Most companies have highly committed and ethical people inside who genuinely want to satisfy both financial and moral responsibilities." And that may be one of the key secrets of RAN's success.

demanding they stop funding RAN lest they find themselves confronting lawsuits and formal challenges to their own tax-exempt status. The IRS rejected the case. The Council on Foundations, a national association of several thousand US-based funders, issued a quick verbal legal opinion to its members that the claims against RAN (and the threats to funders) were groundless. I know of at least one major foundation that made its first grant to RAN — a sizable one — because its staff was outraged at Boise's attempts to squelch RAN's free-speech rights by intimidating its funders.

MARKET CAMPAIGNS IN A BROADER CONTEXT: THE POWER OF NGOS

How have nongovernmental advocacy groups acquired the power to organize the market campaigns that we will be analyzing? The power to tap strongly held ethical values in consumers in order to transform corporate practices? The power to move companies and industries in ways that neither national governments nor international agreements can? The answer is fairly simple. People around the world tend to trust NGOs and other civil society organizations more than business, government, or the media.

The Edelman company is, in its own words, "the world's largest independent public relations firm," with over 2,000 employees in offices around the world.[13] Since 2001, it has been publishing the "Edelman Trust Barometer," an assessment of relative levels of trust in different institutions (business, government, NGOs, and the media). The "barometer" is based on roughly 2,000 interviews each year with opinion leaders in up to 14 countries.

The key question asked in the Edelman survey is "How much do you *trust* each institution to do what is right?" The responses are reported as the percentage of respondents who indicated that they trusted each institution to "do what is right." According to the 2006 report (which also summarizes data from the five previous years), "trust in NGOs, always the most trusted institution in Europe, has steadily increased in the US — from 36% in 2001 to 54% in 2006 — becoming the most trusted institution in the States. Trust in NGOs has also risen significantly in the past year in Canada (45% in 2005, 57% in 2006) and Japan (43% in 2005, 66% in 2006)."

Many other observations in the 2006 report indicate the extent to which NGOs have gained levels of civil society trust over business, government, and the media...and why:

- There is a "deep trust void facing traditional institutions including business, government, and the media."
- In Europe, the gap between NGO credibility and business credibility has grown from a 10 percent difference in 2002 (51 percent for NGOs vs 41 percent for business) to a 14 percent difference in 2006 (52 percent for NGOs vs 38 percent for business).
- Trust in government has been falling precipitously in the US (from 48 percent in 2004 to 38 percent in 2006) and remains at very low levels in Europe (averaging less than 30 percent over the five-year period from 2002 to 2006).
- Trust in the media to do the right thing is even lower in both regions and has also been falling (averaging less than 30 percent in both the US and Europe).
- Trust in NGOs is growing, Edelman staff say, because NGOs are "willing to do what other groups aren't, which is work closer with business to get things done." Increasingly, "they'll cooperate with whomever it takes to get solutions. And they do what they do in the interest of good — they appear interested in solutions for you and me, as opposed to political power or money."
- This relative loss of trust of the business world, according to Edelman, has significant financial costs. "At least 64% of opinion leaders in every country surveyed said they had refused to buy the products or services of a company they did not trust." And half of the opinion leaders surveyed in the US, Canada, France, Germany, and Spain "had refused to accept employment

with a company they didn't trust."
- Edelman states that "the days of delivering a reliable product at a good price being enough to earn a good reputation are over." Trust in a company is a combined product of company behavior, industry reputation, and the country of origin of the opinion leaders. Company behavior — i.e., the manner in which a company engages with its full set of stakeholders — is the only one of those dimensions over which it has control. And full stakeholder engagement is cited by Edelman as "imperative for US companies trying to tap into the concerns and needs of the communities they serve." More importantly, "trust is at the center of comprehensive risk management."

Edelman also noted in its 2006 Trust Barometer that building trust in the 21st century requires significantly different approaches than those used in the past. The growth of peer-to-peer communications through the Internet gives consumers and employees far more credible information about companies than they could previously find. "The consumer," Edelman finds, "has become a co-creator, demanding transparency on decisions from sourcing to new-product positioning."

This growth of an increasingly coherent and powerful transnational civil society has been documented and studied by a number of academics in recent years. Ann Florini, a researcher at the Brookings Institution, calls it "the third force,"[14] which responds to the global need for "*someone* to act as the 'global conscience,' to represent broad public interests that do not readily fall under the purview of individual territorial states or that states have found themselves wont to ignore."[15]

In her anthology on global civil-society case studies, *The Third Force*, Florini and her co-authors question how powerful this transnational civil society is, and they ask how sustainable and how desirable its influence is. They conclude that transnational civil society coalitions, such as those we will see orchestrating both national and international market campaigns, have been particularly successful in "getting otherwise-neglected issues onto the agendas of national governments, inter-governmental organizations, and, increasingly, corporations." Further, "the power of transnational civil society manifests itself at virtually every stage of policy making, from deciding what issues need attention to determining how problems will be solved to monitoring compliance with agreements."[16]

A couple of factors extend civil society's power:
- Improvements in global communications technology, including cable media companies, the Internet, and electronic mail, greatly expand the ability to form coalitions, to organize activities, and to have simultaneous impacts at several points around the globe.
- Transnational campaigns are relatively inexpensive to organize and finance since many of the participants are volunteers, most paid employees work for wages well below what they could make in business markets, and government

funding is often available, especially in Europe.

However, the power of civil society and NGOs is limited by several factors:

- There is no coherent transnational agenda driving the attention of these groups.
- They remain powerful only as long as they retain their credibility, and they don't always get it right.
- Their power is soft and indirect; they gain influence by convincing others to take action, whether those others are governments, intergovernmental organizations, or corporations.

Many people question the legitimacy and accountability of civil society groups. Ann Florini comments that there are no easy means of imposing accountability because "transnational civil society is not subject either to elections or to market tests." Legitimacy often comes from superior knowledge. On-the-ground experience in mine-infested countries gave the global campaign to ban landmines credibility in arguing for the ban. Organizations such as Amnesty International have gained legitimacy by building a global reputation for accuracy and political neutrality. Sustainable forestry campaigners build on the local expertise of social and environmental groups and the academic expertise of international experts, document their claims of inappropriate practices with photographs, and appeal to consumers' deeply felt concerns about environmental destruction.

Another source of legitimacy is implicit government approval, which is conveyed by the legal recognition extended by many governments, though this is a tricky one. Governmental involvement with coalitions and campaigns, whether real or perceived, can quickly undermine legitimacy and cohesiveness.

The question of representativeness is perhaps the toughest. Who do NGOs and other civil society organizations actually represent? For whom do they speak? What gives a group of 30, or 50, or even 1,000 "twenty-somethings" the authority to challenge governments for not acting, to push corporations to change practices that are completely legal, or to seek to impose change that they have not been able to create through electoral processes? How do they compete effectively against democratically elected governments that can claim broad representation of a populace?

At the global level, there are tensions about global and regional representativeness. At the local level, groups advocating responsible mining practices represent different perspectives than miners, and sustainable forestry advocates find themselves opposed by local businesses and local civil society, which depend on continued logging at current levels for employment and for a share of the taxes generated.

But Florini points out that "all civil society advocacy stands or falls on the persuasiveness of the information it provides. Over time, groups whose facts and arguments prove unfounded discredit themselves. The deliberately dishonest and the merely incompetent can certainly do short-term damage, but they are unlikely to have significant, long-lasting influence." [17]

REFLECTIONS

The growth of ethical business campaigns as new mechanisms for transforming the practices of global corporations is an important element of the story I am telling. But it is not an isolated phenomenon. It is, rather, one of a rapidly growing number of mechanisms developed by increasingly powerful NGOs and civil society coalitions that fill an enormous gap in the evolving globalized world. In the absence of a United Nations that can effectively legislate to control the activities of global corporations; in the absence of treaties that bring other forms of international law to bear on corporate behavior; in the absence of legal ability to reject imports on the basis of how they were produced (no matter how nefarious the production practices); and in the presence of clearly evolving consumer and business attitudes supporting more responsible behavior, market campaigns are the instruments of the day for calling attention to irresponsible practices. We will see that they become particularly effective when combined with certification systems.

But enough of the theoretical background! Let's turn to specific and impressive examples of how this transformation is taking place around the world.

4

Birth of It All:
Transforming the Global Forest Products Industry

The first major certification system for social and environmental practices emerged in the forestry sector in the late 1980s and early 1990s. Its birth and early growing pains have been studied fairly closely, and the lessons learned have been used by the crafters of subsequent systems, who take advantage of what was learned and avoid some of the missteps.

The history of the organization created, the Forest Stewardship Council, is intriguing. It sheds much light on both the opportunities and the challenges in building a stakeholder-based global network that serves diverse social and environmental constituencies, meets the needs of business, and transforms a major industry at a pace, and to an extent, that not even the most optimistic of the founders could foresee.

In this chapter we will explore the background issues that led to the creation of the council and its certification system, examine how the certification system works, and look at the measures of its success through the end of 2006. Using vignettes from Bolivia, Russia, China, and other countries, I will illustrate the different scenarios addressed. And I will profile some of the founding organizations, participants in the system, and businesses that have found that corporate accountability associated with FSC certification is critical to their success. The dynamic, and sometimes stormy, relationships between the players have become the basis for new forms of collaborative governance that move well beyond what any individual government or international agency, or even international treaties, have been able to accomplish. At the end of the chapter I will reflect on the continuing challenges that the system faces as it gains in stature and impact.

THE ISSUES

The original focus of the environmental advocacy groups, civil society organizations, and forest products companies that came together to create the Forest Stewardship Council (FSC) was the severe and increasingly recognized problem of tropical deforestation.[1] The Food and Agriculture Organization of the UN estimated that 53,000 square miles of tropical forest (an area the size of the state of North Carolina) were destroyed *each year* during the 1980s, with about 40 percent of that in South America and the rest in Africa and Asia.[2] Deforestation (especially through clearing and burning) contributed about 25 percent of the total release of carbon into the atmosphere. According to NASA data, deforestation also disrupted the hydrologic cycle, leading to less rain and more heat worldwide and contributing to further warming of the atmosphere.[3]

Burgeoning global concerns about deforestation led to considerable governmental attention to regulating logging, establishing protected areas, and reducing the conversion of natural forests into plantations that favored exotic species at densities that effectively eliminated all biodiversity. But it became clear in the 1980s that governments were losing control, unable to implement regulations, maintain the integrity of protected areas, and limit the development of "tree deserts." The loggers, often operating illegally, and the paper companies were winning. As Tim Synnott, first executive director of the FSC, wrote, "Controversies about forestry became a global phenomenon, like the trade in forest products."[4]

In 1984, Friends of the Earth began to call for total boycotts of tropical timber, based on its analyses of the links between UK companies and tropical deforestation. The International Tropical Timber Organization (ITTO), created under the auspices of the United Nations in 1987, was supposed to analyze the problem and propose solutions. As with many UN intergovernmental projects, its work was often constrained by diplomatic delicacy, but one of its first reports, published in 1989, concluded that there were virtually no controls in place in any of the world's tropical forests to ensure that the forests would be logged sustainably.[5] This report further strengthened attempts in Europe and the US to boycott all tropical timber. European governments and the European Economic Commission (predecessor to the European Union) began to consider governmental prohibitions on imports of tropical timber.[6]

But the arguments against the boycotts were also powerful. Some critics asked why wealthy western governments would punish whole countries that were heavily dependent on timber exports. Wasn't the tool too blunt and too damaging to the poor? And if a boycott diminished the market for tropical timber, wouldn't that simply reduce the value of the forests and increase the incentive to clearcut them so people could grow products like soybeans or palm oil that were not banned or boycotted?[7]

Several independent groups started exploring alternative mechanisms for transforming the tropical forestry industry.[8] In 1987, the UK chapter of Friends of the Earth (FoE) published the first edition of a "Good Wood Guide" with the aim of guiding consumers toward timber dealers and retailers who sold "sustainably grown" forest products. The criteria were relatively loose and favored timber from temperate rather than tropical forests. More importantly, the guide listed most of the UK sources, including Harrods and B&Q (the UK's do-it-yourself giant), under the category of companies "that are contributing to the destruction of tropical rainforests."[9] FoE suggested to the ITTO and a group of forest management specialists at Oxford that there ought to be a way to use certification and labeling as mechanisms for improving tropical forest management. The idea provoked great controversy at the ITTO, with strong opposition expressed by members from countries with extensive tropical forests. It also prompted a series of studies, though most were skeptical of the fundamental notion.[10]

BIRTH OF THE FOREST STEWARDSHIP COUNCIL

Meanwhile, a visionary timber entrepreneur, Hubert Kwisthout, set up a small firm called Ecological Trading Company. As he sought to obtain tropical timber in Papua New Guinea that could be reliably labeled as coming from a sustainably managed forest, he wrote a paper proposing the creation of an international forestry monitoring agency that could certify sources.[11]

In 1990, a new North American organization, the Woodworkers Alliance for Rainforest Protection (WARP), took up Kwisthout's proposal and created a Certification Working Group (CWG) to look into the idea. WARP's members represented a broad range of stakeholders, from foresters and woodworkers to environmentalists, wood importers, and dealers in wood products. Their CWG began to develop verifiable criteria for sustainable forestry, a system to certify that those criteria were being met, and the outlines of an organization that would implement the process. These efforts led directly to the creation of the Forest Stewardship Council (FSC) several years later.

The first actual third-party independent certification for "well-managed tropical wood" products was made prior to the launch of the FSC by the newly created SmartWood program of the Rainforest Alliance in 1991. SmartWood's criteria focused on watershed stabilization, sustained yield production, and positive impact on the well-being of local people. The first forest certified to these standards was managed by the Indonesian state forestry corporation, Perum Perhutani, on the island of Java.

SmartWood staff were part of the WARP CWG (see Leadership Profile 4.1). Many of WARP's ideas were incorporated into the standards SmartWood developed, and SmartWood later became one of the first certifiers accredited by the Forest Stewardship Council.

The founding assembly of the FSC took place in Toronto in October 1993. According to Tim Synnott's notes, the 134 invitees came from 24 countries, including 56 people from tropical countries. There were representatives from indigenous groups in Canada, Brazil, and Papua New Guinea; representatives of social and environmental advocacy groups; and representatives of retailing companies, such as B&Q, as well as logging and timber management companies. Although there remained considerable disagreement among the founders (even on questions as fundamental as "Why are we doing this?"), the basic structures set in place were innovative.

The FSC was set up as a membership organization or association and divided into three "chambers": economic, environmental, and social. Both institutional and individual memberships were allowed. There were no limits on the numbers of members, but each chamber was given equal weight, and all major decisions of the association had to be approved by the three chambers. The three chambers were also divided into "North" and "South" sub-chambers in order to guarantee the voices of members from less-developed countries were heard along with those from more-developed nations. The ultimate authority for the organization was a general assembly of the members, convened every three years.

This amazingly democratic structure has served the FSC well. Although some of the General Assemblies held to date have resembled organizational brawls more than quietly deliberative bodies, the FSC has garnered the support of a vast array of forest product and retail companies as well as social and environmental NGOs who have remained engaged and have given the FSC global credibility exceeding that of any other forest certification scheme subsequently created. The general assembly that took place in Manaus, Brazil, in 2005 represented the maturation of this process. There was a better balance of participants from North and South than there had been at previous assemblies, and the weighted-chamber voting system worked flawlessly (with considerable computer assistance). Most of the participants came away pleased with the organization's growing ability to deal with controversial issues.[12]

By the time the council was established, it had developed ten core principles that set out the minimum conditions to be met if a forest were to be certified as well-managed (see Figure 4.1). The principles also reflect the tough negotiations among the diverse participants. The criteria and the indicators for their fulfillment are extensive and far more complicated than they might appear at first. For example, they require that local communities be involved in the assessment of plans for forest management before a certificate can be issued. Protection of biological diversity requires wide-ranging efforts to preserve bird and mammal habitat. And tree plantations cannot be certified if they are planted on forested lands that were cleared after 1994. That was the date set in negotiations to make certain there was no built-in incentive to clear natural forests so the land could be converted to plantations.

It took the FSC nearly three years to negotiate the final broad set of criteria and indicators. The result was not necessarily the scientifically best, environmentally strongest, or socially most ideal set of standards. It was, however, the strongest set of standards that could be developed politically, with balanced representation of economic, social, and environmental interests.

The Toronto founding assembly was just the beginning of the FSC's evolution. Basic outlines for its procedures were approved, including the fundamental principles and criteria for well-managed forestry, and the structure of the certification process. The FSC would not certify directly. Rather, it would accredit (and audit) "certifying bodies" that would do the certification under standards developed by the FSC to implement the principles and criteria. Two kinds of certificates would be issued, following the model that had been developed by Smart-Wood:

  • Forest management certificates would be given to forest management companies and community-based operations based on annual, on-the-ground monitoring of their management practices.

The Core Principles of the FSC

1. *Compliance With Laws and FSC Principles.* Forest management shall respect all applicable laws of the country in which they occur, and international treaties and agreements to which the country is a signatory, and comply with all FSC Principles and Criteria.

2. *Tenure and Use Rights and Responsibilities.* Long-term tenure and use rights to the land and forest resources shall be clearly defined, documented and legally established.

3. *Indigenous Peoples' Rights.* The legal and customary rights of indigenous peoples to own, use and manage their lands, territories, and resources shall be recognized and respected.

4. *Community Relations and Worker's Rights.* Forest management operations shall maintain or enhance the long-term social and economic well-being of forest workers and local communities.

5. *Benefits from the Forest.* Forest management operations shall encourage the efficient use of the forest's multiple products and services to ensure economic viability and a wide range of environmental and social benefits.

6. *Environmental Impact.* Forest management shall conserve biological diversity and its associated values, water resources, soils, and unique and fragile ecosystems and landscapes, and, by so doing, maintain the ecological functions and the integrity of the forest.

7. *Management Plan.* A management plan — appropriate to the scale and intensity of the operations — shall be written, implemented, and kept up to date. The long term objectives of management, and the means of achieving them, shall be clearly stated.

8. *Monitoring and Assessment.* Monitoring shall be conducted — appropriate to the scale and intensity of forest management — to assess the condition of the forest, yields of forest products, chain of custody, management activities and their social and environmental impacts.

9. *Maintenance of High Conservation Value Forests.* Management activities in high conservation value forests shall maintain or enhance the attributes that define such forests. Decisions regarding high conservation value forests shall always be considered in the context of a precautionary approach.

10. *Plantations.* Plantations shall be planned and managed in accordance with Principles and Criteria 1 to 9, and Principle 10 and its Criteria. While plantations can provide an array of social and economic benefits, and can contribute to satisfying the world's needs for forest products, they should complement the management of, reduce pressures on, and promote the restoration and conservation of natural forests.

• Chain of custody (CoC) certificates would ensure that products carrying the FSC logo could be traced back through each stage of processing to forests that were certified to comply with FSC standards.

Figure 4.2. The Forest Stewardship Council's Copyrighted Logo.
Credit: With permission of the FSC.

An FSC logo was designed for use worldwide to identify certified products (see Figure 4.2), and mechanisms were developed to copyright the logo and control its use on products and in communications about forest management practices.

At the national level, the FSC would be represented by FSC national initiatives, independent local organizations dedicated to promoting FSC certification and applying the council's general standards to local forestry types and conditions. National standards could be developed through local consultation, but they would have to be approved by the FSC's international board of directors before they could go into effect. In the absence of approved national standards, certification bodies could apply the generic global standards to the best of their abilities.

As a result of these national initiatives, the phrase "FSC-certified forests" became a commonly used and contentious misnomer. What it means, technically, are forests "certified to FSC standards by an FSC-accredited certification body." Similarly, "FSC-certified products" are "products that can be traced back through FSC-accredited chain-of-custody certification to forests certified to FSC standards."

This complexity masks significant organizational creativity. Rather than having a single global organization that does all the forest management and chain-of-custody certification itself, FSC certification is undertaken by a growing number of for-profit and not-for-profit certification companies on the basis of competitive bids. Of the first four certification bodies accredited in 1995, two were for-profit companies: Scientific Certification Systems in the US, and the worldwide Société Générale de Surveillance, now known as SGS Group. The other two were nonprofit organizations: the Rainforest Alliance's SmartWood program, based in the US, and the Soil Association's Woodmark program, based in the UK. All four offered both forest management and CoC certification, and they often bid against one another in a manner that kept certification costs as low as possible.

By 2006 there were 17 accredited certification bodies around the world, including one each in Russia, Canada, Mexico, and South Africa, as well as seven applicants seeking accreditation. By outsourcing the actual certification and monitoring, FSC has been able to keep its global staff small, fewer than 40 people, while maintaining high standards of credibility. However, some critics of the system argue that this creates potential conflicts of interest between paid certifiers and the companies paying for the certification. The alternative proposed — having the FSC conduct all of the assessments, certifications, and audits itself — was reviewed and rejected, primarily because there were strong doubts that an "FSC monopoly" certification program would keep prices as low. Further, that approach would simply shift the locus of the conflict: companies seeking certification would still have to pay the FSC for it, and the standard-setter would be simultaneously auditing and settling disputes over its own assessments and audits.

Tim Synnott has written a brief history of the FSC (available on the FSC website), and he includes a summary of what was accomplished in the early years:

> During these first years, the FSC framework was laid down: manuals, guidelines, protocols, and contracts for certification bodies, national initiatives and staff; together with the procedures for meetings: formal general assemblies, and less formal annual conferences and working groups. . . . Within a few years FSC was no longer the vision of 1993, or the project of 1996, but an international enterprise with heavy responsibilities.[13]

Synnott notes that the FSC had to deal with tensions between two contrasting concepts: "FSC as a service organization based on accreditation, standards, trademarks, etc., to be run professionally as an enterprise in order to achieve its stated goals" — even if it sometimes offended some of its voting members; and FSC as a global "consensus-based initiative that must reflect the wishes of its members at all times."[14] Much of FSC's success has been its ability to finesse those two dimensions, attempting to provide effective services that provide a "solution" to companies under pressure to improve their forest management practices, and holding together the coalition of civil society groups that lend it credibility.

BUILDING CORPORATE ENGAGEMENT

European timber trade and retailing companies began to show interest in sourcing wood from "well-managed forests" in the early 1990s, partly as a response to the growing public outcries about deforestation. B&Q had financially supported the process that culminated in the creation of the FSC, and it made an early commitment to buying FSC-certified timber at a World Wildlife Fund conference in 1992, even before certified products were available in the market. However, many companies openly opposed the whole notion of certification and labeling, arguing that it was completely infeasible to track forest products from the forest to the market. There was also resistance to the notion that the FSC was independent and separate from the more official standard-setting processes with which companies were comfortable, such as ITTO and ISO.

In 1992, the WWF created the "1995 Club," which consisted of companies that pledged to adjust their buying practices by 1995 so they would source only wood that could be shown to come from well-managed forests. Similar "buyers

Richard Z. Donovan and
the Rainforest Alliance SmartWood Program

Richard Donovan's long tenure as director of one of the Forest Stewardship Council's largest certification bodies, Rainforest Alliance's SmartWood Program, represents the continuation of a professional career sparked, in part, by cutting trees around his grandfather's house in Minnesota to keep the area clear of windfall risk.[15]

The trajectory that both he and SmartWood have followed also reflects his experiences as a Peace Corps volunteer for three-and-a-half years in a Guaraní village of Paraguay. His work has been marked by recognition of the importance of natural resource management for community development, attention to the problems of indigenous communities, and the pursuit of engagement, rather than confrontation, with business.

Donovan (everyone calls him Donovan) was an active participant in the founding of the FSC. As an employee of the fledgling SmartWood program, he attended the initial 1990 meeting of Woodworkers Alliance for Rainforest Protection and joined its Certification Working Group. He participated in SmartWood's pilot certification of the Perum Perhutani forests in Indonesia, managed the development of the last three drafts of the FSC principles and criteria, took them through the international consultative process in 1992, and presented them at the FSC founding assembly in 1993.

SmartWood, under his leadership, became the foremost FSC certifier of small-scale, indigenous, and community-based forest operations around the world. For Donovan, this fulfillment of the FSC's promise to local communities has been "hugely important" for FSC's credibility. He believes that FSC's status in the marketplace is the result of its focus on social issues in the forest products supply chain more than its focus on environmental issues. The protection of indigenous rights, freedom from social conflicts, and assurance of engagement with local communities shields companies from reputational risks even more than visual imagery of non-clearcut hillsides.

But it has been difficult to certify the operations closest to achieving that set of social goals. In the early days, Donovan claims, SmartWood attempted to conduct one small-scale indigenous or community-based certification for each major industrial forest it certified. It was not difficult to do this when national and international agencies covered the costs of the small-scale assessments, but at other times SmartWood had to subsidize the community and indigenous work with revenue earned from the larger forest operations. As the FSC certification arena became price-competitive, it became more difficult to generate subsidies, and SmartWood began approaching foundations to raise the needed funds.

By the middle of 2006, after completing the largest single forest certification in FSC history (the 5.6-million-hectare Alberta Pacific certificate, which encompasses much of the Canadian province of Alberta), SmartWood accounted for 46 percent of the FSC's total area under certification worldwide. With even larger forest management units coming under certification in Russia, Donovan doesn't expect to maintain that share for long. But SmartWood manages the largest number of FSC certificates of any certification body: nearly 500 forest management certificates and 1,400 chain of custody (CoC) certificates, with both numbers growing rapidly every year. (Donovan was also instrumental in the creation of the Rainforest TREES program — a cute acronym for a clumsy name: Training Research Extension Education Systems Program — through which small, community and indigenous forestry operations obtain more affordable access to certification services and certified product markets.)

Donovan admits to one major error in his SmartWood work. He had long believed that, if the FSC were to succeed, it was critical to generate the supply of certified wood before attempting to build the demand. He feared that companies would find it frustrating, and even useless, to commit to sourcing FSC-certified products if there was no supply that they could show to buyers. What he has learned, he admits, is that demand is the most critical component to build. Rainforest Alliance's experiences certifying sustainable agricultural commodities have demonstrated that the rate of certification rises rapidly if newly certified producers find an immediate market for their products. And it has been the ten-year imbalance between supply and demand — with demand greatly exceeding supply — that has given forest managers and forest products companies the incentive to move through certification into ready markets.

The principal challenge faced by SmartWood and FSC's other accredited certification bodies, says Donovan, is the need to continue to raise the quality of the certifications that they perform. With nearly 6,000 FSC-certified forest and CoC operations facing constant scrutiny by civil society around the world, sloppy certification assessments lead to disputes, both formal and informal, in which stakeholders challenge the validity of a certificate. If certification bodies do not consult adequately during the assessment, overlook a forest tenure conflict, or even watch as large and sometimes controversial companies take over already-certified forestry operations, invoking criticism of their practices in uncertified forests, the level of diligence required of the certification bodies continues to mount.

SmartWood faced one difficult situation involving the very first certificate it granted, which went to Indonesia's Perum Perhutani in 1990, well before the formal creation of the FSC. In 2001, SmartWood was forced to suspend the certificate, partly in response to complaints from Indonesian NGOs, and largely on the basis of SmartWood's last on-the-ground assessment of Perum Perhutani's performance. In the end, despite ten years of technical support, Perum Perhutani failed to maintain the level of "production sharing" required as a condition where it was operating in community forests.[16] Another controversy arose when the large Brazilian timber company Aracruz, which has received considerable civil society criticism of its treatment of communities and indigenous peoples, purchased an FSC-certified operation. After an explosion of criticism from Brazilian social advocacy groups, SmartWood asked Aracruz to relinquish the certificate that covered the newly purchased property.

For Donovan, this raises a major challenge that the full FSC Global Network needs to face: What is its most important paradigm for creating change within the forest products industry? What are the requirements that FSC demands for companies attempting to move toward certification? Must all of their operations be totally above reproach and, effectively, certifiable? Or can there be room for major companies, even those with questionable track records (or maybe *especially* those with questionable track records), to be certified on the basis of commitments to changing their practices, then audited diligently to ensure that they fulfill their commitments. The latter option runs the risk of "greenwashing" and the loss of credibility, while the former may make certification irrelevant for those companies and those regions where forest management practices most need improvement.

groups" developed elsewhere in Europe and in the US as a result of "conversations" between conservation groups, retailers, and the timber industry. In Europe, these discussions were driven by only an implied threat of campaigns against the companies, partly, I suspect, because there was a longer history of engagement between environmental NGOs and companies. Progress was slower in North America, in part because of the tightly organized opposition of the American Forest Association, predecessor to the American Forests and Paper Association (AF&PA).

A critical turnaround in North America occurred in June 1998, when the top executives of MacMillan Bloedel (MacBlo), a major Vancouver-based timber and paper company, appeared with representatives of Greenpeace, the Natural Resources Defense Council, and other environmental groups (organized at that time as the Coastal Rainforest Coalition, later ForestEthics). The press conference was called to announce that MacBlo would cease clearcutting on Vancouver Island and elsewhere on the British Columbia coastline and would seek certification of its forest management practices under the principles of the FSC. Commenting on the announcement, Lester Brown, founder of the Earthwatch Institute, wrote:

> Under the leadership of a new chief executive, Tom Stevens, the company affirmed that clear-cutting will be replaced by selective cutting, leaving trees to check runoff and soil erosion, to provide wildlife habitat, and to help regenerate the forest. In doing so, it acknowledged the growing reach of the environmental movement. MacMillan Bloedel was not only being pressured by local groups, but it also had been the target of a Greenpeace campaign to ban clear-cutting everywhere.[17]

Then, as noted in Chapter 1, he asked, "What in the world is going on?"

The Coastal Rainforest Coalition campaign had followed the tried-and-true market campaign strategy: lobby and demonstrate against the purchasers of

MacBlo forest products (including, it is rumored, the *New York Times*, which purchased significant quantities of newsprint from the company), pressuring them to cancel or threaten to cancel orders unless the firm implemented more socially and environmentally sustainable practices.

In the United States there was much less public awareness of the issues involved in deforestation, especially tropical deforestation. And there was much less positive response from the forest industry to the notion of certification and labeling. The breakthrough came with the Rainforest Action Network (RAN) campaign against Home Depot.[20]

RAN's campaign began in the summer of 1992 with a public call to Home Depot to phase out the sale of "old-growth tropical timber." Within months, Home Depot announced that it had begun to phase out the sale of products "that cannot be proven to be forested on a sustainable basis." Specifically, it ceased to sell teak furniture. RAN then turned to a less-successful campaign against the Mitsubishi group of corporations, major owners of forest lands worldwide, but less well-known as a brand in the marketplace.

When RAN returned to its old-growth campaign in 1997, it focused once more on Home Depot, by then the largest home improvement chain in the US, with sales exceeding US$25 billion. By that time the FSC had been established, which gave RAN a goal toward which it could push the company. Working together with Greenpeace, the Sierra Club, and local California campaigners, RAN first focused on stemming the logging of old-growth redwoods in the Pacific Northwest. Home Depot responded publicly that it would no longer sell lumber cut from ancient, first-growth redwood trees in any of its stores nationwide,[21] a commitment it later admitted was not kept.

The pace then picked up. In 1998, RAN published open letters from movie director Oliver Stone, Toronto Blue Jays baseball star Al Leiter, and the rock band R.E.M., which called on Home Depot to take the lead and phase out the sale of all old-growth wood. This was followed by a five-story banner hung in front of Home Depot's Atlanta headquarters and a Christmas holiday "kids campaign" in which 3,000 children from across the US sent letters to Home Depot CEO Arthur Blank, asking for a Christmas gift of healthy forests. The letters were delivered by schoolchildren, who accompanied an activist dressed as Santa Claus. This event was followed by a full-page ad in the *New York Times* headlined "Only a Kid Could Say 'Save the Rainforests' 3,000 Different Ways: Will Home Depot Listen to Just One?" (see page 72).

On March 17, 1999, RAN and other groups organized simultaneous demonstrations in 150 Home Depot stores across the US. At some of these events, demonstrators climbed into the rafters, donned bear costumes, and, speaking through bullhorns, urged shoppers not to buy wood stolen from the bears' forests. Negotiations between RAN and Home Depot became intense, and on August 25, 1999, Arthur Blank announced that Home Depot would stop selling wood products that came from "environmentally sensitive areas" and that it would "give preference to wood that is certified as having come from forests

ONLY A KID COULD SAY 'SAVE THE RAINFORESTS' 3,000 DIFFERENT WAYS.

Dear home depot, please don't sell or buy any old growth trees. Please tell your Suppliers that you don't want any old growth trees because they are important to us. a friend of the trees.

Chloe

Will Home Depot listen to just one?

On December 16, Home Depot's CEO Arthur Blank received an early Christmas present from Santa Claus – a sack filled with over 3,000 letters from children urging him to stop selling products ripped from the world's pristine rainforests.

Home Depot is the largest retailer of products taken from old growth trees, including cedar shingles and Douglas fir lumber from British Columbia and northwestern United States; mahogany doors from the Amazon; and lauan plywood and ramin wood from Southeast Asia. If Home Depot just listened to our children and stopped purchasing these products, millions of acres of ancient rainforest could be saved.

In the past Home Depot has claimed it can't keep track of where products come from. But right now store executives say they're developing a policy that will save ancient trees. Let's hope they're true to their word – and to our children's wishes – by entirely phasing out old growth wood.

Dozens of major U.S. corporations have pledged to stop purchasing and using products made from old growth trees. We urge Home Depot to follow suit and help end a practice as barbaric as slaughtering elephants for their ivory. Because no matter how children say it, the message to save the rainforest is loud and clear.

Aleksandra, 6th grade

Jocelyn, 4th grade

Samantha, 6th grade

RAINFOREST ACTION NETWORK

www.ran.org • 221 Pine St., #500, San Francisco, CA 94104 • 415.398.4404

Building Support for FSC Success
Bruce Cabarle and WWF-US

It was logical for Bruce Cabarle to be a member of the first FSC board of directors, even if it surprised him to be elected at the founding assembly in 1993. A graduate of Rutgers University's undergraduate program in forest management, he later earned a master's degree at the Yale School of Forestry and Environmental Studies and, in the early 1980s, became a timber sale administrator for the US Forest Service. In that position, Bruce had to allow massive clearcutting in US National Forests, and his outrage at the damage they caused to fabulous trout streams in northern Idaho was intensified by childhood memories of trout-fishing trips to those forests with his mother.

Conflicted by his experiences with the Forest Service in the Bitterroot Mountains and his Yale training in more sustainable options for forestry, Bruce left the Forest Service and took a job in Puerto Rico to help set up a state forest service on lands that had been turned over to Puerto Rico by the US federal government. His six-month contract extended into five years of work across three ranges of tropical forest types, from mangroves to cloud forests and down to dry coastal cactus forests. Bruce finished his five years in Puerto Rico as the state forester, supervising 200 staff in eight regional offices…and he was not yet 30 years old.

Bruce then spent eight years working for the Washington office of the International Institute for Environment and Development (IIED) and the World Resources Institute (WRI), into which the IIED program was merged. His work focused on forest management issues in Ecuador, Bolivia, Peru, and Central America, with special emphasis on community-based forestry in each context. The project helped communities validate that they were managing forest resources according to local laws and regulations, provided the technical assistance they needed to gain permission to log, and assisted communities in the search for markets for their products. His 1993 book on tropical forestry, *Surviving the Cut*, written with Nels Johnson, was one of the first to identify community-based forestry as a more sustainable means of protecting tropical forest integrity and biodiversity while providing livelihoods to communities.

Bruce attended the FSC founding assembly in 1993, while on the staff of WRI, and facilitated the participation of a number of Latin Americans. Elected to the first formal FSC board, and then chosen as vice-chairman, he succeeded Chris Elliot, who had agreed to serve only one year as board chair. In those early years of the FSC, it was an "operating board," deeply engaged in day-to-day decision making for the newborn organization. Bruce had the advantage of being seconded to the FSC for a year by WRI to help with the early-stage developments. In that capacity he worked on shepherding the initial principles and criteria (P&C) through an exhaustive international consultation, including ten different international meetings and 1,500 e-mail comments. At the end of the process, the P&C, the initial charter of the

FSC, and the first draft guidelines for certifiers were all approved by 90 percent or more of the founding members.

Bruce moved to WWF-US in 1998 as the initial co-director of the World Bank/ WWF Forest Alliance, which was designed to "reverse the process of forest loss and degradation, increase forest cover and quality, and harness the potential of forest lands to secure livelihoods and bring about lasting reductions in rural poverty, sustainable economic development, and the protection of vital local and global environmental values and services."[18] A core activity of that alliance was the promotion of forest management certification. By 2006 Bruce had risen to the level of managing director for WWF-US's forest program.

WWF had been an early supporter of the notion of a global institution for certifying more sustainable forest management, starting with the publication of *Truth or Trickery*, the first critique of pseudo-claims of sustainability by UK companies.[19] WWF's Forests for Life program, established in 1991, set sweeping goals for bringing forests worldwide under independent certification of sustainable management. Over the years since then, the WWF has focused consistently on the leading-edge issues of forest certification:

- Supporting the initial creation of the FSC.
- Supporting the establishment of national initiatives in the many countries where WWF's conservation focus plays out.
- Helping develop applied FSC standards at the national level (China is the most recent example).
- Working on market linkages for certified forest products, through its Global Forests and Trade Network (GFTN), to ensure the commitment and financial success of forest management operations that become certified.

The forest certification world is small, and Bruce is close to the center of it. While at WRI, he and his colleagues provided consultation services to MacMillan Bloedel, prior to that company's decision to declare a public commitment to FSC standards for well-managed forestry. His role with the World Bank/WWF Alliance channeled significant resources into development of certified forestry in WB-client countries, including the places in Latin America where he had worked before, and during, the creation of the FSC. And his engagement as interim co-director of WWF's GFTN supports thousands of forest owners around the world, both large and small, who are seeking to become certified and to make market links for their certified timber.

His biggest surprise, he admits, is how fast the FSC has grown and how large its impact has been on a global forest products industry that was historically slow to change. "FSC has shaken it up more than ever in its history," Bruce notes, "including their creation of the copycat systems set up to attempt to nullify FSC's market impact." He doesn't believe that anyone at the founding assembly dreamed that its impact would be this great. He regrets, at the same time, that "the FSC didn't realize its own potential even sooner, and took so long to acquire the business savvy to make itself as relevant to business as it has become."

managed in a responsible way." [22] That meant, the company explained, that it would give preference to wood certified to meet the standards established by the Forest Stewardship Council. Given the relative scarcity of wood that met those criteria at that time, Home Depot hoped that its announcement would spur more suppliers to seek FSC certification. It used the "power of the purchase order" to notify its suppliers that wood from uncertified sources would gradually be replaced by wood from certified sources. RAN responded by running a full-page ad in the *New York Times,* congratulating Home Depot for its decision and identifying the retail home improvement suppliers that had not yet made a comparable commitment (see page 76).

Within months, most of the leading home improvement retail chains in the US followed the Home Depot lead, and some made a stronger commitment. As the implications of the Home Depot announcement rippled through the forest products industry, the *Vancouver Sun* editorialized: "Just one statement from retailer Home Depot did more to change British Columbia's logging practices than 10 years of environmental wars and decades of government regulation." [23]

Market campaigns gained greater strength as campaigners were able to promote the FSC as a positive solution for both timber companies and retailers. Greenpeace, for example, began to mention the FSC in much of its forest work around the world. In October 1998, the group blockaded a ship carrying newsprint from British Columbia to Long Beach, California, because much of the pulp for the newsprint came from Interfor, a Canadian company that was logging in the Great Bear Rainforest, which various environmental groups were calling "the largest unprotected temperate rainforest in the world." The Greenpeace press release concluded: "Greenpeace advocates the reduction of wood products consumption, increased rates of paper recycling, use of ecologically-sound non-wood fibers and the use of wood certified under the accreditation of the Forest Stewardship Council as alternatives to the use of fiber from ancient forests." [24] In September 2000, Greenpeace activists shut down an Interfor sawmill by chaining themselves to a loading conveyor high above a wood-chip barge outside a chip mill in British Columbia. They were protesting "the company's ongoing destruction of Canada's ancient rainforests." The press release and subsequent news coverage noted that, in 1999, both Home Depot and Ikea, the Swedish home furnishings giant, "committed to phasing out use of endangered forest products and to buying only eco-certified products to Forest Stewardship Council standards." [25]

Turning to tropical rainforests, Greenpeace campaigned actively against illegal logging in the Amazon River basin, calling the attention of Brazil's national environmental agency, IBAMA, to rafts of illegal logs that Greenpeace's overflights had detected. "Without certification of Amazon forest products by a reputable institution such as the Forest Stewardship Council," Greenpeace argued, "both Brazilian and overseas buyers must assume that they are directly contributing to the destruction of this last great tropical rainforest." [26] In 2001 IBAMA ended *all* mahogany exports from the Amazon except those from forestry operations that were either FSC-certified or in the process of becoming certified. [27]

*O*ur sincere thanks to *The Home Depot*

for recognizing that ancient trees are worth more

in the forests than in their stores.

In a bold policy turnaround, The Home Depot says it will stop selling wood products from endangered forests by the year 2002. Since The Home Depot is the largest lumber retailer in the world, this new wood-sourcing policy will have a profound global impact. The policy sends a message to lumber suppliers and retailers worldwide that it's barbaric and no longer acceptable to sell wood products made from old-growth trees. The Home Depot also recognizes that it's good business to be environmentally responsible, knowing customers want to spend their money with companies who do the right thing.

However, there are many businesses still living in the past. Thousands of lumber retailers continue to sell products made from our disappearing rainforests. These products include cedar shingles and Douglas fir lumber from North America, doors made of Amazon mahogany, dowels and tool handles of ramin wood, and lauan plywood from Southeast Asia.

Without smart business policies like The Home Depot's, our last old-growth forests will be gone forever. Please visit our website and join us in encouraging other companies to meet or beat The Home Depot's example. And show them that the true value of old-growth forests can't be measured in board-feet.

Visit our website and tell these companies that selling old-growth wood is no longer acceptable.

- **HomeBase**
- **Wickes**
- **Menard's**
- **84 Lumber**
- **Payless Cashways**

RAINFOREST ACTION NETWORK

www.ran.org   1-800-989-RAIN

words are not enough

Take action!

Buy wood products with the FSC label and help save the world's forests.

*Brosnan photo donated by Greg Gorman.

C is supported by

WWF®

GREENPEACE

www.panda.org
www.fscoax.org

FSC

The FSC label assures that wood products come from responsibly managed forests.

FSC-SECR-0022
FSC Trademark©1996 Forest Stewardship Council A.C.

NOTHING ELSE IS GOOD
ENOUGH

Only the nonprofit FSC LABEL can guarantee that the wood you purchase comes from a forest that was managed according to the world's highest environmental standards. That's why World Wildlife Fund, Rainforest Alliance, Natural Resources Defense Council and the National Wildlife Federation all support the FSC. Get into the action. Look for the label. For more information visit www.FSCus.org or call toll-free 1-877-FSC-LOGO.

FSC Forest
     Stewardship
     Council

Global Leaders in Responsible Forestry

It wasn't just market campaigners attacking uncertified timber operations who supported the FSC. Celebrities lent their images to positive advertising campaigns promoting the council. Pierce Brosnan, who at the time was playing James Bond in the "007" movie series, lent his image to a life-size poster that was hung in 500 locations throughout the London underground, while FSC-US developed a poster featuring singer and actress Jennifer Lopez (see pages 77 and 78).

RESULTS

Progress in forest certification began slowly and then built quickly. Figure 4.7 shows the growth in hectares certified worldwide, and Figure 4.8 shows the growth in number of CoC certificates for wood- and paper-product manufacturers. By mid-2006, the growth was exponential. Bolivia and Brazil were competing for the honor of having the largest amount of tropical forest under certification. Canada and Russia were competing for the largest area of certified temperate and boreal forests.

FSC's impact can be measured in other ways, as well. By the end of 2006, it had endorsed national initiatives in 38 countries, with 10 more applicants developing the prerequisites for endorsement. Accredited FSC certification bodies had issued certificates in 79 countries: 26 in the FSC North and 53 in the FSC "South" (developing countries plus countries in transition from the Soviet Union). From 1 million hectares under certification in 1997, the area certified had increased to 19 million hectares in 2000, 48 million in 2004, and 82.7 million in 2006, nearly doubling in the last two years. It can be argued, based on World Resources Institute and UN Food and Agriculture Organization data, that the FSC had managed to certify between 10 and 11 percent of the world's working forests (which excludes parks, protected areas, and forested lands that are completely inaccessible).[28]

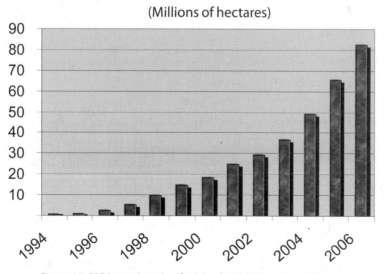

Figure 4.7. FSC Forest Area Certified. Credit: FSC International Center.

Chain of custody certificates are a measure of business uptake for FSC-certified products. From 26 in 1997, the number of CoC certificates increased to 765 in 2000, 3,561 in 2004, and 5,200 at the end of 2006.

The FSC also spurred the creation of a number of competing forest management certification systems, each of which claimed to be based on improved forest management practices and to demand some level of verification of better practices from those it certified (though that was not always the case, as we will see in Chapter 11). The FSC deserves credit for any improvements in forest management practices documented by the competing systems, for there was nothing of that sort underway before the FSC was created, and most observers agree that if the FSC were to fail, most of those groups would disappear as well.

Impacts have varied in different parts of the world. The following is just a small sampling of country-specific results.

Sweden

The Swedish FSC national initiative was the first to complete a full set of national standards; they were approved by the FSC international board in 1998. Sweden quickly jumped ahead in total hectares certified; all 3.5 million hectares of the country's national forests were quickly certified, along with the largest private forest holdings (nearly 5 million hectares). Leaders of the main forest companies, SCA, Bergvik Skog, and Holmen Skog, argued that certification under the FSC was critical to their reputations, even though they did not tend to put large quantities of their certified wood into final markets with the FSC label. This was due mostly to problems with the original chain-of-custody scheme, which didn't serve them well (this is discussed later in the chapter).

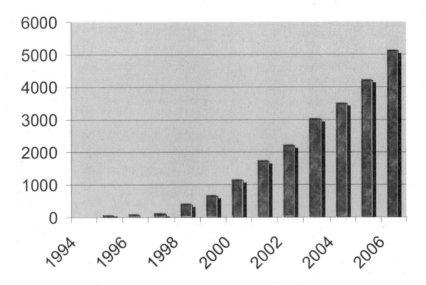

Figure 4.8. FSC Chain-of-Custody Certificates. Credit: FSC International Center.

By 2000, Sweden accounted for roughly 25 percent of all the FSC-certified forests. But that would soon change, as countries with much larger forested areas achieved extensive FSC certification. In 2006 the total area of FSC-certified forests in Sweden reached 10.4 million hectares.[29]

Bolivia

Forest certification in Bolivia moved forward rapidly for a distinct set of reasons. A major forest management project, BOLFOR, was launched in 1994 to create new national regulations, technical assistance, and training for forest management, with strong support from USAID, the US foreign aid agency, as well as Conservation International and the Wildlife Conservation Society. The standards that BOLFOR ultimately established for Bolivia were among the most stringent in Latin America.

In 1995, the Bolivian Council for Voluntary Forest Certification (CFV) was created and became the first recognized FSC national initiative in Latin America. After the government adopted the more stringent BOLFOR regulations, some forestry concession holders relinquished their government concession contracts rather than be bound by the new regulations. But others realized that the gap between BOLFOR standards and FSC standards was relatively small, and they chose to seek FSC certification relatively quickly.

In 2004, there were more than 1.4 million hectares certified under 13 certificates, and 17 companies held CoC certificates. By late 2006, the total certified area had risen to 2 million hectares, all of it in natural forest, which gives Bolivia a right to claim the largest amount of certified natural forest in Latin America. The country's tropical hardwoods earn premium prices in US and European markets, where they are primarily used for garden furniture, decking, and flooring.[30]

Russia

Russia began certification even later than some of the less-developed countries of the global South, but it has been increasing at a stunning pace. And the motivation is market-driven in an unusual way.

The Russians still have relatively strict policies in place for managing forests that have been privatized since the collapse of the Soviet Union. But doubts about the efficacy of Russian state regulation, combined with evidence of illegal logging in the country's far eastern wilderness, have created significant doubts in the marketplace about effective forest planning and management and, therefore, about the social and environmental "quality" of wood that is exported from Russia.[31]

Russian branches of WWF and Greenpeace have been active in monitoring forestry practices in Russia and in encouraging the adoption of FSC certification. In June 2005, I had an opportunity to talk with the managers of some certified forests in northwestern Russia, an area stretching from St. Petersburg to Moscow. Some Finnish companies, such as Stora Enso, which have resisted FSC certification for their holdings and factories in Finland and Sweden, are seeking FSC certification of their wood sources in Russia, primarily, they argue, to offset market doubts about official Russian government processes.

Much of the rapid growth in Russia is being stimulated by a single company, Ilim Pulp, which accounts for 60 percent of the total pulp production of Russia and controls vast tracts of forest throughout the northwest, north, and east. Ilim and some other companies are even arguing for an "FSC-Plus" level of certification. That is, they are willing to pay for the presence of representatives of WWF or Greenpeace on virtually every forest assessment if it will give the world confidence in the validity of certification processes in Russia.

Russia reached 4 million hectares certified by early 2005. It soared to 9.9 million hectares by late 2006 and is projected to reach 15 million in 2007.

Brazil

Brazil holds the largest share of Amazon forests as well as a rapidly dwindling Atlantic forest; it also has extensive plantation forestry in cleared areas of the south. Brazilian companies have increasingly sought certification in order to maintain existing markets and possibly open new ones, especially in more-demanding countries.[32] Unlike the situation in Russia, where European markets are driving much of the certification efforts, 86 percent of the timber harvested from the Amazon is consumed domestically, especially in Sao Paulo state. (For more on the complexity of the Brazilian situation, see Leadership Profile 4.3, which focuses on the Orsa Group, a major player in the Brazilian pulp, packaging, and furniture industry.)

Brazil had roughly 1 million hectares certified to FSC standards by mid-2004. By the end of 2006, the area of certified forest had risen to 3.5 million hectares in 69 forest management certificates. Plantations accounted for 52 percent of the certified operations and 60 percent of the certified area (2.1 million hectares). So Bolivia retained the crown for the largest amount of certified tropical natural forests, but Brazil claimed the largest total amount of FSC-certified forests in Latin America and, effectively, in the developing countries of the FSC South.

Canada

Canadian companies' engagement with the FSC has gone through several different phases. Originally, FSC was advocated most strongly for western Canada, especially British Columbia, as a response to the "forest wars" that erupted in the early 1990s as environmental advocacy groups confronted companies logging the rich temperate rainforests of coastal BC. (The Greenpeace campaign against Interfor, mentioned earlier, was part of this battle.) Canadian forestry operations were technically more sensitive to public pressure because most of the forests in Canada are held as "Crown lands," with companies required to apply for provincial licenses in order to log.[34]

Canadian forest companies resisted FSC and attempted to build their own system through the Canadian Standards Association (CSA). Even before the CSA standards were complete in 1997, however, most environmental organizations

FSC and the Amazon

Roberto S. Waack of Grupo Orsa

Roberto Waack could not have foreseen the impact he would have on the Amazon forest industry when he disappointed his father, an engineer, and chose to study biology at the Universidade de Sao Paulo.[33] Nor could he have anticipated the insights he would gain about certification systems when, in graduate school, he became fascinated with the "new institutional economics" of Oliver Williamson and Nobel laureates Douglass North and Ronald Coase, mentors to his favorite professor, Decio Zylbersztajn.

Roberto may have a genetic predisposition for both biotechnology and Amazon exploration. His paternal great-grandfather came to Brazil in the early 20th century to seek horses for the Prussian Army, lived an adventurous life on the frontier, and never returned to Germany. His maternal grandfather was a naturalist, a pharmacist, and an inventor of medicines derived from snake serum. But Roberto is first and foremost an entrepreneur. He began his first company, Embrabio (Empresa Brasileira de Biotecnologia SA), while still an undergraduate student. The FSC entered Roberto's sights when he began, first as a friend and a volunteer, to help the charismatic Sérgio Amoroso resolve some knotty corporate governance issues in his rapidly growing Grupo Orsa.

Amoroso had taken this paper and packaging company from startup to sales in excess of US$700 million in just a few years. He had risen from an impoverished family and created his companies despite little formal education. He also had a strong commitment to "triple bottom line" social and environmental responsibility. In keeping with this commitment, Amoroso set up Orsa Foundation, contributing one percent of gross sales from all the companies of the Orsa Group to the foundation, which supported preschool and primary education of Brazilian youth at risk.

Roberto Waack became deeply involved with the Orsa Group and was soon named executive director, leading it in its most complex operation: the rescue of the Jari Project. This is one of the most ambitious forest and plantation enterprises ever created in Brazil, encompassing 1.7 million hectares (nearly 4.2 million acres, the area of Connecticut and Rhode Island combined) that straddle the Jari River, 300 miles from the northeast Amazon port of Belem. The Jari Project had been developed in 1964 by Daniel Ludwig, the enigmatic US shipping magnate, in an attempt to show that the Amazon jungle could be made to produce food, fiber, and protein in massive quantities for global markets. The military government of Brazil sold him the land for just US$3 million, about US$0.75 per acre. Ludwig then invested billions in clearing native jungle, planting trees for fiber, and creating some of the largest rice and chicken production operations ever seen. He was noted especially for constructing state-of-the-art pulp-processing and paper-making factories on ocean-going barges, which he shipped intact from Japan to the riverfront of the project.

But the project failed. The trees planted, *Gmelina arborea,* a fast-growing tree from Southeast Asia, did not do well in the shallow and poorly drained Amazon soils. Ludwig's title to the land was questioned by subsequent Brazilian administrations, which made it impossible for him to raise money. He turned the project over to a group of Brazilian businessmen from Sao Paulo in 1981, in whose hands it gradually sank toward bankruptcy. The gmelina was replaced with eucalyptus, but that failed to mature fast enough to keep the banks at bay. Furthermore, global markets had become suspicious of the very idea of pulp and paper from invasive species in the heart of the Amazon.

By the time the Orsa Group acquired the Jari property in 2000, for a payment of one dollar and the assumption of $450 million in debt, there were 140,000 people living on the land, with little employment, virtually no healthcare services, and practically no law or order. The residents lived on earnings from illegal mining, illegal logging, and drug commerce.

Roberto saw the Jari Project as an opportunity for modern sustainable development. Taking advantage of the fact that the eucalyptus had matured, he modernized and rebuilt the pulp plant and sought FSC certification on both the 427,000 hectares of eucalyptus plantation and on 545,000 hectares of natural tropical rainforest. Grupo Orsa developed a variety of plans to generate wealth from those forests, and FSC certification became critical to all of them, including the creation of a 500,000-hectare protected area, free from all logging.

FSC certification allayed the concerns of pulp buyers whose clients might otherwise avoid paper and packaging from eucalyptus plantations in the Amazon region. It assured them that the land had been converted long before the 1994 FSC forest-conversion cutoff date and that forest management on the plantation met all the rest of FSC's social and environmental standards. European markets began buying the full production of Grupo Orsa's exported paper pulp, at a small premium.

Certification also became an important solution for corporate governance. Representatives from the banks holding the company's large debt sat on the board of directors, but FSC's constraints on the rate of exploitation and conditions for harvesting curbed the desires of those board members who wanted to see greatly increased rates of extraction. Further, the FSC's independent auditing of forest management practices gave Grupo Orsa greater credibility with financial institutions such as pension and insurance companies, which offered long-term financing.

Timber harvesting from the natural forests has become a major source of additional revenue for Orsa Florestal, a separate company within the group, which Roberto also runs. It also creates significant additional employment for the local community. Orsa Florestal harvests and sells some 35 tropical species, most of them dense hardwoods, including a number of previously underutilized and little-recognized species. The company has found a burgeoning market in the Netherlands, where rough-sawn tropical hardwood, with its legendary durability, is used for water-related construction, such as docks, locks, and dykes. Much of the wood is also used in high-tech finger-jointing plants in Holland to make doors and window frames. These products carry a 30-year warranty without the need for treatment with the arsenic and chromium chemicals normally used to give wood longevity.

By the end of 2006, Orsa Forestal was producing 2,000 cubic meters of rough-sawn tropical hardwood each month for shipment to Europe, where it earned a 30 percent price premium because it is FSC certified. By the end of 2007, about 5,000 cubic meters will be exported each month.

Seeking greater value from the Amazon forests, Orsa Florestal has built factories to produce starch (using the native manioc plant) and furniture, which will generate additional jobs. The factory producing FSC-certified furniture will be linked to a chain of furniture showrooms that are also being developed. The Orsa Foundation, meanwhile, now employs 150 people in the Jari region and provides a wide range of social services to the populations in the local towns and villages, including both preschool education and specialized technical training in secondary schools.

The new institutional economics that Roberto studied suggests that all economic life is part of a web of institutions that are designed to reduce the "transaction costs" associated with any market activity. In this framework, the rigorous annual FSC monitoring and auditing significantly reduces the cost of assuring clients that they will not be criticized for buying a product from Grupo Orsa and that the forest products are not tainted with any of the most worrisome market defects: illegality, deforestation or other environmental damage, genetically modified organisms, or social conflict around land tenure. According to Roberto, when potential buyers, investors, or financiers hear that a product is FSC certified, "their risk perception goes way down."

Roberto — only 46 years old in 2006 — created yet another company, AMATA, to develop high-value products from the Amazon forests in his search for more opportunities to transform natural forests from a negative asset, worthy only of clearing, into positive assets for investors, local communities, and the environment. His conviction that the FSC is a "new economic institution" critical to sustainable development led him to run for election to the FSC board of directors as a representative of the economic chamber from FSC South. He was elected and began his three-year term in November 2006.

involved in the BC forest wars rejected them. Market campaigns against companies logging in British Columbia and supportive of the FSC were especially effective in Europe. CSA standards were seen as company attempts to avoid the tighter controls of the FSC. Rejection of all forest products from British Columbia became a common theme of the campaigns, which was understandably worrisome to the province. Yet the FSC standard-setting process in British Columbia stagnated around standards that most of the industry rejected. At the end of 2006, progress in certifying forests in BC remained slow.

At the same time, FSC standards were embraced in most of the rest of Canada, with Tembec and Domtar, two of Canada's largest forest products companies, leading the way. Tembec received certification on nine different forest tracts totaling 6 million hectares. Domtar managed to get certificates for 1.6 million hectares spread over seven operations They were joined by Alberta Pacific with the largest single certificate to date, 5.5 million hectares. By late 2006, with little certification taking place in contentious British Columbia, Canada became the world leader in total area certified, with 18.1 million hectares under FSC standards.

China

China is moving cautiously, but expeditiously, toward becoming one of the most important players in the FSC global network. The WWF's China office has been promoting sustainable forestry certification since 2001, when it launched a first China Working Group on Forest Certification in collaboration with the World Bank. Initial progress was slow as the country struggled with the growing influence of global markets, a recognition of the importance of producing in ways that meet international standards, and some governmental resistance to the notion that an international NGO like the Forest Stewardship Council might set those standards.

In 2000 I had the opportunity to meet with a cluster of officials from China's State Forest Administration (SFA). They were interested in learning more about community-based forestry as an economic development model because municipal governments in forested areas of China were creating local enterprises to log and process timber. They were also willing to listen to questions and comments about the prospects for certification of sustainable forest management in China. They were unaware of the FSC and generally unimpressed by the idea of an international organization telling them how to manage their forests. "We have very good technicians in the SFA and researchers in the Chinese Academy of Forestry," noted one member of the group. "We have several universities dedicated to nothing but forestry; we don't think that we need much assistance with creating standards for forest management that are appropriate for the conditions in China."

Three years later, some of the same officials were much more interested in discussing certification. "There are a number of international companies requesting permits for importing timber that's very similar to timber available from China," they commented, "and they're even paying higher prices for it than they would have to pay for wood already available here." Why? Because the companies for whom they were manufacturing furniture, furniture components, and other wood products were requiring that the raw materials be FSC certified. So these international buyers were paying the price of importing the wood from South Africa, New Zealand, and even the US, then exporting the finished products into European and US markets.

In June 2003, the Central Committee of the Communist Party and the State Council issued a "Resolution on Accelerating Forest Development." It said, in part, "We must be active in undertaking forest certification so as to fit in with international standards as soon as possible. . . . The establishment of a certification system for the forests for public benefits needs to be speeded up."[35] In less than two years, the Chinese Academy of Forestry in the SFA had developed a set of standards. By April 2006, a new working group was constituted to seek FSC national initiative endorsement; it began working with the government agencies to have parallel national standards and FSC standards that would be sent for FSC approval in 2007.

Meanwhile, between 2003 and 2006, more than 150 Chinese manufacturing companies received CoC certificates so they could produce certified products for export to global markets or for sale through companies in China, such as IKEA and B&Q, with strong preferences for the FSC.

The first forest management unit certified to FSC standards in China was a small forest (about 950 hectares) assessed by SmartWood in 2003. In 2005, the first large forest, a state-owned unit with 420,000 hectares, was certified, and there were a half-dozen large state forests in the pipeline for FSC assessment and certification.

United States

The FSC has had a tough struggle in the US. Soon after the council's creation, the American Forest and Paper Association (AF&PA) began organizing an industry-led certification system, the Sustainable Forestry Initiative (SFI), which it promoted in US markets as the preferred alternative of most major timber and paper companies. (The SFI is discussed in detail in Chapter 11.) The AF&PA recognized early that it had a problem. A public opinion survey it conducted ranked the major US logging companies among the least trustworthy businesses in the land, only slightly above the tobacco companies. The association realized it needed some kind of public relations response, but the changes in forest practices that the still poorly organized FSC was demanding in the mid-1990s were more than most of the companies were willing to face. They were also, frankly, leery of a system that was partially run, and fully supported, by the very NGOs who had been attacking them.[36]

The demand for certified product from Home Depot, Lowe's, and other major US home improvement companies encouraged some logging companies to take the plunge, beginning with those already following forest management practices that met FSC requirements. One of them was the Collins Companies, a group of small family-owned forest businesses that were already harvesting their forests in ways and at rates that would allow them to continue logging "forever."[37] But solidarity within the industry meant that most of the major firms focused on certification under the SFI, not the FSC.

FSC made considerable progress certifying public lands, especially municipal, county, and state forest lands, with some of them seeking dual SFI and FSC certification. The public lands increased the available supply of FSC-certified timber, but certification of public lands was constrained because it was a point of contention for some of the major environmental NGOs supporting the FSC. They refused to allow certification of national forest lands for two reasons.

• They believed there should be higher standards for public forest lands than

private lands, and these higher standards should perhaps include full protection from logging in some cases.
- They believed that certification would lead to renewed logging in major national forest areas where successful campaigning had virtually eliminated all logging in order to protect endangered species.

By end of 2002, there were only 9 million acres (3.6 million hectares) of FSC-certified forest in the US; by the end of 2003 there was virtually no change. Over the following two years, however, certification began to surge, reaching 13 million acres (5.3 million hectares) at the end of 2004 and 22 million acres (9 million hectares) by the end of 2005.[38]

The paper industry has become the strongest force driving FSC certification in the US. In 2006 alone there were 50 new CoC certificates issued to paper-related firms, including the country's largest printers and paper merchants. And FSC-certified wood is in heavy demand in the US "green building" industry. The US Green Building Council allows only FSC-certified wood in its Leadership in Energy and Environmental Design (LEED) designation process. That wood credit is actively sought in an estimated 30 percent of buildings seeking LEED designation, and at the end of 2006 there were 3,000 commercial buildings in the LEED pipeline for construction.[39]

INSTITUTIONAL MATURATION OF THE FSC

Some friends and other observers may scoff at the notion of the FSC as a mature institution. Scrappy, struggling, overextended, contentious...those adjectives are more likely to spring to mind. But I believe that the initial dream of the FSC as an institution that could transform a global industry while holding itself together in spite of the contending visions of its constituents has largely been achieved.

We can see the level of maturation — and the distance still to go — in the FSC's handling of two difficult issues in recent years. The first is the FSC's major shift in course in response to concerns about its original standards for chain of custody, which were not working well for important participants. The second was the broad-based internal and external review that the FSC undertook to address the question of whether it should be certifying forest plantations.

Chain of Custody

The original standards for chain of custody were designed to ensure that every final product carrying an FSC logo could be traced back to an FSC-certified forest. That meant, for example, that processors of the wood — such as the mill that did the rough sawing of logs, the furniture factory that made final products, and every other intermediate processor — were required to show that they could physically segregate wood that originated in FSC-certified forests from wood that had come from non-certified forests and that they could trace the certified wood through its entire process. In some paper mills handling both certified and uncertified wood-chip inputs, this meant that whole batches had to be run separately with only FSC inputs. For wood and paper processors that were just beginning to work with certified timber, it often meant costly adjustments to their production schedules for small batches of outputs.

In places like Sweden, where the search for efficiency often leads forest products companies to "swap" wood between forest and factory, reducing transportation costs and optimizing species mixes, that chain-of-custody process was even more difficult and costly. One result was that Swedish companies were content to have their forest lands certified, but they didn't tend to put much FSC-certified product into the marketplace, despite the rapid growth in demand for FSC-labeled products.

The first step toward a solution was to create a set of standards that allowed products with high proportions of FSC-certified content (but not 100 percent certified) into the market. These products bore a label specifying what the FSC content was. (I once purchased doors, for example, that were clearly labeled "FSC 70 percent.") This form of "percentage-based claim," however, gave no assurances about the origins or sustainability of the non-certified content. The FSC's environmental chamber was concerned that there were no constraints on the remaining content. In theory, it could come from wood harvested illegally, in the worst possible ways, from forests in social turmoil.

In 2003, some of the Swedish companies said that modifications to the CoC standards were needed if they were to get more of their certifiable wood and paper into global markets. At that time, Sweden had the greatest amount of certified forestland, and FSC staff realized they needed to do something to get a larger proportion of the Swedish forest products into the market with an FSC label.

What finally emerged was a system that met company needs for easier management of FSC flow-through in their plants, at the cost of a stronger set of controls on the content of FSC-labeled products that included material from non-certified forests. This modification in the system took the form of two new standards. One created a "volume-credit" system, and the other stipulated new controls on wood that was not FSC-certified.

The volume-credit system allowed companies to place an FSC logo on products coming out of a mill in direct proportion to the FSC-certified inputs going into the mill over a defined period of time. For example, if the mill could show that 50 percent of the pine or fir it purchased for making windows during a given month or quarter came from FSC-certified forests, it could place the FSC logo on 50 percent of the windows produced with that wood during that period.

From the point of view of some FSC stakeholders, this change came with a high psychological cost. If you purchased a window with the FSC logo on it, you could no longer be absolutely certain that the wood in that window actually came from trees harvested from an FSC-certified forest. You could, however, be confident that by purchasing that window you were providing direct support to the improvement of forest management worldwide. It required trust in the system. To bolster that trust, environmental advocacy groups agreed to the introduction of the volume-credit system only if a system for improving the control of uncertified wood was strengthened.

The "controlled-wood" standard that was later approved by the board stipulates that no uncertified wood used in processing plants under the volume-credit standard could come from forests where any of the following four conditions prevailed:

- There were questions about legality of the harvesting.
- There was any genetically modified timber grown.
- There was any evidence of social turmoil or violation of rights of workers or indigenous peoples.
- The wood came from "high-conservation-value forests" or old-growth forests.

This focus on controlling the uncertified content of products with mixed content became a significant incentive for companies to move toward higher proportions of FSC content. It reduced the advantage for companies using less-costly uncertified inputs and provided positive incentives for "just doing FSC," according to one forest products company executive I interviewed at the 2005 FSC general assembly.

The trade-offs have proven beneficial for the FSC. Swedish companies were quick to pilot the new system, and they have subsequently increased enormously their shipments of FSC-labeled product into the markets. One company built a major new processing installation in the UK, taking rough-sawn certified Swedish timber and milling it, just in time, into the shapes and semi-finished products required by UK retail stores. That same company has begun to sell FSC-certified dimension lumber to Home Depot in the US and is now supplying both FSC-certified bulk paper pulp and FSC-certified finished papers into US markets, where it had had few or no sales previously.[40]

The process of obtaining those trade-offs was neither simple nor rapid. The first drafts of both standards were published on the FSC website and then went into a formal consultation process involving all FSC members, certification bodies, national initiatives, and any certificate holders who wished to participate. Significant problems were identified, conflicts with other standards were identified, new drafts were developed, and meetings were held literally around the world to get further feedback on what the standards stipulated and how they might be implemented. By the end of 2006, test implementation was underway in a large number of forests, many companies were using the draft standards, and the FSC was moving toward final approval within a year.

The volume-credit system proved to be useful in unexpected places. Representatives of the social chamber argued, at the 2005 general assembly, that small-scale, indigenous, and community-based certified forests were finding it easier to convince local mills to become CoC certified because the standards no longer required that they implement costly physical segregation for small batches of certified timber.

Plantations

The issue of certifying plantations has been controversial from the very beginning of the FSC. At the founding assembly in Toronto, representatives of groups such as the World Rainforest Movement argued vigorously against including plantations. From their perspective, a plantation was a biodiversity desert, often a monoculture of invasive and exotic species. Plantations frequently brought about the destruction of natural forests and were sustained with heavy uses of pesticides and other chemicals. Those who supported certifying plantations argued that plantations could take pressure off natural forests and could be developed on land that was already degraded from agriculture or previous excessive logging. In any case, there needed to be standards on pesticides and other chemicals applied to them, as well.

The 2002 general assembly passed a resolution that called for the creation of a working group on FSC plantations policy to review, once again, whether the FSC should continue to certify plantations. The FSC international board appointed the 12-person working group in 2004, drawing on nominations from around the world to ensure the group represented all three chambers (economic, environmental, and social) and both sub-chambers (North and South). Funding for the process came largely from the Netherlands, and the working group began to meet in March 2005.

The group held four formal meetings, in Sweden, Germany, Spain, and South Africa. Stakeholder input came from an extremely rich set of e-mail discussions, with debate varying from clear and cogent to blustery and outrageous. Some 20 formal position papers were submitted by organizations and made available on a special part of the FSC website.[41] At one point, anti-plantation forces lodged a formal request to challenge the certificates of a select group of plantations around the world. This and a litany of other complaints brought every major issue to the fore.

The working group completed its deliberations in April 2006, distributed its draft recommendations for three months of further commentary, and issued a final, carefully worded report in November 2006.[42] It included the following (paraphrased) considerations and recommendations:

- The group said that the distinction between natural forest and plantation was too black-and-white. In reality, there is a continuum of management approaches, from low-impact management of natural forests to high-intensity, short-rotation plantations. The FSC should recognize this.
- Plantations should not be called forests (conceding one of the most strident points of critics).
- The FSC should develop "one integrated set of common Principles and Criteria for all management units," rather than discussing a separate principle (Principle 10) and set of criteria for plantations.
- Managers should strengthen attention to social issues by developing a reinforced "Social Management System" geared to the scale and intensity of the forest or plantation being managed and the local socioeconomic context.

Building a Mature Global Forest Products Certification System

Heiko Liedeker of the FSC

The challenges faced in building a mature social and environmental certification system that is democratic and transparent, that responds to a broad range of stakeholders, and that functions at the speed of the businesses it seeks to transform may seem monumental, even in the abstract. Those challenges were very real for Heiko Liedeker when he arrived in Oaxaca, Mexico, in August 2001 to become the interim executive director of the FSC, following a predecessor who lasted only six months.[43]

Heiko found himself in charge of an organization with a US$2 million annual budget, nearly a million dollars in short-term debt, no money in the bank, a frustrated and angry staff, and growing distrust in the external communities it tried to serve. This was a defining moment for the FSC, and one that could have spelled the end of the experiment it represented.

Heiko brought two kinds of experience that were precisely what the FSC needed at that moment. He was both a trained forester and an experienced businessman. Born in 1960 in the village of Borgfeld, near Bremen in northern Germany, he studied forestry at the University of Munich and the University of New Brunswick, Canada, and forest ecology at the University of Vermont, completing his master's degree in 1988. Stints at the Munich Wildlife Society led to three years in environmental and wildlife management agencies in Saudi Arabia and then to the creation of his own environmental information systems company, which grew to have some 40 employees.

Heiko spent five years with WWF Germany, beginning in 1996. He set up the first stages of the German FSC national initiative and the first German "buyers' group," chaired the WWF European Forest Team, and ultimately ran WWF's European campaign to support the FSC, from Switzerland, in 2000 and 2001. Although the WWF approach was always to collaborate with the forest products industry, rather than be confrontational, Heiko was pleased that the campaign he ran managed to collaborate with the Taiga Rescue Network, Finnish Nature League, and Greenpeace International to put pressure on Pan-European Forest Certification (PEFC), the competing system that was just then being set up.

He was, in his own words, "incredibly naïve" about the challenges he faced when he was invited to an FSC funders meeting outside Washington, which involved many members of the FSC board, and emerged as the interim executive director. He had little awareness of the complicated North-South dynamics of the organization, underestimated its global scope and dynamism, and didn't realize the magnitude and the complexity of the management tasks that faced him. First among them was the decision, made by the board of directors before he arrived, to move the organization's headquarters from Oaxaca to Europe.

The move to Germany was necessary for several reasons. Oaxaca was too isolated from the global standard-setting industry. Because few people knew of the fundamental charms of the small mountain city in southern Mexico, it was becoming increasingly difficult to recruit the technical staff needed. And the location was becoming a reputational liability, as spokespeople for FSC's competitors, SFI and PEFC, belittled FSC as "that Mexican system based in the unpronounceable town."

Working closely with the German branches of WWF, Greenpeace, and the FSC, Heiko managed to obtain generous relocation subsidies from the German federal, state, and local governments (with special support from the German Green Party), eclipsing bids from the Dutch government and the city of Geneva. The package included nearly US$400,000 in direct relocation subsidies, a 25-year rent-free lease on a 24,000-square-foot office building in a park along the Rhine River in Bonn, and another US$350,000 to remodel the building. The move was completed in 2003, with all but two of the Oaxaca staff making the move to Bonn.

The FSC regained financial stability when the Ford Foundation and the Summit Foundation disbursed promised grants ahead of schedule. The debt was eliminated thanks to medium-term loans from supportive organizations, which were repaid by the end of 2005. And when the FSC received the 2005 Alcan Prize for Sustainability, most of the US$1 million proceeds were used to create a stabilizing cash-flow-reserve fund.

The council's functional viability increased as it went through the complicated process of building global accreditation and standard-setting programs. FSC engaged stakeholders around the world, and regained their confidence, when it renegotiated chain-of-custody (CoC) standards to allow volume credits offset by new controlled-wood standards (see main text of this chapter). The industry response was both immediate and huge, and the flow of FSC-certified products into European, North American, and Asian markets increased dramatically.

Since 2001, the number of FSC national initiatives has doubled from 19 to 38 (most in countries of the FSC South), with 10 more currently applying for endorsement. When Heiko took over the reins, there were approximately 24 million hectares of FSC-certified forest and 1,000 companies with CoC certificates. By late 2006, the totals had more than tripled, to 82 million hectares (surpassing 200 million acres) of certified forest and more than 5,000 companies with CoC certificates. The SFI and PEFC were in considerable disarray (see Chapter 11), and FSC certification was ascendant, as shown by its preferred status with the world's largest companies engaged with forest products, including IKEA and Tetra Pak.

Heiko is proudest of what he has done to rebuild confidence in the FSC among members, supporters, donors, and certificate holders and to transform the FSC into an organization with reasonably solid finances and cash reserves. The stability has reached a point, Heiko notes, where the staff in Bonn can let out their collective breaths about whether the payroll will be covered each month and can buy homes in the area. There are continuing challenges, as the servicing needs of the rapidly growing pool of certificate holders increase more rapidly than the revenue to support them. But Heiko believes that the FSC has passed an important institutional "tipping point." The number of companies adopting FSC standards and procedures and seeking certification continues to grow at a rate of 50 percent per year. But they are doing it because "FSC certification is good for business, not just because they are being pressured to do so."

- Management of an FSC-certified plantation must involve a proactive conservation strategy "to prevent, mitigate, and, where needed, compensate" for impacts on ecosystem integrity.
- Managers must have a "clear and robust" consultation process with local stakeholders and a conflict resolution process in place.

No one believes this report of the plantations working group will resolve all the doubts about, or convince all the opponents of the need for, the certification of plantations. But it is a powerful illustration of the way in which advocacy NGOs and businesses can address a contentious issue, develop a transparent and democratic consultation process, and reach conclusions that are both respectful of differences and helpful for moving the certification system forward.

Transformation of Corporate Purchasing

FSC's ultimate success will be determined by the extent to which major corporations transform their purchasing practices for forest products. The evidence accumulating on that front is also very encouraging. Here are some examples:

- Home Depot, the world's largest chain of home improvement stores, with US$90 billion in sales and 235,000 employees in 2005, continues to move large quantities of FSC-certified wood into its supply chain. Each year, Home Depot's chief buyer meets quietly with representatives of the major market campaign groups to report on the company's success in sourcing and selling FSC-certified products. At the 2005 meeting, it was reported confidentially, the total exceeded $1.5 billion dollars, about 7 percent of Home Depot's total wood purchases. FSC-certified sourcing was expanding at more than 30 percent per year. Home Depot has taken an equity position in Columbia Forest Products, a hardwood manufacturing company with the largest certified plywood and panel manufacturing and sales organization in North America (eight manufacturing facilities and one international brokerage group certified by SmartWood to FSC standards).[44]
- Tetra Pak, the world's largest distributor of food packaging, with patented paper cartons for liquids, sold more than 120 *billion* cartons in 2005. Tetra Pak has created a step-by-step system for all its suppliers of wood fiber, which requires both certification and traceability. It audits its suppliers annually on both counts, and in 2005 it could demonstrate that 22 percent of the fiber used in its cartons came from FSC-certified forests. Forests under other certification systems produced 19 percent of the fiber, but only FSC qualifies for Tetra Pak's preferred certification stage. The company is moving as quickly as it can to sourcing only from companies that reach that third stage of preferred certification.[45]
- IKEA, one of the world's largest manufacturers and retailers of affordable household furniture, with 237 stores, 90,000 employees, and 17 billion euros (US$22 billion) in total sales, has established forestry sourcing guidelines that push all of its wood suppliers in a step-by-step process toward the FSC.[46] Al-

though IKEA does not publish how successful it has been in accomplishing that goal, a confidential informant suggested recently that, worldwide, 25 to 26 percent of the wood it bought in 2005 was FSC certified, and it anticipated reaching 30 percent by the end of 2006.

• B&Q, the largest home improvement chain in the UK and the third largest in the world, helped to create the FSC; it is publicly committed to ensuring that *all* the wood or paper products it sells "come from forests independently certified as well-managed according to the standards of the Forest Stewardship Council (FSC), or from recycled materials." [47]

REFLECTIONS

The FSC is the most important example of increasingly successful certification systems that are transforming major industries around the world. It illustrates the potential for global action to change industry practices through collaborative governance that is closer to the reality of industrial globalization than any set of laws and regulations implemented by individual nations. This kind of certification system is arguably superior to a negotiated United Nations treaty, as it is more efficient and less costly than a treaty, it works through markets to provide its services, it depends on market forces to drive companies into its reach, and it builds on decades of global civil society's calls for improved social and environmental practices in the management of the world's forests.

The FSC is not without its detractors, some of whom have disagreed with aspects of the organization's evolution, while others were critical since its initial creation. One group, which includes FSC supporters and members, has set up an "FSC-Watch" website, which is, in their words, "dedicated to encouraging scrutiny of the Forest Stewardship Council's activities. By doing so, it aims to increase the integrity of the FSC's forest certification scheme." This is ultimately healthy, as it provides new public scrutiny and contributes to transparency. Unfortunately, these critics of the FSC are dedicating less attention to the much-less-transparent processes of FSC's competitors, as discussed in Chapter 11.

If forest certification were relegated to the United Nations, or if it were to return to the old days, when individual countries enforced (or failed to enforce) their inconsistent laws and regulations, there would still be critics. The FSC is not perfect, but it has shown that a global standard-setting organization attempting to implement transparent and democratic voluntary governance of a global resource, can modify itself, improve its processes, respond to its stakeholders, and retain its fundamental credibility as the "gold standard" for well-managed forestry. I would argue that we are globally better off with the FSC than without it.

5

Tapping the Ethic of "Fairness": Certifying Global Commodity Trade

Over the past 25 years, the plight of small-scale agricultural producers has become the focus of significant global concern as price competition, technological change, and corporate concentration undercut the livelihoods of hundreds of millions of farmers. The reasons for those changes fill dozens of economics, sociology, and policy tomes. They range from the rapidly increasing concentration of retailers in the global food system, where large-volume global supply chains favor large-scale corporate farming,[1] to fundamental problems in commodity trade pricing, with commodity prices falling for more than a quarter century.[2] For better or worse, the dominance of conservative economic policy for the past 20-odd years has meant the elimination of various price-stabilization regimes, which has undercut the production and pricing of many commodities. According to a European Commission study, "the abandonment of international intervention policies at the end of the 1980s and the commodity market reforms of the 1990s in the developing countries left the commodity sectors, *and in particular small producers*, largely to themselves in their struggle with the demands of the markets" (emphasis added). Today, the study notes, producers live "an unpredictable existence because prices for a wide range of commodities are very volatile and follow a declining long term trend."[3]

Is it possible to have an international trading system in which giant corporate buyers purchase products from small-scale producers at prices that convey the equivalent of a "decent living wage," rather than pitting producers in Vietnam against producers in Guatemala, and both of them against producers in Lesotho, for the sake of a few pennies' difference in prices? Or is it inherent in global economic systems that brutal and cutthroat competition will always squeeze impoverished producers in an inexorable "race to the bottom"?

The Fair Trade movement described in this chapter has become an extraordinary force, using market processes to create an alternative form of international trade that taps the latent search for "fairness" among ethical consumers and businesses while generating market advantages for those who engage in it. Once the haven of small, faith-based volunteer groups, Fair Trade is now embraced by some of the largest food-processing and food-retailing companies in the world. And it is being applied to a rapidly expanding set of agricultural commodities and other products.

In this chapter we will discuss how the certified social and environmental attributes of some agricultural products are making those products stand out in the marketplace from products whose origins are not known by retailers and consumers. Just as the market for wood products with strong social and environmental attributes is steering the forest products industry toward improved forest management practices, the emerging market for agricultural commodities that are "fairly priced" and "sustainably grown" aligns with the pressure from global civil society for greater accountability on the part of food processors and food retailers worldwide.

We will see how a relatively small number of market campaigns focused on industry leaders have, once again, led to rapid growth in the uptake of fairly traded products. We will also see what this means for the certification organizations, for the food-processing companies, and for competitive grocery retailing.[4]

BASIC NOTIONS OF FAIR TRADE

The concept of "fair trade" carries many meanings in contemporary usage. President George W. Bush used the term in a 2006 address to the Chicago Economic Club when he argued that the United States will continue to push for "free and fair trade."[5]

Michigan governor Jennifer Granholm, responding to the president's call for more technical training and tax breaks for corporate research as the best way to increase US competitiveness, said that the president should, instead, focus his attention on protecting automakers such as Ford and General Motors from "unfair foreign competition" and on helping them provide health care and pensions for their workers. "Fight for fair trade," Granholm said. "Fight for our manufacturers. Fight for our automakers. Fight for our American workers."[6]

Reflecting another use, *Mother Jones* magazine identified Chris Martin, lead singer in the rock band Coldplay, as "Fair Trade's Front Man." Martin gathered more than 30,000 signatures for Oxfam's "Make Trade Fair" petition at Coldplay's concerts and presented the full Oxfam collection of more than 4 million signatures to the head of the World Trade Organization at the WTO's 2003 summit meeting in Cancun.[7] That petition, signed by nearly 18 million people by the end of 2005, calls for broad changes in the rules governing international trade, including dramatic reductions in northern countries' subsidies for their own agricultural production, increased access to northern markets for the products of the global South, and less pressure to force open the markets of developing countries under conditions favorable to exports from the North.[8]

However, Fair Trade (capitalized) has a separate history that emerged in the years after World War II, when organizations such as SERRV International (Sales Exchange for Refugee Rehabilitation Vocation), a faith-based US organization, began its work among postwar European refugees with the mission to "promote the social and economic progress of people in developing regions of the world by marketing their handcrafts and foods in a just and direct manner."[9] At approximately the same time, an organization called Ten Thousand Villages was created

Fundamental Principles of Ten Thousand Villages

- We honor the value of seeking to bring justice and hope to the poor.
- We trade with artisan groups who pay fair wages and demonstrate concern for their members welfare.
- We provide consistent purchases, advances, and prompt final payments to artisans.
- We increase market share in North America for fairly traded handicrafts.
- We market quality products that are crafted by underemployed artisans.
- We build sustainable operations using a variety of sales channels, including a network of stores with a common identity.
- We choose handicrafts that reflect and reinforce rich cultural traditions, that are environmentally sensitive, and which appeal to the North American consumer.
- We encourage North American customers to learn about fair trade and to appreciate artisans' cultural heritage and life circumstances with joy and respect.
- We use resources carefully and value volunteers who work in our North American operations.

Source: tenthousandvillages.com/php/about.us/mission.principles.php

by the Mennonite Central Committee, which sought to provide "vital, fair income to Third World people by marketing their handicrafts and telling their stories in North America."[10] Ten Thousand Villages' guiding principles (see above) are similar to those of other Fair Trade organizations. Ten Thousand Villages has grown to encompass more than 160 nonprofit retail stores across the US and Canada, with total sales in 2005–06 growing by 25 percent to approximately US$20 million.[11]

The term "Fair Trade" first appeared in Europe in the 1950s when Oxfam UK began to sell handicrafts made by Chinese refugees, and in the 1960s with the creation of the Dutch organization Fair Trade Organisatie. The latter organization imported the first "fairly traded" coffee in 1973 from cooperatives of small farmers in Guatemala.[12] The German alternative trade organization Gepa was founded in 1975 by five Catholic and Protestant missionary groups. Gepa has grown into Europe's largest "Fair Trade Company," with total 2005 sales of nearly 40 million euros (US$50 million).[13]

In 1989, Ten Thousand Villages, SERRV, Gepa, and other organizations came together to form IFAT so they could share their knowledge and work together to create alternative marketing channels for products from less-developed countries. This cooperation was a hallmark of the movement. IFAT identifies itself as a "global, democratically organized network of Alternative (or Fair) Trade Organizations and producer organizations in Africa, Asia, Europe, Latin America, North America, and the Pacific Rim."[14]

In the 1990s, Oxfam America and Oxfam Canada jointly established a relatively successful catalog-sales operation featuring handicrafts sourced directly from village-level producers around the world, but this effort to stimulate local community economic development using "fair" prices didn't continue for long. Similar stand-alone efforts, such as "Pueblo to People" (which lasted nearly ten years), attempted to expand the market and build direct-sale supply chains from impoverished handicraft producers to ethically motivated final consumers. The definitions of "fair trade" varied, although in most cases producers received higher prices than they would have received through normal commercial handicraft channels.

In Europe, Oxfam developed a multinational network of shops — initially identified as "Oxfam Shops" and ultimately spun off and branded as "World Shops" — whose purpose was to provide direct market access to products from developing countries. The shops also served an educational function, promoting discussion of the conditions under which the products were produced. That network of World Shops has expanded, and there are now more than 2,500 shops in 13 European countries, run by more than 100,000 volunteers under the umbrella of the Network of European World Shops (NEWS), created in 1994.[15]

In the US, the work of these and other "alternative trading organizations" led to the creation in 1994 of the Fair Trade Federation (FTF), "an association of fair trade wholesalers, retailers, and producers whose members are committed to providing fair wages and good employment opportunities to economically disadvantaged artisans and farmers worldwide."[16] The FTF also sees its role as educational and policy-oriented, fostering "a more equitable and sustainable system of production and trade that benefits people and their communities."

The core goals of these organizations, however, have moved well beyond the idea of "relief" or simple charity. The lead organizations have agreed on a formal definition of Fair Trade that makes it clear the movement seeks to transform international trade in fundamental ways:

> Fair Trade is a trading partnership, based on dialogue, transparency and respect, that seeks greater equity in international trade. It contributes to sustainable development by offering better trading conditions to, and securing the rights of, marginalized producers and workers — especially in the [global] South. Fair Trade organizations (backed by consumers) are engaged actively in supporting producers, awareness raising and in a campaign for changes in the rules and practice of international trade.[17]

In retrospect, this early Fair Trade movement was unified by the following characteristics:
- Most, if not all, of the vendors were nonprofit organizations that depended heavily on volunteer staffing. This reflected their specific interest in providing a higher price to producers while not seeking profits for themselves. It also provided a basis for selling products in final markets at relatively competitive prices when compared with the equivalent commercial for-profit products, which were often produced for a lower price on a larger scale.

- There were few, if any, specific formal criteria for what constituted a fair trade product.
- Virtually all the vendors were associated with well-known nonprofit organizations, such as religious groups, social advocacy groups, or other NGOs whose name recognition conveyed legitimacy to their claims that the products represented Fair Trade.
- The products were sold exclusively in "alternative stores" with "alternative brands" and on such small scale that there was little possibility they would grow into a large-scale operation.
- Virtually all of the "alternative" stores sold nothing but Fair Trade products, whatever the implicit definition. This gave them a unity of selling points and reduced the likelihood that final consumers would question or challenge the legitimacy of the claims made for the products.
- By the late 1990s, most of these organizations were concerned that their sales were stagnating, that they had difficulty reaching larger "mainstream" markets, and that the benefits they could deliver to producers were, therefore, severely constrained. These concerns were the subject of many discussions at FTF and IFAT conferences, several of which I attended.

It became critical for Fair Trade to enter mainstream channels, in collaboration with mainstream brands, in order to demonstrate its potential as a new model of international trade. However, if consumers were to be confident they were buying Fair Trade products in mainstream stores, which also sold products for which no social claims were made, there had to be a system for certifying the origin and the trade conditions under which the products had been sourced. The move to mainstream also required a philosophical change. Many proponents of the original "alternative trade" model sought to build a parallel economy outside, and not engaged with, conventional global capitalism. Their goals were to substitute a new model, sometimes called a "solidarity economy," rather than transforming the existing model.[18] That philosophical difference remains in some parts of the Fair Trade movement.

CERTIFIED FAIR TRADE

The challenge of creating an identifiable Fair Trade product that could be sold in mainstream shops and stores, side by side with uncertified varieties of similar products, was first taken up by the Dutch development organization *Solidaridad*. In 1988, *Solidaridad* began importing Mexican coffee into European markets and selling it with a "Max Havelaar" seal to indicate that it had been obtained under specified Fair Trade conditions.[19] Seals of this sort proliferated in Europe, and in 1997, Fairtrade Labeling Organizations International (FLO) was created by the emerging national counterparts of the Netherlands' Max Havelaar in Europe, the United States, and Canada to harmonize the efforts of the "certified" Fair Trade movement. By the end of 2006, FLO had 19 member organizations, each a "Labeling Initiative" responsible for certifying the chain of custody (called "trade certification" in the Fair Trade world); engaging with corporate brokers, processors, wholesalers, and retailers in the supply chain; and promoting the sale of Fair Trade products in a specific country.[20]

FLO and its labeling initiatives focused at first on agricultural products produced in the South and sold in markets of the North, and then began expanding into other products on the basis of local demand. It developed or endorsed Fair Trade standards for ten categories of products: coffee, tea, rice, fresh fruit, juices, cocoa, sugar, honey, sports balls, wine, and flowers. In general, there are two types of standards: standards for producers and standards for trading.

In order to be certified Fair Trade, producers must meet rigorous and comprehensive standards for social and environmental responsibility. They must either be

- a relatively small-scale operation, organized in a democratically functioning cooperative to process and ship products, or
- a larger farm or plantation (for some products, like tea), with all workers represented by some form of democratic organization for labor-management relations.

Both types of producers must meet strict, highly detailed, environmental sustainability standards that ban the use of many chemicals and require other practices, such as economy in the use of water. All certified producers must comply with product-specific standards that set minimum quality and processing requirements.[21]

FLO trading standards stipulate that traders must meet the following requirements:

- They must pay a price to producers that covers the costs of sustainable production at the local cost of living (these prices are negotiated, product by product and region by region, with the producers).
- They must pay a small premium above that price so the producers can invest in social development projects (producer or worker organizations decide, in a transparent manner, how that premium will be used).
- They must provide partial "pre-financing," when producers request it, rather than holding payment until all the product is sold to retailers (as is common in coffee and other markets).
- They must work to develop longer-term commercial relationships with producers that allow for long-term planning and sustainable production practices, rather than leaving producers completely at the whim of "spot markets" from year to year.

FLO has developed a unified European Fair Trade seal. The United States and Canada use their own seal (see Figure 5.2).

FLO Cert, a wholly owned subsidiary of FLO, manages the worldwide inspection and certification of producer organizations that qualify to sell into Fair

Figure 5.2. Fair Trade Logos. Credit: FLO.

Trade markets under Fair Trade producer criteria. FLO Cert also conducts annual audits to ensure that certified producers continue to qualify, and it manages the annual auditing of registered traders in all countries where that task is not handled by the national labeling initiative. Producers pay the full costs of their inspections and auditing; the rest of the system is financed primarily through labeling fees on licensed products, which range from five to ten cents (US) per pound of coffee, for example, from one to several cents per pound of bananas, and comparable prices for other products, depending on total volume and percent of total sales that are Fair Trade. The fees are collected by the labeling initiatives, and a prorated share is sent to FLO and FLO Cert to cover their standard-setting, inspection, certification, and producer support functions.

As of November 2005, FLO was working with 548 certified producer organizations worldwide, representing over 1 million farmers and workers in 50 countries of Africa, Asia, and Latin America. Including their dependents, more than 5 million people benefit from the certified Fair Trade system managed by FLO.[26] On the business side, FLO works with more than 1,000 traders, including exporters, importers, processors, and manufacturers who have been licensed to process and sell labeled Fair Trade products.

The most commonly sold Fair Trade commodity has been coffee. Coffee is the second-most-heavily-traded commodity in the world, exceeded only by oil. In the 2004–05 production year, 5.4 million metric tons of coffee were exported by 50 different countries.[27] These numbers translate to 2.23 billion cups of coffee being consumed each day in the producing and importing countries.[28] Though the overall coffee industry is ruled by multinationals (Kraft, Procter & Gamble, Sara Lee, and Nestlé together buy half the world's coffee beans), almost all recent growth in coffee markets can be attributed to the "specialty coffee" market. According to the Specialty Coffee Association of America, the definition of specialty coffee is relatively clear: "Sometimes called 'gourmet' or 'premium' coffee, specialty coffees are made from exceptional beans grown only in ideal coffee-producing climates. They tend to feature distinctive flavors, which are shaped by the unique characteristics of the soil that produces them."[29]

Building Fair Trade into Corporate Culture

Bob Stiller of Green Mountain Coffee Roasters

Not every company needs to be taught that an ethical approach to business can be more profitable.

Bob Stiller wasn't born into the coffee industry.[22] He got there by drinking the best cup of coffee he had ever tasted, tracing it back to its source, and buying the company![23] This was in 1981, pioneering years in the growth of consumer appreciation for fine-tasting specialty coffee in the US.

From its inception, Bob's company, Green Mountain Coffee Roasters (GMCR), was firmly rooted in the Vermont-based business community of socially responsible firms like Ben & Jerry's Ice Cream, Cabot Farms (a large dairy and cheese cooperative), and Champlain Valley Chocolates (an early US vendor of fine dark chocolate). Though its corporate identity was closely linked to community-mindedness through philanthropy and the respectful treatment of its employees, formal integration of social and environmental practices in its supply chain did not take hold until the 1990s.

GMCR had introduced its own social concerns in its treatment of coffee farmers, offering preferred longer-term contracts to producers in Mexico, Perú, and the Aceh region of Sumatra, in Indonesia. Long before GMCR introduced either certified organic or Fair Trade coffees, it offered a line of "Stewardship Coffee," using its own criteria. It sought to identify growers who were committed to producing high-quality coffee, supported a healthy environment, and were respectful in the treatment of their own workers. In the absence of industry standards for these characteristics, Green Mountain developed its own. Stewardship Coffee was launched in 1992 after a group of employees went on the first of many company-sponsored trips to coffee farms. But those were quiet dimensions of GMCR's corporate practices, difficult to validate externally or to turn into marketable qualities for their products. By the time GMCR began buying significant amounts of coffee certified to organic and Fair Trade standards, Stewardship Coffee accounted for almost a third of the coffee it purchased.

Bob Stiller decided to experiment with a couple of lines of Fair Trade Certified coffees in 2001, after conversations with TransFair USA — and despite the misgivings of some of his senior managers. "Paying a higher price to start," they argued, "is not a logical basis for increasing our profits." However, Bob recognized the potential value of strengthening the economics of coffee producers, and he provided funding for the creation of a cooperative among 100 farmers in Sumatra, who then increased their production six-fold and committed to selling a sizable portion of their coffee to GMCR.[24] By the end of 2002, Fair Trade coffees accounted for 9 percent of GMCR's total coffee sales. By 2006 it was approaching 30 percent. And 85 percent of the certified Fair Trade coffee was also certified organic. Fully 46 percent of their coffee product lines were then Fair Trade and organic.

GMCR focuses on supplying coffee to major grocery chains, to some 7,000 wholesale customers, and by direct mail. Since 2000, it has held a contract with ExxonMobil to supply ready-to-brew coffee at more than 900 convenience stores and 13,000 dealer and franchise stores; it expanded its sales through branded placements in Amtrak trains, Jet Blue Airways flights, and food service companies like Aramark. Gas stations and convenience stores might not seem the logical place to find ethically conscious coffee drinkers, but GMCR's most important growth in sales over the past five years has come from the introduction of organic and Fair Trade Certified coffees, which illustrates how Fair Trade and organic coffees can be a viable business model.

GMCR also attributes a lucrative wholesale contract with Sodexho, a major institutional food supplier, to its line of Fair Trade and organic coffees. Sodexho provides food services to many colleges and university campuses, where demand for Fair Trade is growing as a result of campaigns waged by United Students for Fair Trade and the presence of conscientious student consumers.

A GMCR partnership with Newman's Own Organics (the socially generous company linked to actor Paul Newman and his daughter Nell) proved especially beneficial. The companies developed a co-branded line of six Fair Trade organic coffees. Sales of those coffees, which had been doing well in grocery stores, began to soar in 2005 when GMCR signed a contract to provide *all* the coffee sold in McDonald's 650 New England restaurants.

GMCR is an excellent example of a publicly traded company for which Fair Trade has been an important business driver. In 2006, total net sales rose 39.5 percent to nearly US$225 million; net income grew by 21.7 percent; and share value continued a four-year rise, with an increase in excess of 200 percent from early November 2002

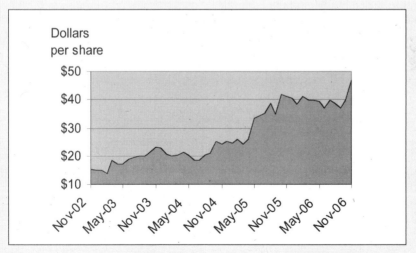

Figure 5.3. GMCR share value 48 months through November 2006. Credit: Yahoo!Finance.

to early November 2006 (see Figure 5.3), raising its market capitalization to nearly US$400 million. Green Mountain was also number one in *Business Ethics* magazine's "100 Best Corporate Citizens for 2006." In fact, *Business Ethics* suggested that GMCR illustrated what their "top corporate citizens" rating system was all about:

> The best-managed firms today — in this era when societal expectations of business are rising — can no longer focus solely on shareholder return. Companies that aim to prosper over the long term also emphasize good jobs for employees, environmental sustainability, healthy community relations, and great products for customers.[25]

Students in my Yale seminar asked Bob Stiller why Green Mountain would commit so clearly to social and environmental accountability when its competitors carried little or none of that burden. Bob's response, after thinking a few moments, was soft-spoken but definitive: "I frankly can't see any other way to engage with my employees, my customers, or my suppliers. If I couldn't run my business this way, I wouldn't want to be in business."

In the last 30 years, the global retail market share of specialty coffee has grown from 2 percent of the market for coffee by value to 40 per cent. In 2005 it represented 20 percent of US coffee imports by volume and 50 percent by sales.[30] The specialty coffee market segment in the US was valued at $11.9 billion in 2005 (up from $1 billion in 1990).[31]

FLO originally set Fair Trade prices for coffee at approximately $1.26 per pound of dry green coffee FOB the point of export. The price for coffee also certified organic was $1.41 per pound. There are slight variations in those base prices from country to country due to transportation costs and local conditions. Producers in South America, for example, don't want to be disadvantaged vis-à-vis producers in Mexico and Central America because of the latter's slightly lower shipping costs to the US, so the South American base price is slightly lower. These prices were originally set to reflect what the average farmer needs to receive in order to earn the equivalent of a living wage. They also include a "social premium" of five cents per pound that the producers' cooperatives or workers' organizations can dedicate to social development projects of their own choice.[32] There is an expectation that the prices will be raised in 2007 to reflect current costs of production.

For all but a couple of the past 18 years, those prices have been consistently above the "Commodity C prices," the mid-grade commercial prices offered by brokers in the New York Coffee Exchange (see Figure 5.4). They were significantly above the commercial prices during the recent coffee crisis, from 2000 to 2005.

Comparable prices for bananas, oranges, cocoa, tea, and other commodities have been negotiated with producer groups on the basis of cost of production and cost of living and are generally well above the spot market prices for those products.

CERTIFIED FAIR TRADE IN THE US

Self-certified "fair trade" coffee has been sold in the United States since 1986 by Equal Exchange, a Massachusetts-based for-profit, worker-owned firm that began selling only "fairly priced" coffees through solidarity networks.[33] Equal Exchange drew its name, and principles, from the theoretical assertion that historical relations of "unequal exchange" must be challenged in order to reduce global inequalities.[34] Though not initially affiliated in a formal way with its European Fair Trade counterparts, Equal Exchange adopted principles and price criteria similar to those articulated by Max Havelaar and other European groups. For Equal Exchange, this pricing approach provided a more equitable distribution of production risk across farmers, intermediate traders, roasters, and retailers.[35]

Equal Exchange was one of the first companies licensed by TransFair USA, the FLO labeling initiative for the United States. A small group of NGOs and coffee roasters, who had been developing their own models of fairer pricing and improved trade relations with small-scale coffee producers, came together at Transfair USA's founding meeting in 1995, which was hosted by the Institute for Agriculture and Trade Policy. The institute was interested in developing alternative, fairer models for global agricultural commodity trade and in launching a line of certified Fair Trade coffee. After a brief hiatus for early organizational efforts, TransFair USA was launched in 1998 and certified Fair Trade sales took off.

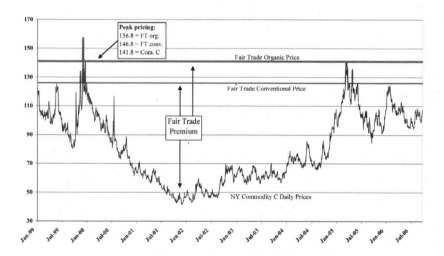

Figure 5.4. Fair Trade coffee prices compared with NY Commodity C Price (U.S. dollars per hundredwieght, Jan. 1999–Oct. 2006. Credit: Author's elaboration on New York Board of Trade data (nybot.com/reports/monthlyData/COFFEE.xls).

Equal Exchange remains one of the five largest vendors of Fair Trade Certified products in the US, though competition for the unofficial title of "largest vendor" became much more acute in 2006, with several candidates jockeying for the honor. Equal Exchange also remains a leader of the set of coffee roasters committed to selling *only* Fair Trade products (the "100%-ers").

TransFair USA is generally credited with creating the first workable model for getting Fair Trade products into the "mainstream" companies and stores beyond the fully committed 100%-ers like Equal Exchange. US Fair Trade coffee imports exploded from less than 1 million pounds in 1998 to an estimated 70 million pounds in 2006 (see Figure 5.5). The rapid growth of Fair Trade coffee in the United States can be attributed to three principal factors:

- Advocacy NGOs organized successful market campaigns to put pressure on companies to adopt lines of Fair Trade coffee and other products.
- A number of coffee roasters and retailers adopted Fair Trade products as a distinguishing characteristic of their businesses for marketing purposes.
- TransFair USA created a sophisticated business-oriented service structure to meet the needs of companies purchasing, processing, and selling Fair Trade products and licensed to use the Fair Trade seal.

Much of this model was replicated in other countries as certified Fair Trade expanded. Each of these factors has limitations and each has contributed in important ways to ongoing struggles within the Fair Trade movement, both in the United States and elsewhere.

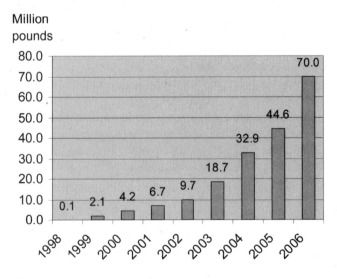

Figure 5.5. Green Coffee Imports to the US certified by TransFair USA (2006 estimated). Credit: TransFair USA.

The Campaigns

It was not easy to convince major coffee importing, roasting, and distributing companies to buy into the notion of Fair Trade. They had their sources, they were generally unchallenged in terms of their sourcing processes, and most coffee consumers were unaware of the exploitation of farmers in the normal business supply chain. However, the collapse of coffee prices worldwide from 2000 to 2005 (apparent in Figure 5.4) brought worldwide attention to the plight of coffee producers. It also raised concerns in the coffee industry about the sustainability of the supply of high-quality coffees.

A "breakthrough" moment for certified Fair Trade in mainstream markets came on April 10, 2000, when Starbucks, the world's largest chain of specialty coffee houses, signed a letter of intent with TransFair USA to offer certified coffee in all 2,700 of its US cafes. This deal was fostered in large part by the social activist organization Global Exchange, which had carried out a year-long campaign to promote it.

TransFair USA staff met with Starbucks repeatedly during 1999 and early 2000, encouraging the chain to "experiment" with lines of Fair Trade coffee in all of its shops, but there was little or no interest. The Global Exchange (GX) campaign focused on Starbucks precisely because it was the largest specialty coffee retailer, with a fifth of all coffee shops in the country.[36] In the fall of 1999, GX approached Starbucks' founder and CEO Howard Schultz and urged him to offer certified Fair Trade coffee in all his stores. The company argued that it wasn't able to find Fair Trade coffee of sufficiently high quality to meet its standards. GX began to organize peaceful demonstrations in front of Starbucks stores in Seattle, the city where the chain had started and where its headquarters are located. GX also began organizing students to pressure college and university administrations to serve Fair Trade coffee in campus restaurants, dining halls, and other food services.

In February 2000, an investigative report by San Francisco's ABC-TV affiliate revealed the use of child labor and scandalously low wages on Guatemalan coffee plantations, some of which, the reporters learned, sold coffee to Starbucks. GX organized protests at Starbucks stores in the Bay Area immediately after the report aired and then approached Starbucks stockholders at their annual meeting in Seattle, asking them to put forward a resolution to offer Fair Trade coffee in their shops. One week later, Starbucks announced a one-time purchase of 75,000 pounds of Fair Trade coffee. GX's response was that for a firm as big as Starbucks, the purchase represented a "drop in the cup." Besides, GX activists told the media, the coffee the chain purchased wasn't, in fact, certified by TransFair USA.

On April 5, 2000, Global Exchange released an open letter to Starbucks that urged the company to purchase coffee certified Fair Trade so it could guarantee it was paying its coffee producers a living wage. The letter noted that Starbucks reported revenues of US$1.7 billion in 1999, with US$164 million in profits, "yet the farmers and workers who make [Starbucks] rich still earn poverty wages." The letter was signed by 84 student, labor union, environmental, church, and other social justice organizations, ranging from Pax Christi USA and United Students Against Sweatshops to Trade Aid New Zealand and Friends of the Earth.[37] GX then worked with other groups to organize 30 simultaneous demonstrations around the country at Starbucks shops, scheduled for April 13, 2000. It also set up a mechanism on its website, innovative at that time, through which faxes could be sent to the Starbucks CEO, urging him to serve certified Fair Trade coffee. Hundreds of faxes were sent. Five days later, Starbucks agreed to stock and sell one line of certified Fair Trade coffee in all its US stores. The GX press release that day announced:

> In a Stunning Concession to Protesters Just Days Before the Launch
> of A National Campaign, Starbucks Agrees to Offer Its Customers
> Fair Trade Certified Coffee by the End of the Year
>
> Human Rights Activists Say Thousands of Poor Farmers
> in the Developing World Will Be Guaranteed a Living Wage
>
> Protesters Now Plan to Turn Their Attention to Other Coffee Retailers[38]

Peet's Coffee, Tully's Coffee, and a host of competing specialty coffee companies soon followed suit, initiating sales of Fair Trade Certified coffee. None of these major vendors were willing to sell only Fair Trade coffees, but their commitment did lead to modest, though inconsistent, growth in sales of certified Fair Trade coffee.

In subsequent years, other NGOs and faith-based groups have worked to promote certified Fair Trade products in the United States.

- Global Exchange, Co-op America, and other NGOs waged a bitter campaign to convince Procter & Gamble, the largest coffee vendor in the US, to introduce a line of Fair Trade coffees. The company has done so, but without much enthusiasm.
- Oxfam America trained student leaders who developed campus campaigns that would persuade colleges and universities to buy Fair Trade coffee for their institutional needs. It also helped launch United Students for Fair Trade, the student-based organization that continues to organize these campaigns, having reached more than 350 campuses in the US by the end of 2006.
- Lutheran World Relief created the Interfaith Fair Trade Initiative to encourage congregations of many faiths to purchase and serve Fair Trade coffee and tea in their institutions and to encourage members to purchase Fair Trade products for their homes. The initial goal was to convince "at least 1,000 congregations of differing religious denominations across the nation" to adopt Fair Trade coffee. In less than three years, the campaign expanded to incorporate 15 major denominations and faith-based organization and to reach 20,000 congregations, where Fair Trade coffee and other products were considered for serving after services. Many members of the congregations also agreed to campaign to get Fair Trade products placed in local stores.[39] Most

of the coffee, tea, and chocolate sold through this interfaith campaign has come from Equal Exchange.

The Business Structure

Another factor influencing the rapid growth of certified Fair Trade in the United States, both in the coffee market and for newly introduced products such as cocoa and chocolate products, tea, and bananas, is the unusual business focus of TransFair USA. Perhaps symbolic of the evolution of Fair Trade more generally, TransFair USA was launched by Paul Rice, a former Central American rural development specialist who later obtained an MBA degree. Under his leadership, TransFair USA has followed a classic business model to expand sales of certified Fair Trade products (see Profile 5.2). In 2006, with a staff of 50 and an annual budget in excess of US$9 million, TransFair USA continues to be a primary force in the further mainstreaming of Fair Trade in the United States.

- In 2005, it convinced Costco, the leading warehouse club store, to convert its principal line of private-label coffee to certified Fair Trade.
- It worked with Dunkin' Donuts, which has more than 6,500 donut and coffee shops across the US, to introduce 100 percent certified Fair Trade coffee in an espresso line that challenges Starbucks.
- It encouraged Sam's Club, the warehouse club store affiliated with Wal-Mart, to introduce a line of certified Fair Trade coffee grown, roasted, and packaged in Brazil.
- It helped Green Mountain Coffee Roasters in its efforts to convince McDonald's to sell *only* certified Fair Trade coffee in its New England region restaurants (see Profile 5.1).

The Fairtrade Foundation, the labeling initiative for the United Kingdom (the other market where dramatic progress has been achieved), has used similar methods to introduce Fair Trade commodities into some of the nation's largest retail venues, including Marks & Spencer, Tesco, and Sainsbury.

RESULTS

For several reasons, there are no reliable estimates of the overall size or impact of the complete Fair Trade movement to date. First, there is no central registry for the various components of the movement. Second, different vendors measure sales at different points in the supply chain. The shops that sell only Fair Trade handicrafts and food products maintain relatively clear records on their final sales, but there is no central clearinghouse that collects and aggregates those sales figures. FLO and TransFair USA, on the other hand, produce voluminous statistics on pounds of coffee, bananas, oranges, cocoa, tea, and other products whose licensed sales they have recorded and verified at the wholesale level, in many cases before final processing. Figure 5.6 shows that commodity certification data converted into estimated retail sales. Unofficial estimates for 2006 suggest that those figures nearly doubled.

Paul Rice and TransFair USA
An NGO that "Works at the Speed of Business"

Paul Rice refused to believe his distinguished Yale professor of economics when the professor taught that there was an inevitable tradeoff between "efficiency and equity." Paul couldn't foresee that his disbelief would send him on a personal journey that, 24 years later, would land him on the cover of *Fast Company* magazine as the three-time winner of its Social Capitalist Award, for himself and for the organization he leads, TransFair USA.[40]

Paul's immediate response to his professor was to spend a summer studying land reform efforts in Nicaragua, where he sought to demonstrate that greater equity in the distribution of land could also be associated with greater efficiency in agricultural production. The Texan, born in Dallas and raised in Austin, graduated from Yale in 1983 and returned to Nicaragua to conduct further research on agrarian reform.

This was the beginning of an 11-year odyssey working with Nicaraguan farmers and rural cooperatives, especially in the coffee regions of northern Nicaragua. It took him through the darkest years of the *contra* war in that part of Nicaragua, where Paul was working with cooperatives that had been created by small-scale farmers who had received agrarian reform lands distributed by the Sandinista government. Funded by European aid agencies, Paul helped the cooperatives develop basic business skills and promote sustainable development. In 1990, Paul organized the shipment of the first 38,000-pound container of Fair Trade coffee from Nicaragua to Equal Exchange in the US. In the ensuing four years, the marketing cooperative he helped set up and run, PRODECOOP, grew from a handful of farmers in its first year, to 200 farmers in its second year, to over 1,000 in its third year and almost 2,500 in its fourth year.

Paul left Nicaragua in 1994 to pursue an MBA at the Haas School of Business at the University of California, Berkeley. While still in the MBA program, Paul developed the formal business plan for TransFair USA. When the business plan successfully drew start-up funding from a major foundation in 1998, Paul was recruited to be Transfair's first CEO; he has remained there for nearly ten years.

Certification organizations in the social and environmental accountability field face two main challenges:

- They must develop the ability to provide certification business services to companies at the speed that those companies want to move, rather than at the generally slower speeds at which nonprofits move.
- They must wrestle with the complicated interaction between advocacy organizations, on which the movement depends for credibility, and the engaged companies who seek to insulate themselves from the bite of the advocates.

Under Paul's leadership, TransFair USA has proven to be a model for engaging with companies in an effective manner, relying on a business structure that draws from classic business development literature and practice. The results are apparent in TransFair's record of successfully expanding the sales of Fair Trade Certified products in the US.

TransFair's management of its ongoing relationships with advocacy NGOs in the Fair Trade movement has been a bigger challenge. Yet TransFair has succeeded, more than any other social and environmental certification system, in moving the fundamental business case beyond reputational risk management. By promoting and communicating the business advantages of Fair Trade certification, TransFair has convinced a growing number of major national importers, manufacturers, and retailers, such as Green Mountain Coffee Roasters, Costco Wholesale, Sam's Clubs (part of Wal-Mart), Dunkin' Donuts, and Wild Oats Markets that it is to their business advantage to sell certified Fair Trade products, even though none of them has been subjected to market campaign activities by the advocacy NGOs. These companies have become the national leaders in expanding mainstream Fair Trade sales within the United States.

Paul is convinced that the empowerment of producers engendered by Fair Trade is as much a part of the success of the movement as the financial value it brings to them. Comparing the mentality within the incipient cooperatives in Nicaragua in the late 1980s with their attitudes today, Paul sees how direct marketing to Fair Trade buyers has helped the producers "hear the market whispering in their ears." This has led to significant improvement in the quality of the coffee and other products they export, a shift to organic cultivation, a focus on the margins they generate rather than on sheer volume of production, increased satisfaction in the role they play in "ethical markets," and further pride in the social development projects that their cooperatives fund in their local communities.

Yet Paul's greatest satisfaction is the way in which TransFair USA has demonstrated the potential for success of a new international business model that links small-scale farmers and farm and factory laborers to the global economy in a powerful, positive alliance with industry. The result: higher family incomes, protected environments, and vibrant communities throughout the global South — without sacrificing the profitability of the companies selling Fair Trade products. As he discusses with major global companies the possibilities for Fair Trade in toy manufacturing; apparel and shoe manufacturing; diamond, gold, and silver sourcing; and even tourism, Paul comments that "we haven't even begun to tap the range of possibilities."

It is no little source of satisfaction, as well, that he has proven his Yale professor wrong. Fair Trade is demonstrating, he notes, that improved equity in international trade can also be associated with improved efficiency in global supply chains. Fair Trade is showing a rapidly growing number of companies that strengthening the supply of ethically sourced products that command premium prices from ethically minded consumers simply makes good business sense.

Figure 5.6. Worldwide Estimated Certified Fair Trade Sales,
by Principal Markets

National Initiative	Est. Retail (Million Euros) 2004	Share of Sales 2004	Est. Retail (Million Euros) 2005	Share of Sales 2005	% Change in Sales 2004–05
Austria	15.781	1.9%	25.629	2.2%	62%
Belgium	13.605	1.6%	15.000	1.3%	10%
Canada	17.536	2.1%	34.848	3.0%	99%
Denmark	13.000	1.6%	14.000	1.2%	8%
Finland	7.553	0.9%	13.032	1.1%	73%
France	69.670	8.4%	109.061	9.5%	57%
Germany	57.500	6.9%	70.855	6.2%	23%
Ireland	5.051	0.6%	6.552	0.6%	30%
Italy	25.000	3.0%	28.000	2.4%	12%
Japan	2.500	0.3%	3.365	0.3%	35%
Luxemburg	2.000	0.2%	2.250	0.2%	13%
Netherlands	35.000	4.2%	38.500	3.4%	10%
Norway	4.786	0.6%	6.734	0.6%	41%
Sweden	5.494	0.7%	9.271	0.8%	69%
Switzerland	136.000	16.4%	143.117	12.5%	5%
United Kingdom	205.556	24.7%	276.765	24.2%	35%
United States	214.603	25.8%	344.130	30.1%	60%
Australia & N.Z.	0.884	0.1%	2.462	0.2%	179%
TOTAL	831.519	100.0%	1,143.571	100.0%	38%

Source: FLO.

One researcher has laboriously assembled cross-movement statistics for 2004 that suggest the total sales in Europe, the US, Canada, and Japan came to US$1.2 billion. Of that amount, approximately US$169 million (or 14.9 percent) were sales of Fair Trade products by alternative trade organizations.[41] The movement-level scale of certified Fair Trade is increasingly apparent in Europe. As of 2005, for example:

- Fair Trade products were available at an estimated 79,000 points of sale.
- In Switzerland, Fair Trade bananas accounted for 47 percent of total banana sales, and Fair Trade flowers were 28 percent of total sales.
- In the United Kingdom, Fair Trade coffee reached 20 percent of ground coffee sales, and Fair Trade bananas accounted for 22 percent of total national sales.[42]

By comparing the Fair Trade price received with the average commercial prices for coffee, cocoa, tea, and fresh fruit, TransFair USA estimates that, between 1999 and 2005, Fair Trade in the US alone has generated well over US$80 million in additional income for producers (see Figure 5.7).

Benefits to farmers and other producers are not limited to the higher prices and the social premium. The Fair Trade Research Group at Colorado State Uni-

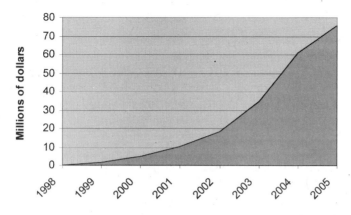

Figure 5.7. Estimated Extra Income Earned by FT Producers from US FT Sales. Credit: TransFair USA.

versity has documented a wide array of social benefits for Mexican participants in the certified Fair Trade system.[43] They include the following advantages:

- Greater access to credit for the expansion of production, given the relative stability of the Fair Trade financial relationships.
- Greater economic and social stability for Fair Trade farmers because of the Fair Trade financial relationships.
- Greater access to training and enhanced ability to improve the quality of their coffee.
- The development of new and beneficial networks of contacts among producers participating in the Fair Trade network.
- Increased access to projects developed by their cooperatives with the social premium.[44]
- Training and marketing opportunities for family members to develop alternative income sources.
- Enhanced family stability.
- Contributions to cultural revival.
- An increase in organizational credibility.
- Access to a broader range of government support programs.

Another group of independent researchers, who gathered data on samples of Fair Trade and non-Fair Trade coffee farmers in Nicaragua, Guatemala, and Peru, found additional statistically significant differences favoring farmers engaged with Fair Trade:

- Fair Trade farmers sold more coffee and received higher prices than comparable non-Fair Trade neighbors.
- Fair Trade farmers made greater investments in land, tools, sheds, livestock, and other farm improvements.

Taking Fair Trade to the Consumer

The Wild Oats Story

Those who would argue that Fair Trade is little more than a charity mission, better met by international development assistance or the philanthropic side of business, should meet Perry Odak, CEO of Wild Oats Markets, Inc.[46]

Wild Oats Markets is the US grocery chain that has been most successful in adding Fair Trade products to its consumer product lines. From the perspective of Odak, this has been a mission-driven profitable success for his company. In 2006, Wild Oats Markets had 115 stores spread across 23 states and in Canada, primarily in the West, but with new stores opening quickly in New England, Florida, Illinois, Southern California, and other metro market areas. It had just over $1.1 billion in sales in 2005, and its stock price has soared from under $6 per share in 2001, when Odak took over, to more than $20 per share in 2006.

Although the Wild Oats company includes about 35 stores under the Henry's Farmers Market, Sun Harvest, and Capers Community Markets brand names (the last only in Canada), the leading edge of its North American image are 70 stores carrying the Wild Oats brand. These full-feature Wild Oats grocery stores focus primarily on products, especially fresh meats and produce, that are all-natural or organic. The organic products are labeled under the standardized US Department of Agriculture criteria. "All-natural" is a label without formal definition, but Wild Oats investigates the supply chain of each and every product so labeled to ensure there are no herbicides, no growth hormones, no antibiotics, and no artificial flavors or colors used in production. Customers nationwide have come to expect that supply-chain diligence.

Perry Odak is not an old-fashioned believer in social or environmental causes above corporate profits. In fact, he is a tough, experienced "turnaround specialist" who had previously demonstrated his executive skills at a Bahrain-based multifaceted investment firm, Invescorp International; at the Belgian arms manufacturer Fabrique National; at the US arms company Browning and Winchester; as well as at the uniquely socially responsible ice-cream manufacturer, Ben and Jerry's. When he took over Wild Oats, his first act was to close down some 30 of its least profitable stores before beginning to build almost as many new ones.

Odak first encountered Fair Trade in 2002 when he sought to replace the coffee previously sold in all of the Wild Oats stores, coffee that he characterized as "of poor quality and cheap." He connected with salespeople at Green Mountain Coffee Roasters (GMCR) through a former colleague and consultant to Ben and Jerry's and made a trip to Mexico to visit coffee cooperatives in order to assure himself of the legitimacy of Fair Trade claims and the integrity of the supply chain. He returned to Wild Oats' Boulder, Colorado, offices with a determination to move the firm into Fair Trade sourcing and sales. Wild Oats stores then began to introduce a double-certified Wild Oats GMCR Certified Fair Trade and Organic line of coffees. He used pictures from that trip and his own experiences to participate personally in the development of the printed materials that would be used in stores throughout the company to introduce the new line.

Coffee procurement costs rose as Fair Trade and organic premiums were paid. Coffees that previously sold for an average of $6 per pound were replaced by coffee priced at $8 per pound on average, with ample point-of-purchase signage and labeling to "tell the story" of increased fairness for coffee producers. In the first year alone, Wild Oats' coffee sales volume increased 20 percent, despite the higher price point, according to Odak, with an expanded profit margin on every pound sold. Stores within the chain embraced the new products quickly, according to Odak, in part because many of their 8,500 employees and managers are "young and passionate" and live the lifestyle.

Wild Oats then began to sell many other Fair Trade products, including bananas in 2004, and chocolate, pineapples, mangos, and teas in 2005. In late 2006 the stores introduced an array of clothing and handicraft products from World of Good, which, while not certified under FLO standards, are considered to be among the reasonably credible "fairly traded" products of their type in the US.

Odak's bottom-line success with these products does match, in fact, his personal and professional ethical values. "Business is the biggest change agent in society now," he notes, replacing everything from churches to governments. "Sustainable and profitable business practices shouldn't make profits off the backs of other people...shouldn't take away from the environment...and shouldn't wait for the government to define and enforce responsible practices."

- Fair Trade farmers had greater rates of electrification in their homes and greater access to potable water.
- Though the average level of education attained by Fair Trade and non-Fair Trade farmers was the same (three to four years in total), a significantly higher proportion of the 10- to 15-year-old children from Fair Trade families were in school compared to those from non-Fair Trade families.
- A higher proportion of the children in Fair Trade families were able to receive medical treatment for common illnesses.
- Fair Trade families in Nicaragua were found to have a significantly more positive outlook on the future for themselves and their children than families not engaged with Fair Trade. In Peru, Fair Trade families felt that they were "holding their own," while non-Fair Trade families felt their conditions had worsened.[45]

REFLECTIONS

The Fair Trade movement and its mainstream market manifestation in certified Fair Trade products illustrate the emergence, and the rapid success, of an alternative, more equitable, and more sustainable form of international trade. Those who would argue, as some have, that Fair Trade simply subsidizes the production of commodities that are already overproduced fail to recognize that the certified socially and environmentally superior product is essentially distinct from comparable products on the shelf or in the bin of a grocery store. Certified Fair Trade and Organic bananas in Wild Oats stores sell at price points well above conventional bananas, even when they are placed side by side. Certified Fair Trade and Organic coffees sell at higher prices on Green Mountain's website, even though they're listed right next to uncertified coffees roasted and packaged by the same company. The exponential growth in sales of certified Fair Trade products indicates that consumers find superior value in ethically responsible products. Their willingness to pay higher prices is no subsidy; it represents a payment level linked to an ethical attribute, or "quality," for which consumers are willing to pay.

But economic theory would suggest that those price premia should draw other entrants into the marketplace — either other Fair Trade vendors willing to sell the retail products at a lower price, or competing labeling schemes that attempt to earn the price premium without necessarily generating the same flow of benefits to producers. In Chapter 11, we will review a number of schemes with which Fair Trade must increasingly compete.

The struggle to maintain the support of leading social and environmental advocacy groups while providing effective and responsive services to business (and competing with the other schemes) is as much a problem in the Fair Trade world as it has been in the sustainable forestry world. Debates among the stakeholders take place continuously.

One discussion focuses on whether coffee (and other products) grown on larger estates should be included in the system, or if the system should be reserved for the "purest form" of Fair Trade, with nothing but poor — and often impoverished — farmers allowed. FLO certifies larger farms or estates in most product categories, including bananas, tea, pineapples, grapes, orange juice, and sugar cane, as long as the hired labor standards of Fair Trade are met. Many producers of coffee and cocoa, and some banana producers, currently in the Fair Trade system fear the impact that would have for their commodity. Should the major banana companies be allowed to compete with small-scale banana farmer cooperatives?

Another controversy swirls around the level of commitment a company must make to Fair Trade before it is allowed to use the label. Some groups fear that major food-processing companies will engage just enough to do some "green-washing" or "fair-washing" of their brands while continuing to sell uncertified products as their major business. If, on the other hand, Fair Trade were limited to the "100%-er" companies, the total benefits generated for farmers over the past six to eight years would be a minuscule fraction of what they have been.

An additional challenge is presented by the uptake of Fair Trade by some of the largest companies in the world, whose social and environmental reputations are under attack for reasons other than the sourcing of their coffee or chocolate. The classic case is McDonald's decision to serve Green Mountain Coffee Roasters

Fair Trade coffee in all its restaurants in New England and upstate New York. Some of my friends quickly e-mailed me after the decision was announced, saying, in effect: "Told you so! Fair Trade will never be a transformative model for capitalism as we know it!" They see McDonald's as the iconic "bad boy" of globalization, encouraging unhealthy eating habits by selling obesity-producing food drawn mostly from exploitative agricultural conditions.

The alternative perspective was voiced in a *Stanford Social Innovation Review* article, which argued that the McDonald's decision represents the definitive movement of Fair Trade "out of its niche and into the most mainstream market of all."[47] The article documented how McDonald's franchise owners wanted to compete better with both Starbucks and Dunkin' Donuts on the coffee front. They chose GMCR's line of Newman's Own Fair Trade Organic coffee because of its taste quality, but also because of its association with social and environmental responsibility. Nell Newman, a co-owner of the brand, summed it up when she said, "I never thought I'd see the day when McDonald's got so excited about organics." When she went to visit some of the restaurants that featured the coffee, "it was amazing to see how enthusiastic the franchise owners were about Fair Trade and organic." And when my friends argued that this was the ultimate debunking of Fair Trade, I simply asked them whether there is another sustainable system in sight that would bring the extra millions of dollars in annual benefits to small-scale, struggling coffee farmers around the world.

The Fair Trade movement is finding ways to deal with these dilemmas, generally creatively, sometimes not. What seems clear from a business perspective is that the system enjoys increasing market recognition, growing institutional stability, and a rapidly widening set of models showing how it can become part of an effective business strategy. And that is at the heart of its usefulness for demonstrating supply-chain accountability to business partners, consumers, shareholders, and financial markets.

Finally, Fair Trade provides an example, in the context of this book, of a socially and environmentally responsible set of products whose uptake by the market appears to depend far less on NGO advocacy than on competitive business practices. With the exception of Starbucks, the companies who were "coerced" because of market campaigns to sell Fair Trade products have *not* been the most important players in the growth of Fair Trade sales. A majority of Starbucks' Fair Trade coffee purchases are related to the requirements of other companies for whom they roast and package private-label coffee, not the Fair Trade sales that occur in the chain's shops. As a result, Starbucks continues to draw the wrath of advocacy organizations because the proportion of its Fair Trade coffee purchases is still very low, leading to charges of "fair-washing" their brand. In its broader effectiveness, beyond advocacy, Fair Trade has moved farther into mainstream business marketing consciousness than virtually any other certification system that we will discuss.

6

Even the Banks Can Do It!
New Accountability in Global Finance

The global banking and finance industry long felt that it had no fundamental responsibility to shareholders and depositors other than to produce strong financial results, and no responsibility to those who borrowed from its members other than to provide efficient service at competitive rates. As recently as 1997, a major study of the "non-financial" factors taken into consideration by financial analysts was considered remarkable because it found and categorized 39 specific non-financial dimensions reviewed by analysts when deciding to invest in, or lend to, a company. This result ran counter to accepted wisdom that decisions were based primarily on financial factors. It demonstrated that when non-financial characteristics of a firm were taken into account, earnings predictions were considerably more accurate. But not one of the non-financial characteristics it found in use referred to the social or environmental characteristics of the businesses bought and sold.[1]

Shareholder groups promoting socially responsible investment, such as the Interfaith Center on Corporate Responsibility, have undertaken many worthy campaigns, but the closest they have come to a focus on banking is their work on microcredit and other programs, which encourage better access to capital for poor families and small enterprises, and their work on predatory lending.

Since the mid-1990s, activists have tried to link environmental issues to financial markets. Friends of the Earth, the global coalition of major environmental groups in some 70 countries, worked with financial analysts on Wall Street and abroad to raise their awareness of the risks associated with the environmental aspects of global investments. But none of the groups attempted to implement a specific set of standards for social or environmental screens at major banks.

Campaigns to reform the lending practices of the World Bank and the International Monetary Fund, national export credit agencies, and regional development banks have been common since the early 1990s. These international financial institutions (IFIs) were somewhat more susceptible to civil society pressure because of their public nature, though activist organizations, such as the Bank Information Center, had to become extraordinarily resourceful to track the activities of IFIs. One of the results of this early pressure on IFIs, in fact, was an effort by the International Finance Corporation (IFC), an arm of the World Bank Group that lends money for private sector projects, to develop a series of Safeguard Principles to guide its lending around the world. Beginning in 1990, IFC developed and published principles on involuntary resettlement and indigenous peoples (1991), safety of dams (1996), a range of environmental issues (1998), and child and forced labor (1998). These principles were, in theory, used by IFC staff to evaluate every proposed lending project and to exclude those that were not consistent with them.[2]

But there were few calls for comparable practices in private financial institutions before 2000, partly because of the competitive confidentiality of their operations, and partly because they seemed extraordinarily difficult to trace. One of the earliest campaigns against private bank lending was organized by the Dutch NGOs Profundo and AIDEnvironment, when they were seeking to stop the financing of Indonesian oil palm plantations by Dutch banking giants ABN AMRO, Rabobank, ING Bank, and what became Fortis Bank. The NGOs reported that vast tracts of forest lands in Indonesia were being cleared and burned, destroying enormous swaths of the habitat of Asian elephants, primates such as orangutans, and other endangered species. Much of the land given in concessions to oil plantation developers was land settled by indigenous peoples, which led to violent displacement of these peoples.[3] ABN AMRO, in particular, was stung by these criticisms because it considered itself one of the most ethical members of the world banking community. WWF added to the pressure. Highlighting the use of palm oil in commercial ice-cream production, WWF asked, in one press release that was picked up widely, "Is your ice cream bad for elephants?"[4]

The period from 2000 to 2003 was a time of extraordinary activity. Numerous reports, declarations, campaign activities, and banking sector responses addressed the issues of social and environmental standards for private international project lending. In 2000, the Rainforest Action Network (RAN) launched a campaign to persuade Citigroup to incorporate environmental screens in its lending programs. Focusing first on destructive forest practices, RAN urged Citigroup, in an April 2000 letter, to recognize that some of its loans were being used to destroy the last remaining old-growth forests, and that other loans were contributing to climate change. When there was no response, RAN placed a series of tough advertisements in major newspapers (see Figure 6.1).

But, as in previous chapters, let's look first at the key issues that prompted NGO action, then at some of the campaign strategies, and, finally, at the resulting standards and implementation mechanisms that emerged.

THE ISSUES

The critique of financial sector actors emerged in the late 1990s, led by the work of Friends of the Earth, Greenpeace, and RAN. The major banks were seen as funding, thoughtlessly, the massive destruction of forest habitat to allow the production of plantation crops, such as oil palm in Indonesia, soybeans in the Ama-

Did you know that someone is using your Citigroup credit card without your authorization?

zon basin, and even coffee in the highlands of Vietnam. NGO campaigns in the United States and Europe reproached banks for providing major project financing for forestry projects that failed to take into consideration the presence of old-growth or high-conservation-value forests and that used unsustainable forest management practices.

The fact that private banks were not themselves actively engaged in the destructive practices (though they funded the companies that were), that governments were encouraging the projects and even guaranteeing some of the loans, and that other banks would step in to support the projects if the major branded banks chose to pass them up did not deter the campaigners.

Private banks were accused of stepping in where even the IFIs increasingly feared to tread. One example was in the financing of hydroelectric dam projects that forced the resettlement of large numbers of people. A report produced for the South Asia Network on Dams, Rivers, and People; Urgewald; and the International Rivers Network illustrated how private banking syndicates, including major US and European banks, were financing unproductive and destructive dams in India, where

> project appraisal by domestic financial institutions is skewed by the vested interests of private contractors and their political allies. International financial institutions focus on privatization in their power sector reforms, and neglect a balanced assessment of all options including efficiency gains. They extend large loans to power utilities and financial intermediaries which in turn fund wasteful and destructive power projects. In some cases…they do not even inform the public, or affected people, about the projects they support through financial intermediaries.[5]

In 1998, the World Bank had directed a globally representative World Commission on Dams to produce a major analysis of the social and environmental effects of dams. The commission summarized its report, issued in 2000, in its own words:

> We believe there can no longer be any justifiable doubt about the following:
> - Dams have made an important and significant contribution to human development, and the benefits derived from them have been considerable.
> - In too many cases an unacceptable and often unnecessary price has been paid to secure those benefits, especially in social and environmental terms, by people displaced, by communities downstream, by taxpayers and by the natural environment.
> - Lack of equity in the distribution of benefits has called into question the value of many dams in meeting water and energy development needs when compared with the alternatives.
> - By bringing to the table all those whose rights are involved and who

bear the risks associated with different options for water and energy resources development, the conditions for a positive resolution of competing interests and conflicts are created.

- Negotiating outcomes will greatly improve the development effectiveness of water and energy projects by eliminating unfavorable projects at an early stage, and by offering as a choice only those options that key stakeholders agree represent the best ones to meet the needs in question.[6]

One dramatic result of this report was that the commission recommended developers carry out a participatory "rights and risks" analysis before the construction of any new dams. This would replace the simple economic cost-benefit analysis that had been typical of most dam planning previously. The commission asserted the rights of communities to give or withhold their "free, prior, and informed consent" before resettlement programs would be undertaken, and it cataloged the environmental damage done by dams but rarely taken into consideration. Although the World Bank chose to ignore the commission's full set of recommendations, the Bank and its allied agencies have been much more reticent to finance new dam projects. As a result, national and regional governments have been turning to private banks to finance the projects, despite the higher cost of private finance.

Private banks were also taken to task for financing huge oil-pipeline projects that were environmentally harmful. There were three cases, in particular, that drew NGO criticism between 2000 and 2003: the OCP pipeline, the Camisea Project, and the Chad-Cameroon pipeline project. More have emerged since then.

- The OCP pipeline project in the Ecuadorian portion of the Amazon basin was developed with both World Bank and private bank support. It has been criticized extensively for both the environmental damage associated with its construction through protected ecological zones and the social consequences for the indigenous peoples, opposed to its construction, along its route. In an independent assessment in 2002, Robert Goodland (one of the people who created the World Bank's own policy guidelines) concluded the environmental impact assessment offered by the pipeline proponents was extensively deficient.[7] However, the Ecuadorian government continued building the pipeline, with significant financial support from a German bank, West LB, and a letter of credit from Citigroup.
- The Camisea Project in the Peruvian Amazon has been described by Amazon Watch as "arguably the most damaging project in the Amazon Basin at the time of writing." The $1.6 billion project includes oil-field development and two pipelines to the Peruvian coast that "cut through an Amazon biodiversity hotspot described by scientists as 'the last place on earth' to drill for fossil fuels."[8] Three-quarters of the planned gas-extraction operations will take place inside government reserves for indigenous people who still live in isola-

tion, and the pipeline passes through six other reserves for indigenous peoples living in semi-isolation. A gas-processing facility on the Peruvian coast was planned within the buffer zone of the Paracas Marine Reserve, Peru's only marine reserve and an internationally important wetland area recognized by the Ramsar Convention on wetlands.

- The Chad-Cameroon pipeline project used World Bank and IFC financing to open a major oil field in Chad and to construct a 650-mile pipeline to the coast of Cameroon. World Bank and IFC financing of $365 million was expected to generate private bank loans of $1 billion, illustrating the close interaction between public and private financial institutions in major project lending. The original routing of the pipeline traversed ecologically sensitive areas, but the consortium building it changed the route at the urging of NGOs and the World Bank. Critics of the project fear that the governments of Chad and Cameroon will use most of the proceeds from oil sales to purchase arms; that the 300-well oilfield at Doba, the start of the pipeline, will seriously disrupt farm production in one of Chad's richest agricultural valleys; and that the rights of settlers at the oil field and all along the pipeline will not be respected.

NGO concerns about global project lending by private banks were brought together systematically, for the first time, when more than 100 civil society groups from around the world produced the Collevecchio Declaration on Financial Institutions and Sustainability in January 2003. Crafted in Collevecchio, Italy, the declaration was released in Davos, Switzerland, in the midst of the 2003 World Economic Forum. A press release from Friends of the Earth (FoE), which accompanied the declaration, stated:

> Up until now, the financial sector has been spared widespread criticism by proponents of environmental sustainability and social justice, who have instead focused on multinational corporations and major financial institutions such as the World Bank, the International Monetary Fund, and the World Trade Organization.
>
> Flying…below the public's radar screen, private banks and investors have been helping underwrite some of the world's most environmentally destructive projects.… As more people know about this, the public will increasingly hold financiers responsible through tried and true tools such as exercising consumer choice, engaging in shareholder activism, and pressuring politicians to reform government regulations.[9]

In the declaration, NGOs demanded that private financial institutions commit themselves to six key principles as a minimum basis for ensuring that they continue to receive their "social license to operate." The Collevecchio Declaration required the institutions to:

- **Commit to sustainability** by integrating "consideration of ecological limits, social equity, and economic justice into corporate strategies and core business areas" and by putting sustainability objectives "on an equal footing to shareholder maximization and client satisfaction."

- Commit to **"do no harm"** by "preventing and minimizing the environmentally and/or socially detrimental impacts of their portfolios and their operations."
- Commit to **responsibility** by acknowledging and bearing full responsibility for the environmental and social impacts of their transactions.
- Commit to **accountability** by becoming accountable to the full set of stakeholders affected by the activities and side effects of companies they finance.
- Commit to **transparency** by making "robust, regular, and standardized disclosure" on their financial decisions, including disclosure of specialized information needed by stakeholders.
- Commit to **sustainable markets and governance** by "supporting public policy, regulatory and/or market mechanisms which…foster the full cost accounting of social and environmental externalities." [10]

The declaration also included a set of recommendations outlining how financial institutions could implement each of these commitments. This document has become the "touchstone" against which subsequent changes in social and environmental policies by banks have come to be measured.

CAMPAIGNS AND RESULTS

By 2003 there were dozens of NGOs around the world campaigning actively to force private financial institutions to adopt higher standards for social and environmental accountability, but the nature of campaign activities varied enormously and, unfortunately, the campaigns were rarely well-chronicled. NGOs have often been too busy, had too little staff, and been too short of the funding needed to hire a scribe to record their activities. Yet we can find evidence of some of the campaigns in the news files of Europe and the United States. Among the US campaigners, the group that has recorded its history most completely is Rainforest Action Network.

RAN and Citigroup

RAN's campaign against Citigroup began, as mentioned above, in April 2000 with a letter to the financial conglomerate's CEO Sandy Weill. At that time, the New York newspaper *Village Voice* noted that RAN was fresh from a successful campaign in which it had been "driving Home Depot so crazy with protests and letters that the company… agreed to stop selling wood from old-growth forests" (see Chapter 4 for a detailed discussion). In analyzing the new campaign focused on Citigroup, the *Village Voice* reported that RAN would highlight a wide range of financing and services provided by Citigroup — for example, bonds that may have helped with the construction of China's Three Gorges Dam (which the IFIs had refused to support because of its egregious social and environmental consequences); financing for Indonesian palm oil plantations; and Citigroup's role as a financial advisor to the Chad-Cameroon pipeline project, "rife with corruption, human rights abuses, and rainforest destruction." [11]

RAN's campaign began with a push to get consumers to cut up their Citibank credit cards and close their Citibank accounts. This was an attempt to affect the bank's consumer business, but RAN was simultaneously getting its messages out to the broader public with every advertisement. The campaign hit an early high point on October 17, 2000, when local groups in 50 US cities held simultaneous demonstrations and issued similar statements to the local media, making the point that "Citigroup continues to operate without basic environmental and social standards despite the American public's demand for responsible financial services." [12] On that day in New York City, groups of students cut up their Citibank credit cards in front of news cameras. Yale University professors and staff in New Haven, Connecticut, announced that they had removed more than $100,000 from their Citibank accounts in protest.

In April 2001 there was a second "Citi Day of Action." RAN claims that there were 80 protest actions in 12 countries on 5 continents. In 2002 the campaign began to exploit anti-Bush sentiment (at the time, President George W. Bush refused to participate in the World Summit on Sustainable Development) with a full-page ad in the *International Herald Tribune*. The ad linked the US president with World Bank president James Wolfensohn and Citigroup president Sandy Weill and described the three as "faces of global warming and forest destruction." The text of the ad stated:

> The face of global warming and forest destruction is a frightening one. More than 25 million people are currently dislocated by flooding rivers as our atmosphere heats up. The West Nile virus can now thrive in the U.S. Severe droughts and massive wild fires have increased. The logging of the world's old growth forests is only adding to our ecological woes.
>
> At the World Summit on Sustainable Development in Johannesburg, South Africa, world leaders will convene to measure the "progress" made during the last ten years in addressing the ecological crisis and consider the fate of the planet. Thanks to James Wolfensohn, President Bush, and Sandy Weill the outlook is bleak.

In November 2002, some 25 activists used bicycle-style U-locks, "kryptonite" chains, and dirt-filled barrels to block the entrances to every Citibank branch in downtown San Francisco during the morning rush hour. They unfurled a banner that said "Corruption on the Inside: Destruction on the Outside." On the same day, activists in Washington, DC, locked the doors of the Citibank branch across the street from the World Bank and scaled the building to unfurl a similar large banner.

RAN pursued Sandy Weill. When he went to his alma mater, Cornell University, to deliver a lecture on globalization, he was greeted by loud protesters. Even when he went on a family vacation to Europe, Weill could not escape. He opened the *International Herald Tribune* and saw his picture in a full-page ad that called

Put a Face
on Global Warming
and Forest Destruction.

James Wolfensohn - President, The World Bank

- Is the largest public funder of destructive fossil fuel projects
- Is stripping protection for old growth forests
- Is masquerading as a "Green Banker" at the World Summit on Sustainable Development

George W. Bush - President of the United States

- Refuses to support the Kyoto treaty to help curb global warming
- Is reversing publicly supported protection of old growth forests
- Refuses to attend the most important environmental summit of the decade

Sandy Weill - Chairman and CEO, Citigroup, Inc.

- Is the largest private funder of destructive fossil fuel projects
- Refuses to establish meaningful environmental banking standards
- Has the power to establish a strong environmental legacy

Now Put an End to It.

The face of global warming and forest destruction is a frightening one. More than 25 million people are currently dislocated by flooding rivers as our atmosphere heats up. The West Nile virus can now thrive in the U.S. Severe droughts and massive wild fires have increased. The logging of the world's old growth forests is only adding to our ecological woes.

At the World Summit on Sustainable Development in Johannesburg, South Africa, world leaders will convene to measure the "progress" made during the last ten years in addressing the ecological crisis and consider the fate of the planet. Thanks to James Wolfensohn, President Bush, and Sandy Weill the outlook is bleak.

World Bank President James Wolfensohn is no "green banker." He's using your tax dollars to fund fossil fuel projects that drive global warming and forest destruction. His team is gutting the World Bank's existing forest policy for a new one that provides less protection and allows old growth logging.

Mr. Wolfensohn has the power to stop this. Any new policy should protect forest ecosystems from logging old growth trees and foster community-based economic development in non-timber products.

U.S. President George W. Bush will not be joining the 100 heads of state attending the meetings in Johannesburg. He is on vacation. President Bush is ignoring the world's climate troubles by rolling back environmental laws to increase corporate profits for his campaign supporters.

President Bush should attend the Summit and face the global warming and forest destruction crises.

Citigroup CEO Sandy Weill provides the money and financial expertise behind controversial fossil fuel projects around the world. As the top funder of the oil, gas, and mining industries, Citigroup uses consumer dollars for projects that destroy pristine ecosystems and contribute to global warming. The Camisea project in the Peruvian Amazon, the Chad-Cameroon pipeline in the African rainforest, and the destruction of Indonesia's rainforests are the real costs of Citigroup "living richly." Unlike top European Banks, such as ABN AMRO, that have policies to preserve endangered forests, there are no serious environmental or social standards under Citigroup's red umbrella.

Cut up your Citibank card and tell Sandy Weill, "Not With My Money" until he meets the financial industry's ecological best practices.

We can and must halt global warming and forest destruction. Future generations are depending on us. James Wolfensohn, President Bush and Sandy Weill have the power to establish strong policies that address the environmental crisis and lead us toward sustainability. The Johannesburg Summit presents an unprecedented opportunity to implement a visionary plan of action that will improve lives and preserve our environment. We must act together to change the face of global warming and forest destruction.

Finance Global Warming?
Not With My Money!

www.ran.org RAINFOREST ACTION NETWORK

him an environmental villain (see page 129). According to one report, Weill later said that explaining this to his grandson was no fun.[13] It is rumored that Weill, disgusted with the continued RAN pressure, turned to his staff and said, "Fix this!"

RAN began airing TV commercials featuring such well-known actors as Ed Asner, Susan Sarandon, Darryl Hannah, and Ali McGraw cutting up their Citibank credit cards. In April 2003, just hours before protests planned for Citigroup's annual shareholder meeting, Citigroup executives met with RAN staff to ask them to cease campaign activities and begin negotiations to develop new environmental standards that Citi would implement. As an act of good faith, Citi agreed to cancel some of the financing it had promised for the Camisea pipeline project in Peru, though it did not remove itself fully from the project. RAN agreed to hold off on campaign activities against Citigroup for 90 days.

Negotiations continued well beyond the 90 days, and on January 22, 2004, the two organizations reached agreement. According to the RAN press release, Citigroup's announced policy changes set a new standard for ecological investment. It became the first multinational bank to prohibit investment in any extractive industry (e.g., oil and gas, mining, logging) in primary tropical forests and to place severe restrictions on destructive investment in all endangered ecosystems worldwide. Citigroup's New Environmental Initiatives also contained the finance industry's first illegal logging policy, which required documentation of legality before the bank invested in any logging or logging-related projects. Finally, the company pledged to audit its climate-changing investments and invest significant capital in renewable energy projects.[14]

In the agreement, Citigroup went far beyond the commitment it had made when it signed the Equator Principles (see the next section), especially with respect to sustainable forest management and forest conservation. In essence, the agreement pushed for greater specificity than the Equator Principles required in areas affecting forestry and then moved beyond the Equator Principles on critical issues of greenhouse gas emissions and climate change.[15]

The Equator Principles

RAN's campaign against Citigroup, and similar campaigns against other private banks, led almost directly to the creation of the Equator Principles in 2002 and 2003. It was a remarkably rapid process that began when Herman Mulder, senior executive vice-president at ABN AMRO and head of its group risk unit, visited the IFC in the summer of 2002 to talk with his old friend Peter Woicke, IFC's executive vice-president. Mulder noted that the IFC's Safeguard Principles for project lending might be a useful starting point if major private project-lending banks were to craft a set of social and environmental practice standards that they would commit to follow.[16]

Within two months, a group of major bank executives were meeting at ABN AMRO's offices in the Netherlands to begin developing a collective response to the pressure they were feeling. At one point they considered naming the standards

"Greenwich Principles," but later they chose "Equator Principles" because of the term's value-neutrality and the fact that it privileged neither northern nor southern countries. Eight months later, after three more meetings, a group of ten major banks — including Citicorp, ABN AMRO, West LB, Credit Suisse First Boston, Barclays — was prepared to launch and endorse the first version of the Equator Principles.

When they were first released, the Equator Principles (EP) were a set of voluntary standards designed by the banking industry, with the assistance of the IFC, to address environmental and social risks in project financing. The preamble to the principles illustrates the extent to which the NGO campaigns and the Collevecchio Declaration were crucial inspirations for this process:

> Project financing plays an important role in financing development throughout the world. In providing financing, particularly in emerging markets, project financiers often encounter environmental and social policy issues. We recognize that our role as financiers affords us significant opportunities to promote responsible environmental stewardship and socially responsible development.
>
> In adopting these principles, we seek to ensure that the projects we finance are developed in a manner that is socially responsible and reflect sound environmental management practices.
>
> We believe that adoption of and adherence to these principles offers significant benefits to ourselves, our customers and other stakeholders.
>
> These principles will foster our ability to document and manage our risk exposures to environmental and social matters associated with the projects we finance, thereby allowing us to engage proactively with our stakeholders on environmental and social policy issues. Adherence to these principles will allow us to work with our customers in their management of environmental and social policy issues relating to their investments in the emerging markets.
>
> These principles are intended to serve as a common baseline and framework for the implementation of our individual, internal environmental and social procedures and standards for our project financing activities across all industry sectors globally.
>
> In adopting these principles, we undertake to review carefully all proposals for which our customers request project financing. We will not provide loans directly to projects where the borrower will not or is unable to comply with our environmental and social policies and processes.[17]

There are nine key principles articulated in the original EP. They are, in brief, that every project considered by an Equator Principles financial institution (EPFI) will be subject to an initial categorization, using IFC social and environmental screens to determine whether it has high, moderate, or low social and environmental risks or impacts. Any project with high or moderate potential risks or impacts then undergoes a formal "environmental assessment," with proposals for mitigation and management measures to reduce the consequences of the project. The industry-specific standards used in such an assessment come from the general IFC Pollution Prevention and Abatement Guidelines as well as from IFC's Safeguard Policies. The principles make explicit a list of the topics to be addressed by the environmental assessment, revealing that the scope is more than just environmental. The topics include baseline environmental and social conditions; protection of human health, cultural properties, and biodiversity; occupational health and safety; socioeconomic impacts; involuntary resettlement; impacts on indigenous peoples and communities; cumulative impacts of existing projects, the proposed project, and anticipated future projects; and a dozen others.

Once that social and environmental assessment has been completed for all projects with potentially moderate or significant impacts, the borrower must prepare an environmental management plan (EMP) that addresses the management of the impacts, risks, and corrective actions required to meet both host country laws and regulations and the IFC standards and guidelines. For all projects with significant potential risk — and for others "as considered appropriate" — the borrower must also show that it has consulted, "in a structured and culturally appropriate way, with project affected groups, including indigenous peoples and local NGOs." Finally, the borrower must agree to comply with the EMP and to provide regular reports on its compliance "prepared by in-house staff or third party experts." These principles were limited to projects with a total capital cost of US$50 million or more.

The rapid development and release of the Equator Principles represented a major breakthrough in public awareness on the part of the banks. They realized that stonewalling about their responsibility beyond the loans themselves was not serving their public relations. An Agence France Presse report quoted Peter Woicke, who said: "In taking this step today, the adopting banks are doing something that financial institutions rarely do. They are stepping forward to take a leadership role on global environmental and social issues. This is unprecedented...even if you use an extremely conservative estimate, this will change the rules of the road for over 100 billion dollars in global investment over the next 10 years."[18]

Yet, not surprisingly, most of the major NGOs complained that these industry-driven standards, developed without direct NGO participation, were too weak. The *Wall Street Journal*, quoting a Citigroup spokesperson, reported that "the banks 'believe that this will lead to more secure investments on the part of customers and safer loans on the part of banks.... Because if you finance something that's dirty or something that harms people, there's a likelihood that the host government or local people will interfere with it or even take it away from you.'"[19]

The *Wall Street Journal* conceded that the decision had been made in the face of mounting pressure from protest groups and described, in particular, the RAN

Bringing "Charismatic Commitment" to the World Bank Group

Rachel Kyte

Those who knew Rachel Kyte in her earlier professional incarnations are not surprised by the energy and achievement she brought to her position as director of the International Finance Corporation's Environment and Social Development Department. At the age of 23, Rachel was named secretary general of the Council of European National Youth Commissions, which built links between youth groups on either side of the Iron Curtain, helping to build the transnational environmental movements that were important in bringing democracy to Central and Eastern Europe just a few years later. In the early 1990s, Rachel coordinated youth input to the Earth Summit in Rio de Janeiro. From there she became the first staff director at the Women's Environment and Development Organization, an international group that advocates for women's equality in global policy. All that before she turned 30.[21]

Born and raised in Aylesbury in Buckinghamshire, England, Rachel went to public schools and graduated from the University of London after studies in history and politics. Although she then went to work for the Economist Intelligence Unit, a business service providing continuous economic and political analysis of emerging market countries so companies can determine investment risk, her broader engagement with social and economic issues was prompted by a volunteer position as the vice chair of the British Youth Council, which soon led to her early professional work with youth across Europe.

The International Finance Corporation (IFC) is the World Bank Group's agency responsible for private sector lending. With a portfolio of nearly US$20 billion at the end of 2005 and more than US$6 billion in new loan commitments that year, the IFC is a major public agency that for many years has been nudged by NGOs to incorporate stronger social and environmental screens into its lending. Rachel has been at the heart of that work since joining the IFC in February 2000 as a lead staff person for the office of a newly created Compliance Advisor Ombudsman. That office was given the independence and the responsibility to assess whether IFC operations had complied with the IFC's own environmental and social policies, standards, guidelines, and procedures. Rachel's experience with those standards made her the natural choice to work with the private banks as they struggled to respond to campaigns for greater social and environmental accountability.

Though the lead responsibility for this work belonged to Meg Taylor, the Compliance Advisor Ombudsman, with the "tremendous support" of Vice-President Peter Woicke, Rachel was one of the key staff who attended all the meetings that led to the Equator Principles, based on the IFC's Safeguard Principles. She was named director of the IFC's Social and Environmental Development Department in January 2004 and then led the revision, between 2004 and 2006, of both the IFC's standards and the Equator Principles. She believes that she illustrates the adage

"Once an activist, always an activist," even when it sometimes drives her more bureaucratic colleagues wild.

Rachel is proud of the way the IFC has been able to take its own newly strengthened standards and convert them into the principles that by mid-2006 had been adopted by, and were being implemented by, more than 40 major bank groups. She watched as the discussions among the bank representatives evolved from "protection against reputational events" to a focus on "better banks with better risk management."

The biggest struggle the banks faced was the difficult process of creating standards that were more than simply a set of boxes to be checked. What they sought instead were standards that could be implemented with a degree of professional judgment at each stage of the loan process. At the IFC this means that the principles are invoked and monitored whenever parts of a loan are disbursed, often as frequently as quarterly. It means that rather than being a broad set of pre-conditions, a one-time check-off, the principles become the basis for a performance contract and a management system. However, they are not a certification system with stakeholder standard setting and independent compliance assessment; they are, rather, a set of supply-side policies designed to address industry risk in the project finance field.

In the consultative process for the revision of both IFC performance standards and the Equator Principles, Rachel encountered high levels of interest from international businesses across the full spectrum of industries because they were beginning to realize the reputational risk they faced on social and environmental issues. NGO input was also significant, and she chuckles at the way NGOs played the banks against the IFC, and vice versa, in the quest for higher standards. She is proud that the IFC has become the international standard setter for social and environmental accountability among commercial banks around the world. And she has achieved all this as she just begins to move into her 40s.

campaign against Citigroup. It also noted the skepticism of RAN staff. "We're glad to see banks responding to pressure that's been brought on them," noted a RAN spokesperson, "but I think you'll find broad consensus around the NGO …community that the Equator Principles don't go far enough. The loopholes are wide open enough for bulldozers to move through." The *WSJ* quoted other activists, who noted that there was no enforcement mechanism "other than the public pressure that comes with a public promise." An International Rivers Network commentator, quoted in the *International Herald Tribune*, argued, "This is a step forward, but we know that the World Bank guidelines aren't strong enough and they don't prevent the banks from financing a bad project." Furthermore, "there is no compliance mechanism and this is a very serious weakness."[20]

JPMorgan Chase and Goldman Sachs

After its success with Citigroup, RAN quickly switched the focus of its campaign to other large US banks, including JPMorgan Chase (now known simply as Chase) and the investment bank Goldman Sachs. It invited them to "meet or beat" the Citigroup environmental policies, seeking to obtain even stronger commitments than those made by Citigroup. In November 2004, RAN placed outdoor billboard ads in Chicago, New York, and Washington, DC, calling on Chase to stop making "investments of mass destruction" (IMDs). Beneath a big red headline reading "Stop IMDs," the ad depicted a larger-than-life version of Chase's logo framing examples of environmental devastation caused by destructive investments (see page 136).

In December, RAN orchestrated an event in which second-grade children from an elementary school in Fairfield, Connecticut, the town where Chase's CEO, William B. Harrison, lived, brought 700 colorful oversize posters to Chase's Manhattan headquarters. The posters were handmade by children around the world and each called on Chase to stop one of its current environmentally harmful practices (see page 137). In an even more personal vein, several RAN volunteers were arrested in March 2005 for stapling flyers to telephone posts in the Greenwich, Connecticut, neighborhood where Harrison then lived. According to the *New York Times*, the flyers showed a photo of Harrison under the word "WANTED," claimed that Chase was responsible for "reckless investment in environmentally and socially destructive projects in dozens of countries," and invited his neighbors to "ask him to do the right thing."[22]

In April 2005, Chase issued a "Public Environmental Policy Statement" that would apply to all new business and to all old business coming up for renewal after September 2005.[23] According to RAN, the policy "sets new best practices on the environment in several critical areas including carbon mitigation and reduction, endangered forest protection, independently certified sustainable forestry as well as land and consultation rights of native communities everywhere." It is also "the first policy of its kind in the financial sector to create a special heading acknowledging 'No Go Zones,' a major step forward in the effort to protect ecosystems that are most valuable intact and untouched by industry."[24] Chase goes beyond the Citigroup commitment by specifying that it will give preference to Forest Stewardship Council (FSC) certification when it finances forestry projects and will require FSC chain-of-custody certification of wood that comes from areas of the world, such as Indonesia, where more than 50 percent of the logging is known to be illegal.

Without the need for an explicit campaign, RAN then entered into discussions with Goldman Sachs, and in November 2005 Goldman agreed to a set of environmental policies that "keeps going where others leave off," according to environmental advocates cited in a report in the *New York Times*.[25] The *Times* went on to say that "the Goldman policy is certainly the most explicit. . . . Chase's environmental policy statement] calls for public policy that 'establishes certainty

Stop IMDs
Investments of Mass Destruction

 JPMorganChase

Go to DirtyMoney.org and tell CEO Bill Harrison to stop profiting from environmental destruction.

Allie, 6th Grade, Dayton, OH

Thanks, Allie.
We couldn't have said it better ourselves.

www.rainforestheroes.com

RAINFOREST
ACTION NETWORK
www.ran.org

for investors and allows significant investments in greenhouse gas reductions.' Goldman endorses a 'strong policy framework that creates long-term value for greenhouse gas emissions reductions and consistently supports and incentivizes the development of new technologies that lead to a less carbon-intensive economy.'"

Insiders noted that the introduction to the Goldman Sachs policy was written by CEO Hank Paulson, who became US Treasury secretary in 2006. It reads, in part:

> Goldman Sachs believes that a healthy environment is necessary for the well-being of society, our people and our business, and is the foundation for a sustainable and strong economy.
>
> Goldman Sachs recognizes that diverse, healthy natural resources — fresh water, oceans, air, forests, grasslands, and agro-systems — are a critical component of social and sustainable economic development. Forests are particularly important for the environment and biodiversity. They are vital to water and air quality, and help regulate climates. Forests are home to thousands of wildlife species, and, at the same time, represent a natural source of timber. The key challenge for society is to manage the competing human demands on land, soil and vegetation without undermining crucial ecosystem functions.
>
> We take seriously our responsibility for environmental stewardship and believe that as a leading global financial institution we should play a constructive role in helping to address the challenges facing the environment. To that end, we will work to ensure that our people, capital and ideas are used to help find effective market-based solutions to address climate change, ecosystem degradation and other critical environmental issues, and we will seek to create new business opportunities that benefit the environment. We will work to identify policy measures that are creative, meaningful and provide real solutions to environmental problems while recognizing the importance of economic growth in contributing to the alleviation of poverty. In pursuing these objectives we will not stray from our central business objective of creating long-term value for our shareholders and serving the long-term interests of our clients.[26]

Although there was virtually no mention of social policies in the statement, outside experts were full of praise for this latest bank commitment. Stanford professor Walter Reid, former director of the Millenium Ecosystem Assessment, wrote that "the emphasis of the Goldman Sachs environmental policy on climate change, biodiversity, and forests should be commended, but what is perhaps most striking is that this is the first-ever policy among financial institutions to include goals related to the conservation of 'ecosystem services'; that is, the benefits we obtain from ecosystems such as clean water, flood control, pest regulation, and disease regulation." Further, he argued, "By steering investments in ways that avoid harm to ecosystem service and by helping to create new markets that would promote the conservation of these services, Goldman Sach's policy will help to align the power of markets with the conservation of these services."[27]

Revising the Equator Principles

Meanwhile, bank-focused NGOs were closely watching the implementation of the Equator Principles, and they didn't much like what they saw. One of their first responses to the banks' collaboration that produced the Equator Principles was to create a matching NGO collaborative, BankTrack, to monitor the continuing evolution and implementation of bank commitments. BankTrack was formed in January 2004 by 12 civil society organizations from ten countries, including WWF-UK, Amigas da Terra (Brazil), Urgewald (Germany), Friends of the Earth (US), and RAN, to pressure financial institutions to play a positive role in advancing social and environmental sustainability. BankTrack's work has evolved in three areas:

- Identifying, tracking, and supporting communities affected by projects financed by private banks that have a negative effect on their well-being, the environment, and their fundamental rights.
- Monitoring policy initiatives aimed at improving banks' performance, such as the Equator Principles.
- Assisting BankTrack member organizations with their own campaigns focused on a specific institution or certain projects.[28]

Within one year of the Equator Principles launch, some 23 global banks and two European public financial institutions had announced their intentions to adhere to the principles. BankTrack published a report, "Principles, Profits, or Just PR?" to commemorate that first anniversary. The report asked whether the banks' public commitments "promoted a true 'Triple P' approach to investments, balancing people, profit and planet in a way that can be called truly sustainable, or are the Principles a mere PR effort?"[31] BankTrack reported clear positive outcomes from the launching of the principles:

- The Royal Bank of Canada decided not to finance the Rosia Montana mining project in Romania because of the social and environmental characteristics of the project, identified in NGO campaigns.
- Citigroup decided not to renew its financial advising relationship with the Camisea Project in Peru.
- Although several EPFIs financed a controversial Baku-Tbilisi-Ceyhan pipeline, a 1,000-mile-long pipeline from Lake Baku to Western Europe with seismic, political, and environmental problems, others that could have been involved chose to refrain.

However, BankTrack staff found fault with the EP implementation on several levels. They began by listing a number of major projects they believed should not have been funded under the EP, but which EPFIs had funded during the first year after they announced their commitment to the principles. The list included the

Caught in the Cross-Hairs, Responding with Flair
Pamela Flaherty of Citigroup

Pam Flaherty, Citigroup's senior vice-president for global community relations, brought two important attributes to the development of Citigroup's environmental and social risk-management processes from 2000 to 2006. First, she had more than 30 years of experience within Citigroup, working at all levels, from managing a retail branch bank to working with external stakeholders from the headquarters offices. And second, she had close professional links with several of Citigroup's CEOs over the years.[29]

Citi's interest in social and environmental issues, she insists, did not begin with the RAN campaign. It had been responding to questions raised by shareholder groups and by socially responsible investment groups for years. Citi was increasingly aware of the maturing of new definitions of corporate responsibility, and there was internal company interest in emerging trends, such as the Dow Jones Sustainability Index, created in 1999. But, she admits, Citi "didn't have a way to crisply describe how we managed environmental issues." Human rights and other social issues were not "at the center of the plate." And she and her staff found other private financial institutions had little interest in addressing these issues, which meant there were virtually no staff people at a comparable level in other banks with whom she could work.

When she met with staff from several banks and from the IFC in Amsterdam in October 2002 to explore the creation of what became the Equator Principles, Pam quickly saw how this could become the "third-party standard for core principles on these issues." She became the internal champion within Citigroup for crafting implementation mechanisms for the principles.

For a woman born in Webster Groves, Missouri, and educated at Smith College and Johns Hopkins University, the opportunities in banking did not seem especially attractive when she received her MA in 1968. With a specialization in economics and Middle Eastern studies, the US Foreign Service seemed a better fit. But while waiting for an assignment after she passed the rigorous Foreign Service entrance examinations, Pam took a temporary job doing economic research at Citibank and never looked back.

One of the internal tensions around the creation of the Equator Principles, from the outset, was between the operations side of Citigroup and the bank's culture. Operations needed the standards, and the implementation mechanisms for them, as quickly as possible. The culture of the bank, however, demanded that a public commitment to the standards could take place only after staff had figured out the full range of implications that might arise from their implementation. Determining those implications was part of Pam's task as well.

Citigroup mainstreamed the Equator Principles by creating an environmental and social risk-management (ESRM) unit, placing it alongside the rest of the risk-management staff in the Citigroup Corporate Investment Bank, and embedding the principles into the credit and risk policy manual and procedures. By the end of that process, the principles became an "internal bible on how things need to be done." Project lenders knew that their careers were on the line if they were not implemented appropriately.

Pam is quick to insist that she couldn't have moved the bank forward as rapidly as she did if it weren't for the assistance of Matt Arnold of Sustainable Finance Ltd. (also profiled in this chapter). Matt provided necessary technical support as the bank attempted to understand what the advocacy groups wanted. He accompanied Pam when she met with a group of NGOs, helped her train staff in implementation procedures, and created a bridge between the cultures of the NGOs and the internal culture in the bank.

Pam recognizes that the revised Equator Principles are just one stopping point on a longer road to increased accountability. She understands that they will continue to evolve, but she insists that if their implementation is to have credibility, they must have some stability, since large projects take many years to develop and then play out. Constant revision and modification requires costly changes in processes and procedures, as well as the training needed to develop internal capability.

Pam and her colleagues were awarded a commendation at the first Sustainable Banking Awards ceremony in June 2006. The awards were created by the *Financial Times* in collaboration with the IFC. The commendation stated: "For exemplary leadership in integrating best-in-class environmental and social policies across the global operations of [Citigroup]. This relatively small team has done extraordinary work in establishing a focus on sustainability across the world's largest banking group. This involved the systematic application of the Equator Principles across key business lines in a global operation with 300,000 employees in 100 countries."[30]

Baku-Tbilisi-Ceyhan project and the Karahnjukar project in Iceland, which would divert several glacial rivers to supply power for a massive aluminum smelter, endangering Icelandic reindeer and one of Europe's last remaining true wilderness areas.

BankTrack recognized that while the Karahnjukar project was technically "not subject to the Principles (as it was not project finance), Barclays [Bank] to its credit recognized that its client Landsvirkjun was explicitly raising funds to construct the dams" and applied the EPs in this case. The project violated four of the EPs, and "Barclays...played a key role in arranging financing to help ensure" it went ahead. "In fact," BankTrack staff concluded, "Barclays may earn money from the deal and not even have to lend any money." The report also listed projects in the Philippines, Thailand, Bolivia, Brazil, Papua New Guinea, and Russia that were receiving financing from EPFIs in apparent violation of the principles.

More generally, the critics excoriated the banks on several dimensions of the way in which they put the principles into practice during the first year of their existence:

- Few of the banks had developed their own implementation schemes, including environmental and social performance indicators.
- Development of full internal policies in many of the banks had been slow, and in some cases the EP had slowed the institution's development of sector-specific policies.
- Relatively few EPFIs had committed to hiring the additional staff needed to implement the EP, with the notable exception of Citigroup and HSBC.
- Few of the banks had developed transparent paper trails for EP documents.
- The EP's failure to require banks to report publicly and regularly reduced the credibility of banks' adoption of the principles.

As the number of banks committing to the Equator Principles rose to 40, criticism of the principles accumulated. With the assistance of the IFC, member banks established a process for revising them. When the principles were first devised in 2003, they were based on "the then-applicable IFC Safeguard Policies," partly to free the banks from the need to modify them whenever IFC revised its policies.[32] In the meantime, the IFC had begun such a revision, partly in response to NGO challenges. After consultations with the EP banks and many other stakeholders, the IFC created new environmental, health, and safety standards and implemented a number of other changes in the existing standards, which were renamed IFC Performance Standards.

The IFC revisions were also driven by an attempt to harmonize standards across the world of project financing, including those of the leading export credit agencies (ECAs).[33] The ECAs, for example, stipulated that standards had to be applied to all transactions in excess of 10 million SDRs (special drawing rights, the IMF monetary measure). This suggested that the IFC and the banks should reduce their thresholds to a similar level.

When the banks began the process of revising the Equator Principles, they first sought to bring them in line with the IFC Performance Standards. The proposed revisions were then discussed at a series of meetings between the NGOs and the banks during 2005. At a final meeting in April 2006, representatives of 18 EPFIs met with representatives of 12 NGOs to discuss a "final draft" of the revised standards. Through BankTrack, the NGOs prepared a formal set of responses to the draft.[34] A revised set of Equator Principles was released in July 2006, and within weeks virtually all the banks that had signed on to the original EPs renewed their commitment to the new set of principles.

From the point of view of the IFC, "the revised Equator Principles have now incorporated, and are fully consistent with, IFC's environmental and social Performance Standards, ensuring that there is one, consistent standard for private sector project financing."[35] They also incorporated specific changes driven by NGO criticisms:

- A tenth principle was added, requiring each EPFI to report publicly "at least annually" about its EP "implementation processes and experiences." There was one big condition: "taking into account appropriate confidentiality considerations." This is interpreted in a footnote to mean at least the number of transactions screened and the level of risk of significant impact associated with each transaction will be revealed.
- The principles are extended, at least nominally, to renewals or upgrades of lending on projects with significant social and environmental impacts, as well as to finance advisory activities.
- The revised principles require independent expert reviews of the required social and environmental assessments of projects with a high potential for negative impacts.
- The revised principles require the creation of grievance procedures for receiving and addressing concerns raised by affected communities.
- The threshold for project lending is reduced from US$50 million to US$10 million.

The revised Equator Principles left the NGOs feeling that the banks were faced with "a unique opportunity to address both the shortcomings of [the original set of principles] and the IFC's Performance Standards," but they found that the EPFIs "failed to grasp this opportunity." NGOs praised some of the revisions, such as the expansion of the EPs to include financial advisory services and renewals of previous projects with significant social or environmental impacts, as well as the lending itself. But given the success of campaigns focused on individual banks, such as Citigroup and Chase, that resulted in environmental policies covering far more than project lending, the NGOs lamented the unwillingness of EPFIs to extend the reach of the principles beyond project finance.[36]

REFLECTIONS

The market campaigns to transform fundamental banking practices have been some of the most effective ever seen. The global banking community has recognized, and accepted, its shared responsibility for the social and environmental impacts of direct lending and other financial services that it undertakes. That the NGOs involved are less satisfied than those we have seen in other campaigns is directly attributable, I would argue, to the fact that the Equator Principles are not, in fact, a certification system. Yes, they have been modified to respond to some of the strongest criticisms of the advocacy NGOs, but the changes fall far short of producing a transparent system in which third-party verification of each bank's compliance with its public commitment can bring greater credibility to the system.

The current version of the Equator Principles will provide *some* risk reduction for the banks that have subscribed to them, but not nearly as much as a certification system would. Such a system, featuring greater active engagement with the NGOs and better verification, may still seem impossible to the banks, given

Pioneers in the Implementation of the New Banking Standards

Matt Arnold and Sustainable Finance Ltd.

"Our business is one that didn't exist five years ago because there was no demand for the services that we supply," observes Matt Arnold, co-founder and partner in Sustainable Finance Ltd., a firm that now has 20 staff and 40 major clients in the banking and broader finance field.[37] Five years previously, when he was an executive at the World Resources Institute, Matt convened a group of commercial and investment banks to discuss the role of banks in protecting the environment. Their responses at that time were modest. "Our direct footprint is very small," they argued. "As for investments, we comply with the law, and equity markets take care of the rest.... Leaders are rewarded and laggards punished through changes in value.... We as banks are not accountable for the environmental and social impact of our clients."

What a difference five years can make! Change has been driven in part by the withering criticism banks have received for their roles in controversial projects like the Three Gorges Dam in China, the Camisea Project in Peru, and the Asia Pulp and Paper plant in Indonesia. The digital revolution in communications means that the voices of local community groups with complaints about big projects are broadcast quickly and heard worldwide.

Gradually, Matt believes, the banking and finance community is starting to realize that attention to the social and environmental dimensions of the projects they fund is actually good business. A client's inattention to environmental and social problems may be an indicator of poor management and a potential credit risk. At the same time, projects that have positive social and environmental outcomes can pay well on many levels.

Out of nowhere, Sustainable Finance Ltd. has become a major support to financial services companies wrestling with the challenges of sustainable development. Matt helped Citigroup develop its landmark environmental policy, announced in 2004, which emerged from intensive dialogue with market campaigners and the formation of the Equator Principles. In 2006, he joined forces with a British company doing similar work for ABN AMRO and others.

Sustainable Finance provides a bridge across the enormous gap in language, culture, and values that separates market campaigners and financial institutions. Matt believes there is an enormous opportunity for these institutions to transform risk to the environment and to vulnerable communities into reward for lenders and investors.

At first, it all seemed too daunting. The initial response of bank staff was: "Those pesky NGOs don't know what they're talking about!" But, Matt notes, experience has shown that the best thing to do is talk with the critics, who are often quite creative and have useful ideas. In the beginning, bank staff needed the language of the NGOs "translated" into a language they could understand. They needed to learn to dialogue, to explore alternatives, to seek solutions. The support of a group like Sustainable Finance has proven critical in many of these market-campaign situations.

Matt Arnold's trajectory to his Sustainable Finance position began in Chapel Hill, North Carolina, where he was born into an academic family in 1961. Both his parents were professors at the University of North Carolina's Medical School. He attended Harvard College, studied psychobiology, and spent a year after graduating on "walkabout" in Australia, New Zealand, and Thailand "to find the meaning of life." He then found himself selling IBM computers to Bankers Trust in New York City. Later, dual master's degrees — first in business from Harvard Business School, and then in international affairs from the School of Advanced International Studies at Johns Hopkins University — landed him an internship in the US Environmental Protection Agency. That in turn led to the creation of an NGO, partially supported by the EPA, called the Management Institute for Environment and Business, which was the beginning of the work he has done since.

After merging his NGO into the World Resources Institute in 1996, Matt became chief operating officer of WRI in 1998 and a senior fellow in 2002. At that point he began his consulting with major companies on social and environmental sustainability. To formalize his current business, he joined with two partners, Glen Armstrong and Leo Johnson, both former staff at the International Finance Corporation who had worked on the development of the Equator Principles. Though their firm is technically based in Shrewsbury, Shropshire, in the United Kingdom, all 20 staff members work from their home offices, scattered across the US, UK, Netherlands, France, and Canada. That, of course, permits them to assert on their website that they have offices in "Continental Europe, the United Kingdom and North America, with key staff in Washington DC, New York, Shrewsbury, Edinburgh, Paris, Amsterdam and Toronto."[38] And more recently in Brazil, Mexico, and South Africa!

The services that they offer fall into four categories, which are common among "implementing organizations" supporting certification systems:

- They provide "policy and strategy" advice to banks and other financial institutions, helping them target where they want to be on the social and environmental spectrum.
- They become an "inside friendly critic," helping the firm assess possible alternative responses to the criticism likely to come from outside critics.
- They provide risk-management support services, often web-based and web-driven, to help a company's staff develop the skills needed to undertake in-house social and environmental risk assessments. In this way, Sustainable Finance has trained literally thousands of bankers.
- In those cases where companies have not yet developed internal capacity, Sustainable Finance will provide transaction-specific risk assessments.

Each of these services provides vital transition capability for firms that seek to respond both efficiently and creatively to market campaigns.

Matt feels that the biggest challenge faced by many of these companies is the fear that they will be forced to respond in a way that will cripple them in the face of their competition. There is discomfort with the issues, fear that the NGOs will never be satisfied, and often strong internal resistance from senior bankers who think they will lose business. In this regard, it was a stroke of brilliance that Citigroup, rather than responding on its own to the RAN campaign, brought together 10 major banks to make the first commitments to the Equator Principles and encouraged its competitors to join the club of Equator Principles financial institutions.

But the final challenge, Matt notes, is for banks to develop standards for behavior that are lofty, aspirational, and yet tangible enough to be measured. Echoing the advice of Rachel Kyte, Matt believes that, given room for professional judgment, evaluating the implementation of the standards should be based on the "integrity of the management" of the financial institutions. Do they provide the senior management support, the resources, and the staff to conduct social and environmental scrutiny in an honest and effective way? Without that integrity, even elaborate checklists will have little impact on the fundamental practices of the firms.

traditional banking practices, but no one in industry thought that wood or coffee or seafood could be traced reliably either. NGOs have shown significant capacity for discovering and revealing the internal responses of the EPFIs to the Equator Principles, as well as EPFIs' continued engagement with projects that, in principle at least, should be covered by the EPs. And it's likely that implementation of the Equator Principles will continue to draw criticism from BankTrack and its members until a stronger, more transparent system is in place.

There also remain a significant quantity of financial services to which the principles do not yet technically apply. By not moving to cover those services as well, EPFIs are inviting further advocacy campaigns.

The other major failing of the EP system is that some of the world's largest project lenders have still not committed to them. Chinese and Indian banks are among the most important institutions outside the EP fold, and some bank commentators suggest that they are particularly "tone deaf," at this point, to the international criticism of lending practices that fail to consider social and environmental consequences. How long that will last may depend on the ability of local and international NGOs to call global attention to the consequences of their practices, especially as Chinese and Indian banks seek to gain respect and the ability to participate in Western financial markets.

The transformation that has taken place among the major banks that *have* committed to the Equator Principles was well-illustrated in a February 2005 presentation by André Abadie, at that time the head of the Sustainable Business Advisory Group at ABN AMRO. Abadie laid out the learning curve his bank had gone through over the previous five years. A key slide from his presentation is shown, with his permission, in Figure 6.5.

There were three drivers behind the ABN AMRO bank's "sustainability journey," according to Abadie:

- A fundamental desire within the bank's corporate culture to be a responsible corporate citizen.
- Recognition that not doing business with the right clients could lead to reputational risk.
- Awareness that the trust that is needed for a bank's "franchise value and license to operate" is both of critical importance and of considerable fragility, for it can be lost overnight with poor business decisions.

ABN AMRO's journey toward a sustainability business case began when bank staff engaged with Friends of the Earth. It led them to define policies on specific loans, such as those for Freeport-McMoRan and Asia Pulp and Paper. They then began formulating sector-specific policies for forestry, mining, and oil and gas. These policies were superseded by adoption of the Equator Principles.

Seen another way, the journey took them from "value destruction" at a time of "innocence" to pursuing the business case for sustainability, which takes them well beyond the Equator Principles. Finally, the business case for sustainability focuses on adding value to the firm by first improving effective risk management, which must include sustainable risk-management policies, processes, and tools. The sustainability case can then be transformed into increased profits by looking for sustainable finance possibilities with responsible clients. It is hard to imagine that the NGOs could argue the case any better than that.

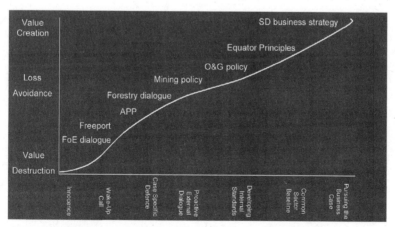

Figure 6.5. ABN AMRO's Sustainability Learning Curve. Credit: Presentation by André Abadie, head of ABN AMRO Sustainable Business Advisory, at the Rockefeller Foundation, February 16, 2005.

7

Can Tourism Be Tamed?
Toward a Sustainable Tourism Stewardship Council

Tourism is arguably the world's largest service industry, and it represents one of the most remarkable economic and social phenomena of the last century. The UN World Tourism Organization (UNWTO) estimates that the total number of international tourist trips grew from 25 million in 1950 to 763 million in 2004. Estimated total receipts from international tourism rose from US$2 billion in 1950 to US$623 billion in 2004. France, Spain, the United States, China, and Italy, in that order, received the largest numbers of tourists. Total international tourist receipts in the United States were US$75 billion in 2004; for Europe they exceeded US$360 billion.[1] And those numbers do not include domestic tourism travel and expenditure. The US Bureau of Economic Analysis estimates that the total value of tourism goods and services produced in the United States during 2004 was US$544 billion.[2]

Tourism is an extraordinarily complicated and fragmented industry. The following are among its most important characteristics:

- Worldwide, it tends to be dominated by "outbound tour operators" — companies that organize and sell tours to individuals and groups at their places of origin, and who then contract with airlines, hotels, and travel services at the destination. Prominent among them are Thomas Cook Tours in the UK, TUI Group in Germany, Accor Tours in France, and American Express Vacations, Globus Tours, and Lindblad Expeditions in the US.

- "Inbound tour operators," their local equivalent, are companies at travel destinations that organize and sell tours to individuals and groups, including some outbound tour operators and individuals who contact them from origin countries. With the rapid growth of Internet-based reservation systems, inbound operators have gained much greater ability to connect directly with travelers.

- Much of the growth in tourism in the last 50 years has occurred because of "mass-market tourism" and "all-inclusive tours" in which large groups of tourists are flown in chartered aircraft to large (often internationally owned) hotel properties on exotic beaches. These tourists rarely leave the property during their stay. This class of tourism is considered the most damaging in environmental, cultural, and social terms, and the least beneficial to the local economy at the destination.[3]

- The alternatives to mass-market tourism are given many names: ecotourism, nature tourism, adventure tourism, responsible tourism, and ethical tourism, among others. They differ in their specific definitions but share notions of environmental conservation, respect for local culture and engagement with local communities, and a concern for local economic benefits.
- "Greenwashing," in the form of unsubstantiated first-party claims of social and environmental responsibility by tour operators and hotel owners, is rampant in the industry.

THE ISSUES

Although tourism can, in theory, be an important source of employment and income growth, as well as poverty alleviation, there are many negative aspects of tourism that are often overlooked. According to the United Nations Environment Program, environmental impacts of tourism begin when

> the level of visitor use is greater than the environment's ability to cope with the use within acceptable limits of damaging change. Uncontrolled conventional tourism poses potential threats to many natural areas around the world. It can put enormous pressure on an area and lead to impacts such as soil erosion, increased pollution, discharges into the sea, natural habitat loss, increased pressure on endangered species and heightened vulnerability to forest fires. It often puts a strain on water resources, and it can force local populations to compete for the use of critical resources.[4]

Social and cultural impacts include:
- Change or loss of indigenous culture and values when "religious rituals, traditional ethnic rites and festivals are reduced and sanitized to conform to tourist expectations.... Once a destination is sold as a tourism product, and the tourism demand for souvenirs, arts, entertainment, and other commodities begins to exert influence, basic changes in human values have been seen to occur."[5]
- Anger in tourism destinations when tourists, out of ignorance or carelessness, fail to understand or to show respect for local customs or values.
- Conflicts between tourism land uses and traditional land uses, especially in areas such as coastal zones, which are often popular destinations for tourists, when the choice has to be made between development of the land for tourist facilities or infrastructure and local traditional land use. The local population often loses out in the competition for these resources as the economic value of tourism often counts for more.
- Prostitution and sex tourism focused on the sexual exploitation of children and young women and men has paralleled the growth of tourism in many parts of the world.
- Tourism can contribute to the creation of "sun, sand, and sea sweatshops," in which labor rights of workers in tourism facilities are abused, minimum wage laws are violated, and overtime work is forced on employees.[6]

Despite the size of the industry and the scope of the problems it can cause, re-markably little attention has been paid to corporate social and environmental re-sponsibility in the tourism field. The UNWTO, the intergovernmental body led by ministers of tourism, published a "global code of ethics for tourism" in 1999. It articulated a "universal right to tourism" as well as the rights of the workers and entrepreneurs in the tourism industry. And it argued that "tourism resources" are a "common heritage of mankind," with no qualifications for the rights of tra-ditional residents.[7] However, there is little evidence of formal uptake of that code of ethics by the tourism industry, no independent monitoring of its application, and no marketable recognition for tour operators that may be guided by it.

Conservation International's Center for Environmental Leadership in Busi-ness (CELB) has helped tour operators create an organization that engages some 20 leading outbound and inbound tour operators who have committed to sus-tainable development. The Tour Operators Initiative for Sustainable Develop-ment has published a guidebook for managing environmental and social issues in the accommodations and marine recreational sectors, and it has developed guidelines for supply-chain management and sustainability reporting for tour operators.[8] Its "Statement of Commitment to Sustainable Tourism Develop-ment" expresses a pledge to observe broad principles that include striving to "an-ticipate and prevent economic, environmental, social and cultural degradation," as well as monitoring, measuring, and reporting publicly on these issues.[9] Now located within the offices of the UNWTO, the initiative has shied away from call-ing the guidelines "standards," and it offers no mechanism for identifying what companies may, or may not, be applying them.

There are only a few actions that can be identified as market campaigns for higher social and environmental accountability in the field. Tourism Concern, a small and valiant UK nonprofit, has spent some 15 years attempting to call atten-tion to the problems embedded in most forms of tourism.[10] In 1999 and 2000 it crafted the concept of "Fair Trade in Tourism," which focused on the conditions faced by workers in the tourism industry, and it has drafted a preliminary set of principles for this area.[11] The group commissioned a study on labor standards and social responsibility in tourism in 2004 and then came up with the clever "sun, sea, and sand sweatshops" concept, which highlights its efforts to improve the lot of underpaid local workers in the industry.[12] And it has occasionally taken on corporate leaders, writing letters to the UK Federation of Tour Operators (FTO) and to the Hilton Hotel chain. Goaded by Tourism Concern, the FTO has encouraged all its members to publish their social policies on their websites.

Another UK group calling for more responsible tourism is Tearfund, The Evangelical Alliance Refugee Fund was created in the 1960s, has been linked to Cliff Richard and the "Live Aid" concerts, and since 2000 has handled major UN High Commission on Refugees projects in Afghanistan, Eritrea, Ethiopia, Mo-zambique, and Sudan. Tearfund issued a "Call to Responsible Tourism" in early 2002 that urged tour operators to "take their social responsibilities more seri-ously." The group's consumer research in the UK found that 52 percent of British travelers would be more likely to book a holiday with a company that had a written code to guarantee its efforts to "[provide] good working conditions, protect the environment, and support local charities in the tourist destination." Although support for local charities harkens back to old-fashioned corporate social responsibility (CSR), invoking the "market for virtue," Tearfund also found that three in five travelers were willing to pay more for their holiday if the money went to "the preservation of local environments, good wages and working conditions for workers, or to a local charity." Research among British outbound tour operators found that of 65 tour companies studied, only half had responsible tourism policies, and many of those were "so brief as to be virtually meaningless."[13]

Tourism Concern maintained, in a 2006 issue of *CSR Asia Weekly*, that signs of CSR in tourism "are appearing all over the place." It noted that there has been an increase in the number of hotel and tour operator websites "proudly displaying responsible practices and social policies."[14] But it also argued that "voluntary codes of practice are a waste of time unless they are monitored and evaluated, preferably by an independent third party."

The broader concept of "sustainable tourism" has recently come into use to describe, according to the National Geographic Society, "tourism that sustains or enhances the character of a destination — its environment, culture, aesthetics, heritage, and the economic well-being of its residents."[15] The UNWTO defined the term formally to include three distinct dimensions. As quoted on the Eco India website:

Sustainable tourism should:
1. Make optimal use of the environmental resources that constitute a key element in tourism development, maintaining essential ecological processes and helping to conserve natural heritage and biodiversity.
2. Respect the socio-cultural authenticity of host communities, conserve their built and living cultural heritage and traditional values, and contribute to inter-cultural understanding and tolerance.
3. Ensure viable, long-term economic operations, providing socio-economic benefits to all stakeholders that are fairly distributed, including stable employment and income-earning opportunities and social services to host communities, and contributing to poverty alleviation.[16]

The concept of "ecotourism" entered the tourism lexicon late in the 20th century. In an early description of the phenomenon, a *New York Times* reporter wrote that ecotourism "promises the traveler an opportunity to help save the planet and get a suntan in the process."[17] A "kinder, greener tourist" was emerging:

The ecotourist is asking tougher questions of tour companies, perhaps choosing only those that funnel a portion of their profits to local conservation projects. The ecotourist is more likely to choose low-impact transportation: a canoe rather than a cruise ship, walking rather than a Land Rover. And the ecotourist prefers small, locally owned lodges to huge hotels or resorts owned by multinational corporations.[18]

Defined most succinctly as "responsible travel to natural areas which conserves the environment and improves the welfare of local people,"[19] ecotourism may be "the most profound intellectual innovation ever to have occurred within tourism."[20] In this context, ordinary tourism is simply travel undertaken for pleasure. "Nature tourism," distinct from ecotourism, is travel to unspoiled places to experience and enjoy nature. And "adventure tourism" is "nature tourism with a kick," involving a degree of risk-taking, athleticism, and endurance.[21]

Ecotourism has become everything that mass-market tourism isn't. Rather than massive beachfront hotels, it tends to feature smaller facilities, attractively designed using sustainable local materials. Rather than isolating tourists from local communities in all-inclusive resorts, it features engagement with local culture, nature, and communities. Rather than despoiling the environment, it seeks to protect and enhance it.

Ecotourism came of age internationally when the United Nations declared that 2002 would be the International Year of Ecotourism, highlighted by a World Ecotourism Summit in Quebec City, which I had the pleasure of attending. At that summit, delegates approved and issued a Quebec Declaration on Ecotourism. It recognized that ecotourism is a subset of sustainable tourism, but with the following additional characteristics:

- Contributes actively to the conservation of natural and cultural heritage.
- Includes local and indigenous communities in its planning, development and operation, and contribut[es] to their well-being.
- Interprets the natural and cultural heritage of the destination to visitors.
- Lends itself better to independent travelers, as well as to organized tours for small size groups.[22]

To this, Martha Honey, former president of the International Ecotourism Society (TIES), would add that "authentic ecotourism" is sensitive to the host country's political environment and social climate, and it supports human rights and international labor agreements.[23]

Yet not all ecotourism is created equal. The term has also been used to describe massive government projects in Southeast Asia that destroy shorelines and force local residents to move from their ancestral lands in order to attract tourists. Third World Network, a highly respected NGO based in Malaysia, has argued that ecotourism is an "ecological and economic trap." In general terms, developing a country around ecotourism may not only disrupt local economies, but also leave the developing country more indebted. The Third World Network explains that "to set up such tourism projects and to establish the necessary infrastructure to service tourists, more and more foreign loans are needed, which just add to the already overwhelming financial burden of countries. Meanwhile, many case studies show that the economic benefits from ecotourism have been highly overrated, and there is simply not enough money for the conservation of natural and cultural heritage and the improvement of public services." [24]

An even harsher critique comes from an analysis of the nature and impacts of ecotourism in the tiny nation of Belize. Based on extensive interviews with eco-tourists and ecotourism facility operators, it came to the following conclusions:

> The idea that ecotourism can benefit the environment and bring devel-opment through a reliance on self-reflexive travelers is questionable. Eco-tourists, like other types of tourists, are primarily interested in them-selves. It was clear that the main concern of travelers to Belize was how the holiday benefited them in a variety of ways, such as hedonistic pursuits, the capacity for self-reliance and organizational skills, and the building of character. In many ways they were engaged in a performance, portraying themselves as environmentally aware and culturally sensitive. In fact, it was clear that they were keen to impress their peer groups at home with tales of their self-denial and tenacity, and to display their genuine concern for the environmental welfare of the planet and the cultural wellbeing of the communities that they visited. [25]

The cultural impacts are also far more complex than most ecotourist advocates are prepared to admit.

> The image of a pristine paradise of silver beaches, turquoise water, palm trees, and primeval rainforests, and welcoming and exotic locals is de-signed to attract overseas visitors. . . . This invention of national identity to ensure that ecotourism remains an economically viable industry has a di-rect impact on the domestic political order in Belize. . . . Images of Mayan customs, traditions and histories are used by national governments to at-tract visitors. In contrast, those same governments have criticized Mayan communities in Belize for their lack of Western-style development. At-tempts by Mayan communities to engage in the development process (in-cluding ecotourism) in any meaningful way have been directly frustrated by their involvement in ecotourism. [26]

CERTIFICATION IN THE TOURISM SECTOR

Tourism certification systems of various kinds have evolved in recent years, espe-cially for sustainable tourism and ecotourism, in response to criticism of the in-dustry on both environmental and social grounds. In fact, by the end of 2005 there were some 80 different programs around the world that claimed to certify some aspects of tourism. They ranged from the Green Globe program, created in 1994, which operates worldwide and covers almost every aspect of tourism from airlines to car rentals, cruise ships, golf courses, restaurants, and vineyards. An early entrant in the field, and organized as a for-profit company, the original Green Globe had no standards and did no audits; companies received a Green

Globe plaque to display and the right to use the logo simply by purchasing membership in the Green Globe organization.[27] Reorganized and upgraded as "Green Globe 21" in 2001, following ample criticism at the Mohonk conference on sustainable tourism and in the writings of Martha Honey (see profile 7.1), Green Globe began to require members to develop environmental management systems (EMS) and to have their companies undergo third-party audits to ensure they were meeting their own EMS benchmarks, but as of early 2007 it had neither environmental performance standards that must be met nor social dimensions of any kind.[28]

Farther along the spectrum toward legitimate certification with clear standards and auditing mechanisms, there is the national tourism certification program of Costa Rica, Certification for Sustainable Tourism (CST), which was created by the Costa Rican government's Tourism Institute in 1995. It covers mass tourism, sustainable tourism, and ecotourism, and it was designed "to differentiate tourism sector businesses based on the degree to which they comply with a sustainable model of natural, cultural and social resource management."[33] The standards, which are primarily performance based, cover more than 150 criteria in four general categories: physical and biological engagement of the company with its local environment; implementation of sustainable management policies; programs to involve clients in its sustainability efforts; and the interaction of the company with local communities.[34] CST offers five levels of certification, each signified by a single leaf, with few facilities able to reach the top-level "five leaf" distinction (see Figure 7.1).

Another variant is the nonprofit, but non-governmental, Green Deal program of Guatemala.[37] This is a certification system created by a local NGO, Asociación Alianza Verde, with technical assistance from Conservation International and the Rainforest Alliance, and funding from USAID. It covers a combination of environmental management system issues and performance-based criteria on both environmental and socio-cultural issues. The Green Deal program focuses on standards related to the sustainability of construction materials, reduced use of water and energy, protection of wild fauna and flora, reduction of waste and treatment of wastewater, and active environmental education programs.

Figure 7.1. The CST "Five Leaf" Certification Plaque.

Building the Ethic of Sustainable Ecotourism
Martha Honey of the International Ecotourism Society and the Center for Ecotourism and Sustainable Development

Although many have written paeans to ecotourism, extolling its virtues and describing its wonders, there may be no one who has contributed more to establishing clear distinctions between tourism "greenwashing" and authentic ecotourism than Martha Honey. Serving in the dual posts of executive director of the International Ecotourism Society (until the end of 2006) and founding co-director of the Center for Ecotourism and Sustainable Development, Martha has been one of the strongest voices for, and one of the most dedicated developers of, certified ecotourism, despite some personal misgivings about whether certification can truly transform the tourism industry.

Martha's dedication to making the tourism industry more responsible might seem unusual if you didn't know her previous activist history. Born in Orange, New Jersey, and raised in Connecticut by parents who were a social worker and an academic, Martha graduated from Oberlin College, where she studied history, participated in the 1960s civil rights movement, volunteered in the Mississippi Civil Rights Project in 1964, and joined the peace movement in Philadelphia, all before graduate school, where she studied African American Studies at Syracuse University. A fellowship took her to Tanzania during the heyday of President Julius Nyerere. Martha spent a total of ten years there, working as a journalist, writing for the *Washington Post,* the BBC, Associated Press, and the Manchester *Guardian*, while completing her graduate study with a PhD from the University of Dar es Salaam.

The challenges facing tourism in Tanzania were often a focus of her research and writing. The Nyerere government struggled with the ways in which tourism might become part of the African socialism it was building. Tourist destinations such as majestic Mount Kilimanjaro and the wildlife-filled Serengeti Plains drew millions of visitors, but the benefits to local communities remained limited, and at times the tourism competed with sustainable local livelihoods. Early variants of contemporary ecotourism seemed to offer a useful compromise.

In 1983, as Nyerere planned to leave office, Martha and her family moved to Costa Rica. Ecotourism was on the rise there, and she again asked herself the fundamental question raised by most ecotourism advocates: Can ecotourism become a truly effective tool of both conservation and poverty alleviation? Costa Rica was attractive to her not only because of its interest in ecotourism, but also because it had an unbroken history of 100 years of democratic government, it had well-developed social programs such as national health care, and it had eliminated its army.

Little did she know that the Reagan administration's response to the Sandinista government of Nicaragua would involve Costa Rica as one of the two bases for the anti-Sandinista *contra* forces. A significant part of her writing while in Costa Rica described how the US government was transforming Central American societies through its foreign aid programs. She also wrote a book on an incident at La Penca, on the border of Nicaragua, where her journalist husband, Tony Avirgan, was nearly killed in an attempt on the life of one of the anti-Sandinista leaders, Eden Pastora.

Martha's first book on ecotourism, *Ecotourism and Sustainable Development: Who Owns Paradise?* was published in 1999.[29] In it she evaluates the ways in which the world travel industry is "going green" and then analyzes the evolution of ecotourism in some of the places where it is most developed: Costa Rica, Ecuador (the Galapagos), Cuba, Tanzania, Zanzibar, Kenya, and South Africa. She concludes that ecotourism has become "the most rapidly growing and dynamic sector of the tourism market," but appropriate development (including community participation) takes longer than many private developers are willing to wait. She found that "ecotourism…[was] far from fulfilling its promise to transform the way in which modern, conventional tourism is conducted," but excellent models were being built, some local communities were being empowered and their members' lives improved, and protected areas and fragile ecosystems were receiving more support.[30]

Martha was invited to become a member of the board of the International Ecotourism Society (TIES) in 2000. TIES is the leading international membership organization, providing technical services to ecotourism operators worldwide at the same time as it promotes appropriate, sustainable ecotourism. Then, working with the Institute for Policy Studies' program on ecotourism, Martha organized the first-ever global conference on certification of sustainable tourism and ecotourism. Held at the Mohonk Mountain House, near New York City, the conference produced what is now called the Mohonk Agreement, a proposal for the development of an international certification program for sustainable tourism and ecotourism, including a preliminary set of guidelines and principles. (The agreement is discussed in the main text of this chapter.)

In 2001 Martha and Abigail Rome published an introduction to tourism certification and a survey and analysis of some of the best-known eco-labeling and certification programs then present in the tourism field.[31] That was followed in 2002 by an edited volume on setting ecotourism standards in practice.[32] In both of these books, Martha struggled with the critical issues raised about the problems of certification for ecotourism. Can it be made accessible to small-scale and community-based operations? What is the appropriate community to which ecotourism operations must relate? How can the existing systems for certification be accommodated? And how can the weaker systems be identified?

In 2003, the TIES board asked Martha to become the organization's executive director. In that same year she worked with colleagues at Stanford University to create the Center for Ecotourism and Sustainable Development (CESD), with offices in Washington DC and Stanford, California. CESD was designed to complement TIES as a research organization studying the most important issues in building ecotourism and the related certification systems. For the following three years, Martha ran both organizations in a personal whirlwind of globe-trotting, making presentations to almost every major conference on the topic, as well as soul-searching, as she explored potential solutions to the problems that arose.

By 2006, Martha was encouraged by the prospects for setting stronger standards to improve the social and environmental impacts of tourism. Tour operators were finding, she noted, that the traveling public was increasingly aware of the critiques raised about conventional tourism, and rapidly growing numbers of travelers wanted to travel in socially and environmentally responsible ways. Rather than having to do the due diligence themselves, both travelers and tour operators wanted to see a global system for evaluating social and environmental practices that was both clear and credible.

Martha is optimistic about the prospects for creating a global accreditation system for sustainable tourism and ecotourism, as called for in the Mohonk Agreement, that would identify certification systems meeting a common set of international principles and criteria, and that could be adapted to the unique circumstances of different countries and regions.

Among the lessons she has learned over the years is that the greatest vulnerability of *all* the existing systems is their lack of financial viability. None of the small country-specific tourism certification programs have found a way to raise sufficient fees to cover their costs. Those that have been subsidized by governments, as part of public efforts to draw more tourism, find that government funding is a mixed blessing. But it may be the only way to give both legitimacy and viability to tourism certification efforts.

Martha remains convinced that, under the proper conditions, the hopes raised for ecotourism 15 and 20 years ago in Costa Rica and Tanzania can still be fulfilled. It could be a form of tourism that conserves natural resources and creates sustainable livelihoods. Her personal and professional commitment gives us hope that it will happen.

Launched in 2002, Green Deal set standards for hotels, restaurants, community projects, and tour operators. Most of the first ten Green Deal businesses certified in 2002 were located in the Mayan Biosphere Reserve area. In 2004 the program was taken to the whole nation, and by December 2006, 40 firms had been certified and 20 more had begun the process of certification. This voluntary program is now the official tourism certification program for all of Guatemala, recognized as such by the Guatemalan Tourism Institute, and Green Deal staff are providing technical assistance to counterparts in Mexico and El Salvador who are creating comparable programs in each of those countries.

A leading stand-alone ecotourism certification program evolved in Kenya. Organized by Ecotourism Kenya, a nonprofit linked to the travel industry, it included some 160 ecotourism facilities as members in late 2006. Ecotourism Kenya created an "eco-rating" system with three levels of achievement (bronze, silver, and gold). By late 2006, only 31 of the members had qualified for bronze level certification, and there were no facilities certified at either silver or gold

Certified Ecotourism Pioneer
Karen Lewis of Lapa Rios Ecolodge

When keyboard musician Karen Lewis left Minneapolis for the wilds of Costa Rica in the early 1990s, she had just accomplished one lifelong goal: after 20 years of teaching and playing as a church organist, she was finally invited to join a distinguished local chamber orchestra. The end of that career proved to be the beginning of a new starring role as one of the Western Hemisphere's most successful and highly decorated ecotourism pioneers.[35]

Karen and her husband, John, a prosperous but frustrated attorney, sought to recreate in their lives some of the satisfaction they had felt as Peace Corps Volunteers working in rural communities of Kenya from 1968 to 1970. They sought work that would satisfy their passion for linking environmental conservation with community development. After visiting leading ecotourism facilities in Africa and Central America, in 1990, they had the opportunity to purchase nearly 1,000 acres of endangered lowland rainforest on the southern tip of Costa Rica's Osa Peninsula, accessible at that time only by boat from the banana port of Golfito.

The threat to the rainforest came primarily from the expansion of cattle ranching in the region, as well as the rampant illegal trade in endangered species, including toucans, scarlet macaws, and howler, spider, and squirrel monkeys. Although Costa Rica's Corcovado National Park lay within 30 kilometers, local residents were barely aware of the value of the remaining rich biodiversity.

Creation of Lapa Rios Ecolodge involved nearly three years of work with local architects and contractors who were familiar with thatched roof "palapa" structures and were willing to build in a manner that maximized the use of local materials and minimized impact on the forest. Karen and John engaged with the understandably suspicious local farmers and laborers by providing a sizable loan to the village to cover the cost of construction of the area's first schoolhouse.

The first years were lean ones in terms of financial success. The lodge attracted the heartier travelers, who were not averse to the cross-water access and starkly simple villas and who appreciated the vigorous educational hiking tours through the local hills and down to the nearest beach, 300 feet below. Yet there was no certification system available to validate the sustainability of their practices or to permit systematic comparisons with those of other facilities. The Costa Rican CST wasn't created until several years after Lapa Rios opened.

Karen and John decided to apply for CST certification soon after the system was set up in 1997. By 2000, according to Karen, they "barely" qualified for CST certification at the second-highest "four-leaf" level, and in 2005 they became one of the two highest-rated hotel facilities in Costa Rica, earning the rare "five-leaf" CST certification, shown in Figure 7.1. That distinction brought more. Lapa Rios was named to the 2005 Conde Nast Reader's Choice Awards for the "Top 10 Hotels in Mexico & Central America" and was included in the Andrew Harper Travel 2005 list of the "World's Best Hotels, Resorts, and Hideaways." Capping a good year, in November 2005, Lapa Rios received a US State Department award for corporate excellence as a

US company operating overseas that exhibited "the highest standards of conduct in…good corporate citizenship, exemplary employment practices, responsible environmental stewardship and practices, and contribution to the overall growth and development of the local economy."[36]

When asked what CST certification has meant for financial returns from the property, at first Karen holds her hand up to her eye with fingers held in a circle to signify "zero." But with a bit more prompting, she talks enthusiastically about how it has engaged her staff creatively, led to internal economies, provided a much-needed auditing of their own sustainability practices, and, more recently, has begun to draw clients who recognize and appreciate the certification.

The CST requirement to measure and post all water and energy usage, by villa and by support facility, changed staff practices in ways that continue to improve years later. Staff were proud of the practices and took pleasure in explaining them to visitors. The culture of wildlife conservation became part of the knowledge base of most of the staff; it became an important theme in the local school they helped to build; and it has helped the lodge draw skilled and dedicated staff from around the country. "Why even the gardener, our oldest employee, stops visitors to show them interesting bird and butterfly species, which he can name correctly!" says Karen. The CST documentation requirements for water and energy consumption, sourcing and disposal of food and other materials, and continuous improvement over time provide, according to Karen, "the best internal audit I could ever get with respect to moving staff and management toward the property's original goals."

One of their most interesting staff-led innovations arose when her kitchen staff came to Karen and said, "We need pigs." Aghast, at first, at the suggestion of introducing pigs into their carefully preserved environment, Karen learned that pigs would help dispose of the sizable amount of kitchen waste and that pig manure, properly handled, would generate methane, which could then be used for cooking, replacing very expensive bottled gas brought from many miles away. So, today, Lapa Rios has a pig cultivation project located near staff housing, a few hundred yards from guest housing. The methane generated from closed composting of the manure provides most of the cooking gas needed for the staff kitchen that feeds 55 people every day. Locally raised pork is occasionally part of the lodge's gourmet menu.

The most difficult aspects of qualifying for certification involved finding ways to measure and validate what they were doing, especially on the level of engagement with the local community. It has led them to find creative ways to empower their staff to become community leaders, and it has involved them in solving a number of the social ills in the local area.

Their sustainability practices are clearly more expensive, Karen insists. Using local teak and thatch for the four-story main palapa and the villa roofing means replacing them every five or six years, rather than every 15 or 20 years, which would be the case with conventional commercial materials. Sourcing organic foods, as well as biodegradable soaps and personal products, was much more expensive at their distant location in the earlier years. But as more competitive sources of those products begin to appear in Costa Rica, the prices are falling.

"The largest impacts of certified ecotourism for us," Karen concludes, "are the hard-to-measure ripple effects that it has had throughout our local area. By buying local, using local and sustainable materials, creating local jobs, and creating a context in which staff seek to create implements and equipment from local materials, we have a positive impact on our own performance and a much larger impact on our local community." The ultimate satisfaction comes when the owners of neighboring (and competing) ecolodges admit to her, especially in the last few years, that "it looks like we really need to get certified, too."

level.[38] The program covers hotels, lodges, camps, and smaller local facilities. Certification begins with a self-assessment, which is then audited on-site according to criteria that increase in stringency and complexity at higher levels of certification. The standards emphasize "sustainable use of resources and protection of the environment; and support to local economies through linkages and building of capacity of local communities and employees."

It was in the context of this variety of fundamentally unrelated and difficult-to-compare national, regional, and global programs that the Mohonk Conference on Certification of Sustainable Tourism and Ecotourism brought together representatives of the industry in 2000 to discuss what was needed to create globally credible principles and criteria. Several decisions were made by the participants, who came from 20 different countries and represented many of the leading attempts to create certification in tourism. They agreed to work together to create a set of principles that sustainable tourism certification systems should incorporate in order to be legitimated; they also added separate principles required for sustainable ecotourism. The resulting Mohonk Agreement (see Figure 7.2) has proven to be a remarkable set of guidelines, crafted in just a few days of feverish activity.

The conference participants then delegated to the Rainforest Alliance the task of conducting a set of global negotiations to determine how the Mohonk Agreement might be communicated widely, broadened or sharpened as necessary, and made an element of a global system for determining whether claims of sustainability could be tested against a set of well-developed standards.

After two more years of diligent global work led by Ronald Sanabria of Rainforest Alliance's Costa Rica office, the Rainforest Alliance released the results of its deliberations, which included stakeholder discussions at the World Ecotourism Summit held in Quebec City in May 2002. The recommended global system has the following general characteristics:

- A new Sustainable Tourism Stewardship Council (STSC) will be established as a global institution for developing and certifying compliance with a full set of multi-stakeholder standards for sustainable tourism.
- The standards for sustainable ecotourism will include fulfillment of all those

Mohonk Agreement:
Proposal for an International Certification Program for Sustainable Tourism and Ecotourism

Mohonk Agreement

A framework and principles for the certification of sustainable and ecotourism.

Background

This document contains a set of general principles and elements that should be part of any sound ecotourism and sustainable tourism certification programs. This framework was unanimously adopted at the conclusion of an international workshop convened by the Institute for Policy Studies with support from the Ford Foundation. It was held at Mohonk Mountain House, New Paltz, New York on November 17-19, 2000.

Workshop participants recognized that tourism certification programs need to be tailored to fit particular geographical reasons and sectors of the tourism industry, but agreed that the following are the universal components that must frame any ecotourism and sustainable certification program.

1. Certification Scheme Overall Framework

Basis of Scheme

The objectives of the scheme should be clearly stated. The development of a certification scheme should be a participatory, multi-stakeholder and multi-sectoral process (including representatives from local communities, tourism businesses, non-governmental organizations, community-based organizations, government, and others).

- The scheme should provide tangible benefits to tourism providers and a means for tourists to chose wisely
- The scheme should provide tangible benefits to local communities and to conservation
- The scheme should set minimum standards while encouraging and rewarding best practice
- There is a process to withdraw certification in the event of non-compliance
- The scheme should establish control of existing/new seals/logos in terms of appropriate use, an expiration date and, in the event of loss of certification, withdrawal
- The scheme should include provisions for technical assistance
- The scheme should be designed such that there is motivation for continual improvement—both of the scheme and of the products/companies to be certified

Criteria Framework

- Criteria should provide the mechanism(s) to meet the stated objective(s)
- Criteria used should meet and preferably exceed regulatory compliance
- Criteria should embody global best practice environmental, social and economic management
- Criteria should be adapted to recognizing local/regional ecological, social and economic conditions and local sustainable development efforts
- Criteria should be subject to a periodic review
- Criteria should be principally performance-based and include environmental, social and economic management process elements

Scheme Integrity

- The certification program should be transparent and involve an appeals process
- The certification body should be independent of the parties being certified and of technical assistance and assessment bodies (i.e., administrative structures for technical assistance, assessment and auditing should avoid conflicts of interest)
- The scheme should require audits by suitably trained auditors
- The scheme should require mechanisms for consumer and local community feedback

2. Sustainable Tourism Criteria

Sustainable tourism is tourism that seeks to minimize ecological and socio-cultural impacts while providing economic benefits to local communities and host countries. In any certification scheme, the criteria used to define sustainable tourism should address at least minimum standards in the following aspects (as appropriate):

Overall

- Environmental planning and impact assessment has been undertaken and has considered social, cultural, ecological and economic impacts (including cumulative impacts and mitigation strategies)
- Environmental management commitment by tourism business
- Staff training, education, responsibility, knowledge and awareness in environmental, social and cultural management
- Mechanisms for monitoring and reporting environmental performance
- Accurate, responsible marketing leading to realistic expectations
- Consumer feedback

Social/Cultural

- Impacts upon social structures, culture and economy (on both local and national levels)
- Appropriateness of land acquisition/access processes and land tenure
- Measures to protect the integrity of local community's social structure
- Mechanisms to ensure rights and aspirations of local and/or indigenous people are recognized

Ecological

- Appropriateness of location and sense of place
- Biodiversity conservation and integrity of ecosystem processes
- Site disturbance, landscaping and rehabilitation
- Drainage, soils and stormwater management
- Sustainability of energy supply and minimization of use
- Sustainability of water supply and minimization of use
- Sustainability of wastewater treatment and disposal
- Noise and air quality (including greenhouse emissions)
- Waste minimization and sustainability of disposal
- Visual impacts and light
- Sustainability of materials and supplies (recyclable and recycled materials, locally produced, certified timber products, etc.)
- Minimal environmental impacts of activities

Economic

- Requirements for ethical business practice
- Mechanisms to ensure labor arrangements and industrial relations procedures are not exploitative, and conform to local laws and international labor standards (whichever are higher)
- Mechanisms to ensure negative economic impacts on local communities are minimized and preferably there are substantial economic benefits to local communities
- Requirements to ensure contributions to the development/maintenance of local community infrastructure

3. Ecotourism Criteria

Ecotourism is sustainable tourism with a natural area focus, which benefits the environment and communities visited, and fosters environmental and cultural understanding appreciation, and awareness. In any ecotourism certification scheme, the criteria should address standards (preferably mostly best practice) for sustainable tourism (as per above and at least minimum standards for:

- Focus on personal experiences of nature to lead to greater understanding and appreciation
- Interpretation and environmental awareness of nature, local society, and culture
- Positive and active contributions to conservation of natural areas or biodiversity
- Economic, social, and cultural benefits for local communities
- Fostering of community involvement, where appropriate
- Locally appropriate scale and design for lodging, tours and attractions
- Minimal impact on and presentation of local (indigenous) culture

required for tourism in general, but will also carry more stringent social, educational, and community-involvement requirements.
- Given the large existing number of tourism certification programs, some of
which are considered to be excellent, the STSC will not create a wholly new
global certification system but will focus on accrediting existing programs
that meet the highest standards (and, implicitly, disaccrediting others).
- The STSC will begin as an international network, based on national and regional tourism initiatives already in place; this will lead to the creation of an
STSC Association, which would be an international office designed to facilitate marketing, training, and information sharing among existing certification schemes.
- STSC accreditation will then provide a basis for identifying and distinguishing, for both consumers and tourism mass-marketers, those facilities around
the world that best fulfill the negotiated set of standards for sustainable and
responsible ecotourism.[39]

Since then, the pace of implementation has picked up. Rainforest Alliance has
developed further standards, dubbed Mohonk II, in conjunction with the Sustainable Tourism Certification Network of the Americas, which was launched at
a meeting in Bahia, Brazil. It includes representatives of groups supporting sustainable tourism from 10 Latin American countries, Spain, and the United States.
The network has developed nearly 100 "baseline criteria" that it believes all
tourism certification systems should take into consideration, including environmental, social, cultural, and business-policy criteria.[40] A study of potential solutions to the funding problems of country-specific and region-specific tourism
certification programs will be completed in early 2007, and a business plan for
launching the STSC should be ready by mid-2007.

REFLECTIONS

The process of creating a certification system for sustainable and responsible
tourism and ecotourism differs in several interesting ways from the processes we
have seen for sustainable forestry, agricultural commodities, and international
project finance. Although, like those others, it was set in motion by the criticism
of a few small, articulate, and valiant advocacy groups, where are the major market campaigns to move companies toward the emerging standards for certification? Who are the targets? Where is the leading edge of the pressure for change in
the industry?

It is a common complaint among those promoting certified sustainable
tourism and ecotourism that "not many tour companies see the need for certification." This feeds into the difficulties the national certification schemes have
faced when seeking sufficient funding to cover their costs. Without significant
scale of operation, which means hundreds or thousands of certified operations
rather than dozens, the cost of the system is too great for a small number of certified participants to bear.

Building Global Tourism Certification

Tensie Whelan, CEO of Rainforest Alliance

Tensie Whelan is only the second CEO in Rainforest Alliance (RA) history. She succeeded Dan Katz, RA's charismatic founder, in 2000. She is, however, the person who has put RA on the global sustainable tourism map. It now epitomizes the kind of business-oriented environmental NGO that has emerged in recent years as an important player in the certification revolution.[41]

Rainforest Alliance was created in 1986 "to protect ecosystems and the people and wildlife that depend on them by transforming land-use practices, business practices and consumer behavior."[42] In earlier chapters we have touched on RA's important work in the area of certifying sustainable forest management through its SmartWood program. The RA certification system for coffee and other commodities will be discussed in Chapter 11 as a competitor to Fair Trade certification. Yet the organization's efforts to transform the travel and tourism industry have been its biggest challenge and perhaps its greatest opportunity to change global corporations.

Tourism — the elixir of super-wealthy travelers as well as the stuff of brutish louts — might seem, at first, distant from the mission of an organization called Rainforest Alliance. For Tensie, however, sustainable tourism and ecotourism provide creative alternatives to the socially and environmentally destructive tourism that seems to sprout on every gorgeous coastline or in every pristine valley. Ecotourism provides one more way for communities to make a living from forests kept intact. Making larger-scale tourism sustainable lessens the destructive impact of tourist facilities, conserves biodiversity, and is another arena where certification systems can be brought to bear.

The Rainforest Alliance's Sustainable Tourism Program, as noted on its website, works with tourism entrepreneurs and community-based businesses in Latin America, providing training and information on environmentally and socially sound management, in order to help them gain access to and be more competitive in the marketplace, while contributing to the conservation of the local culture and nature.[43]

This work takes Tensie far from her New York City roots. Born and educated in that city, Tensie earned an undergraduate degree at New York University in political science, then a master's degree in international communications from American University in Washington, DC. Her early work as an environmental journalist in Sweden and then Costa Rica, with particular focus on the links between environment and development, have given her powerful insights into the dilemmas faced by the poor and by struggling entrepreneurs in Latin America and elsewhere. Five years as the leader of the New York League of Conservation Voters, one of the most politically powerful conservation organizations in the state; three years as VP for Conservation Information at the National Audubon Society; and her current chairmanship (on a volunteer basis) of the Brooklyn Bridge Park Conservancy taught Tensie about the links between local, regional, state, and international environmental concerns, links echoed in RA's domestic and international work. Under her direction, RA has grown from a staff of 45 to 200-plus, with an annual budget that rose from $4.5 million to well over $20 million.

RA is *not* a market campaign organization; its focus is to help businesses large and small adopt improved practices. Its principal tool is certification. The biggest challenge for efforts to certify sustainable tourism and ecotourism operators, according to Tensie, is the fragmentation of the world travel and tourism industry and the lack of pressure on the industry to develop, validate, and market more sustainable practices.

Engagement with governments is also a challenge. While forest management certification moved rapidly without government involvement, governments are deeply involved in regulating and promoting their tourism industries. The national and regional tourism agencies competing for global tourist revenues are quickly becoming the point of entry for tourism certification in many countries.

In the end, the biggest challenges come with success. Rainforest Alliance certifies the ecological practices of Chiquita, one of the three largest global "bananeras." RA can show how Chiquita's banana-growing practices have improved environmentally, relative to their competitors. But Chiquita is also the target of great political animosity because of its corporate history as the United Fruit Company, which was linked to the CIA's overthrow of the Guatemalan government in the 1940s. RA's SmartWood program now certifies more than 1,500 FSC forest management units worldwide, including a majority of the FSC's smaller indigenous and community-based certificates. As the system grows, local and international advocacy groups are challenging the validity of more FSC certificates, including those issued by SmartWood. And so it is likely to be with sustainable tourism.

If, however, the construction of the Sustainable Tourism Stewardship Council continues at its present pace, if the United Nations Environment Program and the UN World Tourism Organization continue to recognize its potential significance, and if Rainforest Alliance can maintain its track record of non-hostile engagement with businesses large and small, the transformation of the global tourism and ecotourism industry is no more impossible than the transformation of forestry, finance, and agricultural commodity trade seemed to be a decade ago.

This may be the great, unresolved conundrum of tourism certification. Until powerful advocacy campaigns develop, focused on major outbound tour operators or key tourism destinations, it may be too much to expect that a demand for certification will arise, that industry will recognize the need for certification, and that certification will have real market value to the participating firms.

Government funding may be more available for tourism certification than for other forms of private voluntary certification. The tourism sector is such an important source of investment and, under the right circumstances, export earnings that governments have an interest in ensuring that each country's tourism sector is competitive in the current market. But even some of the better government-supported tourism certification programs, such as Costa Rica's CST, are languishing. People I interviewed from the Costa Rica tourism industry (who preferred to remain anonymous) complained that there is a long list of properties seeking certification, but not enough staff at the National Tourism Institute to conduct the audits and convey the certificates. Monitoring of those already certified has lapsed to the point of uselessness for the same reason. Changes in the leadership of the Tourism Institute and of Costa Rica's government have meant reduced budgets for, and only lackadaisical interest in, certification.

The UN World Tourism Organization and the UN Environment Program have wavered in their engagement with and commitment to tourism certification, undoubtedly reflecting hesitation on the part of their member governments to create a private voluntary system, driven by NGOs and the tourism industry, that governments do not control directly. In the context of what we have learned over the past ten years, there is a certain shortsightedness in that institutional response. The global tourism industry and its major corporate players are vulnerable to a dramatic and powerful attack from well-positioned international NGOs. It's not that there are no social and environmental problems in the industry; they just have not yet drawn the attention of advocacy groups who understand how to organize and launch market campaigns against the industry leaders. And there's little reason to believe that oversight will last for long.

8

Accountability Comes to Mining: Building an Assurance Process

I am on record, I must admit, arguing that the mining sector is one place where voluntary certification is not likely to work. "How can one trace mineral products to the market," I wrote, "when mining firms rarely sell their products directly to consumers?"[1] This was, I am happy to report, a failure of imagination on my part. In this short chapter we will see how the shared learning of market campaign organizations produced a brilliant little campaign that has shaken up the global mining industry.

That's not to say that the industry wasn't aware of the problems it faced. In fact, there have been more attempts to deal with both the perception and the reality of social and environmental problems in the mining industry than there were in other sectors before many of the sector-specific campaigns were launched. This may be a result of the mining companies' particular exposure to high levels of governmental regulation. In recent off-the-record conversations with mining company leaders, I found the sustainability and social responsibility vice-presidents of several of the major mining companies especially conscious of the costs of long and delayed processes to obtain permits to mine, which are linked closely to the notion of a "social license" to operate. However, the systems they patched together for themselves, in pursuit of improved practices in the industry and improved respect from the general public, had little transparency and even less credibility. As a result, their attempts to improve their global image provided very little reputational risk reduction, either for themselves or for their clients down the supply chain.

The tale of the mining accountability campaign is the story of another small, smart NGO that simultaneously crafted a market campaign that convinced the industry something new had to be done and orchestrated a process that is building toward a globally useful system that may transform the mining industry in ways that will meet the demands of global civil society. This work built on at least a hundred years of advocacy by dozens of civil society organizations around the world. To describe the results as something that came only from the new market campaign and new corporate engagement is unfair to all those who had applied pressure before. But I would argue that the mining industry has moved more rapidly in the past two years than at any previous time.

169

THE ISSUES

The litany of problems associated with mining and minerals extraction has filled hundreds of books.[2] The industry itself cataloged the problems it faces in a massive self-study on mining, minerals, and sustainable development (MMSD), completed in 2002 for release at the World Summit on Sustainable Development in Johannesburg. Among the industry's own conclusions, the following stand out:

- The mining and minerals industry faces some of the most difficult challenges of any industrial sector — and is currently distrusted by many of the people it deals with day to day. It has been failing to convince some of its constituents that it has the 'social license to operate' in many parts of the world.
- Indigenous lands have been and, many would say, are still under threat from all sorts of exploitative uses, including mining. Land is often used without the consent of indigenous peoples.
- Resettlement has often been accompanied by landlessness, unemployment, homelessness, and loss of access to common resources.
- Some companies in the minerals sector may have colluded in a variety of illicit activities — bribery to obtain licenses and permits; to get preferential access to prospects, assets, or credit; or to sway judicial decisions.
- Few areas present a greater challenge than the relationship between mining companies and local communities. The legacy of abuse and mistrust is clear.
- Some mining companies have been accused of human rights abuses, for actions taken either independently or in collusion with governments. Some of the worst cases have occurred when companies have relied on national security forces to gain control over land or defend established premises.
- Miners rights are also threatened by difficult and dangerous working conditions, with a long history of labor-management conflict, particularly in authoritarian states.
- Mining produces very large volumes of waste, so decisions about where and how to dispose of it are often virtually irreversible.
- Even the best modern [mining] operations may have some undesirable environmental impacts, and good practice has far to go before it spreads to all parts of the industry.
- In many ways far more troubling are some of the continuing effects of past mining and smelting. These sites have proved that some impacts can be long-term and that society is still paying a price for natural capital stocks that have been drawn down by past generations.[3]

Critics of the MMSD process and report began with the assertion that sustainability means less mining, not more. And, they added, "a truly sustainable global society will take fewer minerals from the earth each year. Instead of requiring ever-growing amounts of minerals and fuels, a sustainable economy will use materials much more efficiently, reducing waste to a bare minimum, and rely more on recycling, reuse and renewable energy technology."[4]

Truly global action around mining began to be organized more effectively in 2001 with a conference hosted by Earthworks (at the time called Mineral Policy Center), a Washington-based NGO with a strong reputation for advocacy on behalf of local communities and the environment in the face of mining operations, especially within the United States. The conference brought together activists from some 20 countries, ranging from community activists fighting mine expansion in Peru to Canadian and Australian mining-watch NGOs with long records of struggling against the mining industry. Three conclusions emerged from the meeting, which I was privileged to attend.

The first conclusion was that there was a clear need for greater networking among these groups to get beyond the occasional loosely structured, and expensive, conference phone calls that had been their principal prior method of communicating. An Internet-based listserv was created that has become an inexpensive vehicle for sharing stories, tactics, and appeals for assistance under the rubric of the Global Mining Campaign (GMC).

The second conclusion was that many participants were profoundly skeptical about the appropriateness of developing a voluntary certification system to regulate mining. Although conference organizers had invited speakers who described the emerging success of the Forest Stewardship Council as a vehicle for transforming the forest products industry, many of the participants felt that engaging with a mining industry they had been attacking relentlessly was not a wise or useful strategy.

The third conclusion reached by some of the participants was that they needed to make a coordinated effort to hold the mining industry accountable on a global basis, and they were interested in exploring the use of market and corporate campaign strategies. This work began as an effort to monitor industry-commissioned efforts like the MMSD project, which many NGOs viewed with skepticism. But it also led to direct engagement with the mining industry sponsors of MMSD and a negotiated agreement through which NGOs participated in an industry-sponsored conference to consider the MMSD findings. Subsequently, a number of these NGOs began to consider the potential for using market strategies to advance their objectives.

It is worth noting that the outcomes were somewhat contradictory. Some NGOs that were skeptical of market campaigns continued to participate in campaign planning. Whether the conclusion that a market campaign could get results was prescient will be seen in the next year or two, as a balanced stakeholder process seeks to build consensus on standards and procedures. Earthworks and other NGOs, cautioned by the skepticism, decided to go ahead and see what might develop in any event.

THE CAMPAIGN

Over the course of the two years following the conference, Earthworks explored the possibility of developing a certification system for mining. The group hired a new international campaigns coordinator, Payal Sampat, in late 2002, and the first shot in the campaign, across the figurative bowsprits of companies in the gold and silver supply chain, came in June 2003. Earthworks (at that time still called Mineral Policy Center) and Tiffany & Co. organized a meeting in New York that brought together representatives of retail jewelry companies, other corporate consumers of gold and silver (such as major electronics manufacturers), representatives of the finance and insurance industry, and mining advocacy NGOs to discuss the need, and the possibilities, for putting pressure on mining companies to improve their social and environmental practices. No mining company was invited to that meeting.

There were four presentations over the course of a half day: an aspirational introduction from Michael Kowalski, chairman and CEO of Tiffany, on the reasons why higher standards were needed; a discussion of the strengths and weaknesses of the Kimberley Process, which seeks to identify and reduce the flow of diamonds from "conflict zones," especially in Africa, where they are seen as a means of financing guerilla forces; a presentation on how certification systems were emerging in comparable natural resource arenas, such as forestry, environmental toxics, and agricultural commodities; and a visually vivid and powerful illustration of a "theoretical campaign" that could be waged against current practices in the mining of gold and silver if something wasn't done to improve those practices. About two-thirds of those present subsequently agreed to participate in the next stages of developing a campaign for the mining industry.

Earthworks then drew up, in collaboration with this first group of interested parties, a vision statement, "Responsible Sourcing, Investing, and Insuring in the Minerals Sector," that embodied a first set of principles (see Figure 8.1).[5] The purpose of the vision statement was to produce an initial consensus among stakeholders in the minerals industry before the group began to approach the mining companies themselves. Within months, the list of organizations and individuals committed to the vision statement grew to impressive length.

No Dirty Gold

The outlines of a market campaign began to emerge later in 2003. Earthworks developed a partnership for this work with Oxfam America, a larger organization with stronger international name recognition. With input from focus groups and media consultants, NGO staff came up with the name of the campaign, which was a simple and straightforward expression of its intent: No Dirty Gold. It was launched just before Valentine's Day in February 2004, primarily in Washington, DC, New York City, and Boston, and it drew significant media attention immediately.

The first stage of the campaign was simple. A number of volunteers walked along main jewelry shopping avenues, such as Fifth Avenue in New York, one of the symbolic hearts of the world jewelry business, and distributed several thousand full-color postcard-size flyers that said, on one side:

Don't tarnish your love with dirty gold.

Figure 8.1.

Vision Statement: Responsible Sourcing, Investing, and Insuring in the Minerals Sector

Representatives from corporations, nonprofit organizations and philanthropic foundations recently initiated a dialogue aimed at improving the performance of the mining industry on environmental, social and human rights issues. A statement embodying their vision follows.

Society uses metals and other minerals for a wide variety of purposes, and it is in society's interest to make sure that they are obtained, produced and used in environmentally and socially responsible ways. This includes respect for recognized codes of human rights, including workers' rights and indigenous peoples' rights.

We believe that natural resources should be developed in a manner that respects the needs of current and future generations. We seek to protect those places where mining should not occur. We recognize the societal benefits that accrue from the use of recycled content and existing above-ground sources, and support their greater use. We also recognize the potential risks associated with sourcing minerals from non-responsible sources.

We seek to develop and promote solutions to a number of critical issues relevant to mineral extraction and use, recognizing that as we move from vision to solutions, greater definition and specificity will be necessary. These issues include:

- protecting natural water bodies from mine tailings and wastes, including the risks associated with long-term water treatment and with the chemicals used in mineral extraction and processing;
- respecting the need to preserve ecologically and culturally significant areas;
- establishing environmental protection and management standards for operating mines, including comprehensive closure plans and full funding for cleanup as a pre-condition of mining;
- developing protocols and implementing practices for informed community decision-making that respect the rights and interests of affected communities, including independent socio-economic and environmental impact assessments and audits;
- adhering to human rights protocols and standards, including workers' rights and indigenous peoples' rights; and
- promoting the use of recycled content and life-cycle analysis.

Access to information on the impacts of mining and the life-cycle of materials made from mined products is essential to informed decision-making and to our ability to realize our vision. Therefore, we recognize that central to establishing these responsible practices is the creation of information systems to help track the sources of metals and other minerals, and to monitor extraction, transportation, refining and disposal practices throughout the life-cycle of the mineral.

While we acknowledge the complexity of the chain of custody for minerals, we recognize the need for investors, insurers, retailers, consumers and others to know the origins of these minerals and to understand the associated environmental, economic and social impacts. This understanding and information will provide all involved with the ability to assess mining projects and choose minerals and mineral products that have been sourced and produced responsibly.

(November 19, 2003, Version)

Leading the Jewelry Industry
Toward Greater Sustainability

Michael Kowalski of Tiffany & Co.

It is rare for the CEO of a high-profile company to step out ahead of his or her industry to confront a set of problems that the rest of the industry would prefer to ignore. But Michael Kowalski learned early in his time at Tiffany & Co. that there's no way to sweep a problem under the rug if you are running a highly branded company linked to a controversial industry. Having worked for Tiffany & Co. since 1983, one of the first tasks he faced after becoming executive vice-president in 1992 was a brand-management crisis that erupted when a whole line of chinaware, hand-painted in a Paris atelier, was found by Environmental Defense to have "eye-popping" levels of lead in its glaze.[6]

Constant attention to reputational risk has to be second nature for senior management of a company like Tiffany, where the value of the brand may be as high as 77 percent of the company's total capitalization.[7] Kowalski's response was to spend a million dollars on a new laboratory in which samples of every shipment of china to Tiffany are now tested before they are put on sale. Tiffany was able to offer a merchandise credit to all 406 people who had purchased one or more pieces of the problem china, which sold for $1,200 per five-piece setting.

It surprised both the jewelry industry and the mining industry, nonetheless, when Kowalski, now CEO and chairman of Tiffany & Co., published an open letter to the chief of the US Forest Service in the *Washington Post* in 2005. The letter opposed a mining project that had received preliminary approval from the Forest Service and that would have dug miles of tunnels beneath the Cabinet Mountains Wilderness Area in northwestern Montana, despite vehement opposition from a large coalition of advocacy groups and local businesses. They feared, and Kowalski concurred, that the mine would discharge millions of gallons of waste water per day into pristine trout streams and hold vast quantities of "toxic sludge" in holding facilities of "questionable durability."[8]

In my conversations with Kowalski, it became clear that he understands, better than any other CEO I have met, that without a certification system for the sourcing of precious metals, Tiffany & Co. will remain exposed to reputational risk and danger to its brand value beyond what it wishes to bear. Tiffany & Co. has done just about everything an individual company can do to protect its sourcing from potentially damaging products. It became part-owner of a diamond mine in Canada to reduce the risk that there would be "conflict diamonds" in its stores, and Kowalski established a policy of "zero tolerance" for diamonds of questionable provenance that might come from conflict zones. Tiffany & Co. also decided to source most of its gold from a cyanide-free gold mine.

Yet he still reminds his senior management of what he calls, hypothetically, "the Mike Wallace moment," referring to the senior reporter on *Sixty Minutes,* the CBS News investigative journalism program. "Do you mean to tell the world," Mike Wallace would be saying, microphone in the face of the executive he was interviewing, "that you really didn't know the buildup of toxic tailings at your mine might some-day break out of the holding tank and destroy one of the finest remaining salmon fisheries in the Northwest and poison the water of hundreds of communities?" For Kowalski, the ultimate risk reduction comes from having a clear set of standards, backed by social and environmental stakeholders, coupled with independent third-party certification that his suppliers are meeting those standards.

Kowalski's collaboration with MPC/Earthworks and other NGOs has included co-sponsoring the meeting of NGOs, jewelers, and investors in 2003; organizing meetings with senior officials from the mining sector; and sponsoring independent research, such as the development of a framework for responsible mining that maps out specific steps companies can take to address the environmental and human rights challenges facing the sector.[9] He and his colleagues have also worked closely with other companies in the jewelry industry to encourage their support for the development of a certification system. And Kowalski has sought out progressive actors in the mining sector. He is well aware that finding and collaborating with leaders in this sector is critical to success. His voice is quiet and persuasive, and he has chosen to employ the iconic image of Tiffany & Co. to lead the jewelry industry toward higher levels of sustainability.

The flip side of the card simply read:

Gold mining is one of the most destructive activities in the world today.

The production of one gold ring generates 20 tons of waste.
Tell the gold industry you want an alternative to dirty gold!

It directed interested persons to a newly created website, nodirtygold.org, that provided information (in both English and Spanish) on the social and environmental impacts of gold mining and gave people the opportunity to sign a pledge to pressure companies to end dirty gold mining practices.

At the same time, Oxfam, Earthworks, and the No Dirty Gold campaign, which involved community groups around the world, released a 30-page report entitled *Dirty Metals: Mining, Communities and the Environment,* which described the amount of newly mined metals consumed each year by an average US citizen (21 metric tons) and the ways in which mining "damages landscapes, pollutes water, and poisons people." It also provided suggestions for "what concerned citizens can do to clean it up."[10]

CNN's Headline News network picked up the story immediately, showing a blowup of the card, running a header across the bottom of the screen that said "No Dirty Gold This Valentine's Day," and repeating an interview with Payal Sampat throughout the day. Forbes.com ran a story that afternoon, taken from the Reuters wire, which quoted Keith Slack of Oxfam, who pointed out that "the symbol of your enduring love should not have to come at the expense of clean drinking water or respect for human rights."[11] A Knight-Ridder Washington bureau news article on the action and the report appeared in a half dozen Knight-Ridder newspapers from Miami to San Jose, California. The *Village Voice* in New York headlined its story "Toxic Gold." A story even appeared the next day in the Elko, Nevada, *Free Press*, in the heart of Nevada mining country, with more of a tilt toward the mining industry responses.[12]

The industry press also picked up the campaign story quickly, and without great pleasure. On February 11, the National Mining Association, the US industry's leading trade association, issued a rejoinder in a press release entitled "Modern Gold Mining Practices Contradict Critics," which asserted that "the 'gold standard' for objectivity and factual information has been abandoned by these groups."[13]

Thanks to Earthworks' Global Mining Campaign links to community organizations fighting mines in other countries, similar actions took place that week in Kyrgyzstan, Ghana, Peru, and among Native American groups in Nevada, with campaign materials available in Russian and Spanish as well as English.

At that time, the campaign did not target any specific jewelry store or chain. Focus groups had shown that most consumers had "zero consciousness" of the social and environmental impacts of gold mining, so the campaign was deliberately less hard-hitting. Rather, it emphasized branding gold as "dirty," knowing that that approach would reinforce the concerns in the jewelry and electronics industries about their sourcing of the metal.[14]

The campaigners also realized that they were dealing with a luxury item, not an essential good, like wood or food. Brand value and marketing were central features of the jewelry-buying transaction, and campaigners theorized that jewelers would move to protect their brand and their products especially quickly.

Campaigners also tried a somewhat different strategy than that used by market campaigns in other sectors. Starting in 2003, they tried to recruit corporate leaders to support the campaign before there was any public activity. In retrospect, campaigners noted that this pre-campaign activity was of limited use in securing actual commitments to change mining practices or consent to a process in which new standards would be set by a broad range of stakeholders. It took the threat of an attack advertisement to get corporate commitments, with the exception of Tiffany & Co. and Helzberg Diamonds. But the early activity presented the campaign to jewelers, and even some in the mining sector, as a serious attempt to seek solutions. It was harder for companies to write off the campaign.

The No Dirty Gold campaign has continued, focusing on annual events, like Mother's Day and Christmas, when purchases of gold jewelry peak. A second thrust, which drew the attention of graduating college students to the social and environmental implications of gold class rings, was launched later that year, with postcard-size flyers distributed on campuses (see Figure 8.2). Another important constituency read of the campaign in the September 2004 issue of *Southern Bride* magazine, which included an article, with a strong graphic from the No Dirty Gold campaign, that explained how the No Dirty Gold campaign was offering a "way for brides to make a difference in the lives of other women around the globe." It suggested socially conscious brides use vintage jewelry, a noble form of recycling that does no new damage, until it was possible to buy gold "that comes from a mine that doesn't endanger the environment, respects workers' rights, and minimizes dangerous health risks for miners."[15]

At about the same time, Earthworks CEO Stephen D'Esposito and Michael Kowalski of Tiffany quietly began to organize meetings with senior management of the leading gold mining companies. In those meetings they argued the need for stronger steps to counteract the negative reputation of the gold mining industry and presented the ways in which "some kind of" certification system might give them a reputational risk-management tool that could meet their own needs as well as those of their clients in the jewelry and electronics industries.[16]

During these discussions, D'Esposito and Kowalski emphasized the motivations and interests of their respective organizations and sectors. D'Esposito stressed the need for high standards and an independent certification system as value added for Earthworks and many NGOs. Kowalski underlined the need for a system that was credible and independent and could withstand scrutiny. Kowalski also indicated that Tiffany would be willing to pay a premium price for gold and silver certified to a set of standards, and he invited the mining companies to participate in the development of those standards.

It was interesting to find that, during these and other discussions taking place at this time, a number of the mining companies maintained a fairly non-defensive position. They were not averse to working with NGOs, jewelry retailers, and representatives from other sectors to develop standards and certification. In fact, some companies saw this as a system that could potentially provide some

Figure 8.2. No Dirty Gold class rings ad. Credit: NoDirtyGold.org, with permission.

form of public validation for steps they were already taking, particularly at new operations.

Council for Responsible Jewellery Practices

The 2005 No Dirty Gold campaign began, again, in February, just before Valentine's Day. Campaigners welcomed a new partner, "Ms. Goldzilla," a 10-foot-tall macabre puppet representing a crazed gold-hungry shopper, who chatted with passersby in Washington and New York while volunteers distributed thousands more postcards urging "Don't Tarnish Your Love with Dirty Gold." Reinforcing the effort was a small report that estimated the gold sold each year at Valentine's Day created 34 million tons of waste. Concerned consumers were again encouraged to sign the No Dirty Gold online pledge.

A number of leading companies and associations in the jewelry and mining sector responded to the campaign with the May 2005 creation of a new industry-led program and organization, the Council for Responsible Jewellery Practices (CRJP). (Although some observers argue that industry members had been planning this response before the 2005 No Dirty Gold campaign, it is clear the campaign was a catalyst for the new organization.) The objective of the CRJP was "to promote responsible ethical, social and environmental practices throughout the diamond and gold jewellery supply chain, from mine to retail." [17] CRJP quickly defined a set of principles on business ethics, social performance, and environmental performance and produced a 16-page code of practices. Since any company that was a member of CRJP was required to comply with those principles, the organization was following the model of other second-party, industry-led assurance schemes.

No social or environmental NGO participated in the development or governance of the CRJP, nor in the development of the code of practice. NGOs were simply asked to provide comments on documents drafted by CRJP. As a result, the new organization suffered from the same fundamental lack of credibility as other industry-led attempts to take control of reputational risk management. A further blow to credibility was the fact that an implementation mechanism would not be developed until 2006. (As of early 2007, it was still a work in progress.)

NGOs were also concerned that there was no threshold or basis for entry into CRJP. Members were not required to demonstrate any commitment to standards or best practices. The only requirements for membership were that a company was active in the jewelry industry, was willing to pay a fee, and had expressed a commitment to some relatively vague language regarding social, environmental, and ethical performance. Within a relatively short time, CRJP had a membership of jewelry retailers, jewelry traders, and mining companies with mixed public reputations. Once this diverse cast of characters was in the room together, they tried to establish a basis for participation.

One possible explanation for these problematic origins may have been that CRJP emerged from a small, informal working group of diamond mining, trading, and retailing companies that had been working together on issues related to conflict diamonds. As a behind-the-scenes working group of self-proclaimed "early adopters" of new standards for diamond sourcing, there was little risk in their association. But once this group morphed publicly into CRJP, with both retailers and mining companies (including some with very controversial mines) in the process, the risks of association were considerably increased. As one NGO executive, meeting with CRJP leadership, asked, "How will you respond to reporters from the *Financial Times* when company X, now a member of CRJP, has a major mining accident? Aren't your reputations now joined at the hip?"[18]

Before, during, and after CRJP's founding, NGOs hammered away at the lack of an entry threshold for CRJP and the lack of any real NGO role. As of this writing, and as a result of dialog between campaign leaders and CRJP, an operating truce is in place. CRJP is participating in a new initiative (IRMA — discussed later in this chapter) to create a certification system, with all key sectors fully involved. This has been viewed as a positive step by many NGOs.

The Golden Rules

The No Dirty Gold campaign began to escalate in fall 2005, with a full-page ad in the trade magazine *National Jeweler* that showed two wedding rings and the caption "Love. Romance. Commitment. Destruction. We need to clean up the gold mining industry before it tarnishes the jewelry business" (see page 180). The ad called on jewelers to sign a statement of principles on responsible sourcing, which included a commitment to the creation of an independent, third-party, verification system. This set of principles, which campaigners were calling "The Golden Rules," was quite a bit shorter than the CRJP code, but it included specific details, such as a ban on dumping mine waste in rivers and oceans, free prior and informed consent to mine development by local communities, no forced displacement of communities, and full financial guarantees by mining companies to cover the costs of cleanup and mine closure.[19] Tiffany & Co. and Helzberg Diamonds were among the first to sign.

By late 2005, some 60,000 people had signed the No Dirty Gold pledge, and campaigners began to involve these supporters, contacting them through their e-mail addresses and requesting that they call or write to jewelry companies that had not agreed to the campaign principles. The supporters were to ask the companies why they weren't willing to commit publicly. The campaigners told the companies that an ad published in early 2006 would identify "leading" and "lagging" companies in the effort to clean up gold mining. "Leading" companies would be those that had signed the No Dirty Gold statement of principles and intentions. More companies agreed to the campaign principles to avoid being named a "laggard." In addition, Earthworks and Jewelers of America led a behind-the-scenes effort to organize an in-person discussion with key NGO and jewelry sector leaders to talk through the issues raised by the "golden rules" commitment.

In October and December 2005, the *New York Times* published a series of feature articles on gold mining around the world and in Nevada. The first, on

Love.

Romance.

Commitment.

Destruction.

**We need to clean up the gold mining industry before
it tarnishes the jewelry business.**

Cyanide, contaminated water, and displaced communities probably aren't what you want your customers thinking about when they consider buying gold jewelry. But that's becoming more and more likely as media coverage and public awareness of the mining industry's irresponsible practices grow. As a jewelry retailer, you know better than anyone how important it is to maintain consumer confidence in gold. What can you do to preserve gold's glowing reputation? Visit www.NoDirtyGold.org/retailers and urge the mining industry to make real reforms that respect local communities and the environment. You'll be protecting a very important relationship: the one between you and your customers.

www.NoDirtyGold.org/retailers **dirty** gold

October 24, was a powerful 5,000-word piece, "Behind Gold's Glitter: Torn Lands and Pointed Questions," that was especially critical of Newmont Mining Company, then the world's largest producer of gold.[20] It also called attention to the problem of cyanide leaching, the environmentally dangerous technique used by most gold mining companies to separate gold from waste material. The report cited one of the worst gold mine disasters in history, in Romania in 2000, when mine waste "spilled into a tributary of the Danube River, killing more than a thousand tons of fish and creating a plume of cyanide that reached 1,600 miles to the Black Sea."

The second article, "Tangled Strands in Fight over Peru Gold Mine," appeared just one day later and focused on issues of corruption and pollution at Newmont's Yanacocha gold mine in Peru, the second largest in the world.[21] That same night, PBS, the main public television network in the US, aired a stinging critique of Newmont's problems in Peru on its popular *Frontline* program. *The Curse of Inca Gold* featured Father Marco Arana of GRUFIDES, a No Dirty Gold campaign partner based in northern Peru.

A third *New York Times* article in December, entitled "A Drier and Tainted Nevada May Be Legacy of Gold Rush," focused on Barrick Gold and the fact that it was pumping out, and wasting, 10 million gallons of water a day from the aquifer that surrounds one of its mines in Nevada, a state that suffers from an acute water shortage.[22] No Dirty Gold campaign staff could not have elicited better support if they had written the articles themselves.

To make matters worse — or better, depending on your perspective — a small group of mining industry lobbyists tried to ram pro-mining legislation through the US Congress in late 2005. The provision could have led to millions of acres of publicly held lands in the western United States being sold off to mining companies and other corporate interests. It couldn't have come at a worse time for the mining industry, or at a better time for key NGOs participating in the No Dirty Gold campaign. Earthworks sent a message to jewelry sector leaders, alerting them to the fact that if this proposal became law, they were likely to see growing numbers of protestors at jewelry stores, particularly if lands near national parks, wilderness areas, and iconic landmarks were at risk. In response, Jewelers of America let congressional leaders know that it opposed the provision.

This unprecedented step was a clear sign that things had changed, that jewelers were beginning to take public responsibility for mining policy, that the retail jewelry industry and the mining advocacy NGOs could find common cause, and that the campaign was beginning to have benefits beyond what organizers had anticipated.

In February 2006 the ad on "leaders" and "laggards" appeared in the *New York Times* (see page 182). Tapping the emotions of Valentine's Day once again, it offered another compelling image: a locket on a chain, open to show a sign "Danger, Cyanide." The caption read:

There's nothing romantic about a toxic gold mine.
Leading jewelers agree: It's time to clean up gold mining.

The leaders listed were Tiffany & Co., Helzberg Diamonds, Signet Group (with 1,875 stores, including Kay's Jewelers), Fortunoff, Cartier, Piaget, Van Cleef & Arpels, and Zale Corp. The laggards list included Rolex, Wal-Mart, JCPenney, Sears/Kmart and four others. The 2006 campaign again featured a big drive on college campuses to get students to focus on the ethical problems behind their gold class rings.

There's nothing romantic about a toxic gold mine.

Leading jewelers agree: it's time to clean up gold mining.

It doesn't make for a pretty story, but the truth is that irresponsible mining practices are tarnishing your gold jewelry. Gold mining is one of the dirtiest industries in the world — it contaminates drinking water, destroys traditional ways of life, and uproots people from their homes. Producing gold for one wedding ring alone generates on average 20 tons of toxic waste. Not very romantic, is it? But there is a brighter side. Leading jewelry retailers are now urging the gold mining industry to make real reforms that respect human rights and the environment. Ask your favorite jeweler what they're doing to support responsible gold mining. If they haven't added their name to the growing list of leading retailers, you can take your business elsewhere. Because when it comes to your gold jewelry, you want nothing but the beauty to shine through. www.NoDirtyGold.org

Retailers who are leading the way:	
✦ Tiffany & Co.	✦ Cartier
✦ Helzberg Diamonds	✦ Piaget
	✦ Van Cleef
✦ Signet Group	& Arpels
✦ Fortunoff	✦ Zale Corp.

Retailers who are lagging behind:	
✦ Rolex	✦ Sears/KMart
✦ Wal-Mart	✦ Jostens
✦ Fred Meyer Jewelers	✦ QVC
	✦ Whitehall
✦ JCPenney	Jewellers Inc.

Oxfam America

EARTHWORKS

Forging the "No Dirty Gold" Campaign
Payal Sampat of Earthworks

It is hard to imagine a more appropriate person than Payal Sampat to lead the No Dirty Gold campaign to its quick and significant success. Payal was born in India, the largest gold-buying and gold-consuming country in the world. She inherited, at birth, heirloom gold jewelry handed down from her grandmother and great-grand-mother. That inheritance has given her a profound understanding of the symbolic cultural and historical meanings that gold can have, far beyond the awareness of contemporary critics who see it as a luxury and a trifle.[30]

Payal studied English literature at St. Xavier's College of Bombay University and later campaigned with the Bombay Environmental Action Group. Although some members of her extended family argued that it was "outlandish" for an Indian woman to undertake that environmental work, a postgraduate scholarship to Tufts University for a master's degree in environmental policy brought her to the United States and set her on the course that eventually took her to the No Dirty Gold campaign.

When she finished her studies at Tufts, she went to work for the Worldwatch Institute, Lester Brown's organization, which was staffed, in her words, by some of the most brilliant people in each and every field of environmental sustainability. Her work with them, as a writer and researcher focused on water and mining issues, provided a "fantastic training ground," she argues, for the campaign she would later lead. Hired by Earthworks in 2002, when it was still known as Mineral Policy Center, Payal took the job of international campaigns director at a time when the form of the markets campaign was still unclear. It began to take shape after the June 2003 workshop at the Ford Foundation that first put gold and silver consumers and retailers together with NGOs to discuss how responsible mining practices might be brought to the fore.

Payal maintains that the design of the campaign also benefited from the experiences of market campaigns around forestry, sweatshops, fair trade, and other sectors, which, by then, had been in place for ten years and more. "We could meet with other campaigners, discuss our specific challenges, and then 'cherry pick' from their experiences in our evolving campaign," she explains. "And," she adds, "it also helped to be married to a labor rights campaigner who led international anti-sweatshop campaigns for UNITE [the apparel workers' union]."

Payal's mother, a communications specialist in Bombay, returned to the university to complete a PhD in her late 40s. Her mother may have contributed, through family learning, to the very powerful messaging and imaging that have been the core of the No Dirty Gold campaign. Although some pro bono assistance has come from branding consultants, the basic messaging and imagery were developed by campaign staff and then executed with the assistance of Resource Media and Big Think.

Payal's father, an engineer, would certainly appreciate Payal's command of the technical details of the social and environmental damage associated with gold mining. Drawing from the *Dirty Metals* report, which she helped write, she speaks eloquently and passionately of the damage done to watersheds by riverine tailings disposal and acidic mine drainage, to air quality by sulfur dioxide emissions from smelters, and to communities by violence against mine activists and protesters.

One of the more challenging aspects of Payal's work has been to ensure that Earthworks' efforts to engage with companies and seek their collaboration in the creation of new voluntary standards will lead to real and meaningful improvements on the ground, benefiting the communities and ecosystems affected by mining. In most other campaigns, the market advocacy to transform company practices is led by campaign organizations dedicated to that task. Those who create standards and set up certification systems normally belong to different organizations. However, both sides of the mining campaign were headquartered at Earthworks, with the assistance of many partners, most notably Oxfam America.

Payal's inherited gold jewelry will now be passed to her daughter, Leela Sampat Hensler, born in 2006. By the time Leela reaches the age when she can begin her own environmental campaigning, we can be confident that Payal will not find her interest "outlandish"! Even then, the campaign that Payal and her colleagues organized under the name "No Dirty Gold" is likely to be recorded as one of the more brilliant and effective of this period.

Framework for Responsible Mining and the Initiative for Responsible Mining Assurance

There was also progress taking place on the other side of Earthworks' efforts: the creation of social and environmental mining standards developed by a full range of stakeholders. In October 2005, an expert group brought together by Earthworks and Tiffany & Co., and led by the Center for Science in Public Participation (CSP[2]), released *Framework for Responsible Mining*, a review of the full range of critical issues in the mining and minerals sector.[23] The framework is especially useful because it provides a series of "leading edge" practices that could generate significant environmental and social improvements if they were implemented. The report was designed as a background guide for a stakeholder process, not as a substitute for that process. It addresses four overarching questions at length:

- Is mining an appropriate land use in specific cases?
- How can we ensure environmentally responsible mining?
- How can we ensure that mining results in benefits to workers and affected communities?
- How can we ensure good governance on both corporate and governmental levels?

The Mining Certification Evaluation Project (MCEP), a similar effort to develop standards and an approach to certification in Australia, was launched by WWF

Australia, Oxfam Australia, and a small group of mining companies, including BHP-Billiton, Placer Dome, and Rio Tinto. MCEP was not seeking to develop a full-blown certification system itself; instead, it was testing approaches to certification at active mines in an attempt to evaluate how a system might work at specific mine sites. The outcome of this process was a lessons-learned paper.[24]

As for the mining industry itself, the International Council for Mining and Metals (ICMM) and the Mining Association of Canada (MAC) were beginning to develop company-specific tools for their members. While these are inherently first- or second-party tools, some of them may prove to be useful if incorporated into a third-party system. ICMM was working on a set of sustainability principles and a system to report on the implementation of these principles. MAC has been trying to complete second-party audits of compliance with association-developed standards on key issues like emergency response and information disclosure.[25]

During this period, Earthworks, BHP-Billiton, Placer Dome, WWF, CRJP, ICMM, and CSP[2] organized a series of three meetings among stakeholders to start a cross-sector dialog that might eventually lead to agreement on a system of standards and third-party verification. The meetings, which took place in September and December 2005 and June 2006, came to be called the Vancouver Dialogue because the first and third meetings took place in Vancouver.[26] Participants were not required to commit themselves to any standards or any outcomes from the meetings, but they did seek to reach agreements that would catalyze the next steps among a broader multi-sector group. They also built common understandings of alternative tools; selected a few key issues to discuss in greater depth; shared the experiences already accumulated in similar processes that had had less NGO participation (such as the attempt by the International Council on Mining and Minerals to develop an "assurance system"); and sought common agreement on basic definitions and goals. For example, participants developed the following preliminary definition of the differences between "assurance," "verification," and "certification":

- Assurance was defined as an outcome that enables all stakeholders to be confident that what a company/organization/operation says it is doing is what it is actually doing.
- Verification was defined as a system that confirms that a company/organization/operation's actual performance matches its stated performance and is critical to achieving assurance.
- Certification was defined as documentation that identifies that a company/organization/operation meets certain agreed standards or criteria.[27]

The third meeting of the Vancouver Dialogue involved a larger group and saw a series of breakthrough discussions and decisions.[28] Participants formally created and launched the Initiative for Responsible Mining Assurance (IRMA). Although IRMA comes from a process focused on gold mining, representatives of the copper and nickel trade associations were actively engaged in the meeting, and all agreed the new initiative would develop a system applicable to all types of metals mining. As stated on the organization's website:

> IRMA seeks to create an independent, third party assurance system to ensure that mines operate in an environmentally and socially responsible manner. IRMA seeks to develop a system with input and support from all key sectors. The following principles would underpin this system:
> - Independent verification;
> - Fair and equitable distribution of benefits to communities (including Tribes/First Nations and indigenous peoples) while respecting and protecting their rights;
> - Effective responsiveness to potentially negative impacts to the environment, health, safety, and culture; and,
> - Enhancement of shareholder value.

With a coordinating committee composed of representatives from the mining and jewelry industries, from NGOs focused on mining and community organizations, and from the main mining union, IRMA began to work on draft standards, a verification system, and initial pilot testing of the standards, with an ambitious deadline of June 2007.

REFLECTIONS

The experiences in the mining sector present several encouraging dimensions for the "certification revolution." First and foremost is the fact that it was a major company exposed to brand risk that initiated the search for a certification system that would validate what it was attempting to do on a company basis. The role of Tiffany & Co. has been critical here.

The No Dirty Gold campaign, which has moved the mining industry by moving the jewelry industry, was accomplished at relatively low cost. The principal players' total expenditures on the campaign were effectively under US$1 million over the first two years.[29] There were other expenses in developing Earthworks' *Framework* document, and there will be considerable expenditure as IRMA develops a full set of standards and designs a new verification and certification organization. But the global economics of transforming a major industry look much better in light of the effects of the No Dirty Gold campaign.

CRJP's decision to participate in the IRMA process is probably evidence, in part, that its industry-led second-party assurances were not enough to protect its members from the challenges to their brands and to their core business that were created by the campaign. On the other hand, the IRMA process will, itself, be much stronger because of CRJP participation.

There is no guarantee that IRMA will be completely successful. However, it offers further evidence of how the certification revolution may transform even large, entrenched, and resistant industries when civil society pressure combines with stakeholder-based standard setting.

9

Can Certification Systems
Reduce Global Poverty?

As we have been seeing, certification systems are relatively new tools that have evolved globally to encourage and reward higher levels of social and environmental accountability among producers of all sorts. To date they have been most effective in altering the performance of otherwise unreachable transnational corporations in industries with natural-resource-based production, such as forestry, agriculture, fishing, mining, and tourism. In this chapter we explore the question of whether these systems, which have not generally been designed explicitly to alleviate poverty, can, in fact, help poor people, either individually or in community-based and small-to-medium production units.[1] The broader question is whether these systems, developed largely in the global North, have become — or could become — important tools for alleviating poverty in diverse international contexts.

We will take another look at both certified Fair Trade agricultural products and certification of well-managed forestry by the Forest Stewardship Council to analyze their impact on the poor and their ability to contribute, directly and indirectly, to the alleviation of poverty through an asset-based approach called "building natural assets." We will also look at the emerging certification systems in tourism and mining, but to a lesser extent. Standards have not yet been codified in these industries, though there has been considerable movement toward that end in both cases.

BUILDING ASSETS AND ALLEVIATING POVERTY

The notion that one can alleviate poverty by building the assets of the poor, which may seem obvious, is actually a relatively recent phenomenon. From the early 1960s up to the present, most programs designed to alleviate poverty saw it in a deficit context: the poor have too little income to meet their basic living needs, too few skills to earn that income, or too little motivation (given the social and economic conditions in which they live) to rise out of poverty. The policy implications of that deficit-based theory of poverty seemed simple: give the poor temporary sources of income, allowing them to raise their levels of consumption somewhat, until they can "get back on their feet" and then work their way out of poverty. The ugly fact that this method never seemed to work didn't deter governments from spending billions of dollars on these income-based programs in developed and developing countries around the world in an attempt to alleviate poverty.

In the early 1990s, however, a different perspective on poverty emerged. It also seemed tautological on its face: the poor were those who didn't have access to the assets from which they could derive a decent living. Articulated most clearly by sociologists and economists in the United States and the United Kingdom, the asset-based theory of poverty alleviation grew relatively rapidly as a basis for a very different kind of program.

The theory was first conceptualized around the financial assets of the poor.[2] In this context, an asset is a valuable stock that can be conserved, expanded, or improved and drawn upon as needed. Personal financial savings are the most logical and simple example. Many assets can also be transferred from one generation to the next. But in all societies, control and ownership of assets are unevenly distributed.[3]

The fact that the poor have much lower levels of financial assets or have physical assets, in the form of homes, tools, or vehicles, with considerably less financial value goes farther to explain their low levels of income than almost any other factor. Programs designed to increase the assets of the poor — whether the micro-lending programs that received the Nobel Prize for Peace in 2006 or the increasingly popular "individual development accounts," in which government agencies provide incentives for poor people to save — have been shown to have significant, positive, long-term impacts for helping individuals and families move from abject poverty to higher, more sustainable standards of living.[4]

The concept of poverty linked to "natural assets" was developed most clearly in the early years of the 21st century.[5] Natural assets include not only forests, farmland, and fields, but also environmental assets, such as the biodiversity-conserving and watershed-improving capabilities of a standing forest; the ability of rivers, oceans, and the atmosphere to dilute and carry away pollution; and the agro-biodiversity of farming that preserves old strains of crops. The theory of poverty alleviation through building natural assets asserts that there is no conflict between poverty alleviation and environmental protection. In fact, it argues that both goals can be advanced best when dealt with in a way that links sustainability with poverty alleviation. From this perspective, environmental degradation is a major cause of poverty throughout the world, rather than primarily a result of poverty. In the words of James Boyce, one of the pioneers in this field, "Strategies for building natural assets in the hands of low-income individuals and communities can simultaneously advance the goals of poverty reduction, environmental protection, and environmental justice."[6]

Experts working in this field find that there are four main routes to increasing the amount and value of natural assets in the hands of the poor.[7] They are:
- Investment in, or improvement of, the natural resources to which the poor already have access (this investment could mean helping farmers become more productive in the use of the small plots of land they have by teaching them about organic production techniques or intensive gardening).

- Redistribution of natural resources from others to the poor (agrarian reform, in which underused farm resources are transferred to those who could produce much more on them in sustainable fashion, is a classic example).
- Internalization of the benefits (and avoidance of external costs) associated with the natural resources that affect the poor (providing payments for watershed-improving and biodiversity-conserving sustainable forest management by the poor serves both goals).
- Appropriation of rights of access for the poor to open-access resources. Some of the best examples of this form of poverty alleviation would come from proposals like the "Sky Trust" of Peter Barnes, in which firms are charged for the pollution they emit into the air; they pay for the emission-dilution capacity of the atmosphere, which belongs to all, and the funds recovered are distributed equitably to all citizens.[8]

These experts recognize that building natural assets may require, or may contribute to, building social or community assets. This includes establishing the community organizations that bring benefits of strengthened "social capital" to the poor. These go far beyond the solely economic benefits of turning natural resources into natural assets in the hands of the poor.

From a strictly economic perspective, certification systems could possibly internalize (and, hopefully, monetize) the economic benefits associated with more sustainable production techniques (such as the biodiversity-conserving benefits of improved forest management) and avoid the negative economic consequences of unsustainable production (such as the water-polluting consequences when stream beds and shorelines are inadequately protected).[9] There is a rapidly growing body of formal and informal analysis of certification systems that allows us to assess their impacts and implications for producers and consumers in greater detail than was possible even a couple years ago. This literature suggests that building natural assets may require, and is often facilitated by, social and political processes well beyond those captured by the strictly economic analyses.[10]

As we've noted before, from a governance perspective, certification systems may be seen as attempts to create non-state market-driven systems to govern the use of natural resources.[11] And from a sociological perspective, certification systems create new commodity networks that transform the producer-consumer chain in ways that build on progressive ideas and practices related to trust, equality, and global responsibility.[12] But in neither case is there a clear indication that the poor reap the benefits of certification, especially in terms of access to, and control of, natural assets.

I believe that as we evaluate the impact of certification systems, we must consider two levels of analysis. We can ask, first, broad framework questions at the macroeconomic and macro-social level, such as:

- **Context.** Does the system alter the implicit or explicit regulatory context within which natural resource management decisions are being made?
- **Internalization.** Does it alter the ability of natural asset managers to internalize external benefits and costs?

- **Market access.** Does it change the access that producers have to markets that value that internalization?

But it is important, as well, to ask the "narrow" framework questions that focus on issues directly linked to impoverished and disempowered people and communities:

- **Minimal entry level.** Does the certification system specifically privilege or provide benefits for small-scale, community-based, or otherwise disempowered producers?
- **Minimal impact level.** Are the changes in context designed to improve the ability of impoverished or disempowered people and communities to develop sustainable livelihoods?
- **Scalability.** Can the impacts be scaled up so that large numbers of small-scale producers are capable of benefiting?
- **Costs.** Are the actual (or likely) costs of participation reasonable for small-scale and impoverished producers?

In the following sections we will re-examine several of the certification systems we studied in earlier chapters in order to assess their potential poverty-alleviating abilities, keeping in mind both the broad framework questions and the narrow ones as a basis for the evaluation. Not surprisingly, we will see rather different impacts, as well as the possibility for significant positive impacts that depend on how the systems evolve.

Experiences in Certified Forestry

In the first 12 years of its activities, as we saw in Chapter 4, the Forest Stewardship Council (FSC) has had success that many observers consider remarkable — even startling. By mid-2006, the FSC had certified the forest management of more than 200 million acres (82.6 million hectares), roughly 10 percent of the world's working forests. The rate of growth in certified acres remains higher than 40 percent per year. More than 5,000 wood-processing firms had established chain-of-custody certification under the FSC, assuring consumers that products reaching the market with an FSC label can be traced back to FSC-certified forests. FSC initiatives and standard-setting exercises were underway in more than 70 countries. And there were more than 20,000 forest products in global markets that carried FSC labels.[13]

Does FSC certification bring extra economic benefits to certified forest owners and to producers of products from the lumber and paper from those forests? And are these benefits available to small-scale forest land owners, community forests, or indigenous forests? Ample anecdotal evidence suggests that, in 2006, the demand for FSC-certified timber for dimension lumber and paper products was still considerably greater than the supply. Economic theory suggests that a price premium would arise, and there was, again, anecdotal evidence that significant price premiums were being paid, especially to those suppliers who could provide large quantities to major buyers.

It is extremely difficult, however, to gather systematic data on price premiums for the simple reason that it is not in the interest of either the supplier or the purchaser to admit that price premiums are being paid. The mills and manufacturers who buy FSC-certified timber are constantly seeking to obtain the lowest possible price; they won't publicly offer to pay a price premium. Sellers of certified timber prefer not to publicize the availability of a premium because they don't want to see the premium disappear as more sellers enter the market. However, off-the-record discussions with both sides indicate that the economic benefits come in the form of greater assurance of access to markets and, in a large number of cases, actual higher cash prices that are being paid quietly and consistently.

FSC's influence on sustainable forest management, and its potential impact on poverty alleviation, has not simply been through its own standards development and certification system. The success of the FSC has forced non-FSC companies to create copycat systems that compete with the FSC for the minds and hearts of consumers, financiers, stockholders, and insurers. These systems continue to evolve, rapidly, in the direction of more sustainable management of forests. So any evaluation of the FSC's impact must include the fact that those firms that have resisted FSC standards have been forced, instead, to create alternative "standards," which represent, in most cases, significant improvements in their own environmental management of forests, even when they don't reach the "gold standard" established by the FSC. Two examples of these alternative systems are the Sustainable Forestry Initiative of the American Forest and Paper Association[14] and the Programme for the Endorsement of Forest Certification (formerly the Pan-European Forest Certification system).[15] Does this general "raising of the bar" for forest management practices bode well for poorer forest landowners?

There are two critical poverty-related questions we can ask the FSC in 2006, 13 years after its founding and 10 years since it provided its first formal certificates.

- To what extent has the distribution of FSC-certified hectares been concentrated primarily in the FSC North countries, where forest management practices may have already been significantly higher than global averages? On the face of it, to the extent that a concentration in the North appears, there is less likelihood of major poverty alleviation impacts, though one wouldn't want to overlook the possibility of poverty alleviation *within* countries of the FSC North.
- To what extent has the distribution of FSC certificates, either for forest management or for chain-of-custody, been concentrated in the FSC North? If the number of certificates, independent of average size, is concentrated in the North, there is, again, less evidence of poverty-alleviation potential.

Figure 9.1. Global distribution of FSC certified forests in 2000 and 2006

	December 2000		November 2006	
Millions of hectares certified				
FSC North	18.333	75.0%	41.183	49.9%
FSC South	6.110	25.0%	41.385	50.1%
of which tropical forests	n.d.	n.d.	10.613	25.6%
Total	24.443		82.569	
Number of certificates:				
Forest Management				
# of countries with certificates	37		74	
# of certificates in FSC North	190	66.9%	428	49.8%
# of certificates in FSC South	94	33.1%	432	50.2%
of which tropical forests	n.d.	n.d.	205	23.8%
Total forest management	284		860	
Chain-of Custody				
# of countries with certificates	49		73	
# of certificates in FSC North	815	71.6%	3624	70.0%
# of certificates in FSC South	323	28.4%	1554	30.0%
Total chain-of-custody	1138		5178	

Source: Author's elaboration of data from the FSC International Center.

Figure 9.1 illustrates the answers to some of these questions. One of the broadest critiques of the FSC is that its greatest successes to date have occurred *not* in the tropical regions for which the system was initially designed, but rather in the temperate and boreal forests of the global North. Less than 20 percent of the total acreage certified by the FSC through the beginning of 2002 was located in the FSC equivalent of the South.[16]

Early success with certification was heavily concentrated in the FSC North, effectively the more developed OECD countries (other than Mexico). A total of 75 percent of the hectares certified, 67 percent of the forest management certificates issued, and 72 percent of the chain-of-custody certificates were located in the FSC North. By late 2006, however, a major change can be seen. For the FSC, as we noted in Chapter 4, the "FSC South" includes not only all OECD developing countries, but also the countries in transition from the former Soviet Union. By 2006, the FSC South had taken the lead by a small margin in total hectares and total forest management certificates. This is clearly a result of the rapid rates of growth in certification in Brazil, Bolivia, and Russia. And it occurs despite the increased certification of forests in the US and Canada.

Given that the strongest market for FSC-certified products remains the relatively more developed FSC North, and that it is often more efficient to ship logs, rather than finished products, to market and to provide milling close to the final market, it is less surprising to find little change in the distribution of chain-of-custody certificates. It is important to recognize, however, that the quadrupling of total CoC certificates from 2000 to 2006 has taken place in both FSC North and FSC South, with quintupling increases from 323 certificates to 1,554 in the South, not quite matched by rates of growth in the North.

As of 2001, according to Chris van Dam, a leading scholar from the FSC South, only 12 percent of the total number of forest management certificates had been earned by campesino communities or indigenous peoples organizations, and they represented only 3 percent of the total area certified.[17] One observer concluded that, "despite the declared intentions at the start when the FSC was first created, forest certification has ended up benefiting the richer countries, larger firms, and temperate and boreal forests (rather than tropical forests)."[18] The FSC was not able to provide current data on changes in the proportion of certificates held by community-based or indigenous groups, and it is, in fact, a bit difficult to specify.

As of late 2006, 25.6 percent of the area certified in the FSC South consisted of tropical forests (that is 12.9 percent of the total global area certified). Other data suggest that in early 2006, 121 of the total number of certificates (14 percent of the total number of certificates) and 4 percent of the total area certified came from forests held in "communal ownership." These data, however, would not include the 1.6-million-hectare Kayapó tract in Brazil, certified late in the year. That tract alone would raise the proportion to 5 percent of the total.[19]

There are several further arguments to consider in response to the critique that the FSC is not having the same effect in areas with greater poverty as it is in the developed North. First, there is little doubt that the forest management practices in place in Europe and in some parts of the United States, the result of long histories of environmental campaigning and on local and national legislation, made it easier for the forest management firms in those locations to meet FSC standards earlier, and with less effort, than companies in places where the de facto legal requirements were less demanding. It is also true that larger-scale brand-name Northern forest products companies have been the explicit focus of the market campaigns of environmental and social NGOs in the global North, beginning, for example, with companies in Sweden that were extremely sensitive to market campaign pressure and became some of the earliest of the FSC large-scale certificate holders. Both of these factors may have inadvertently shaped the pattern of early success in the forest management certification movement.

Second, a growing body of evidence suggests that low-income forest communities derive considerable benefits from engaging in FSC certification efforts, even if their aspirations for premium prices and greater market access are not fully met. One study documents, for example, that a sample of approximately 50 community forestry enterprises that achieved FSC certification have benefited on several levels:

- Certification has given greater voice to indigenous groups historically left out of forest policy deliberations.
- Many communities have reinvented their businesses, enhanced their products, and established new partnerships through the certification movement.
- FSC standard setting, under international supervision, has raised greater

attention to forest tenure and livelihood rights, conditions of employment, and worker health and safety than had been achievable under prior processes.
- There have been major benefits for communities in industrial concession areas, especially with respect to community relations and worker's rights.
- In some places, as in Bolivia, communities benefit from certification as a substitute for governmental audits and controls over their access to public forestlands.[20]

And third, as we have seen, the pattern of FSC certification has changed significantly between 2000 and 2006. As FSC has grown, the proportion of forests certified in the FSC South has grown disproportionately.

Nonetheless, the challenges for community-level certified forests remain striking.[21] The costs of initial certification assessments and annual auditing are especially high, relative to potential benefits, for communities that are small and/or remote. The costs of changing forest management practices to meet certification guidelines are, in some cases, quite expensive, and they represent investments with uncertain payoff, given the limited price premium realized by community-based or small-scale certified enterprises. As plantation certification continues to expand, the price competitiveness of small-scale and community enterprises may diminish further unless they are able to implement value-added processing of the timber into products of higher value. The story of San Juan Nuevo, in Mexico, is an encouraging example (see Profile 9.1).

Forest management certification alone cannot provide a definitive solution to the issues of tenure reform, violation of indigenous rights, or perverse incentives or subsidies that encourage overharvesting. However, communities have benefited from the rights-strengthening dimensions in the principles and criteria for FSC certification. Studies of community-based forest enterprises in Sweden and Canada show that the strongest benefits from certification are reaped by communities that already have secure title and access, developmental support, and quality natural assets.[25] The communities with the lowest initial levels of social, natural, and physical capital derived the least benefit from certification.

One narrower issue at play here is whether the FSC should focus its collective energy on promoting small-scale and community-based certification. This was a major element of contention during the FSC's early years, when local forest community advocates and community enterprise supporters — especially in places like Mexico, where the FSC was headquartered until 2003 — derided the FSC's decision to focus on expanding total certified acreage, even if that meant giving priority to large-scale certifications of natural forests and plantations. In retrospect, it is relatively easy to assert, but difficult to demonstrate, that the resulting changes in global perceptions of the standards that need to be applied to the management of the world's forests could have been achieved if the FSC had focused primarily on certification for the benefit of small-scale, community-based, or other impoverished natural resource owners. Without a rapid increase in the supply of certified forest products from temperate and boreal forests, it is

Community-based Indigenous Success Under the FSC

The Story of San Juan Nuevo

One of the best success stories for community-owned certified forestry may be found in the town of San Juan Nuevo in the Mexican state of Michoacán.[22]

San Juan Nuevo is a community that rose from the ashes of a volcano, Paracutín, that emerged from a cornfield in 1944 and covered most of the original San Juan and its surroundings with ash and lava. The Purépecha indigenous community has lived in the area for many thousands of years, practicing indigenous land ownership and communal production practices for much of that time.

Although cornfields and avocado plantations abound in the area, the principal source of contemporary income for the community is a community forestry enterprise (CFE) that draws from some 28,000 acres (12,000 hectares) of nearby forested land that San Juan Nuevo was given by the Mexican government to replace the farmlands destroyed by Paracutín. Visitors to the community find an amazing blend of "strong indigenous traditions with an entrepreneurial orientation and a culture that emphasizes higher education for its young people."[23] Essential to the history and success of the CFE is a common property framework under which the forest is considered a common resource that belongs to all members of the community, known among themselves as *comuneros*.

Initially the forest assets were under a logging ban, but the abundance of pine species did yield a lucrative pine-pitch industry in which many members of the village participated. When logging became legal again, in the 1970s, there were stringent requirements for permits to log; but when the San Juan Nuevo *comuneros* began to log in 1976, they were unsuccessful in marketing through a local cooperative and decided to create their own stand-alone community enterprise.

The forest business they began to build grew slowly into a successful, value-adding company that included a drying kiln, a molding and furniture factory, a pallet and crate factory, a chip mill, and a pine-resin distilling plant. In 1999, the San Juan Nuevo community operations were among the first indigenous community facilities certified by the Rainforest Alliance's Smartwood program to FSC standards for both forest management and chain of custody. Since then it has been shipping a growing proportion of its FSC-labeled processed products into markets in the US, often at a healthy price premium.

Certification has meant more than just market access and higher prices for San Juan Nuevo. For the managers of the company, the certification solved a number of community decision-making dilemmas in a manner that has been repeated in common-property forest communities in other states of Mexico, such as Oaxaca and Chiapas. When some *communeros* have pressed for higher rates of logging so that community profits and employment might be increased, the FSC certification process, which dictates the maximum amounts of each major species that can be harvested each year, provides a conflict-resolution process that local residents see as much easier than the "battles" they fought in years past.

San Juan Nuevo has created a virtually full-employment economy with its forest management and forest product industries. Most of the 900 salaried positions in the community enterprises are filled by *comuneros* and their children. In addition to providing income to local households, the profits of the enterprise are used in ways that strengthen communal assets. A large share is invested in the enterprise, to buy new machinery, vehicles, and maintenance. Another share is invested in diversifying projects, such as irrigated peach and avocado orchards, a peach and avocado packing plant, and both ecotourism and deer breeding. These new enterprises, also communally owned, employ the women and children who aren't picked up by the forest products industry. A further share of the profits, which varies from year to year, is invested in computers for schools and road infrastructure within the community.

These enterprises face some major challenges. It has been difficult to increase the number of women employed in the wood product mills. The indigenous practice of rotating community responsibilities has made it difficult, at times, to maintain the quality of the managerial staff drawn from a relatively small community. Wood products entering Mexico under the North American Free Trade Agreement have lowered prices in Mexican markets, but this competition may have been offset by expanded openings in the US markets for FSC-certified products from the community enterprise.

The model of San Juan Nuevo, a blend of indigenous and modern entrepreneurial practices, is being developed by many other CFEs in Mexico. "Little wonder," writes David Bray, one of the many outside experts who have studied this case. "This form of indigenous sustainable capitalism is showing that indigenous peoples such as the Purépecha can compete successfully in national and international markets, preserve modernized forms of ancient practices, and deliver a diverse and productive ecosystem to the next generation of Purépecha and to the world."[24]

unlikely that major retailers would have committed to giving preference to certified forest products.

The broader issue is whether certification alone can offset the full range of market disadvantages faced by small-scale, low-technology community enterprises in a global forest products market increasingly dominated by large-scale or plantation-based timber supply and manufacturing operations. There is ample anecdotal evidence, and some systematic evidence, that certification does alter the context within which community-based forest enterprises operate, and that it can provide access to markets where price premiums are paid. But it is also clear that organizational changes, technology enhancement, skill-level development, and quality-control improvements are necessary in order to take advantage of the certified markets.[26] It would be inappropriate to ask that the certification institutions, such as the FSC, be responsible for all these local improvements. But it may be quite appropriate, and necessary, to expect that national and multilateral development programs that seek to use certification as a tool for poverty alleviation should focus on the full array of factors needed to take advantage of the tool.

A related concern is the suggestion that there does not exist a mechanism for "fair trade" pricing of forest products certified to the highest social and environmental standards, especially when they may come from small and impoverished communities or producers. As one critic noted, certification implies that the producer takes on rigorous commitments to respect international standards that generate external environmental benefits for the rest of the world, but consumers make no commitments to pay for those benefits.[27]

Experiences with Certified Fair Trade

Fair Trade certification, whether of coffee or other products, has been designed from the outset to focus on the small-scale, often poor, producers and poor workers. As we saw in Chapter 5, to receive the Fair Trade Certified seal of approval, coffee roasters must pay a minimum of US$1.26 per pound to producers at the site of production for dry, unroasted coffee beans. That minimum rises to US$1.41 if the beans are also certified organic. For most of the past ten years that price has been well above the commodity "C" price for coffee in New York, at which most coffee is bought and sold. During the period from 2000 to 2004, when prices fell to historic lows, the effective Fair Trade price was double the market commodity price; according to anecdotal evidence from some places in Central America, it was nearly three times the price actually received by farmers from commercial brokers. Comparable minimum price guarantees have been negotiated for cocoa, tea, bananas, sugar, and a number of other fruits.

Certified Fair Trade must meet other conditions as well. Fair Trade certification of producers is open primarily to very small-scale producers organized in democratically managed cooperatives or, in the case of plantations, to those that have well-established worker-management agreements. They must commit to improved environmental management of their farms, with strong price incentives for moving to certified organic production. To qualify for the Certified Fair Trade label, buyers must agree to pay a significant share (up to 60 percent) of the purchase price of the coffee at the moment of purchase, if the farmers request it, rather than holding the products until they are sold and paying only after they have been sold. Buyers are also encouraged to establish longer-term purchasing arrangements with their coffee producers in order to increase the stability of income flows.

An important dimension of Fair Trade certification that made it more attractive to small-scale producers is the fact that the full costs of the registry, assessment, and monitoring were initially born by the system, not by the producers. The 20 national initiatives of Fairtrade Labeling Organizations International (FLO) negotiated a "labeling fee" of US$0.05 to US$0.10 per pound for each pound of coffee that carried the Fair Trade label. There were comparable labeling fees for other products. Worldwide, this generated millions of dollars in annual revenues that cover much of the administrative cost of the system.[28]

Using certified Fair Trade coffee as an example, the benefits to participating producers would appear, at first, to be obvious. Doubling the price for coffee that is placed in Fair Trade markets should generate direct and immediate benefits for the producers, and the available evidence suggests that this is generally true. There is, however, research that suggests Fair Trade processes have a considerably broader set of impacts on the coffee producers who are able to participate in Fair Trade markets. According to a report from the Colorado State University Fair Trade Research Group, case studies that examined the impact of participation in Fair Trade marketing on nine cooperatives (with total membership in excess of 20,000 coffee producers) supported the following conclusions:

- Fair Trade not only raises family incomes of those who participate relative to those who do not; it also generates family benefits from the social development projects organized by the cooperatives with part of the price premium. The benefits included small credit programs for family emergencies, training that has facilitated diversifying sources of income, and marketing assistance to develop alternative sources of income.
- Fair Trade has promoted enhanced family stability through new employment opportunities, increasing employment for additional family members (especially when the coffee is also produced organically, which requires additional family labor), and lessening the tendency of family members to migrate from the coffee-producing regions.
- There is evidence that Fair Trade has promoted community-level benefits, including the strengthening of social networks, improved community health, and diversification of local economic opportunities.
- Fair Trade appears to have strengthened democratic institutions and the empowerment of poor people in the coffee-growing regions where it is most concentrated. Continued certification of producers requires monitoring visits, and some co-ops have been decertified when members complained that internal practices had lost their democratic nature.
- The international recognition brought by Fair Trade seems to give producer organizations increased credibility with government and other external organizations, which can lead to improved access to financial resources for developing processing facilities for the coffee.
- Finally, a commonly reported benefit is an increase in self-esteem among the coffee producers themselves, as well as renewed pride in coffee farming as a sustainable livelihood.[29]

Critics of Fair Trade processes often confuse the older, less-well-specified Fair Trade efforts with those that have relatively clear standards and procedures. But some of their critiques ring true, nonetheless. Certified Fair Trade may be self-limiting in terms of market access because of contradictions in its own internal goals. Certified Fair Trade limits itself, by current rules, mostly to the smallest producers and their cooperatives. Some coffee wholesale buyers and roasters have argued that this does not generate the highest-quality coffee, nor is it likely to provide coverage of a significant share of the total world supply of coffee.

A second criticism is that Fair Trade certification reinforces a reformist approach to globalization by encouraging the consumption of products shipped long distances rather than those that are locally produced.[30] The question is largely trivial in the case of coffee, since there is virtually no coffee produced in the global North, but it illustrates the competing agendas. Reforming the trade process by improving the prices received by a small proportion (at present) of the producers in those markets may give legitimacy to trade that some believe will never be fundamentally more equitable. "Greenwashing" and "fairwashing" the image of major transnational corporations by giving them credibility on the basis of Fair Trade in a very small proportion of their purchases may have a similar effect.

The counterargument is that Fair Trade pricing, and ultimately sustainable-production pricing, may represent the most important example of an approach that could bring greater equity to fundamentally inequitable trading relations. If producer groups worldwide were to build alliances with international NGOs for the negotiation of fair, long-term, sustainable prices, the inequities inherent in the monopsonistic purchasing at both local and international levels might be partially offset. Consumers, financiers, stockholders, and insurers become the ultimate court of financial appeal for the appropriateness of these practices. Whether their motivation is altruistic, business-instrumental, or fear of NGO advocacy, firms can reap tangible economic benefits from fair-trade pricing over the long run, as we have seen throughout this book.

Experiences with Ecotourism Certification

Few industries are more dependent on the natural assets of local economies than tourism. And few industries have attempted to compete on the basis of environmental sensitivity more than the tourism industry, especially the niche component generally called "ecotourism," which we discussed in Chapter 7. Can certification of ecotourism and other tourism under some form of sustainable tourism stewardship council provide tangible benefits to poor or impoverished communities?

There are certainly high hopes that ecotourism will help alleviate poverty. A spokesperson for the Ghana Tourism Board characterized ecotourism as "a panacea for rural poverty."[31] UNESCO is developing cultural and ecotourism projects as part of its Poverty and Human Rights Program.[32] Under Conservation International's Critical Ecosystem Partnership Fund, many millions of World Bank dollars have been invested in projects, including ecotourism support projects, that "illustrate the natural and mutually beneficial links between biodiversity conservation and poverty alleviation."[33] And the 2002 Québec Declaration on Ecotourism recognized that many of the areas that draw ecotourists are "home to peoples often living in poverty who frequently lack adequate health

care, education facilities, communications systems, and other infrastructure required for genuine development opportunity." At the same time, it affirmed (in
classic long-winded "declarationese") that ecotourism, if managed in a sustainable manner, "can represent a valuable economic opportunity for local and indigenous populations and their cultures and for the conservation and sustainable use of nature for future generations and can be a leading source of revenues
for protected areas."[34]

But will certification of ecotourism improve its potential for poverty alleviation? If we return to Martha Honey's now increasingly accepted characterization
of real ecotourism as distinct from "greenwashing," ecotourism involves the following facets:

• It involves travel to natural areas.
• It minimizes impact of the travelers' presence.
• It builds environmental awareness.
• It provides direct financial benefits for conservation.
• It provides financial benefits and empowerment for local communities.
• It respects local culture.
• It is sensitive to the host country's political environment and social climate.
• It supports human rights and international labor agreements.[35]

In narrow terms, only the fifth item in this list suggests potential poverty alleviation; in broader terms of building natural assets, at least four of the eight characteristics increase the likelihood that communities could benefit from ecotourism
in ways that might alleviate poverty.

Whether the effort to certify ecotourism will provide significant benefits for
communities will depend on the nature of the system that evolves and its costs. If
it is analogous to certified Fair Trade, where the principal costs of certification
are financed by labeling fees paid by consumers and borne by the accreditation
agency, there could be significant opportunities. It is not likely that accreditation
alone would counter all the structural obstacles faced by community-based ecotourism operations. But standards that are global, that can easily be indicated on
the websites through which a rapidly increasing portion of all ecotourism is sold,
and that create a context in which major operators have an incentive to involve
local communities in tangible ways, could assist with the development of sustainable livelihoods in those communities based on natural assets.

Certification of Mining Operations

As we saw in Chapter 8, there has been a long history of organizing to discourage
mining companies from the most egregious of their environmentally damaging
practices. In recent years, some of the most effective work has been done by
groups like Earthworks, in Washington, DC, which developed a series of guide-
books for local communities faced with mining problems.[36] The Initiative for
Responsible Mining Assurance (IRMA), described in Chapter 8, holds considerable potential to help alleviate poverty. If, for example, IRMA uses the analysis

and recommendations of the *Framework for Responsible Mining*, developed by Earthworks and others, as a starting point for its standard setting, it will be addressing an extensive list of negative social impacts. The authors of the *Framework* cataloged the following examples of social problems associated with mining:

- Increased poverty "through a degraded environment on which, in many cases, community subsistence depends."
- Loss of land and sustainable livelihoods.
- Increased internal economic inequality.
- Destabilized internal power relations.
- Worsened economic dependency from the boom-and-bust of the mining operation.
- Worsened militarization because of mine security conditions.
- Displacement, forcible eviction, or forced relocation.
- Accelerated in-migration of outsiders with differing socio-cultural values.
- Exposure to new health risks.
- Increases in alcohol and drug use, prostitution, gambling, and other criminal activities.
- Human rights abuses.
- Loss of cultural cohesion and possible loss of sacred places.
- Breaches of core labor standards, use of child labor, forced overtime, etc.[37]

The "leading edge" approaches recommended by the *Framework* are likely to have significant positive impacts on mining processes if IRMA adopts them as part of the standards it is developing. Those recommendations include the following approaches:

- Protect indigenous rights with respect to land and natural resources.
- Require free, prior, and informed consent as a local pre-condition for prospecting, exploration, and opening a mine operation, and at each subsequent phase of mining and post-mining activities.
- Establish continuous processes for consultation on the ongoing activities of a mine, using approaches that are culturally appropriate.
- Provide sufficient resources to enable local communities to evaluate proposed mining activities, including resources for participation and funds for hiring independent experts.
- Require full disclosure of information to local communities, in culturally appropriate forms and locally accepted languages.
- Provide accurate information on employment opportunities, especially for women, indigenous people, and marginal groups.
- Establish binding contracts between mine companies and local communities, enforceable in local courts systems, with mutually acceptable arbitration procedures.
- Establish clear specifications for local benefits and compensation.
- Recognize women's rights and address gender-related risks (this might

require gender impact analyses, gender impact audits, and equal compensation for women-headed households, among other actions).
- Recognize the rights of small-scale or artisanal miners, if present, and address risks to their livelihoods.
- Avoid resettlement if at all possible, but provide detailed advance-impact analysis if voluntary resettlement is required, and do not require legal title as a precondition for resettlement compensation.
- Avoid mining in areas where the use of military forces or excessive security forces is required to maintain operations.

This impressive list of recommendations, each extensively documented in international law and international human rights agreements, provides an excellent basis for avoiding many of the impoverishing dimensions of mining and for allowing local communities to benefit as much as possible. How many of them will ultimately be part of the IRMA standards is not yet clear.

Summary

The potential for existing and emerging certification systems to alleviate poverty, in terms of the macroeconomic (or "macro") and narrow (or "micro") questions listed at the beginning of this chapter, is summarized in Figure 9.2.

The FSC is strong on the "macro" level, largely because it has been negotiated by producers, NGOs, and industry representatives to transform fundamentally the nature of sustainable production and conservation in the industry. It is, however, weak on "micro" dimensions (other than scalability), and its direct poverty-alleviating effects are still to be demonstrated. Certified Fair Trade, on the other hand, was developed explicitly to provide direct market access for small-scale and often impoverished producers; its strongest characteristics range across the micro dimensions that ensure the system alleviates poverty.

Whether new certification systems for sustainable tourism and ecotourism and for the responsible sourcing of minerals develop into strong tools for poverty alleviation will depend on the specific nature of the systems that emerge. In both cases there are grounds to believe they *could* become effective tools for poverty alleviation. It remains to be seen whether the ongoing negotiations will take them in that direction.

RESPONSES TO THE CHALLENGES

A number of organizations have come up with interesting responses to the challenge of designing a certification system that might significantly improve the ability of small-scale and impoverished producers to build their assets. Although these solutions were developed for individual certification systems, they could possibly be applied to others.

Efforts to reduce the costs of certification for small-scale timber operations are advancing rapidly in the US Midwest. The Minneapolis-based Community Forestry Resource Center is experimenting with a form of umbrella certification

Figure 9.2. Criteria for Assuring that Certification Systems Alleviate Poverty

Fundamental Dimensions	Certification System			
	FSC	Fair Trade	Tourism	Mining
MACRO DIMENSIONS				
Context Does the system alter the implicit or explicit regulatory context within which natural resource management decisions are being made?	Strong	Weak	Strong	Strong
Internalization Does it alter the ability of natural asset managers to internalize external benefits and costs?	Strong	Weak	Strong	Weak
Market access Does it change the access that producers have to markets that value that internalization?	Strong	Strong	Not clear yet	Not clear yet
MICRO DIMENSIONS				
Minimal entry Does the certification system specifically privilege or provide benefits for small-scale, community-based, or otherwise disempowered producers?	Weak	Strong	Weak	Weak
Minimal impact Are the changes in context designed to improve the ability of impoverished or disempowered people and communities to develop sustainable livelihoods?	Weak	Strong	Weak	Weak
Scalability Can the impacts be scaled up so that large numbers of small-scale producers are capable of benefiting?	Strong	Strong	Not clear yet	Not clear yet
Costs Are the actual (or likely) costs of participation reasonable for small-scale and impoverished producers?	Weak	Strong	Not clear yet	Not clear yet

that would provide the full range of FSC certification services at a cost as low as US$0.20 per acre per year. The center proposes to offer these services to several thousand landowners simultaneously. The key to the model is its recognition that, for small landowners, logging occurs relatively infrequently. The center's team of consulting foresters provides initial certification assessments based on a sample of the landowners. The foresters will gradually develop forest management plans for all, but they would be monitored simply on the basis of a sample of those landowners who had actually done some logging each year. If successful, this model will respond to key cost concerns of small-scale landowners in both the North and the South.[38]

The Tropical Forest Trust (TFT) has created another model for improving access to certification for communities in the global South. TFT is a not-for-profit organization, based in London, that "sells" its services directly to the forest products industry. Working initially with firms in Southeast Asia that were trying to clean up the supply chains for their tropical timber, TFT contracted to teach existing local suppliers how to ensure that their logging was, first, fully legal; they then worked with the suppliers to move them toward FSC certification. For example, TFT has helped several suppliers for the European furniture manufacturer Scancom become FSC certified.[39] It has been especially successful in navigating the difficult waters in Malaysia, where significant criticism of the FSC has centered on the certification of concession lands where indigenous land claims had not been fully resolved.[40] Recent FSC certifications there, facilitated by TFT, have been the result of innovative schemes that integrate local communities by pursuing certification of nontraditional forest products as well.

The brilliance of the TFT model is that it is almost completely supported by the firms whose supply chains are being improved. TFT has also earned the trust of European and US environmental NGOs, which are willing to accept that the companies purchasing timber from communities working with TFT, but not yet certified under the standards of the FSC, are making good-faith efforts to move their supply toward the FSC's style of well-managed forests. Advocacy campaigns against some of these firms have been halted, pending the results of TFT work on the ground. And TFT has recently developed contracts with US retail forest product firms that wish to improve the sourcing of their imported tropical products, such as luaun plywood, a material widely used for doors and subflooring.

Certified Fair Trade institutions have considered the possibility of monitoring working conditions on coffee estates, using mechanisms analogous to those now in place to monitor tea plantations, mostly in India and Sri Lanka. The expansion of Fair Trade certification is driven, in part, by offers by major coffee roasters to purchase significantly larger quantities of Fair Trade coffee if suppliers improve conditions on farms that are larger than the micro-farms of the co-operatives presently enrolled in the Fair Trade Registry. The same is true in the Fair Trade banana market; there are potential buyers for Fair Trade bananas, but they require a supply that is considerably larger than what current small-scale, cooperatively based producers are able to provide.

The potential changes could offer an opportunity to respond to the criticism that Fair Trade certification limits itself to a niche market by not offering to certify larger coffee producers (who do produce most of what is presently considered the best coffee in the world). The dilemma, however, is a classic one. Given that there is a large oversupply of coffee, of varying quality, from farmers presently certified, would certification of coffee estates mean that the impoverished small-scale coffee farmers who still cannot place their coffee in Fair Trade Certified markets are being abandoned? Would the potential improvement of working conditions for hundreds of thousands of day laborers on coffee estates offset the reduced benefits for some on family-owned micro-farms? Would the overall expansion of the Fair Trade market make the Fair Trade criteria a mainstream, industry-recognized fundamental quality criterion, expanding sales for all producers on the Fair Trade Registry, small as well as large?

REFLECTIONS

Building certification systems to negotiate stakeholder-based social and environmental standards and provide independent third-party certification that those standards have been fulfilled does have the potential to build natural assets for the reduction of poverty and injustice. However, each of the systems reviewed must overcome challenges to its ability to achieve these goals, in part because poverty alleviation was not necessarily among the goals for which they were initially established (with the exception of certified Fair Trade).

Superimposing a poverty-reduction goal and a focus on the poor and disempowered is a relatively heavier burden for the FSC than it is for Fair Trade certified. Whether poverty reduction becomes a focal point for the emerging certification systems in ecotourism and mining will depend on the standards that are set in the next few years. The groups and individuals involved in developing these systems will have to consider not only which functions are critical for the accrediting and certifying organizations, but also which asset-building functions will need additional support programs to help poor communities take advantage of the opportunities provided by certification.

10

Certification Opportunities and Challenges Encountered in Other Arenas: Fisheries, Toxics, and Labor

Over the past few years, I have discussed, at universities and with foundation colleagues, the potential for the combination of certification systems and market campaigns to transform 21st-century industries. The opportunities to build certification systems and create market campaigns that would call attention to problems in products, or in the supply chains for products, that companies would be just as happy to ignore, appear limitless. The following are a few diverse examples of areas where people would like to see this approach tried.

Certified temporary labor suppliers. A system certifying companies that provide temporary help to businesses could focus on equal opportunity selection; training programs for upgrading skills; and healthcare, life insurance, and pension benefits provided. Much of the temporary work industry provides none of these labor benefits, even when their "temps" are people with relatively high levels of technical skills. Given the increasing importance of temporary work in economies around the world, which some call the "informalization" of the labor market in both wealthy and poor countries, the creation of guidelines for temporary labor suppliers could turn these jobs, often critically necessary when businesses have to deal with temporary labor shortages, into "decent work" that provides flexibility for both the worker and the company. One could easily imagine companies in this field attempting to achieve a "price point" for their services that is superior, and thus potentially more profitable, by becoming certified to a set of labor standards for their industry and guaranteeing, in that way, a higher quality of temporary worker for the companies that seek them.

Consumer-certified health insurance companies and health maintenance organizations. An undergraduate student proposed this system as a result of his parents' dismal experiences getting health insurance programs to cover their healthcare costs. Hospitals and clinics have long had to meet certain minimum accreditation standards covering the state of their facilities, the training and experience of their staff, and the nature of their record keeping. But there are no similar standards and guidelines for the management of healthcare insurance and health maintenance organizations (HMOs). A stakeholder-based process involving insurance companies, healthcare facilities, HMOs, consumer groups, and academic healthcare specialists could determine what standards should apply to the following dimensions of the system, among others:

- The time that passes between submission of a health insurance claim and the payment, or other formal response, for that claim.
- The structure and timing of the appeals process when an HMO or insurance provider refuses to cover a particular service.
- The availability of live personal respondents (whether local or off-shore out-sourced) to answer questions about coverage and payment processing.

Such a system could also standardize how companies present comparable information on

- services covered,
- rates of reimbursement,
- exclusions from coverage, and
- healthcare *results* achieved by each company, including statistics that adjust for age, sex, and race or ethnicity on
  - mortality and morbidity,
  - hospitalization rates for major illnesses (where good preventive care reduces the rates), and
  - the frequency *and* success rates of most major surgical and clinical procedures

so that consumers (and businesses) could make easier and more reliable choices between insurance and HMO plans. (I know, I know, it would be difficult to compile, organize, and publish the kind of information that this might require. But remember, Home Depot didn't think it could keep track of the place of origin of every stick of wood it sells, but it now does. And Starbucks claimed, when first approached, that it couldn't trace each bag of coffee back to the family farm or cooperative from which it was sourced, and now it does!)

Truly certified used cars. Many car dealers sell "certified pre-owned" vehicles, but there are widely varying definitions for the term. Sometimes it means the dealer has subjected the car to multi-point testing and is prepared to provide a limited warranty for the vehicle with respect to all those points. Sometimes it seems to mean nothing more than that the car was, in fact, owned by someone previously. But imagine the possibilities for engaging a nonprofit Consumers Union or automobile association and representatives of the used car dealers association of a country (if such an organization existed) to develop a set of specific standards covering many of the factors that make the purchase of a used car both scary and uncertain. For example, certification could verify the following points:

- All local (state or provincial) laws have been observed with respect to proper documentation, accuracy of mileage information, and reports on previous repairs.

- A specific set of tests (such as compression tests on one or more cylinders, searches for oil or coolant leaks, and electrical tests) have been done and the results revealed, transparently, on the papers that accompany the car.
- A strong and uniform warranty is provided to the buyer, guaranteeing a period of cost-protected operation of the car.

Verification could be done on the basis of a required set of records for each car, including original work done on it, name and coordinates of the previous owners, and repair records for that vehicle throughout the warranty period, as well as spot checks on any vehicle carrying the logo in the dealer's lot.

The certification, with trademarked label, could be provided, for a small fee, by the certifying agency. It is reasonable to expect that buyers would pay considerably more for a vehicle that carries such an assurance. One could even imagine the creation of a nationwide repair service for vehicles carrying the certification, with electronic accounting of expenses and chargebacks to the original dealer that provided it.

Market campaign pressure could focus, first, on the major branded automobile dealerships and then move to large dealers in used cars alone. There would be significant marketing advantages to being the first to provide this kind of certification, and if experience proves true, the demand for vehicles certified in this way could consistently differentiate more responsible vendors. Competition in the marketplace among vendors of cars certified this way would gradually reduce the surcharge to something close to the real costs of providing the service, including record keeping, auditing, and verification.

Certified small-loan financial institutions. We reviewed the Equator Principles, which set social and environmental standards for major financial institutions' large-scale project lending, in Chapter 6. But what about the individual consumer who seeks consumer credit? Most countries have a host of government regulations for this sector, but some firms continue to be accused of "predatory lending."

One type of predatory lending occurs when financial institutions make secured loans to people who are clearly incapable of amortizing the loan, either because of the level and irregularity of their income or because of other characteristics of their financial record. Consumer credit companies, whether they are independent or branches of major banks, profit from this business because the security offered (a home, a car, jewelry, or other assets) is worth considerably more than the loan, yet the loan conditions mean borrowers forfeit the entire security if they fail to meet the terms of repayment.

A certification system for fair and affordable credit might include standards covering the following aspects:
- Minimum and transparent terms of creditworthiness based on financial record scores or other third-party measures that would vary with the level of the interest charges on the loan.

- Fair-value stipulation for the security provided by the lender for the loan, including procedures for independent auctioning of the security, and repayment to the borrower of value that exceeds the unpaid balance of the loan.
- Uniform and transparent procedures for calling in the loan, with mediation and other dispute resolution techniques that reflect the state of the art in the industry.

Verification could involve auditing a random sample of loans and loan histories each year, plus a dispute resolution mechanism for those who believe that the terms of the certification have not been met.

Social development organizations and faith-based groups — especially those focused on enhanced justice and poverty alleviation for a community's poorest residents, who are most likely to be affected by predatory lending — could campaign for such a system. The benefits of the system would be the identification of a set of responsible practices for the small-loan industry, the opportunity for responsible businesses to obtain third-party independent verification of their compliance, and the market advantages that should come with that.

Certified Corporate Partners for a "Mayor's Fitness Council." Imagine a city government publicizing the links between fitness, nutrition, and obesity by challenging local companies to become certified partners in the city's campaign to dramatically increase the physical fitness of its citizens. There could be standards for the kind of nutritional food that would be made available to workers at the place of business as well as opportunities for pursuing fitness-related activities. Certified partners would receive public recognition for their commitment to set up educational and informational programs and to provide incentives to workers for participating in them. Fitness breaks of 30 minutes each day would be one form of encouragement. Or employees who complete specified physical fitness programs might be given cash awards or extra days off each year. Verification of compliance could involve annual monitoring of company programs linked to the certification, with occasional interviews with employees to make certain the company is providing the opportunities promised.

The benefits of such a program would go beyond the cost savings from a healthier workforce. They might include brand-enhancing public recognition, increased loyalty from both employees and customers, and recognition of the contributions this makes to community health.

Market campaigning to encourage participation could be undertaken by existing community-based NGOs, churches, and even schools that would identify and praise the companies that choose to participate, while questioning publicly those that do not.

A certification system of this sort already exists, but is not well-known. The Mayor's Fitness Council of Austin, Texas, has set an ambitious citywide goal: "Austin will be the fittest city in America by 2010." One of the programs created to bring about that goal is a Mayor's Fitness Council Partner Certification Program, which is, according to the City of Austin website, "a mutually beneficial alliance between the Mayor's Fitness Council...and organizations in Austin to optimize the health and fitness of our citizens." The Mayor's Fitness Council "will provide tools, expertise, and support," while "certified partners will implement MFC evidence-based certified programs that will help improve the health and fitness of their organizations through better nutrition and increased physical exercise." [1]

Why would these five hypothetical certification programs be voluntary systems rather than regulatory government systems? In some places they might not be needed if government regulations fulfilled most of what a voluntary system could provide. The fact that they seem even minimally needed, and potentially credible, indicates that in many places the regulatory structure has not reached the level of consumer protection or social responsibility that these systems could bring. In many cases, the suggested certification system would tap the ability of companies to improve their performance in ways that produce private benefits for them, on several levels, and public benefits.

In this chapter we will look more closely at three certification systems at different stages of development in order to illustrate how certification is being embraced and implemented in production areas that seem quite different from those we have already considered. In each of these three cases, the evolution has been different, rates of progress have varied, and major challenges remain, but the current status is encouraging.

The first case study focuses on the Marine Stewardship Council (MSC). The MSC was created shortly after, and for many of the same reasons as, the Forest Stewardship Council. Had things gone better for the MSC in its first seven or eight years, it would have warranted a full chapter in this book. But, frankly, when I was first planning this book in early 2004, the MSC appeared to be on the brink of collapse. Had it collapsed, I might have done a thorough forensic analysis of what went wrong. As it happens, the MSC changed leadership and retrenched significantly in early 2004. Its new leadership has brought it roaring back into the middle of the marine conservation fray, offering a renewed hope for transforming the ocean-caught seafood industry at a time when some writers have found the oceans perilously close to becoming "empty" of commercial stocks of fish. [2]

The second case study focuses on a series of attempts to create a certification system for labor standards in the apparel industry, responding to practices at firms like Nike (as noted in Chapter 1). The global apparel industry has been an extremely difficult industry to transform, partly because of its acutely competitive structure, with very small profit margins and fragmented production. Several attempts to move portions of the market toward more responsible labor practices, including the creation of codes of conduct for sewing contractors, have had relatively little success in reducing "sweatshop" conditions. But there has emerged a new and promising effort by the Worker Rights Consortium, a US-based NGO closely affiliated with a student-based organization, United Students

Against Sweatshops, that may transform the way apparel workers are treated, despite the cutthroat competitiveness of the industry.

The third case study highlights the emerging attempt to clean up the toxics associated with the production and recycling of electronic equipment, especially computers. A market campaign has been operating in this arena for nearly ten years, with some positive response from industry leaders. What is new is the emergence of a clearer set of standards. Future campaigns will now be able to push a wider array of companies in the industry toward these standards.

What we will see in each of these examples is how lessons are being learned and shared across campaigns and certification systems, and how companies are also watching the campaigns and developing new ways to anticipate them, offset them, and, in some cases, come to terms with them.

THE MARINE STEWARDSHIP COUNCIL

The Marine Stewardship Council, like the Forest Stewardship Council, began as a project of the World Wildlife Fund. WWF had been calling attention to the rapidly depleting ocean fisheries, and other environmental organizations were increasingly aware of the problem. The UN Food and Agriculture Organization estimated that 75 percent of the world's fisheries are fully exploited, overexploited, or depleted. It seems clear to many that "harmful fishing practices are by far the most important threat to ocean and fishery health."[3]

Formation

In 1996, WWF's Global Endangered Seas Project and Unilever, the world's largest processor of ocean-caught fish, launched a project (which ultimately became the Marine Stewardship Council) that would attempt to identify the conditions needed to reduce overfishing and create a market-driven process toward sustainable fisheries. This was of interest to Unilever, in part, to ensure that it would have sustainable supplies for its own business.[4] But the company had also been under considerable pressure from Greenpeace because of its annual purchase of more than 300,000 metric tons of frozen whitefish at a time when the global scale of fisheries depletion was starting to become clear.[5] In response, Unilever committed in 1996, even before the principles and criteria were established, that it would purchase all its fish from sustainable sources by the end of 2005.

In 1997 the MSC was set up formally and began a two-year consultative process to draft a set of principles for sustainable fishing.[6] The principles ultimately articulated were relatively simple:

1. A fishery must be conducted in a manner that does not lead to over-fishing or depletion of the exploited populations and, for those populations that are depleted, the fishery must be conducted in a manner that demonstrably leads to their recovery.

2. Fishing operations should allow for the maintenance of the structure, productivity, function and diversity of the ecosystem (including habitat and associated dependent and ecologically related species) on which the fishery depends.

3. The fishery is subject to an effective management system that respects local, national and international laws and standards and incorporates institutional and operational frameworks that require use of the resource to be responsible and sustainable.[7]

Figure 10.1. Logo of the Marine Stewardship Council. Credit: By permission of the Marine Stewardship Council.

Implementation of these principles, and their related criteria, proved considerably more difficult in practice.

The MSC became a stand-alone non-profit organization in 1999, and it began to explore and assess fisheries that might be certified. The first fishery certified, in 2000, was the western Australian rock lobster fishery, which was under strict governmental guidelines, including seasonal closures, minimum size requirements, and a ban on catching breeding females. Comprehensive data on the fishery had been kept since the 1960s, and those data enabled fishery scientists to predict catches accurately and to ensure that controls were adequate to keep the fishery operating at sustainable levels.[8] This was one of MSC's early successes, and was a relatively uncontroversial fishery to certify. It was important to Australia, because at that time the country shipped from AUS$300 million to $400 million worth of lobster to markets in Taiwan, Japan, Hong Kong, China, and the US. This was nearly 20 percent of Australia's total fish exports.[9]

In 2001, MSC certified its second fishery, the New Zealand hoki fishery. This was much more controversial. Hoki is New Zealand's most important fish export, and the New Zealand government had strictly controlled the total hoki fishery for many years. Hoki is a whitefish, also known as hake or blue grenadier, which sold primarily to the US and Europe. (One prominent client was McDonald's, as hoki is the fish you are most likely to find in McDonald's Filet-O-Fish sandwich.)[10]

The hoki certification was quickly challenged by the Royal Forest and Bird Protection Society, New Zealand's leading environmental group, because, it alleged, deep-water hoki trawling also caught, and killed, large numbers of seals (initially estimated at more than 5,000 seal deaths per year).[11] The MSC quickly replied, in the press, that there were ten "corrective action requests" included in its certification of the hoki fishery, and one of them included a reduction in the seal bycatch. The managers of the fishery had agreed to that condition, with a clear timetable for accomplishing the reduction.[12] But the challenges to MSC certifications had begun.

Crisis

Some observers believe that the dominance of Unilever in the initial financing of the MSC and in the setting of standards led the MSC to certify fisheries that met Unilever's needs rather than maintaining truly sustainable fisheries goals.[13] In the 1990s, campaigns for more sustainable fishing (with the exception of the early Greenpeace campaign against Unilever) took a broad and general tone. Their message was that the seas were being depleted, commercial fishing needed to be restricted, and more sustainable rates and processes were needed for ocean fishing. There was virtually no company-specific campaigning that might create a significant demand for seafood from certified, well-managed fisheries. As a result, WWF helped create the system for certification, and it then focused on helping Unilever source seafood that was certified. It did not play the role of a market campaign organization.

What is clear is that the MSC, in its early years, did not actively encourage other marine conservation groups, especially those associated with specific fisheries, to participate in its governance or standard setting. And that decision foreshadowed a number of problems that soon arose.

MSC's third certified fishery, Alaskan wild salmon, drew far less criticism. Alaska had assiduously resisted allowing salmon aquaculture in its offshore waters, partly because of the evidence that aquaculture was damaging wild salmon populations.

At this time, fishery certification was increasingly welcomed by the press, especially in Europe, though not immediately by the fishermen. According to Rose Prince of the *Daily Express* in London, England:

> The response from the fishermen was at first hostile — and with good reason. The Marine Stewardship Council was set up by Unilever (whose subsidiary companies Bird's Eye, Walls, and Iglo make fish fingers for the whole of Europe) with environmental campaigners the World Wildlife Fund. Multinational companies and environmentalists are not fishermen's friends by tradition.
>
> "It was originally thought to be an unholy alliance with commercial interests and the fishing industry was not enamoured," says John Goodland, Chief Executive of the Shetland Fisherman's Association. "But now the industry has been convinced that the MSC is independent, both self-managing and self-funding; it is becoming clear that the concept makes sense… Everyone wants to see well managed fisheries and the advantages of the logo and increased sales is not lost on them." [14]

By the end of 2004, the MSC had certified 12 fisheries as sustainable, but the uptake in the market was far less than what was anticipated from the early successes with Australian rock lobster, New Zealand hoki, and Alaskan wild salmon. By Unilever's own admission, eight years after its commitment to sell *only* certified, sustainably harvested, ocean seafood, barely 4 percent of its sales were MSC-certified.[15] According to Rupert Howes, who became executive director of the MSC in early 2005, there were growing difficulties with matching supply and demand; the supplies were not always available when retailers wanted them, and some certifications were for fisheries for which there was no great demand. Unilever's attempt to introduce hoki as a replacement for endangered cod in British markets, for example, failed so badly that it was forced to withdraw all sales of hoki in the UK. British consumers argued that hoki had neither the flavor nor the consistency of their beloved cod, even though there was growing awareness that North Sea cod was in serious danger of being completely fished out.[16]

There was also growing opposition from environmental groups to some of the newly certified fisheries, such as the Alaskan pollock fishery. Pollock is another whitefish, much in demand as a replacement for cod and as a source of surimi. The Alaskan pollock fishery is the largest fishery in the US and the second most abundant in the world, after the Peruvian anchoveta fishery. But environmental groups objected that the pollock fishery took food away from the endangered Steller seal population and that the certification process failed to consider the impact of pirate Russian trawlers, which were common in the area, on the sustainability of the fishery.[17] Objections from local environmental groups were rising, notes Howes. "The problem is that we were attempting to create a common set of global standards for fisheries, rather than a different standard for each fishery; and we continuously ran up against local NGOs who, based on local knowledge, wanted us to set the bar higher."[18]

The MSC's most severe crisis came in early 2004, when two consultancy reports commissioned by its principal funders severely criticized the organization's procedures and practices. One of those reports, commissioned by the Oak Foundation, the Homeland Foundation, and the Pew Charitable Trusts — all major US-based marine conservation funders and important funders of the MSC — found a litany of problems:

- MSC's claim of certifying sustainable fisheries was, in most cases, not justified under its own definition of sustainability.
- MSC's Principle 2, which called for fishing operations to maintain the structure, productivity, and diversity of the marine ecosystem, was "routinely not met."
- MSC's Principle 3, involving compliance with national laws, was not being upheld; fisheries that were not in compliance had been certified.
- Fishery certifiers had "too much flexibility" in determining how the principles and criteria were applied.
- MSC was not viewed as credible by key environmental stakeholders because they felt that MSC's practices failed to include them in a substantive way.[19]

A second report, commissioned by the Packard Foundation, the US funder that had been the principal supporter of the MSC since its initial creation, was only slightly less critical. Focused more on the lack of market and policy success, this report noted:

- MSC had established, at best, a toehold in European markets, and none of the major retail grocery chains carried MSC-labeled product.
- Policy changes in fisheries management regulations linked to the MSC had, as of the end of 2003, occurred in only two countries, Australia and New Zealand.[20]

The funder-commissioned reports also proposed a series of detailed recommendations for getting the MSC back on track.

Renewal

The MSC board took a series of steps to implement the recommendations.[21] It conducted a global search for a new executive director, and found one, Rupert Howes, in London. It determined that MSC needed to develop a new set of sustainability scoring indicators. It needed a better way to track its progress on corrective action requests, needed to improve the quality and consistency of its assessments, and needed to be able to demonstrate tangible environmental benefits associated with its certifications. The changes were timely, and huge improvements were visible almost immediately.

By the middle of 2006, MSC had certified 21 fisheries using new, tougher assessment methods. These included, in addition to those already discussed, North Sea herring, South African hake, US North Pacific halibut, US North Pacific sablefish, and the Mexican Baja California red rock lobster. Fish caught in these 21 fisheries accounted for approximately 6 percent of the total wild-capture fisheries in the world; for some fish species, the proportions are much higher. Fully 42 percent of global wild-caught salmon and 32 percent of prime whitefish came from MSC-certified fisheries by 2006. There were 400 MSC-labeled products being sold in 26 countries, although the labeled fish included only about 3 percent of the total catch in the certified fisheries.[24] Another 16 fisheries were undergoing assessment at that time, including: Pacific albacore tuna (the first tuna that might be certified), British Columbia wild-caught salmon, California chinook salmon, California and Oregon Dungeness crab, Chilean hake, a Japanese snow crab and flathead flounder fishery, Maryland striped bass, and a lobster fishery in the UK.

The link between certification of a fishery under MSC standards and environmental improvements was strengthened by a study undertaken by a UK consultancy in collaboration with MSC staff.[25] The study focused on developing tools and methodologies to measure the environmental or ecological impacts of certification to the MSC standard and then cataloging and assessing current evidence that the MSC eco-labeling program results in positive outcomes (benefits) for the environment.[26] The results were encouraging. For six fisheries that had been certified long enough to have a post-certification audit, quantitative indicators of environmental change were developed to measure the magnitude of the change that had occurred. Many of the gains found were classified as operational results of the certification, including reduced numbers of discarded fish; return toward sustainability of bycatch species; improving benthic (ocean bottom) diversity; and continued absence of illegal, unreported, and unregulated vessels within the fishery zone.

The MSC has followed a financial model that funds virtually all of its expenses through donations from foundations, government agencies, other NGOs, and some corporations. Although it levies a small fee on the use of its label, that fee raises, as of 2006, an inconsequential part of its total budget. That has made it

Rebuilding the Core of Well-Managed Fisheries
Rupert Howes at the MSC

Rupert Howes was a busy man during his first two years as executive director of the Marine Stewardship Council. For a man who wanted to be "anything but an accountant" when he left the university after studying economics, who worked in marine archaeology in Australia for a while, and then inevitably spent six years as an accountant at KPMG, the challenge of rebuilding and reinvigorating the organization that some funders had called "the most effective investment for transforming the market in seafood" has been both satisfying and exhausting.[22] "When you see the possibility of creating a world where there is no market for unsustainable seafood," he notes, "it's hard to take your foot off the gas."

In the first 20 months that Rupert was at the helm of the MSC, he managed to regain much of the credibility that it had lost through questionable certifications (even some of MSC's harshest critics admitted his success). He brought MSC out of a severe financial crisis that had forced his board to let one-third of the staff go before he even arrived. And the organization managed to double the number of MSC-labeled products available around the world. Rupert was then presented with the supreme challenge of sustainable fisheries: When Wal-Mart, the world's largest retail vendor of seafood, committed publicly in 2006 to source *all* the wild-caught ocean seafood it sells in the United States solely from MSC-certified fisheries within three to five years, Rupert and MSC had to determine whether Wal-Mart's commitment could be achieved without lowering standards or alienating the global marine conservation NGO community that closely watches every step MSC takes.

The bridge between Rupert's stint as an accountant and his success at MSC was a master's degree in environmental technology from Imperial College (London), three years at the International Institute for Environment and Development (in London), and eight years at Forum for the Future, an organization that Rupert calls "one of the most effective sustainable development organizations in the UK" (also in London). A "life-long Londoner," Rupert was delighted when he was head-hunted from the Forum to take the reins at London-based MSC in October 2004. Luckily he's no stranger to travel, as in his first two years he traveled more than 200,000 miles as he raised funds, reestablished contacts with once-critical NGOs, and rebuilt a system that almost disappeared in 2003 and 2004.

"Ocean fisheries depletion is," he believes, "the second-largest and most important global sustainability problem, after climate change." It is not only an immense ecological problem, but is also one of the world's most difficult livelihoods problems, affecting hundreds of millions of people who live in coastal communities and are significantly more impoverished now because of the commercial depletion of their livelihoods and their food stocks.

It is far more difficult to certify sustainable fisheries, monitor the implementation of the standards, and demonstrate the positive impacts of the certification process, argues Rupert, than it is to carry out comparable certification of, say, sustainable forestry. MSC's biggest challenge has been establishing the size of a fish stock, understanding its relationship with all other elements of the regional marine ecosystem, and then creating a globally consistent set of standards that covers everything that varies from fishery to fishery. This explains, he notes, why they are now in the sixth iteration of their assessment methodology in little more than ten years, reflecting a continuous process of learning by doing.

One of MSC's proudest achievements (though not without controversy), and an illustration of the complexity of the problem, was the certification of the Patagonian toothfish fishery around the South Georgia (or Malvinas) Islands in the South Atlantic. Better known in the United States as Chilean sea bass, the toothfish is seriously endangered in the Antarctic and Pacific regions. A number of reasonably successful campaigns have dissuaded chefs and consumers from buying it. For example, "Take a Pass on Chilean Sea Bass," a campaign in the United States, organized by the National Environmental Trust, convinced many major chefs across the US to sign a pledge to avoid the fish.[23]

MSC was able to establish that the South Georgia Islands fishery involves a population distinct from the endangered ones and that it could be managed sustainably. There are now only 16 boats allowed in the fishery. Each of them carries an independent observer; they fish only six months of the year; and they use long lines that are weighted to sink quickly, which avoids damage to bird populations that otherwise go after the bait on the lines before they sink. Albatross deaths from the fishery have been reduced from hundreds every year to virtually none. BirdLife International calls the South Georgia Islands fishing practices a model that should be copied.

The changes were underway before MSC's assessment of the fishery took place, and further modifications were required by MSC. But MSC certification now provides validation of the improved practices for world consumer markets. MSC-certified Chilean sea bass is available to the chefs and family kitchens of the world that have made it one of the most popular fish of all time. The premium price that MSC-certified Chilean sea bass brings is an important global signal to those who continue to use unsustainable practices in the still-endangered Patagonian toothfish fishery and in other fisheries.

"Who could have believed a dozen years ago," Rupert argues, "that a small nonprofit organization with barely 30 staff could provide a tool this powerful to transform an entire global industry by tapping market forces to make business sustainable?"

very difficult for the MSC to expand as rapidly as market conditions seem to permit. For example, it works closely with Wal-Mart, which has notified all its seafood suppliers that it is seeking to purchase only MSC-certified wild-caught fish. That has brought great new interest in MSC certification from many fisheries that sell to Wal-Mart but are not presently certified. Whether they are able to meet MSC standards may determine whether they are able to continue to sell to Wal-Mart. That "power of the purchase order," according to Rupert Howes, MSC chief executive, "is the most important market force for greater sustainability."[27] However, MSC does not have the financial ability to meet this new demand for certification assessments and oversight unless retailers like Wal-Mart provide financial assistance to cover those costs. (This problem has cropped up for other certification systems, including certified Fair Trade, which has had to deal with an extensive backlog of producers seeking certification.)

By the end of 2005, Unilever was able to announce that it was buying 46 percent of its fish from MSC-certified sources, largely on the basis of purchases of newly certified Alaskan Pollock. Ironically, it also announced that it intended to sell most of its European frozen food business, which would dramatically reduce its purchases of seafood from all fish sources.[28]

The MSC represents an excellent example of both the perils and the possibilities of using certification systems to transform the exploitation of a fundamental natural resource. It continues to succeed because of rapidly growing global awareness of the precipitously declining fish stocks in so many of the world's fisheries. With the exception of the initial Greenpeace campaign against Unilever, which was clearly successful in that it moved Unilever to work with WWF to create the Marine Stewardship Council, there has been relatively little market campaigning to draw attention to specific companies or to pressure them to source MSC-certified seafood.[29] So what is the immediate incentive for other companies to favor the MSC?

As we will see in Chapter 12, advocacy campaigns to transform Wal-Mart never had an explicit focus on its seafood purchases, though seafood sourcing became an important part of the negotiated concessions to improve environmental dimensions of its business. Whether Wal-Mart's MSC commitment can transform the seafood industry as hoped, forcing other grocery chains to adopt MSC certification, will probably depend more on the development of a sustainable financial model at the MSC than on vigorous campaigns to move individual companies to commit to the sales of certified seafood. The most likely financial change could come from higher licensing fees for its logo and greatly increased volumes of labeled product in the markets. The existence of a reinvigorated MSC system, with renewed credibility, also raises the possibility of successful market campaigns directed at other retailers and restaurant chains now that there is a rising supply of certified seafood. Consumers may see uncertified commercial seafood as a likely contributor to ocean fish depletion. It will take many more years to realize Rupert Howes' goal of *no* market for fish harvested unsustainably. But an important first step in the direction of what could become the seafood "tipping point" is falling prices for seafood of unknown provenance.

CERTIFYING LABOR PRACTICES IN THE APPAREL INDUSTRY

"Sweatshops" is a term that is more than 100 years old. Generally defined as a shop or factory where employees work long hours under poor conditions, it was discussed in an 1892 *Scribner's Magazine* article entitled "Among the Poor of

Chicago," which concluded that "division of labor is good. . . . Scattering of workers from great groups into smaller groups is good;. . . prevention of theft is good,
and cheapness of garments is good," but "unwholesome atmosphere, moral and
material, is bad; insufficient wages is bad; possibility of infection is bad, and
child-labor is (usually) bad. How shall the good be preserved and the bad cured
or alleviated?" [30]

Since the 20th century responded, in most industrialized countries, by establishing minimum wages, workplace regulations, and the abolition of child labor,
the sweatshop now exists as an illegal, hidden operation in those countries. In
other parts of the world without comparable effective legislation, it is a place
with oppressive working conditions.

There has been a major anti-sweatshop movement in the US and in Europe
for many years. It has taken many forms and engaged many civil society organizations.

In Europe

The Clean Clothes Campaign (CCC) was formed in 1989 by solidarity and
women's organizations in the Netherlands and the UK when they took up the
case of a garment factory lockout in the Philippines. By 2005, CCC had become a
coalition of some 200 organizations across Europe that focus on workers' rights
worldwide. They pursue their objectives by
  • pressuring branded apparel companies to ensure that their garments are pro-
    duced under decent working conditions,
  • raising consumer awareness of working conditions in the global garment and
    sportswear industries,
  • exploring legal options that would compel governments and companies to
    become ethical consumers, and
  • supporting workers, trade unions, and NGOs in producer countries. [31]

The principal mechanism used by the CCC is the organization of "urgent appeals" based on complaints from workers and local NGOs affected by poor factory conditions. In 2005, for example, the international secretariat focused on 29
new appeals for assistance for workers in factories in 17 countries, including
China, Bangladesh, Lesotho, Haiti, Indonesia, Nicaragua, Tunisia, and Turkey. [32]
Its actions on those cases included writing letters to factory managers, writing
letters to the branded companies sourcing from them, lobbying companies
sourcing from them, placing case updates on the CCC International Secretariat
website (cleanclothes.org), and launching action requests on the website. The
CCC website includes company-by-company updates on the latest trouble situations in their factories, with a bit of history and suggested actions to take.

CCC spent eight years collecting code-of-conduct information from the garment and sportswear industry and comparing codes developed by companies
with its own set code-of-conduct recommendations. [33] It has been highly critical
of the company-specific independent social audits that monitor compliance

with good labor practices, which are used by most companies that create their own codes. In a 2005 report, *Looking for a Quick Fix*, CCC concluded that contracted independent social audits are "failing to deliver" as a tool for assessing compliance with the companies' own codes of conduct, "especially in determining violations of freedom of association, excessive and forced overtime, abusive treatment and discrimination of workers."[34]

In the United States

The problems of inadequate company-sponsored monitoring were made vivid for many in the US in November 2006 when *Business Week* ran a cover story that associated suppliers from China with sweatshops.[35] The story detailed how attempts by brand-name companies to manufacture in China under their own labor standards, and with their own contracted monitoring, were being undercut by factory managers who maintained double records, one for their internal use and a different one for the monitors. It included tales of corrupt "corporate responsibility consultants," who resolved one manufacturer's problems with Wal-Mart for a fee, creating false audit reports that satisfied the buyer, even though wages remained below the minimum and workers continued to put in forced overtime. One compliance manager reported to *Business Week* that the proportion of suppliers actually caught submitting false payroll records had risen from 46 percent to 75 percent in the previous four years.

The US anti-sweatshop campaign has been, in some ways, narrower than that in Europe, with a particularly strong focus on one component of the apparel industry: clothing that bears the trademarked names and logos of colleges and universities. Union-affiliated groups, such as the National Labor Committee, had been campaigning for many years for better standards and better monitoring across the board. The National Labor Committee had specialized in a process that identifies, publicizes, and criticizes especially egregious labor practices that can be linked to widely known apparel brands, but its impact had been limited.

The student-led college-focused portion of the movement is generally recognized as beginning with, or at least taking new energy from, student demonstrations and demands at Duke University in late 1998 and early 1999.[36] Duke students had campaigned to have the university create conditions that would ensure the highly profitable Duke regalia industry was not associated with sweatshops. The university responded, in March 1998, with a commitment to adopt a "far-reaching code of conduct…to insure that products bearing its name are not made in sweatshops." The lead student group, then called Students Against Sweatshops, first praised the decision. But as the details of the code became apparent (including its links to the controversial Fair Labor Association process, discussed below), the Duke students staged a protest at the university president's office in January 1999, seizing the office overnight and alleging that the code the university proposed to implement was much weaker than what had originally been promised. In particular, the original code would have required the university to release the names of all factories where any of its 700 licensees were producing their products. The new code, crafted by a licensing attorney linked to the emerging industry-based Fair Labor Assocation (FLA), eliminated that requirement, making independent monitoring virtually impossible.[37]

By the end of 1999, students from more than 100 colleges and universities, organized as United Students Against Sweatshops (USAS), called for their universities to leave the FLA and join an alternative organization, the Worker Rights Consortium (WRC), which sought to provide more stringent monitoring under a tougher code of conduct for factories worldwide that supplied licensed products bearing the symbols of their universities.[38] Some observers associated with the FLA publicly belittled the WRC's ability to match the resources and reach of the corporate-backed system.

The dilemmas faced by these efforts in Europe and the United States are closely linked to the fundamental dynamics of the contemporary apparel and sportswear industries. These industries are extraordinarily competitive and enormously fragmented at both the producer and the retailer level. Although the Wal-Mart case study in Chapter 12 will reveal a company with considerable monopsony power — that is the ability to demand lower prices from producers because of the volume of its purchases — most brand-name apparel and sportswear retailers claim they do not account for a large-enough proportion of the sales in their markets to be able to raise prices to the level needed to cover the costs of non-sweatshop labor.

Time and again, confidential conversations with representatives of the social auditing industry lead to the same conclusion. Anti-sweatshop groups place pressure on brand-name retailers to raise the standards in the factories of their suppliers, but those retailers are not willing to pay a higher price for products produced under those conditions. The suppliers know that they must meet the standards if they want to continue to sell to the retailers, and they sign commitments to raise standards. But they also know that they can't abide by the standards and still make a profit at competitive prices. Monitors come and monitors go; the supplier shows as much compliance as it can. But it also knows that the retailer wants, first and foremost, a price-competitive product. When suppliers do attempt to implement higher standards — allowing unionization, reducing piecework quotas to more humane levels, and raising labor pay — they cannot find markets, under present circumstances, for the products they produce at the slightly higher prices that result.

This fundamentally discouraging scenario was explored in a much-heralded *New York Times* story in 2001, which focused on a factory in El Salvador that was a source for apparel sold by Gap.[39] When challenged by critics on conditions in the factory, Gap insisted on certain improvements. Where the workers had been required to work "18-hour days in an unventilated factory with undrinkable water" for US$0.55 per hour, they were now working in a factory that was "breezy and clean," with other improvements as well. But wages had risen only to US$0.60 per hour. Workers still worked long hours with high production quotas, and earnings were still not sufficient for the young workers, mostly women, to live on. That, noted the authors, "demonstrates the limits to good intentions when first-world appetites collide with third-world realities."

The social auditing that has evolved over the past ten years in an attempt to remedy this situation has suffered from another fundamental flaw. It has assumed that factories abide by the required company codes of conduct as soon as they sign a formal commitment to do so. Auditing usually occurs only after complaints have been registered, most often by trade unions and women's organizations outside the factory. But under the existing rules of the FLA and most company codes of conduct, the audit visit is announced in advance, giving factory managers time to prepare. Auditors are only allowed to speak to factory workers under supervised conditions in factory reception rooms. Until recently, there was no requirement that factories demonstrate they were already implementing the code of conduct, no pre-assessment before certification to confirm they were meeting the code, no engagement with local civil society organizations, and no allowance for interviewing workers outside the potentially inhibiting conditions of the factory.

However, a new approach was established in early 2006 by the Worker Rights Consortium. Its Designated Suppliers Program represents a major breakthrough in apparel manufacturing certification, with the potential, finally, to transform the apparel industry in ways comparable to what we have seen in other industries.

Before looking at the WRC approach, let's study the bitter campaign that was waged between the Fair Labor Association and United Students Against Sweatshops (together with the Worker Rights Consortium) from 2000 to 2006.

Fair Labor Association

The Fair Labor Association was started in 1998 by a small group of apparel and sportswear companies, a group of universities and colleges, and a group of NGOs concerned with worker rights and sweatshop conditions. It was an outgrowth of a White House Apparel Industry Partnership (AIP), launched in 1996 by the Clinton administration, to set up a common system of voluntary labor standards, for use at home and abroad, that would assure consumers that the clothes and footwear they bought was not made in sweatshops. The AIP had been created after a line of clothes associated with Kathie Lee Gifford, a prominent US television personality, was found to come from sweatshops in both New York and Central America. From the outset, organizers envisioned that manufacturers meeting the standards would be entitled to sew a certifying label inside the apparel.[40]

By the middle of 1998, however, the FLA working group, which included sports and apparel makers Liz Claiborne, Nike, and Reebok as corporate participants, could not agree on fundamental terms and conditions, such as the extent and frequency of monitoring visits and whether the basis for wage calculations should be the local minimum wage or an estimated "living wage." Members also disagreed about corporations' responsibility for insuring workers' rights to free association (unionization) in countries like China, where worker rights were very limited. And there was even contentious disagreement over the constitution of the board of directors, with non-corporate members (unions and human rights organizations) demanding a clear majority on the board to give it credibility. Observers suggested that at several points the negotiations almost collapsed.[41]

In November 1998, confounding the expectations of critics, the Fair Labor Association was born out of a proposal put forward by 9 of the original 18 members of AIP, and without significant labor union participation. The Union of Needletrades, Industrial, and Textile Employees (UNITE), the apparel union that had spent two years working with AIP, refused to accept the standards and procedures adopted by the group. The union objected to the failure to specify that workers should receive a living wage and to the failure to require that companies speak up for the rights of workers to organize in countries where that right is suppressed. Five US NGOs, including Business for Social Responsibility, the Lawyers Committee for Human Rights, and the International Labor Rights Fund, joined in founding the FLA. Several of them voiced support for the FLA as a first step, but not the ultimate solution.

The FLA's formal standards are simple and remain essentially the same five years later, taking up less than one page.[42] They cover forced labor, harassment or abuse, nondiscrimination, health and safety, freedom of association and collective bargaining, wages and benefits, hours of work, and overtime compensation. It was left to each participating company to interpret the broad aspirational statement on standards in terms of its own code of conduct. The related "principles of monitoring" required that companies monitor only 30 percent of their factories over the first three years, and 5 to 10 percent of their factories per year on average after that. Critics pointed out that this would mean an average factory might be monitored only once every 10 to 20 years. Companies were allowed to pick the monitors they wanted to use, and there was no requirement that the results of the monitoring be revealed publicly, though companies were supposed to send the confidential results to the FLA. Many of the monitors were expected to be major accounting firms, though the companies were "urged" to involve local NGOs and human rights groups.[43] Within a few months, 17 colleges and universities, including Harvard, Yale, Princeton, Duke, and Notre Dame, had announced that they would join the FLA, in many cases publicly citing the pressure from student groups.[44]

There was widespread rejection of the legitimacy of the FLA process. Reflecting on the fact that companies would only be required to pay the local minimum wage or the local industry standard, whichever was higher, the Interfaith Coalition for Corporate Responsibility, a powerful advocate for corporate transformation that had participated in the AIP and that represents and advises church-related investment funds totaling several hundred billion dollars, rejected the FLA immediately. According to the coalition's spokesperson, the FLA appeared to be a system "that could lock in place insupportably low wages."[45] Students at many colleges and universities began concerted attacks against the FLA. Demonstrators at Brown University succeeded in convincing officials to withdraw from the association if it did not meet more stringent conditions.[46] Students at the University of Pennsylvania occupied the university president's office and held it for a week until the president agreed to withdraw from the FLA.[47] And the chairman of Nike, Phil Knight, withdrew a planned gift of US$30 million to the University of Oregon when the university refused to join the FLA and chose, instead, to associate with the Workers Rights Coalition.

National perspectives on the effectiveness of the FLA varied widely. Supporters claimed that "apparel and footwear factories overseas have slowly improved working conditions" in response to the highly vocal anti-sweatshop movement. Monitoring groups claimed that pressure from companies like Nike and Gap succeeded in reducing the amount of child labor, the use of dangerous chemicals, and the number of workers forced to work 80-hour workweeks.[48] Opponents saw these efforts as little more than "window dressing" because there was no transparency in the process, monitoring firms weren't digging deeply enough, and there was no disclosure of either the results of monitoring or the remediation that followed negative findings. Other than anecdotal evidence, there was little to show that anything was changing. By the end of 2005, United Students Against Sweatshops and its allies had become a formidable foe of the FLA, with a constantly updated website (fla-watch.org) that criticized FLA's every move.

Nike actually implemented labor standards and monitoring that exceeded the FLA requirements, perhaps responding to the drubbing it had taken in the mid-1990s (see Chapter 1). Richard Locke, an MIT professor who was given unparalleled access to Nike processes, wrote in 2003 that the company had established a Corporate Responsibility and Compliance Department that included some 85 people dedicated to labor and environmental compliance, all located close to the factories from which it was sourcing shoes and clothes.[49] Since 2000, Nike had required a "preliminary, pre-production inspection of factories to see if they meet Nike's standards for a clean and healthy workplace, respectful labor-management relations, fair wages and working conditions, and minimum working age."[50] The in-house monitoring was supplemented by outside consultants, such as PriceWaterHouseCoopers, who audited the factory's wages, overtime, benefits, and the age of its employees. All suppliers were graded on these social and environmental issues as well as on quality, price, flexibility, and on-time delivery, and the grading system determined where future orders would be placed.

Three years later, Professor Locke analyzed the across-the-board impact of this monitoring process by Nike, once again using Nike's internal data. Unfortunately, he and his co-authors reached disheartening conclusions. Statistical analysis of the data from Nike's internal audits for over 800 factories in 51 countries suggested that even these audits, presumably biased in favor of the company's efforts, were insufficient: "monitoring alone appears to produce only limited results."[51] The average Nike supplier complied with only 65 percent of Nike's weighted list of some 80 criteria. "Some factories appear to be almost in complete compliance with Nike's code of conduct," Locke and his colleagues wrote, "while others suffer from endemic problems with poor wages, excessive work hours, harassment, etc."[52] Factories in the Americas had higher levels of compliance (77 percent on average); those in South Asia much lower (58 percent). After further analysis of Nike's internal "compliance rating" system, which in theory allows managers to steer orders to those factories that showed the greatest compliance with Nike standards, the analysts found that "workplace conditions in almost 80 percent of its suppliers have either remained the same or worsened over time."[53]

Worker Rights Consortium

The Worker Rights Consortium, meanwhile, grew slowly into an organization that gave universities, in its own language, "effective enforcement of *their* manufacturing codes of conduct" (emphasis added), with "accurate, thorough, timely and impartial assessments of conditions" in the factories producing collegiate apparel. Universities were encouraged to set up their own codes, based on a WRC model code. Where it identified problems, WRC would "work with licensees, factory managers, workers and worker advocates to eliminate violations and move the factory toward compliance," often "without any need for direct engagement by universities."[54]

The WRC "model code of conduct" is four pages long and provides considerably more detail than that of the FLA.[55] The most important differences from the FLA code and FLA practices appear to be the following:

- Wages must "provide for essential needs and establish a dignified living wage for workers and their families."
- Working hours may not exceed 48 hours per week and must permit one day off in every seven-day period.
- Overtime must be demonstrably voluntary, and overtime must be paid at one-and-a-half times the hourly compensation rate.
- Health and safety provisions must comply with local regulations or with US occupational safety and health regulations, whichever is more protective.
- There is a specific code of women's rights, which stipulates equal remuneration and benefits and equal opportunity to fill the positions of male workers, no pregnancy tests or forced use of contraception, and maternity leave with guaranteed return to former employment without loss of pay and benefits.

The WRC's governing board is made up of five members representing university affiliates (elected by a caucus of representatives from affiliated universities), five independent labor rights experts (selected by the WRC advisory council), and five student representatives (elected nationally by USAS members). In 2006, the advisory council consisted of 26 representatives, including US and international labor rights experts, NGO leaders, anti-sweatshop groups, and labor unions. Corporate apparel vendors and licensed suppliers are not represented.[56]

By 2006, the FLA claimed 194 participating colleges and universities; the WRC 157, but 69 of the FLA colleges and universities were also affiliated with

WRC. This resulted in curious anomalies. Notre Dame, an original FLA affiliate, was now solely affiliated with the WRC. Harvard worked with both; Yale with only the FLA. Among Canadian institutions, Guelph was with the WRC, University of Alberta worked with the FLA, and University of Toronto with both. There were as many denominational colleges with the FLA as with the WRC. And within the University of Wisconsin system, Madison, LaCrosse, and Stevens Point worked solely with WRC; Milwaukee and Oshkosh worked with both.[57] One can only assume that affiliation with both organizations covers a wider range of suppliers and that the institutions accept that some of their suppliers comply only with the weaker standards.

In January 2006, WRC made an important breakthrough when it introduced a Designated Suppliers Program (DSP), designed with, and backed by, USAS. The DSP was created to address the principal weakness of all ex-post auditing and monitoring (i.e., monitoring that is done only after complaints are registered), as well as the critical questions of frequency and depth of auditing. Under the DSP, apparel bearing university logos must be sourced from a set of designated factories that have demonstrated *in advance* their full and consistent respect for the rights of their employees under the terms of the universities' own codes of conduct; have shown "demonstrable respects for the rights of association," as evidenced by the presence of a legitimate representative union or other representative employee body; and pay a living wage. Universities participating in the DSP are expected to commit to paying prices slightly above industry norms so that factories can afford to meet these standards. The universities will also be asked to commit to long-term relationships with the factories to allow a reasonable degree of financial stability and job security.[58] The WRC released a strong analytical study that shows the resulting small increase in price makes little difference to the purchasers of logo-emblazoned products.[59]

Initial response to the DSP has been positive. By September 2006, 30 of WRC's university members had expressed their willingness to sign on to DSP. A Duke University director of trademark licensing and store operations reflected a common sentiment when he argued that existing code-based systems were not having the effect desired because "to tell a factory to comply with a certain labor provision, but not provide it with the income necessary for it to comply, is absolute folly."[60]

The DSP takes labor standards certification along the trail already followed by the FSC, the MSC, and Fair Trade. Suppliers must demonstrate in advance that they are implementing the somewhat more costly standards and be assessed in advance as complying. Just as Fair Trade producers must meet conditions in order to be certified by FLO, factory owners will be given the key incentive — guaranteed higher prices from buyers — that will allow them to move to higher wages, better worker representation, and compliance with the other WRC standards.

Nonetheless, it is taking a while for the apparel industry to understand the logic of product differentiation for social and environmental qualities. The

Tackling the Tough Job of Factory Auditing
Heather White, founder of Verité

*"Verité is an independent, non-profit social auditing and research organization estab-
lished in 1995. Our mission is to ensure that people worldwide work under safe, fair and
legal working conditions. Where Verité auditors identify exploitation of workers or
health and safety violations in the workplace, we develop concrete steps to correct
them through a combination of trainings for management and workers, education
programs and remediation programs."* — Verité website, August 2006

The creation of a nonprofit organization with this mission and its accompanying
goals and strategy is a far cry from Heather White's reality during the 15 years she
was running the Pacific Trade Group, a company she founded in San Francisco to
source products from China for companies like Williams Sonoma and Pottery
Barn.[62] That company was consistent with her 1980 Harvard College degree in East
Asian Studies. In the early 1990s, Heather began work on her master's degree in international political economy, studying with MIT professor Richard Locke, who is
well known for his critiques of the social and environmental conditions in factories
such as those of Nike. Heather founded Verité in 1995 as she completed her MIT
studies.

I had an opportunity to witness the energy and idealism behind Heather's organization when we each made presentations to students at Duke University and at
the University of North Carolina in the late 1990s. Verité was set up to provide more
honest, more open, and ultimately more effective monitoring of labor conditions
around the world. Many of the for-profit alternatives that were already operating at
the time had multiple levels of engagement with the companies that sought their
expertise in factory audits. These for-profit auditors were also doing accounting, financial audits, and quality management consultancies for the companies, which
tainted the auditors' credibility for challenging the practices of the companies' suppliers. It's not surprising that some activists believed their social audits were done
"with a wink and a nod."

Because of the independence it could offer, Verité was one of the first auditing
groups that the FLA turned to when it was created. And, true to its integrity, Verité
withdrew from the list of FLA auditors when it saw the weaknesses of the FLA
system.

Over the years, Heather has become skeptical about companies' commitments
to conduct real, meaningful audits. "The companies are looking for cheaper, simpler, more local audits," she asserts, "as they slash their budgets for compliance
mechanisms." Her first client was Kathie Lee Gifford, the US television personality,
who asked Verité to develop a strategy for responding to criticism of the conditions
under which her line of clothes was produced and to design a program for remediation. But when Verité determined that her problems were not just a few factories in
Central America but at least 600 factories in China, Ms. Gifford turned to public relations firms rather than creating a real mechanism for addressing the problems.

"The companies are learning faster than the NGOs," Heather believes, and they are learning how to escape or evade the pressure that NGOs can bring. "Given the constantly changing nature of the challenges in social auditing, and the need for new solutions in response, the models must also change every couple of years." For example, she points out, more and more of the apparel manufactured around the world is coming under the control of a few giant, increasingly powerful cartels, such as South China Garments — which controls production in Lesotho, Zambia, and Madagascar — or the Dada Group from South Korea. "No one appears to be developing a model appropriate for that new reality," she says.

She believes the WRC Designated Suppliers Program, which certifies compliance with high labor standards, offers much promise. "The fact that it is organized and run by an independent board without industry influence is one important dimension. And the other is their focus on requiring that the conditions be established and audited in advance of the certification, rather than the passive certification used in most codes of conduct and the 'gotcha' climate that it creates."

After ten years of work in social compliance assessment, Heather turned over the leadership of Verité to a successor, Dan Viederman. She joined the company's board, but recently she resigned from that board in order to set up a new nonprofit enterprise that will strengthen the ability of local organizations overseas to conduct the kinds of strong and principled audits that Verité set out to do. Helping them develop workplace education and training programs, and assisting them as they bid for and deliver social audits, will keep alive the hope that social auditing can have some impact on the conditions in factories overseas.

companies supplying the colleges and universities affiliated with WRC are "dead set against" the new approach, thinking that it contradicts market economics.[61] I suspect they will learn a slightly more sophisticated market economics involving products differentiated by ethical qualities, but perhaps no more quickly than the sustainable forestry, ethical commodities, and banking and finance industries took to learn this important lesson.

The fragile state of campaigns for better labor standards remains a disappointment for the certification revolution. The WRC Designated Supplier Program is the most encouraging development in recent years. But it may also fall short of what is needed to create true market demand for more ethically sourced apparel. It doesn't offer, for example, a distinguishing label that DSP participants can sew into their garments and use in their advertising, so it is missing a critical element that would permit suppliers to distinguish their products in the general apparel market, or in the university-linked apparel market on which it originally focused. Yes, it may be that specific colleges and universities can raise the prices they charge for items bearing their logos. They will probably lose little market, since presumably all of the apparel and sportswear carrying that logo will be at that price point. And there's little sign of price sensitivity among those who prefer a Yale logo over a Harvard logo, and vice versa. But the lost opportunity will consist of a reduced ability to spread beyond college and university logo markets to the broader apparel market. There it is critical to have a certification system that gives both the factory and the ultimate retail vendor a means of distinguishing ethically branded apparel, produced under DSP, from conventional apparel that is subject to the extraordinary downward pressure on prices felt by conventional producers.

CAMPAIGNS AGAINST TOXICS

Environmental health issues, where the impacts of environmental problems directly affect the lives of humans in their workplaces, their homes, their schools, and even their places of worship, have extraordinary motive power that cuts across political lines. As we learn about the impacts of chemicals in our lives and the power of market campaigns to transform companies, a wealth of corporate campaigns against toxics have developed. Many of them focus on the many uses of specific chemicals (like polyvinylchloride or PVC); others cluster around particular sectors, such as the healthcare sector (Health Care Without Harm [HCWH] has organized a coalition of groups to address the issue of toxics in healthcare facilities). Here is a partial list of environmental health issues that campaign organizations are working on:

- Campaigns to eliminate toxics in cosmetics, especially phthalates and other chemicals capable of crossing the mother/baby barrier during pregnancy, cleverly organized as the Not Too Pretty campaign (nottoopretty.org).
- Campaigns to remove toxics from construction materials, such as arsenic-treated wood and PVC in building materials; see, for example, healthybuild ing.net.
- Campaigns focused specifically on PVC, such as besafenet.com/pvc.htm
- Campaigns promoting pesticide-free and organic foods, especially in school meal programs, such as spcbweb.org, farmtoschool.org, and healthyschools .org.
- Campaigns to reduce and eliminate the use of mercury in medical instruments, part of HCWH at noharm.org.
- Campaigns to create toxin-free clinics, such as the Green Guide for Health Care (gghc.org).
- Campaigns that link environmental health concerns with socially responsible investing, such as the Investor Environmental Health Network (investor environmentalhealthnetwork.org).
- Campaigns focused on the accumulated "pollution in people" based on chemical analysis of "body burden," organized by the Environmental Working Group (ewg.org), among others.
- Campaigns to eliminate the flow of toxins into the atmosphere from incinerators, such as GAIA, the Global Anti-Incinerator Alliance (gaia.org).
- Campaigns to reduce toxicity in the manufacturing, use, and disposal of electronic equipment, such as the ComputerTake Back Campaign (computer takeback.org).[63]

The magnitude of the networks involved in this work is staggering. GAIA includes 360 member groups in 66 countries. HCWH has 450 member associations in 52 countries. Greenpeace has raised toxics to one of its top five campaigns, and it has offices in 41 countries. The 68 country offices of Friends of the Earth also have a major focus on toxics. And IPEN, the International POPs Elimination Network (POPs refers to "persistent organic pollutants"), has 350 member organizations worldwide.[64]

To make the discussion of anti-toxics campaigns manageable, we will focus here on recent efforts to reduce the presence, and the impact, of toxics in electronics. Important elements of this effort relate to our discussions throughout this book.

Electronic Waste

Electronic waste is the "dark side of the digital age." According to Ted Smith of the Silicon Valley Toxics Coalition (SVTC), "the fruits of our high-tech revolution are pure poison if these products are improperly disposed of at the end of their useful life."[65] In its early years, the electronics industry had a reputation for being one of the "cleanest" industries. There were no large smokestacks, no movement of large quantities of natural resources, no apparent refuse and effluents of the sort found in most manufacturing industry. It wasn't until the 1980s that people became aware of the hidden downside of the electronics industry in the form of toxic chemicals in the electronics workplace, chemical leaks from electronics plants, chemical "plumes" in the air above the manufacturing plants, and the problem of recycling the whole array of electronic products for which durability is short and built-in obsolescence an important part of the industry's financial motor. Yes, the amazing technological progress achieved worldwide in electronics is part of the explanation for the short useful life of many pieces of electronic equipment. But the accumulation of discarded equipment in homes and in landfills poses new threats. And some of the mechanisms for disposing of obsolete equipment — exporting it to poor countries for destruction and recycling of valuable basic materials, or using prison labor to do the same tasks — are causing new environmental health problems and severe social justice issues at the points of recycling.

No product epitomizes the problems posed by obsolete electronics better than the personal computer, with its peripheral equipment such as monitors and printers. It is estimated that in the United States, more than 160,000 computers (and televisions) become obsolete *every day*. US government researchers estimate that three-quarters of all computers ever sold in the country remain stockpiled, awaiting disposal. Should every computer owner in the US attempt to discard his or her obsolete computer at the same time, "the nation would face a 'tsunami' of e-scrap, presenting a major budgetary and environmental crisis" for state and local governments.[66]

Discarded computers and their monitors, especially the older models with cathode ray tubes (CRTs, similar to the screens in conventional televisions), are hazardous waste. They contain significant concentrations of lead and other

Stripping Electronics of Its "Clean" Veneer
Ted Smith of the Silicon Valley Toxics Coalition

Ted Smith's trajectory from one-time college football player, passionate about his identity as an athlete, to global leadership of the campaign to reduce toxics in the electronics field seems remarkable even to him.[67] Ted is the co-founder of Silicon Valley Toxics Coalition (SVTC) and was executive director of the group for more than 20 years. The history of the movement to eliminate toxics in the production and disposal of electronic equipment, especially computers, is closely associated with the growth of SVTC, which began as a small neighborhood group in California's "Silicon Valley" in 1982.

Neighbors in the vicinity of a Fairchild Semiconductor plant in San Jose, California, began to notice a high number of strange birth defects and cancers, and they organized to find the source. What they learned is the material of nightmares: the water they were drinking was contaminated with potentially carcinogenic chemicals that had apparently leaked from storage tanks at local electronics manufacturing plants. What had been considered a blessedly clean industry, without smokestacks or dust or heavy traffic, was actually producing "a chemical bomb" in the water of nearby affluent neighborhoods. By the end of the investigation, officials had found high levels of trichloroethylene, which is suspected of causing cancer, in the groundwater near the Fairchild plant, at a former Intel Corporation plant in Mountain View, and at a Hewlett-Packard Company plant in Palo Alto.[68]

Frustrated as a "jock" when his post-college athletic career failed to develop, Ted worked as a volunteer with Volunteers in Service to America (VISTA, sometimes called the "domestic Peace Corps) in the 1960s and then obtained his law degree from Stanford Law School. He had been practicing law for ten years in Silicon Valley when his wife, Amanda Hawes, also a lawyer, began to find more and more cases of occupational illnesses in the area among computer industry workers exposed to the chemicals used in the production processes.

SVTC took off after 1982. At first it helped develop new local ordinances that forced electronics companies to contain their toxic agents and give the public information about the toxic chemicals used on site. These laws were adopted locally throughout California, then by the state, and then in federal legislation. SVTC contributed significantly to the development of the 1986 U.S. Superfund Law, which forced companies to pay the costs of cleanup. Ironically, Santa Clara County, SVTC's home base, became the site of the largest number of federally designated Superfund toxic cleanups for any county in the country.[69]

SVTC broadened its focus over time from electronics manufacturing to the full life cycle of electronic products, from mining through manufacturing to final disposal. It became increasingly concerned about the health risks associated with computer disposal and recycling of computer components and materials, especially when shipped overseas or undertaken by prisoners. SVTC initiated the Computer TakeBack Campaign in 2001 as a broad-based initiative that would require consumer electronics manufacturers and brand owners to take full responsibility for the life cycle of their products.

After stepping down from the executive director job at SVTC, Ted worked to launch an International Campaign for Responsible Technology (ICRT), which is focusing on the full life cycle of a much wider range of technologies. ICRT raises questions of enterprise risk management associated with toxic chemical use and disposal, with the goal of reducing the chance of unsafe substances getting into the market. ICRT is also beginning to address worker rights and human rights throughout the global electronics supply chain.

It has been Ted's experience that working with the "big name" companies in the computer and electronics industries is considerably more productive than attempting to modify production processes in the factories of their suppliers. He has especially appreciated the responsiveness of Hewlett-Packard and Dell as they become more aware of the brand risk they run if they fail to lead on issues of worker safety in both production and recycling. "In recent years," he argues, "there have been unbelievable changes in some of these companies just with the little bit of pressure that we have been able to place upon them." Apple Computer, on the other hand, remains close to the bottom of the list for most of the campaigners because of its unresponsiveness. "They appear to have fallen back on an early-1990s model of defensiveness," Ted says.

These successes with the industry have created much more interest and enthusiasm among the anti-toxics campaigners. Compared with the early days of SVTC, there is now a much larger number of NGOs working in the field. According to Ted, "That gives us much better ability to organize working groups on national and international policy, market campaigns, exports and prison labor, procurement standards for electronics for colleges, universities, and governments, as well as the basic work on the elimination of toxic materials in production, where the movement began."

---

heavy metals. The 315 million computers that became obsolete between 1997 and 2004 are estimated to contain more than 1.2 *billion* pounds of lead; 70 percent of the heavy metals, including mercury and cadmium, found in US landfills comes from discarded electronic equipment.[70]

Some people might ask: "Why not just export it?" There are poor people around the world who might benefit from the jobs created by this massive recycling opportunity. The reasons for not exporting begin with the international treaty that bans the export of hazardous waste. The Basel Convention on the Control of Transboundary Movements of Hazardous Wastes and Their Disposal was adopted in Basel, Switzerland, on March 22, 1989.[71] The convention was developed in response to international scandals regarding hazardous waste trafficking that began to occur in the late 1980s; it went into force on May 5, 1992. The

Figure 10.2. Man sweeping toner out of a printer cartridge in Guiyu, China, December 2001. Toners are made of carbon black — a class 2A probable carcinogen according to the International Agency for Research on Cancer. The toner billows in his face all day long, and he has no respiratory protection of any kind. Cartridges are later dumped by the river. Credit: SVTC, et al., *Exporting Harm: The High-Tech Trashing of Asia.* Copyright Basel Action Network.

United States participated in its drafting and is a signatory, but the US electronics industry lobbied successfully against its ratification by the US Senate, even though it had been ratified by the full European Union (and by most of its members individually), for a total of 61 ratifying countries through the end of 2005.[72] An initial loophole in the convention allowed massive quantities of electronic waste to be exported for "recycling," which was considered "further processing."

Another Basel Convention ban on the export of hazardous waste for recycling was approved by most OECD countries (the more developed countries of the world) and 71 non-OECD countries, including China, and went into effect in 1998. Again, unfortunately, the United States refused to recognize this ban. And China ignores it, leading to local conditions reflected in Figures 10.2 and 10.3.

The solution adopted by most US-based computer companies has been, until recently, to export e-waste, mostly to Asia. In 2002, SVTC and the Basel Action Network released a groundbreaking report that documented the health and environmental impacts on communities throughout East Asia dedicated to recycling materials contained in computer-linked electronic waste, which was shipped almost entirely from the US since most other developed countries respect the Basel Convention.[73] "While the U.S. has instituted programs at home to prevent environmental injustice," the report pointed out, "U.S. policy has actually promoted such injustice on the global stage." The US government policies "appear to be actually designed to promote sweeping the E-waste problem out the Asian back door." The study reported that the primitive means these communities used to recover copper, lead, cadmium, mercury, carbon black (from toner cartridges), and other valuable metals were, in fact, tragic in their impact: "The open burning, acid baths and toxic dumping pour pollution into the land, air and water, and expose the men, women and children of Asia's poorer peoples to

Woman about to smash a cathode ray tube (CRT) from a computer monitor in order to remove the copper-rich yoke at the end of the funnel, Guiyu, China, December 2001. The glass is laden with lead, but the biggest hazard is the inhalation of the highly toxic phosphor dust coating inside the CRT. Monitor glass is later dumped in irrigation canals and along the river, where it leaches lead into the groundwater. Credit: SVTC, et al., *Exporting Harm: The High-Tech Trashing of Asia.* Copyright Basel Action Network.

poison. The health and economic costs of this trade are vast and, due to export, are not borne by the western consumers nor the waste brokers who benefit from the trade."[74]

A second solution undertaken in the US was to engage prison labor in breaking down and recapturing the heavy metals in computer-related electronic equipment. Prisoners work for very low wages and are generally exempt from federal and state regulations on basic working conditions.

Both these solutions have the additional disadvantage of reducing the demand for safe and efficient recycling services for electronic equipment in the United States.

Market Campaigning on Electronic Waste

Market campaigns against electronic toxins from computers, based on the early work of SVTC in Silicon Valley, developed slowly. They picked up pace considerably as SVTC, Greenpeace, and their allies focused on the computer manufacturers, demanding that they become responsible for the safe recycling of what they manufactured. SVTC played a leading role, developing and releasing, with effective media attention, a series of reports on the most critical issues, from the presence of brominated fire retardants in the dust on *every* computer tested and the poisons in personal computers and televisions that are released with inappropriate recycling, to the hazardous conditions in electronics factories in places like Mexico, to which the industry is moving.

The Computer TakeBack Campaign was launched in 2001 by a coalition of 15 NGOs that focused in one way or another on toxics in the environment; conversations with staff of several of the groups suggested that SVTC again played a critical leadership role.[75] Dell Computer became one of the campaign's highest-profile targets, but not just because it was among the largest computer manufacturers in the world. Campaigners knew that Dell's just-in-time marketing and production modes, and its internal management systems, allowed the company to retain, and update, the name and contact information for virtually every individual and company that had purchased its equipment, allowing it to track the life cycle of the equipment better than most manufacturers.[76]

In 2003, SVTC released a report that made an explicit comparison between the electronics recycling of Hewlett-Packard (HP) and that of Dell. At that time, HP's recycling was being done by a California firm, Micro Metallics; Dell's recycling was being done by UNICOR, a US federal prison-based industry. Research for the report found that UNICOR's techniques — such as manually smashing leaded glass in CRTs (similar to the technique shown in Figure 10.3) — exposed inmate workers to high risk of toxic contamination and injuries and were "practices disturbingly similar to those found in developing nations."[77] UNICOR refused to allow industrial hygienists to inspect its facility, and it refused to provide air-quality tests. In a move that reflected conditions at sweatshops in other industries, UNICOR workers were warned not to talk with SVTC inspectors and were told that if they did talk they would "suffer disciplinary action or loss of job."[78]

Micro Metallics, on the other hand, allowed the industrial hygienist to inspect freely and provided air-monitoring and employee blood/lead test results. Micro Metallics used mechanized crushers that greatly reduced worker exposure to toxics. It hired union workers, paid a living wage, created ergonomic work stations for production-line tasks, and developed transparent health and safety programs that welcomed public inquiry. Its long-term relationship with HP suggests that it is not impossible to do effective electronics recycling under safe and humane conditions, and to do it within the US.

One week after the results of the study were made public in the *New York Times*,[79] Dell announced that it had cancelled its contract with UNICOR and that it would no longer rely on prisons to supply workers for its computer recycling program.[80] The US federal government continues to channel most of its recycling to UNICOR.

Apple Computer became a second major target of the campaign. In June 2005, campaigners flew airplanes trailing large banners over a Stanford University graduation ceremony at the school's football stadium, where Apple CEO Steve Jobs was the keynote speaker. The banner read "Steve — Don't Be a Mini

Player — Recycle All E-waste!"[81] Apple was cited in the accompanying press release for poor design and ineffective takeback programs. The iPod was held up as an example: consumers cannot replace the batteries easily when they no longer hold a charge, making the device obsolete and requiring careful disposal of the whole device, which few consumers understand.[82]

A major breakthrough came in February 2003 when SVTC and the Basel Action Network (BAN) announced "a responsible way to get rid of that old computer."[83] They created an Electronics Recycler's Pledge that called for "no export, no dumping, and no prisons." In fact, the pledge required much more than public commitment to a set of standards for "true stewardship." It also demanded a fairly intrusive "qualification process" by BAN itself before recycling companies would be listed on BAN's website as "E-Stewards & Responsible Recyclers." Recyclers must pledge to observe the following nine points:
- No dumping or incineration of hazardous wastes.
- No export from developed to developing countries, directly or through intermediaries.
- No e-waste to prisons, directly or indirectly.
- Put in place an environmental management system certification or comparable system.
- Commit to using the most efficient and least polluting recovery processes available globally.
- Implement visible tracking of hazardous e-waste throughout the processing chain.
- Provide adequate assurance (e.g., bonds) to cover liability for accidents or costs of closing down the facility.
- Support legislation calling for extended producer responsibility.
- Support programs and/or legislation reducing the use of toxic waste.[84]

To qualify for the E-Stewards list, applicant companies must give BAN complete information on their internal environmental management processes, information on the final destination of all the hazardous waste removed in recycling, and documentation on assurance or bonding for liability. The company can be listed only after BAN has reviewed the information and ascertained that there are no questions about the final destination and processing of the hazardous waste. Despite the intrusiveness of the process, there has been good demand for listing. Some 15 companies signed the pledge and qualified for listing when the program was launched. By the middle of 2006, some 35 processing companies, with hundreds of processing sites and drop-off points in 20 states and several provinces of Canada, were listed.[85]

Focusing on electronic equipment manufacturers, SVTC and the Computer TakeBack Campaign began in 2001 to issue an annual "Computer Company Report Card" that tracks the progress of computer and electronics companies on social and environmental indicators. Their technique has been to survey major companies, but their results are limited to those companies that return the survey. The 2005 Report Card, for example, covered 10 major brand-name computer manufacturers; five other companies (Fujitsu, NEC, Philips, Samsung, and Sharp) chose not to return the survey. Companies were ranked on the basis of their responses in three key areas: takeback programs, recycling and disposal systems, and elimination of toxic materials in manufacturing processes. HP and Dell ranked at the top of the list, with HP ahead significantly on the basis of the quality of its broad takeback program. ViewSonic, IBM, Sony, and Apple fell into a middle range. JVC, Panasonic, Gateway, and Acer ranked at the bottom of the list across all categories.

One distinctive characteristic found in the latest survey is that many of these companies sell into, and abide by, European and Japanese responsibility laws, which require full, free takeback and recycling. But most of these companies refuse to endorse or support comparable legislation in the US, even though it would not undercut market competition because it would presumably affect all of them equally.[86]

On the use of toxic materials, such as lead, mercury, cadmium, brominated flame retardants, and PVC, most of the companies surveyed indicated that they would abide by new European Union regulations restricting the use of hazardous substances, which went into effect in mid-2006. But it remained unclear whether they would apply the same restrictions on equipment shipped to markets outside the EU, including the entire US market.

Greenpeace, which is (surprisingly) not a member of the Computer Take-Back Campaign, began to issue its own "scorecard" on the major computer manufacturing firms, highlighting those with better practices, and identifying and criticizing those with the worst practices. The Greenpeace approach is based solely on public information (mostly website-based) about the companies' continued use of toxic materials and their electronic waste recycling policies. In the August 2006 report, Dell received the highest grade among computer manufacturers, but it was still only a "7" on a scale running from 1 (worst) to 10 (best).[87] Apple (2.7), Acer (2.3), Motorola (1.7), and Lenovo (1.3) were the four worst-rated computer companies in the world. Dell scored especially high on the recycling component because it had announced that it would have voluntary recycling available worldwide by November 2006.

The results of the Computer TakeBack Campaign have been encouraging. By 2006, most of the major computer manufacturers had some form of recycling program in place, even when it was not required by law, though many limited it to their business clients and to certain countries, such as the US and the UK. Some have begun to reduce their use of the worst toxics, but much more remains to be done.

There is, finally, a broader global campaign emerging that promises to link the lessons learned in Europe and the US to e-waste campaigns elsewhere in the world. The International Campaign for Responsible Technology, of which SVTC is a founding member (and which *does* include Greenpeace), brings together like-minded organizations in at least eight different countries, from the US and

Mexico to Thailand and the UK. They are committed to increasing the knowledge, capacity, and participation of those most directly affected in the global electronics industry to ensure the responsible design, manufacturing, and disposal of electronic products.[88]

There is, as yet, no full performance-based certification system that consolidates the principles behind the demands placed by the NGO community on individual companies, and none that recognizes, and respects, the Basel Convention. The International Association of Electronics Recyclers (IAER) claims to have the "first and only certification process designed exclusively to conduct third party audits of electronics recycling facilities,"[89] but it is an ISO-style certification that only confirms management systems are in place without requiring proof that toxics are being properly dealt with in practice. There is more on IAER in Chapter 11, where we examine second-party industry-based systems that don't have much impact, except among those who don't understand the fundamental problems.

Market campaigns on toxics in electronics have been successful in pushing for more responsible recycling, but the standards for that recycling remain relatively vague in the positive sense. That is, it is clear that environmental and social advocacy organizations don't want to see more toxic electronic waste exported from the consuming countries; they don't want to have unprotected prison labor performing those tasks; and they want to see reductions in the use of toxics in electronics as rapidly as may be technologically (and politically) feasible. But there has been no negotiation of standards that clarify the criteria by which the industry will be judged. There is no certification system that would give consumers a clear choice among manufacturers — other than the "scorecards" created by some groups, which lack the monitoring and auditing critical to a credible certification system — and there is no clear seal of approval for companies that reach the highest standards. Right now, this appears to be a major lost opportunity, especially given the evidence that companies in the electronics industry are sensitive to consumer disapproval of inappropriate practices.

REFLECTIONS

In this chapter we have considered a number of potential areas for market campaigns combined with certification systems, just a few out of the hundreds that have been proposed. We can draw a number of lessons that may be useful from the three case studies, which reveal well-developed market campaigns with differing levels of certification systems.

With the exception of the Marine Stewardship Council, the organizations examined here have just begun to explore the potential range of campaigns and full-fledged certification systems linked to the campaigns. So long as there is value associated with what consumers and other businesses consider to be socially and environmentally preferred practices, there will be a business case for participating in certification systems, whether or not advocacy groups have established a market campaign to press for adoption of more ethical practices.

Meanwhile, the range of techniques for exercising that pressure grows daily with the experiences of advocacy groups and the exchange of that information worldwide at the speed of the Internet.

Not all campaigns and not all certification systems are quickly successful. The Marine Stewardship Council had to restructure and refocus before it could begin to show major results. Most other certification systems have faced similar crises that required significant modification of their policies (i.e., the modification of the chain-of-custody system for the Forest Stewardship Council discussed in Chapter 4, and modification of the governance structure of the international certified Fair Trade movement, seen in Chapter 5).

It may be more difficult to create certification systems in some areas than in others. More than 20 years of campaigning for stronger global standards in the apparel and sportswear supply chain has produced, at best, limited results. Until recently, neither the FLA nor the WRC approaches to standard setting and monitoring have had significant impact on the industry. Each has been able to claim minor, temporary victories, but the cumulative impact has been negligible. The Designated Supplier Program of the WRC offers great promise, although there are concerns about major missing elements, such as a logo to distinguish certified products in the marketplace.

Certification systems ignore the importance of advocacy NGOs at great risk. The most telling critique of the Marine Stewardship Council, when it almost collapsed in 2004, was the lack of NGO support for its procedures and its outcomes. The WRC, I suspect, will need to broaden its base of support beyond the United Students Against Sweatshops if it hopes to extend the impact of its emerging certification system beyond college- and university-licensed products.

Some certification systems suffer from a lack of tangible benefits to industry, as the FSC, the MSC, and Fair Trade did in their early years. These latter systems took off when their processes, their credibility, and their labeled products began to give companies a competitive edge in the market. And this occurs largely, I would argue, because they are able to bring to the marketplace a new product whose ethical origins are clearly distinguished.

Some certification systems suffer from organizational issues at various times in their development. The result is that companies are less willing to trust their commitment to new standards will be managed effectively and at reasonable cost. Other systems suffer from structural issues in the industry, such as the extreme competitiveness of the apparel industry. But I am convinced, in that case, that creative product development and marketing could overcome those structural characteristics. As soon as we are talking about distinguishable products that carry enhanced social and environmental qualities, the opportunity for different price points becomes clear.

Finally, the ability of smart advocacy groups to use persistent pressure to change the most egregious practices of individual corporations, as in the case of Dell's prison-based recycling effort, and then to extend the change to other firms in the industry, continues to be a major force that is far from spent.

11

Industry Push Back, and the Failure of Second-Party Certification Efforts

There was a time in the mid-1990s when social and environmental NGOs in the United States thought it would be better to attempt to create a single, over-arching certification process, a "big tent" that would encompass multiple com-modities and services.[1] Advocates hoped that consumers, the expected drivers of the systems, would be less confused if there were a single system, patterned roughly on the Nordic Swan certification in northern Europe. Although such a complex effort was expected to cost much more to set up, NGOs believed the re-duced costs of educating consumers about a single system might offset those start-up costs.

In reality, it is unlikely that a single overarching certification system would have succeeded. Given the pattern of industry response to the most socially and environmentally responsible systems we have seen in the past ten years, a coordi-nated industry resistance to a "big tent" certification process would probably have muted the impact of industry-specific campaigns and blunted the ability of single-sector certification systems to achieve what they have in fact achieved.

Even those single-sector systems described in earlier chapters, some of which have been accepted by corporations as verifiable forms of corporate accountabil-ity, have not grown without resistance. Companies that were the targets of mar-ket campaigns have responded by attacking the legitimacy of the NGOs behind the campaigns, although without a great deal of success. More importantly, in virtually every field we have covered, from forestry and fisheries to mining and toxics, the strongest and most demanding standards have been countered by in-dustries' creation of their own less-demanding standards. By establishing these systems, industries claim to be setting high levels of responsibility, but without requiring major changes in corporate practices. Despite the companies' huge in-vestments in alternative systems, virtually none of the copycat systems have achieved legitimacy in the eyes of civil society and the marketplace.

The battle still rages, and the proliferation of certification schemes, labels, and claims of responsible practices and, effectively, the pursuit of greater ac-countability confirms the fact that companies feel pressure to produce evidence of social and environmental responsibility in the sourcing of the products they sell. The challenges to the leading certification systems, those with the strongest standards and greatest NGO support, are serious and costly to counteract. Once again, credible NGOs play a crucial role in distinguishing between legitimate and bogus standards and certification processes.

In this chapter we'll examine some of the challenges to NGO legitimacy by companies facing market campaigns and look at a few of the less-credible certification systems set up for forestry and agricultural commodities in an attempt to give a veneer of accountability to significantly smaller changes in practices than those required by the leading certification system in each sector.

CHALLENGING NGO LEGITIMACY

We saw in Chapter 3 how Boise Cascade attempted to undermine Rainforest Action Network by attacking its tax-exempt status and threatening to attack foundations it believed were supporting RAN. The attack backfired because it brought RAN a spurt of new funding from donors outraged by Boise Cascade's unconstitutional attempt to silence its strongest critic.

Another good example of this kind of broad-spectrum attack was described in a story published in the *Financial Times* during the 2007 World Economic Forum. Headlined "Gold Miner Calls for Regulation of 'Rogue' NGOs," the story quoted Peter Munk, chairman of Barrick Gold, the world's largest gold mining company. Munk said that "the rapid proliferation of small groups that did not explain their funding, aims or methods had created an urgent need for a system of regulation that would hold them to the same standards of transparency as the companies and governments they criticized."[2] He also argued that "these NGOs are threatening more and more projects, and the local population is left behind with no hope." Rather than attack all NGOs, Munk distinguished between "groups such as Amnesty International and the Sierra Club," which had "played an invaluable role and adhered to high standards of behavior," and the smaller organizations, whose activities not only impeded economic development in some of the poorest countries in the world but also created in effect a "new global tax" by raising the prices of all raw materials.

In a longer interview, published on the *Financial Times* website, Munk elaborated further. He was particularly upset because social and environmental opposition was increasing at a time when commodity markets were strong, prices were rising, and rapid expansion of production made good sense. His strongest argument was that the "rogue NGOs" were depriving local communities of the employment and other benefits of expanded mining investment, benefits ranging from "restaurants and hotels, from education to health, from infrastructure to super-structure."[3]

The number of ironies in this blast at "rogue NGOs" are almost too many to list:

- The No Dirty Gold campaign, which has been the single most effective prod to the gold mining industry, was developed in part — and quite publicly —

by Oxfam America, an NGO that Munk would probably place on the same level of credibility and accountability as Amnesty International.

- The Sierra Club, mentioned so approvingly, has been active in campaigns to reform the mining industry, taking on Barrick itself on a number of occasions, always in collaboration with local community groups such as the Shoshone Indian Nation, independent prospectors, and local ranchers "working to counter attempts by Canadian mining corporations such as Placer Dome [which merged with Barrick in 2006] and American Barrick to force locals off the land."[4]

- On the same day Munk made his statements at Davos and gave the extended interview, Barrick's largest new gold-mining project, the Pascua Lama mine that straddles the Argentina-Chile border, was being blocked by hundreds of local citizens because Barrick's oversize mining vehicles were destroying local roads. Many of the protesters were arrested, including men, women, and children, all from the local communities; many returned the next day to block the roads again. In fact, if one runs through the catalog of recent Barrick mining operations that have been blocked or held up, virtually all of them were blocked by local citizens who did not want the mine opened, despite the promises of employment and other benefits.[5]

- Finally, there may be a "global tax," as Munk describes it, but the cost of socially and environmentally responsible mining is more appropriately called the "real price of mined commodities." NGOs are calling for companies to internalize the social and environmental costs of mining activities that they have been passing on to local people and the planet for far too long.

There is little evidence that this kind of attack on the NGOs building ethical business campaigns has generated any negative response (to the NGOs) from governments or international bodies, but there is continuing concern that some governments may attempt to impose constraints of the sort that Munk and others might seek.

INDUSTRY-LED CERTIFICATION SYSTEMS

The more common response from industries facing a campaign for stronger social and environmental standards has been to create a countervailing system of standards that appears to be as good as the campaigners' system, but which leaves the industry in control and effectively requires less of the companies in the industry. These "second-party certification systems," described in Chapter 1, range from those that do little more than wave a magic wand over the members of an industry association, proclaiming that all members are now certified, to others that integrate most of the characteristics of the legitimate third-party independent systems, but fall short in critical areas.

In Chapter 10 we examined the industry-led Fair Labor Association that certifies labor practices in apparel factories. The most extensive history of competing systems is found in the forest products industry, and industry-led systems also compete with certified Fair Trade coffee and agricultural products. Let's examine both of these areas briefly to see how these systems emerge and why they fail to gain real traction.

Forest Products

As described in Chapter 4, the Forest Stewardship Council (FSC) was created in 1993, the culmination of a process that began some three years earlier. The US forest products industry was very conscious of the evolving attempt to improve forest management practices and saw certification as a major challenge to the entire US industry. Soon after the creation of the FSC, the American Forest & Paper Association (AF&PA) published a set of forest management principles that it encouraged all members of the association to follow. These principles tended to emphasize environmental management systems and discretionary, flexible performance guidelines.[6]

However, as the markets campaigns against Home Depot and other forest products retailers in the US intensified, the industry association realized that it was going to require something with more validity than these simple assurances. In 1994, AF&PA increased the scope of the principles and published "Implementation Guidelines," and the next year the association's leadership announced that all its members would be required to abide by the quickly evolving principles and guidelines, renamed the Sustainable Forestry Initiative (SFI). This was essentially what one pro-SFI observer called "mandatory first-party attestation."[7] That is, all the members of the association had to do was assure the AF&PA leaders that they would follow the guidelines. Even so, AF&PA claimed that 10 of its 250 member companies withdrew from the association and another 15 were dismissed, though it never published the names of the companies in either category. In 1999, AF&PA began to encourage, but did not require, third-party certification to its standards.

During this time, AF&PA company representatives belittled the requirements set out by FSC, then headquartered in Oaxaca, Mexico, as "those Mexican standards that we certainly wouldn't want to use," and some argued that if FSC's respect for the rights of indigenous people were transferred to the US, "most American timber companies could 'kiss their lands good-bye.'" In response to the idea of a chain-of-custody system, they claimed that "having to trace every stick of wood from forest to final use was 'simply un-American.'"[8]

When Home Depot announced its preference for FSC-certified forest products over SFI products in August 1999 — followed within months by similar announcements from Lowe's and seven other major US do-it-yourself chains; home construction companies such as Kaufman and Broad Homes Corporation and Centex Corporation; and Andersen Corporation, the largest wood window manufacturer in the US — the SFI system was sidelined. In truth, although a majority of the wood sold by most of those companies still came from AF&PA members and, therefore, presumably SFI-compliant companies, the principal retailers were not prepared to advertise that fact or to claim that SFI-compliant wood provided any verification of more sustainable forest management.

From 2000 to 2006 the SFI program went through a series of major adjustments, which brought its standards closer to those of the FSC. At the same time, AF&PA sought to generate greater legitimacy by creating a quasi-independent Sustainable Forestry Board (SFB) as its standard-setting authority. At one time, the SFB included such credible members as M. Gustave Speth, dean of the Yale School of Forestry and Environmental Studies, Peter Seligman, CEO of Conservation International, and Steve McCormack, CEO of The Nature Conservancy (TNC). But both Speth and Seligman left the SFB quietly when the AF&PA rolled out an SFI label, effectively proclaiming SFI certification, before the SFB majority felt that either the standards or the verification processes were ready. McCormack remained on the SFB, arguing publicly that he wanted to use TNC influence to raise SFI standards. At the same time, TNC continued to seek FSC certification on most of the forest lands it acquired in the US and internationally.[9]

Environmental NGOs opposed the SFI system loudly and constantly. They dismissed the industry-led process as placing "a fox in the hen-house," arguing that it was completely non-transparent and had no chain-of-custody requirements that would give any assurance about the origins of forest products coming through the SFI system. Social development NGOs pointed out that SFI standards had no social content, no protection for indigenous lands, no requirement for local community engagement, and no labor requirements. A large and persistent problem was "gate wood," timber that was purchased from unknown sources "at the gate of the mill." SFI members refused to be responsible for its provenance, and they refused to exclude it from what they would sell with an SFI label.

Over time, the SFI has come to resemble the FSC more closely in both appearance and function. Modest social standards have been introduced. FSC introduced "volume credit" chain-of-custody processes, and the latest SFI standards now have the same. FSC introduced the concept of "controlled wood" for uncertified sources, so that at least the supply chain is free of timber associated with illegal logging, genetically modified trees, social conflicts, and high-conservation forests. SFI now has standards for excluding wood from "controversial" sources.

In January 2007, responding to great dissatisfaction within the US and Canadian forest products industries at the lack of market uptake of certified SFI products, AF&PA proclaimed the SFI a "fully independent" nonprofit organization with a 15-member board, two-thirds of whom had been handpicked from "outside interest groups such as environmental and conservation groups."[10] In fact, the board included seven CEOs of timber or land companies, two academics, a state forester, and four representatives of environmental organizations that have long worked closely with the industry, in addition to McCormack of TNC.[11]

The environmental NGO attack on the SFI became even more acute. The

Alliance for Credible Forest Certification, made up of Greenpeace, American Lands Alliance, Dogwood Alliance, National Wildlife Federation, ForestEthics, the Natural Resource Council of Maine, and Rainforest Action Network, set up the "Don't Buy SFI" website.[12] It provides extensive information on why SFI certification is still weaker than FSC certification, including a dozen or more systematic comparisons of the two systems.

By the end of 2006, SFI had issued only five or six chain-of-custody certificates, though it claimed that 127 million acres of forest land had been certified independently to its standards in the US and Canada. In 2005 and 2006, the AF&PA and SFI began to lose their control over major companies with forest land holdings in the US. The Potlatch Corporation, a major integrated forest products company certified under SFI guidelines, obtained FSC certification on all of its lands, resigned from the AF&PA, and, it was rumored, was about to drop its SFI certification. As we will see when we look next at industry alternatives in Europe, the greatest attrition involves companies that have been staunch supporters of the copycat certification but have found FSC market demand and price premiums much more attractive.

The principal European counterpart to SFI was Pan-European Forest Certification (PEFC), a program created in 1999. Initially, it developed standards not all that different from FSC standards, although it was generally considered much easier to achieve the requirements for certification. PEFC certification processes were undertaken in a dozen European countries, from Sweden and Finland to Austria and Italy.

In 2005, PEFC morphed quietly into a completely different organization. Renamed the Program for Endorsement of Forest Certification (still PEFC), it no longer pretended to be a standard-setting organization. Instead, unlike FSC or SFI, the new PEFC relies on local standard-setting processes (or "schemes," as it refers to them on its website) in a number of countries around the world, which vary enormously in their comprehensiveness and legitimacy. It has no minimum requirements on such critical issues as the rights of indigenous peoples, protection of high-conservation-value forests, and chain-of-custody processes, and provides no limits on the size of clearcuts, the use of GMO trees, or the use of pesticides and other chemicals. By the end of 2006, PEFC had endorsed what it described as:

> 33 independent national forest certification systems of which 22 to date have been through a rigorous assessment process involving public consultation and the use of independent consultants to provide the assessments on which mutual recognition decisions are taken by the membership. These 22 schemes account for over 196 million hectares of certified forests producing millions of tonnes of certified timber to the market place making PEFC the world's largest certification scheme.[13]

It offers no transparency at all about who has done those assessments, what the results have been, or what the requirements are. It is, again, the magic wand.

SFI=
Same old Forest Industry

Destroying Forests, Deceiving Consumers

SFI-Certified Land, Vancouver Island, British Columbia, Canada. Garth Lenz.

Have you seen ads for the "Sustainable Forestry Initiative" (SFI) by the timber industry? Now see what's behind many wood and paper products sold to you as "SFI-certified." **Do these forests look sustainable to you?**

Conservation organizations representing millions of Americans agree: SFI and its new certification standard aren't legitimate measures of responsible forestry.

SFI "certifies" environmentally destructive practices: things like large-scale clearcutting and toxic chemical use, logging of old growth and endangered forests, and replacement of forests by industrial plantations.

And there's no guarantee that products marketed as SFI-certified actually come from SFI-certified forests. Over half of SFI companies' wood comes from non-SFI forests; yet substantial amounts of it can still be sold with SFI claims or labels.

SFI is little more than a misleading, multi-million dollar marketing scheme created by the American Forest & Paper Association. SFI really means **S**ame old Forest Industry. Don't buy it.

SFI-Certified Land, Coos River Watershed, Coastal Mountain Range, Western Oregon. Francis Eatherington.

SFI-Certified Land, Rogue River Watershed, Cascade Mountain Range, Southwestern Oregon. Francis Eatherington.

Get the facts. www.dontbuysfi.com Don't Buy the SFI.

NRDC · RAINFOREST ACTION NETWORK · SIERRA CLUB · FORESTETHICS · American Lands Alliance · GREENPEACE · Dogwood Alliance · NATURAL RESOURCES COUNCIL OF MAINE · EPIC

In 2005, a WWF International comparative analysis of the FSC and the PEFC focused on three characteristics:

- Whether the scheme drives significant improvements in forest management on the ground.
- Whether the scheme design meets, at a minimum, WWF's core values on meaningful and equitable participation of all major stakeholder groups, reliable and independent assessment, certification decisions free of conflicts of interest, transparency in decision making and reporting.
- Whether the system delivers consistency across countries.[14]

The results of the comparison were summarized succinctly:

FSC meets the abovementioned three key elements of fundamental importance to WWF. PEFC demonstrated inconsistency, was more difficult to measure due to lack of transparency, and, in most cases, was inferior to FSC. WWF can therefore only recommend FSC to consumers, forest owners, governments, companies, financial institutions and other concerned stakeholders as delivering on credible forest certification. . . .

"Despite positive improvements within several certification schemes in the last few years, the results of the tests show that the different PEFC schemes are highly inconsistent in quality and comprehensiveness and that PEFC as a system cannot guarantee well-managed forests. This makes it impossible for WWF to recommend PEFC to forest managers, buyers and consumers, even though individual PEFC national schemes like the UK and Sweden perform better than other PEFC national schemes," added Per Rosenberg, Director of the WWF Global Forest and Trade Network.

A somewhat less charitable assessment was provided by the European environmental NGO Fern in two studies, the first in 2001 and the second in 2004. The first Fern report, written before the PEFC morphing took place, analyzed not only FSC and PEFC, but also the Canadian Standards Association (CSA) certification system and the SFI system. That report was harshest in its assessment of PEFC:

No overall performance-based standard exists to which PEFC standards must adhere. The criteria and indicators developed in the Pan European Process are used as a basis for the PEFC. However, these criteria concentrate more on putting systems in place than on outcome. No minimum environmental or social thresholds have been defined. This absence of an overall performance-based standard has led to widely different national standards, some of which are better than others. Of even greater concern, is the certification process itself. No clear rules are described on how certification should take place. This has led to the situation where, in some countries, almost all forests have been certified without a visit by a third-party certifier (Germany); while in other cases forests are listed as certified although certifiers have not yet been accredited (Sweden and Finland).

Another concern is that the PEFC system gives one group of stakeholders (notably the forest owners and wood-processing industry) the opportunity to dominate the process, thereby violating one of the principles of certification endorsed by governments and industry.... Clearly the PEFC is an organization by and for private forest owners or their associations.[15]

Fern gave the SFI higher grades than PEFC in 2001, saying that SFI "can be considered a worthwhile initiative as it has led to some measure of improvement in forest management." In the end, however, Fern concluded that SFI's weak, flexible, and open-ended standards and lack of attention to social issues meant it was "not a credible certification and labeling scheme."

Three years later, Fern revisited the four certification schemes originally studied and also assessed the Australian Forestry Standard (AFS), the Brazilian national standard (CERFLOR), the Chilean national standard (Certfor), and the Malaysian Timber Certification Council's program (MTCC), all of which had been "endorsed" by the PEFC. Fern's summarized findings found little new:
- Each of the eight had different forest management standards, with different procedures and labeling rules.
- Most of them certified the status quo, thereby undermining the concept of certification.
- All of them, save the FSC, allowed current conversion of forests to plantations.
- Half of the schemes were not transparent, for neither the standards themselves nor auditing reports were available on websites.
- Social issues, such as land rights and user rights, were not addressed or were not sufficiently addressed by any of the schemes, "although FSC again [was] well ahead of its competitors."
- Most of the eight, with the exception of the FSC and the CSA, did not involve broad sets of stakeholders outside the forest products industry itself in the development of their standards.[16]

The market uptake of different forest certification schemes remains imbalanced. The only one for which there is widespread public acceptance, strengthened market access, and demand that persistently exceeds supply is the FSC system. The giant publishing company Time, Inc., has established public policies that will move it toward using only paper that is certified to one or another of these standards; but it has also made it clear to all its suppliers that it will move to FSC-certified paper as quickly as the expansion of FSC supply permits. Major global companies such as Ikea and Tetra Pak have created formal, structured, stair-step programs for their suppliers, with time limits for moving from step to step. And in both of these stair-step systems, supplying FSC-certified wood, pulp, and paper is the only way to reach the highest step. Suppliers must reach that step within four or five years or they will be passed over for other suppliers who do reach it.

Coffee and Other Agricultural Products

In Chapter 5 we traced the evolution of the Fair Trade movement, especially the certified Fair Trade component of the movement, which is part of the certification revolution. A proliferation of labels claiming comparable improvements has challenged the movement's efforts to certify the fairness and the ecological sustainability of agricultural production, as well as Fair Trade's attempt to create an alternative global commodity-pricing mechanism.

In view of the rapid growth in demand for certified Fair Trade products in both US and European markets, it is not surprising that competing certification schemes have evolved, generally at the behest of leading companies in the field. The list is long, but we will look at a select few.

I must also admit that deliberate decisions within the Fair Trade movement may have given impetus to the competing systems. For example, certified Fair Trade was initially created to benefit primarily small-scale, often impoverished, producers organized in democratically run cooperatives. As the demand for certified Fair Trade products surged, other farmers with larger farms complained that they had no way to demonstrate social and environmental responsibility through the Fair Trade system. Fair Trade's international regulatory agency, FLO, has been willing to create standards for larger coffee farms, similar to what it created years earlier for tea plantations. But the coffee farmers themselves, especially those from Latin America, have resisted the notion of certifying coffee estates. This reduces or eliminates access to the Fair Trade system for most larger, independent coffee estates ranging in size from a few dozen to thousands of hectares. If these larger producers are to demonstrate their social and environmental responsibility in the marketplace for ethical coffee, they have had to find an alternative certification system that would serve their needs. Nevertheless, Fair Trade coffee producers are convinced that close association with the smallest-scale producers, those who suffer most at the hands of *coyote* intermediaries, brings them access to a special element of the ethical marketplace that would be lost if Fair Trade coffee came from farms of all sizes.

Rainforest Alliance Certified. With much regret, I must classify the agricultural certification program of the Rainforest Alliance in this category of industry-friendly systems that compete explicitly with Fair Trade, and not always with ethically clear claims of "fairness" in production.[17] I have high praise for the Rainforest Alliance's work on FSC certification and the emerging Sustainable Tourism Stewardship Council, but there are several aspects of its certified agricultural program that make it much easier for industry to adopt and use its label, and few aspects that benefit producers, especially small-scale farmers and farm workers.

There is no doubt that the Rainforest Alliance Certified system sets environmental standards that are a significant improvement over conventional agricultural production. They fill the gap, the founder of the Rainforest Alliance once told me, between the small number of producers who are willing to pursue strictly organic production and the large number of producers who know and use only chemically laden production techniques. (It is critical to note that the vast majority of certified Fair Trade coffee sold in the US is also certified organic under the requirements of the USDA Organic label.)

Rainforest Alliance agricultural certification requires that producers reduce the use of agrochemicals, such as pesticides, herbicides, and chemical fertilizers. It requires the introduction of integrated pest management systems; bans the cultivation of genetically engineered crops; and bans the use of most World Health Organization Category I and II agrochemicals, recognized persistent organic pollutants, and any chemical on the Pesticide Action Network's "Dirty Dozen" list. It requires stringent protection of wildlife habitat, coffee production only under shade cover, and strong measures for water conservation.

Unfortunately, Rainforest Alliance social standards are remarkably similar to many of the labor standards discussed in Chapter 10, which have had little tangible impact on the actual conditions under which work is done and workers are paid.[18] They range from statements of the importance of the Universal Declaration of Human Rights to requirements that there be written policies, known to the workers, on hours worked; no mandatory overtime; no outsourcing of labor to get around these criteria; freedom to associate and form labor unions as provided by ILO conventions; on-site housing for permanent workers; access to education for school-age children living on the farm; and fairly standard international health and safety provisions. Because of the presence and use of agrochemicals and other toxic substances, Rainforest Alliance standards have unusually detailed requirements for the training, handling, and disposal of these chemicals. They also, unlike the labor standards discussed in Chapter 10, require both prior certification to its standards and annual auditing. However, the closest that Rainforest Alliance certification comes to Fair Trade's "living wage equivalent" for farmers is a requirement that local minimum wages be paid on coffee farms.

The business press has openly recognized that Rainforest Alliance certification offers a cheaper method for access to ethically motivated consumers. The *Financial Times* has reported on several occasions that Rainforest Alliance certified coffee is available for considerably lower prices, precisely because it carries no guaranteed floor price for producers. One reporter, discussing both Rainforest Alliance and Utz Kapeh, a certification system set up by the Ahold grocery chain (and described below), noted that, "for retailers, the range of certifications available allows them to capture a larger share of the ethical consumer market by offering a product that…is priced much lower than a Fairtrade product."[19] One estimate, in a *Guardian* article otherwise highly complimentary to Rainforest Alliance, noted that Kraft Foods, Rainforest Alliance's largest customer, pays about 20 percent less than the Fair Trade price, under typical market conditions.[20]

The most damaging dimension of Rainforest Alliance's agricultural certification processes are its willingness to accept minimal proportions of certified agricultural product content in the final products that carry its logo. Yuban coffee, a very popular lower-grade canned coffee available nationwide in the US, proudly advertises on the front of its cans that 30% of the contents are Rainforest Alliance Certified. What are consumers to believe about the other 70% of that coffee? That it is pesticide-laced and irresponsible in its water use? In neither of the other certification systems with which RA is associated, FSC forest certification and the Sustainable Tourism certification, would it allow the use of its logo with such a low bar. And neither organic certification nor Fair Trade certification allow anything other than 100% certified content in labeled products. This misjudgment on the part of RA is, I believe, a serious blow to the integrity of the certification revolution.

It would be unfair to call Rainforest Alliance certification of agricultural products an industry-led process. But it is not unfair to suggest that the Rainforest Alliance has found a way to undercut Fair Trade certification, to reach ethical consumers with a process that provides fewer benefits to farmers and farm workers, and to give mainstream companies a cheaper, less beneficial way to show some levels of accountability.

Utz Kapeh. Another, more recent, entry into the coffee certification world is a system called Utz Kapeh, which is said to mean "'good coffee' in a Mayan language," though I have not been able to find a Mayan linguist who agrees. Created largely with the financial support of Ahold, the giant Dutch food retailer,[21] the Utz Kapeh certification system focuses primarily on traceability through on-site documentation and management systems, together with computer-based linking of purchasing data from both buyers and sellers.

The environmental standards required of Utz Kapeh certified farmers are far weaker than those of either Fair Trade or Rainforest Alliance. Utz Kapeh's standard 3.C.1, for example, explicitly announces that genetically modified coffee plants, though not presently available, would be allowable so long as farmers obey local regulations on their use.[22] Any kind of chemical fertilizer may be used as long as an external, technically qualified advisor has determined the quantity of fertilizer to be used (5.A.1). No chemical pesticides or fungicides banned in the European Union, the US, or Japan may be used, but any that are acceptable in those three markets are acceptable on coffee farms if they are applied "according to the label" (7.A).

The social dimensions of Utz Kapeh require only that the appropriate responsible person on the farm be aware of national legislation for wages, working hours, child labor, etc. Anything allowed under national law is allowed on Utz Kapeh farms, including working hours in excess of the International Labor Organization's maximum of 48 hours in any "peak harvest periods" (10.F.1). Other ILO conventions on the treatment of workers are more strongly incorporated into Utz Kapeh standards, such as ILO convention 87 (on freedom of association) and convention 98 (on the right to organize).

There is no stipulated or recommended price for Utz Kapeh certified coffee.

Rather, its website suggests that the farmer and the Utz Kapeh registered buyer "explicitly agree upon the premium that is paid for the Utz Kapeh certification." So there is no guarantee of any premium for any farmers.

Common Code for the Coffee Community Association (4C Association). The concerns of the mainstream coffee producer associations and the European coffee industry have been reflected in the creation of yet another coffee certification system, the Common Code for the Coffee Community Association (or "4C Association"), which was formally launched in December 2006.[23] The purpose of the 4C is "continuously improving the level of sustainability in the production, processing and trading of all green coffee." It is focused on what it calls the "mainstream coffee industry" (as opposed to the specialty coffee industry, where companies like Starbucks are industry leaders), and its initial 37 members represent a "Who's Who" of the European coffee manufacturing industry and the largest conventional coffee associations in the leading producer countries, including Brazil, Colombia, Indonesia, Mexico, Ethiopia, and Guatemala. The standard-setting process, developed over the previous two years, was led and financed by the German and Swiss aid agencies. Partners also include Oxfam, Rainforest Alliance, the International Institute for Sustainable Development, and the largest conventional coffee vendors: Nestlé, Kraft, Sara Lee, and Procter & Gamble.[24]

It remains unclear how the "common code" they propose to release will interact with the existing standard-setting organizations. But it is certainly another piece of evidence that social and environmental certification has become a critical mainstream element in a very large industry. Whether the 4C code will be capable of reaching and maintaining the standards established by the Fair Trade system or even the Rainforest Alliance's certification is doubtful.

REFLECTIONS

We could expand the list of competitive certification processes to cover many other industries.

- The work of the Silicon Valley Toxics Coalition is being countered by the International Association of Electronics Recyclers, who in 2006 produced "Release 2" of its own standards for Certified Electronics Recyclers.[25] This new version, similar to the first, requires the creation of a recycling-oriented environmental management system, but it contains none of the social and environmental performance measures stipulated by SVTC or the Computer TakeBack Campaign.
- The Marine Stewardship Council has faced opposition from national and international fisheries industry associations who object to the stringency of its standards.
- Second-party industry standards in mining, like the International Cyanide Management Code, created in 2005 and first implemented in January 2007, have earned little credibility because there was virtually no civil society

participation in their development.[26] Yet the cyanide standards may now be-come important components of the emerging Initiative for Responsible Mining Assurance, discussed in Chapter 8, which has extensive NGO and other civil society participation.

This is, I believe, simply the hallmark of growing competition for defining ac-countability in supply chains. Companies and industry associations can no longer proclaim that their "codes of conduct" are all that businesses throughout their supply chains and, ultimately, consumers need to be certain of their respon-sible management of social and environmental issues. In this new era of cer-tified corporate accountability, the proliferation of standards and stakeholder processes, and the quest for credibility and legitimacy, set the new business battlefield, shaped and constrained by ever-more-powerful civil society organi-zations reflecting the changing expectations of this generation. And competition among those standard-setting processes will combine quests for the moral high ground and the efficient delivery of certification services in ways that reward and encourage the highest level of accountable practices.

12

The Mother of All Campaigns:
Taking on Wal-Mart and the Looming Domination
of Big-Box Retail Stores

Market campaigns, as we've seen in previous chapters, have been most successful when they focus on a limited set of products or product lines whose supply chains are relatively easy to trace and when they are associated with highly branded companies. We also saw that some of the most effective campaigns have been organized against the last stage of the supply chain, the retail stage, because of the growing scale, concentration, and branding of major retail companies. Home Depot was an early and classic example. Staples, a leader in the office supply industry, was another. Both those retail chains were the focus of campaigns targeting a small set of the products they sell: lumber and other wood products in the case of Home Depot; office paper products in the case of Staples.

But how does one influence the social and environmental practices of highly branded companies that may have 50,000 different products in a single giant retail store (as measured by differing "SKUs" or "stock keeping units"). More importantly, how does one take the level of social and environmental responsibility beyond the sourcing of a few products and shift the focus to a much fuller range of issues, such as labor practices in the retail outlets, the environmental characteristics of the retail stores they build, the impact that they have on the community's pre-existing businesses, and the broader social impact they have on local demand for public services, including school enrollments, contributions to local tax bases, and locally subsidized health and medical services?

BIG-BOX RETAIL

Retail stores of this type are generally described as "big-box retail" outlets.[1] The principle characteristics of "big-box retail," identified in a Columbia University urbanism lab, include the following:

- Each store typically occupies more than 50,000 square feet, with common ranges between 90,000 and 200,000 square feet. (For comparison, there are 27,000 square feet in the box inside goal lines and sidelines on a standard US football field; there are 43,600 square feet in an acre.)
- These companies, and their stores, derive their profits from high sales volumes rather than price markup.

- The stores are generally located in large, windowless, rectangular, single-story buildings with standardized and recognizable facades.
- They rely strongly on car-driving shoppers, so there are usually many acres of paved parking around each store.
- They favor no-frills site development that omits any community or pedestrian amenities.
- They seem to be everywhere and unique to no place, be it a rural town or an urban neighborhood.
- From an urban planning perspective, they have a profound impact on the character of a community.[2]

It seems that big-box retail stores have boomed in both size and variety because they offer low prices and great shopping convenience to an increasingly time-deprived society.[3] They are also known as "value retailers," "superstores," and "category killers." The last term refers to the fact that after a big-box store opens in a community, pre-existing local shops that compete in the big box's key categories often go out of business. Home Depot has frequently been accused of bankrupting local hardware stores and forcing small lumber yards to move or close. IKEA, the low-cost furniture and home equipment vendor, competes strongly across many categories, in particular challenging already existing department stores. And Wal-Mart, the largest corporation in the world, is accused of being a local category-killer in several arenas, from groceries and pharmacies to meat markets, fish shops, and various local gift and service businesses. In Europe there has been a similar surge of big-box retail vending with B&Q and Tesco in the United Kingdom, Carrefour in France, Obi in Germany, and, of course, IKEA, based in Sweden. With the exception of IKEA, however, the average size of the European big-box retail stores is considerably less than that found in the United States.

The phenomenon of the big-box store has emerged relatively recently, though many of us can remember the early Sears, Roebuck and Montgomery Ward department stores of half a century ago. What has changed in the global organization of the economy is the rapid growth and the extraordinary concentration of category-killer retailing. It was only 30 years ago that I taught my economics undergraduate students, from the textbooks of those days, that the emerging ideal model for economic development was closely associated with the vertical integration of manufacturing businesses; significant economies were achieved by firms that owned the entire process, from mines to smelters, steel mills, and production facilities that manufactured products made of steel, including appliances and automobiles. The antithesis of development was the situation where a company produced only raw materials, which were then sent off to someone else, often in another state or another country, for the processing and manufacturing that would add value and take the product to its final retail condition. In general, in those days, single companies did own a larger proportion of the supply chain for a finished product, and they tended to have more control over the retail pricing of their products. Competition occurred between the appliance stores associated with a single brand, like General Electric or Westing-house, rather than among vendors of many brands. Today, that model seems quaint. Competition, and development, occurs among those who can produce increasingly standardized products at the lowest possible price.

Over the past 10 to 15 years, the concentration of retailing in an ever-smaller number of big-box superstores has shifted the locus of pricing power from the major branded manufacturing firms to the giant retail stores. This has coincided with, and been driven in part by, the growing importance of private-label brands. Sears, Roebuck was the most successful retailer of private-label brands in the last century, with its Kenmore line of appliances and its Craftsman line of tools signaling the shift from retailing someone else's brand to contracting with some-one to manufacture to your specifications and placing your own brand on the final product, even when the final product is essentially identical to one that you may have been selling under the manufacturer's brand. Private-label brands are one of the most rapidly growing elements in appliances and prepared food marketing, and there is evidence that this is also a growing trend for general mer-chandise. Private-label manufacturing represents the ultimate shift from name-brand products, where the manufacturer retains some price control, to retail-driven manufacturing, where the manufacturer is wholly at the mercy of the retailer's designs and willingness to pay. The larger the retail business, both in terms of total sales and number of outlets, the greater the power to design and in-troduce private-label products.

Big-box retail stores represent a concentration of category-killing retail func-tions and private-label contracting, and the pre-eminent example of this genre, for better or for worse, is Wal-Mart.

FOCUS ON WAL-MART

Wal-Mart is now the world's largest corporation by total sales (or turnover), ex-ceeding the total sales of General Motors, the long-time leader, even before GM's recent precipitous decline. What makes Wal-Mart such a target for corporate campaigners, though, is its cutthroat corporate culture, which, in its own words, drives every penny of excess cost out of production.

Wal-Mart is the most prominent example of the growing primacy of retailers in the supply chains for products of all kinds. There are many other examples, as discussed above, but Wal-Mart has been the most successful if we measure suc-cess by rates of increase in total number of stores and total sales. It has grown to a scale that gives it the power to dictate not just the shape and form of new prod-ucts but also the prices that it will pay, and that suppliers must accept, if they want to continue to receive orders from their largest customer.

Wal-Mart is extolled by financial analysts as a brilliant innovator of new methods for supply-chain management, using the latest technology for inven-tory control, radio-frequency-identification (RFID) tagging, and standardiza-tion of information flows with its suppliers.[4] By forcing its suppliers to adopt and implement its processes, it is transforming the field of global logistics.

The campaign to transform Wal-Mart into a more responsible retailer has been going on for many years, but it was only in April 2005 that major campaigning organizations in the United States turned their full attention to Wal-Mart. The results have been dramatic.

In this chapter we will see how Wal-Mart has responded to the challenges to its brand brought by literally dozens of increasingly coordinated groups. It is a fascinating story of aggressive steps and calamitous missteps, of Wal-Mart turning its competitive internal culture into a weapon against the campaigns themselves, and of glimmers of possibility that the world's largest corporation might become a world leader on environmental grounds, though perhaps not on social grounds. And it is a story of the challenges confronting the campaigners themselves as they face the prospect of success: if Wal-Mart does change, in response to their pressure, it might become a paragon of environmental practice and improved social practices, made stronger in its international competitive success precisely because of that transformation. It is a story of global transformation that reinforces the lessons from earlier chapters and raises new questions about their long-term efficacy.

THE ISSUES

Why has Wal-Mart become such an important target for social and environmental campaigners? The answers are as complex as they are vast. There are so many dimensions of the Wal-Mart model for growth and domination in the markets in which it works that there has emerged a huge literature that provides a litany of criticisms.[5]

First and foremost are its labor practices, which galvanized its most powerful critics, the labor unions in the US and elsewhere that have been battling for improved wages and benefits in its stores and in many of the factories, especially in China, where the largest share of its products are manufactured. Wal-Mart has also been challenged on the low level of benefits it provides to the majority of its workers. It is hurt by its poor environmental image, particularly for the negative impacts it has on fisheries and on local communities. It has been chastised for the high levels of tax subsidies it manages to coax from state and local governments. And the "Wal-Mart effect" on local economic development, national economic policies, and the future of both manufacturing and services in America, as well as in the world's globalized economy, raises concerns for many people, inside and outside the business world.

Labor Practices

Wal-Mart's corporate culture is intensely opposed to organized labor. James Hoopes, a Babson College business professor, has noted that Wal-Mart's cost of business runs well below that of its competitors. Part of this advantage is the result of innovations in distribution systems and sophisticated sales and shipment tracking, but a large proportion of those cost savings come from lower labor costs.[6] The company trains its managers to fight off unions by telling them they are "expected to support the company's position," even though it may mean "walking a tightrope between legitimate campaigning and improper conduct."[7] When labor organizing seems to be gaining ground at a store, Wal-Mart flies "labor relations teams" to the scene by private jet to undercut the union efforts.[8]

The impact of Wal-Mart's anti-union practices is not limited to its own employees. The company threatens unionized industries in Wal-Mart's supply chains for a wide variety of products, and in the retail stores of competitors. In 2005, a significant factor driving the long and difficult California strike against Albertson's and other grocery chains was the attempt by Albertson's and the others to cut back union benefits in order to remain competitive with Wal-Mart.

In its quest to keep labor costs down, Wal-Mart has been repeatedly sued for illegal labor practices, including the following:
- Illegally altering thousands of employee time cards to reduce payroll.[9]
- Violating child labor laws.[10]
- Violating state laws requiring time for breaks and meals.[11]
- Engaging in illegal and deceptive practices to counter union organizing efforts.[12]
- Coercing employees to work overtime without pay.[13]
- Conspiring with contractors to recruit and hire illegal immigrants to clean stores and then cheat them out of overtime pay.[14]
- Paying significantly lower average wages to female workers in all categories, and discriminating against women workers for promotions to management positions.[15]

In most cases, the suits have been settled out of court or the judge has ruled against Wal-Mart.

Environmental Concerns

Wal-Mart is considered a threat to the environment because its attempts to drive down the costs of products that come from extractive industries (i.e., forestry for wood and paper, fisheries, and mining for gold and silver jewelry) accelerate the destruction of environment, communities, and human health. In part it does this by encouraging domestic producers to move their production to less-developed countries where environmental protection is often less stringent. More generally, Wal-Mart's relentless pressure on suppliers to lower costs tilts the competitive playing field against producers who prefer to use more sustainable practices, who pay living wages with decent benefits, and who spend their money in local communities and create local jobs.

Wal-Mart is the largest vendor of seafood in the US. By pressuring seafood suppliers to lower their costs, Wal-Mart encourages the most damaging practices of the commercial fishing industry, including long-line fishing with terrible by-catch damage, bottom trawling that drags heavy nets across the sea floor, and fish farming that has been associated with heavy pesticide and antibiotic use, destruction of wild fish runs, and contamination of fish from tainted feed.[16]

Wal-Mart is also one of the largest retailers of pork, chicken, and beef. Through the cost-cutting pressure it places on producers of these products, with the constant threat to purchase overseas if prices are not brought down in local markets, Wal-Mart perpetuates the cruelest farming practices. It has been associated with some of the worst practices in this business, including bribery, fraud, and the destruction of records.[17]

Tax Subsidies

The issue that irritates the largest number of local citizens across the political spectrum is Wal-Mart's deliberate strategy to generate major subsidies from state, local, and federal governments in order to reduce its costs. According to a report of the US Congress Committee on Education and the Workforce, in 2004, Wal-Mart employees were eligible for an estimated $2.5 billion in federal assistance because their wages were so low and the number of hours they worked so few that they fell below the poverty lines specified for major anti-poverty programs.[18] According to the report, if we assume that most Wal-Mart employees take advantage of the federal programs for which they are eligible, one 200-employee Wal-Mart store may cost federal taxpayers $420,750 per year. This includes, on average, the following items:

- $36,000 a year for free and reduced-cost lunches for the children from the 50 families (25 percent of those 200 employees) who would qualify for the school lunch programs.
- $42,000 a year for low-income housing assistance.
- $125,000 a year for federal tax credits and deductions for low-income families
- $100,000 a year for additional expenses for programs for students.
- $108,000 a year for additional federal health care costs of state children's health insurance programs (S-CHIP).
- $9,750 a year for additional costs for low-income energy assistance.

At the local level, Wal-Mart seeks, and often gets, a wide assortment of subsidies from local officials who assume that Wal-Mart will generate significant numbers of new jobs and other local economic growth. The subsidies include free or reduced-price land, infrastructure (such as access roads and water or sewer lines), tax-increment financing that returns to Wal-Mart the increases in tax collections at the local level, property tax abatement, state corporate income credits, sales tax rebates, and tax-exempt bond financing.[19] Although much of the information needed to estimate the full extent of those subsidies is confidential, one study of a sample of 91 Wal-Mart stores, Supercenters, and distribution facilities found that they had received a total of $245 million in recorded subsidies from local economic development agencies, an average of $2.8 million per store.[20]

Unfortunately, the assumption that Wal-Mart creates significant increases in the number of jobs and related retail activity does not stand up to the test of research. There is a large and growing body of studies that shows the placement of a Wal-Mart Supercenter *may* increase employment by some 30 to 50 low-wage employees (after the closing of competing businesses is accounted for);[21] but there is even more evidence that the net impact is broadly negative. A study by two Penn State professors analyzed what happened to poverty rates in all counties across the US between 1989 and 1999. While they found that the booming economy of that decade, especially the latter half, reduced average poverty rates from 13.1 percent to 10.7 percent, those counties that had one or more Wal-Mart stores before 1989 or that gained one or more during the 1990s had higher average poverty rates and less reduction of poverty than those that were "Wal-Mart-free." Controlling statistically for all the other potential explanations for poverty-level changes, the authors of the study concluded, "We find that the presence of Wal-Mart unequivocally raised family poverty rates in US counties during the 1990s."[22]

The Wal-Mart Effect

The sheer size of Wal-Mart draws attention. According to the "Forbes Global 2000" for 2005, Wal-Mart's total sales that year exceeded $285 billion, making it the largest corporation in the world as measured by sales, larger even than the oil giants BP, ExxonMobil, and Royal Dutch/Shell, and 32 percent larger than General Motors, the long-time US total sales leader.[23] Its total worldwide employment of 1.6 million made it the largest private company in the world by number of people employed. By market capitalization value, it was the eighth largest company in the world, with total value of $218 billion, half that of the world leader, ExxonMobil. Its $10 billion in profits ranked it 11th in the world, behind only the oil giants, Citigroup and General Electric. Within its category, retailing, its total sales were nearly four times greater than those of its nearest competitor, Home Depot; six times larger than those of its closest general-merchandise retail competition, Costco and Target; and more than eight times larger than those of its closest non-US competitors, the Aeon Group of Japan and PPR, the luxury goods retailer based in France. According to Wal-Mart's 2005 annual report, it had more than 3,600 stores in the US, including Sam's Clubs; nearly 3,200 stores outside the US; and plans to add 530 new stores in 2006 — nearly 1.6 new stores per day.[24]

Wal-Mart sells over 30 percent of all household staples (such as toothpaste, detergents, and cleaning products) sold in the US; its share may reach 50 percent by the end of the decade.[25] It is the largest seller of groceries in the US, and its sales of prescription drugs make it the third-largest pharmacy operator.[26] It is the largest seller of toys, furniture, jewelry, dog food, and many other consumer products.[27] And Wal-Mart accounts for nearly 25 percent of the apparel market in the US, including sales of jeans, blouses, sweatsuits, and underwear.[28]

Wal-Mart's domination of those markets gives it unprecedented monopsony power. This is the theoretical economic power that accrues to the single most powerful buyer of specific products. Leading manufacturers of the products it sells cannot afford to lose their largest client, and Wal-Mart takes direct advantage of that to negotiate prices below those that the manufacturers charge Wal-Mart's lower-volume competitors.

The *Wall Street Journal* highlighted the problem that dependence on Wal-Mart sales creates for its suppliers in a story that opened: "If Wal-Mart Stores Inc. just sniffles instead of sneezes, its suppliers sell fewer tissues."[29] The story went on to describe Wal-Mart's decision to cut $6 billion from its inventory costs, which forced many of its principal suppliers to lower their announced sales targets and revise profitability estimates before issuing second-quarter reports for 2006. As a result of Wal-Mart's inventory adjustment decision, Procter & Gamble saw its stock fall by more than 3 percent (Wal-Mart purchases make up 16 percent of P&G's total sales). Spectrum, which includes Rayovac, Nature's Miracle, Remington, and Spectra among its 20-odd brands, saw its stock plunge 26 percent (Wal-Mart is the single largest buyer of its products, accounting for 18 percent of its total sales). Wal-Mart accounted for more than 20 percent of the annual sales of five of its major supplier companies: Playtex Products (28 percent), Clorox (27 percent), and Hasbro, Revlon, and Tootsie Roll Industries (each with 24 percent).[30]

Wal-Mart tactics have made it a threat to state and local governments as well. As it runs out of places to locate new stores, or upgrade old stores to Supercenters, in the South, Southwest, and rural Midwest of the US, it is investing millions of dollars in campaigns to influence county and municipal governments in other parts of the country to provide the approvals necessary, and subsidies whenever possible, for the construction of new stores. When it cannot obtain the approval, it tries to go around the local authorities with voter referendums or other initiatives that undercut local authority. In Inglewood, California, for example, when the local authorities refused permits for a new store, Wal-Mart sought to bypass the local government with a referendum process that would have excluded the land it had purchased from local control. Wal-Mart lost.[31] Even *Business Week,* in a 2003 editorial titled "The High Cost of Low Prices," expressed concern about Wal-Mart's powerful impact:

Shoppers love Wal-Mart Stores Inc. Its policy of "everyday low prices" saves consumers billions of dollars every year, helping to keep the nation's inflation rate low. But its methods of squeezing out those low prices — paying salaries below the poverty line, building superstores that crush local mom-and-pop shops, and pushing manufacturers to the wall for savings are generating a strong backlash. So, too, is the exportation of the Bentonville (Ark.) behemoth's Southern-style cultural conservatism into big-city and suburban regions of America that hold different social values. There's a growing sense that Wal-Mart may be too powerful. If the company is to continue to succeed, it may have to focus more energy on dealing with these concerns.[32]

Wal-Mart seeks to exercise its influence over state and federal governments, too.
- It invested a reported $1.26 million in the 2003–4 elections, making it the single largest contributor to federal parties and candidates.[33]
- According to the Center for Responsive Politics, Wal-Mart's political action committee, the second largest in Washington DC, makes 85 percent of its contributions to Republicans.[34]
- When faced with major class-action suits, including the largest class-action suit ever filed (on behalf of 1.6 million women who had been Wal-Mart employees and who alleged rampant gender discrimination), Wal-Mart invested millions in efforts to change federal law to limit class-action suits.
- According to a *Wall Street Journal* report, Wal-Mart is constantly attempting to push through legislation that benefits its business, including laws that would permit Wal-Mart to become a banking company, treaties that would remove all tariffs on imported manufactures, legislation to ban union-organizing activities outside retail stores, and regulations that would protect it from enforcement of immigration law.

With all these issues in play, the multifaceted campaign to transform Wal-Mart began in April 2005, with a blast of advertising from two major unions and the creation of WalMartWatch.com and WakeUpWalMart.com.

THE CAMPAIGN

Many groups had been campaigning against Wal-Mart for many years before a formal coordinated campaign was announced in 2005. Some NGOs had sought to encourage state legislatures and city councils to enact laws that would require big-box retailers (almost always with a principal focus on Wal-Mart) to contribute minimum levels of support to cover the health benefits of their workers, so that the public burden of covering those costs for uninsured, or badly insured, workers would be lessened. Others built campaigns to help communities with "site fights," blocking the establishment of new Wal-Mart stores and Super-Centers. The National Education Association explained the negative impacts of Wal-Mart on schools nationwide. The National Organization for Women organized its campaign against Wal-Mart on women's issues, claiming that Wal-Mart should be called a "Merchant of Shame." And the New Rules Project, organized by the Institute for Local Self-Reliance, focused on the local business consequences of the opening of Wal-Mart stores, issuing nearly 200 press releases and comments on Wal-Mart activities between 2002 and 2005. The Los Angeles Alliance for a New Economy pushed for higher standards for Wal-Mart activities in Southern California and led the coalition in Inglewood that defeated Wal-Mart's attempt to override local community control.

In early 2005, however, the anti-Wal-Mart campaigns took on considerably more force as two major labor unions — the Service Workers International Union (SEIU) and the United Food and Commercial Workers (UFCW) — launched new efforts to coordinate and consolidate the work across the United States.

The UFCW had been attempting to unionize Wal-Mart stores for many years, but with little or no success. The only Wal-Mart retail store in North America successfully unionized, in a process validated by the Canadian government, was in Jonquière, Quebec, 150 miles north of Quebec City, in October 2004.[35] Wal-Mart's response was to announce immediately that it would consider closing the store if it was "not able to reach a collective agreement that is reasonable and that allows the store to function efficiently and ultimately profitable [sic]."[36] Within weeks the store was closed. The only successful partial unionization had taken place in Jacksonville, Texas, in 2000, when the meatpacking department of one Wal-Mart store voted to join the UFCW. Wal-Mart immediately announced a major change nationwide, eliminating all on-site meatcutters and instead shipping pre-packaged meats from distribution centers. The unionized meatcutters in Jacksonville were let go.

The Center for Community and Corporate Ethics did the initial coordination for a campaign that became known as Wal-Mart Watch. It drew together student groups, anti-sweatshop groups, anti-sprawl groups, environmental groups such as the Sierra Club, and broader citizen-action organizations such as Common Cause and the National Partnership for Women and Families.[37] The SEIU helped launch the campaign website, WalMartWatch.com, after SEIU president, Andy Stern, committed $1 million to the start-up of the campaign. The UFCW then launched its own website, WakeUpWalMart.com.

While the two unions shared a combative spirit, their duplicate websites illustrated one of the underlying tensions of the campaign from the start: the inability of SEIU and UFCW to work closely together and to coordinate their activities. Nevertheless, over the first 16 months of the campaigns there was a whirlwind of largely independent activities undertaken by the members of both coalitions; both issued a barrage of press releases, generally in agreement with one another, and both effectively brought significantly greater attention to their complaints. To the surprise of many observers, the unions publicly stated they would no longer focus primarily on organizing Wal-Mart workers into unions; rather, they would publicize to the general public the conditions faced by Wal-

Mart workers and the broad range of problems that made Wal-Mart, from their perspective, a danger to the American economy.

In September 2005, Wake-Up Wal-Mart sent an open letter to Wal-Mart CEO Lee Scott.[38] The letter, which was published in the *Benton County Daily Record,* the local newspaper for Wal-Mart headquarters in Bentonville, Arkansas, set out six demands:

1. **Living Wage.** Pay all Wal-Mart workers a fair living wage so they can support their families.
2. **Affordable Health Care.** Provide all workers comprehensive, affordable health insurance coverage so they can care for their families and no longer be forced to rely on taxpayer-funded public health care.
3. **End Discrimination.** Ensure equal opportunity and equal pay for women and people of color in your workforce at all levels through a stringent and independent monitoring process.
4. **Zero Tolerance on Child Labor.** Adopt a zero tolerance policy and institute an independent monitoring program to stop the exploitation of child labor in the United States and abroad.
5. **Buy American.** Establish a "Buy America" program that annually increases the percentage of "Made in America" goods purchased by Wal-Mart so as to help protect American jobs.
6. **Respect Communities.** Work with local communities to effectively address Wal-Mart's negative impact on issues like traffic, sprawl, the environment, and local businesses.

Also in September, campaigners widened their focus to Wal-Mart's international impact on factories around the world, especially in China. The International Labor Rights Fund filed a novel international class-action suit against the company in state court in Los Angeles, drawing attention to Wal-Mart's lax enforcement of its own code of conduct in suppliers' factories. The lawsuit argued that Wal-Mart's published code of conduct created a contractual relationship between the company and thousands of workers employed by contractors who were supposed to comply with the code.[39] In the lawsuit, workers from Bangladesh, China, Indonesia, Nicaragua, and Swaziland claimed that the Wal-Mart code was violated repeatedly. They alleged that they were not paid the minimum wage in their countries, as stipulated in Wal-Mart's rules for suppliers; that they were not paid overtime; and that some were beaten and locked in their factories by managers. The overseas workers were joined in the suit by workers from California grocery stores who alleged that they had suffered cuts in their pay rates and their benefits so that Wal-Mart could maintain its low prices, and that those prices were partly attributable to violations of Wal-Mart's suppliers' code of conduct.[40]

Wal-Mart's Early Response

The organizers had announced their intentions well before the April 2005 launch of the campaign, and one of Wal-Mart's first moves, in December 2004, was to

Justin Ward of Conservation International's Center for Environmental Leadership in Business

Conservation International's (CI) attempt to persuade Wal-Mart management to establish more sustainable environmental practices didn't make much headway until the national campaign against Wal-Mart began to take shape in the fall of 2004.[41] Then Justin Ward, vice-president for business practices at CI's Center for Environmental Leadership in Business (CELB), was given the task of leading a cross-divisional CELB team focused on Wal-Mart.[42] It was in September 2004 that CELB and BluSkye Sustainability Consulting, Wal-Mart's other major consultant on sustainability issues, made their first presentation to Wal-Mart senior management. They couched their proposals in terms of both bad practices and business risks.

Providing these environmental consultation services for major businesses is a key function of CELB, comparable to the role of Sustainable Finance, Ltd., for major financial institutions. When market campaigners were targeting Office Depot's paper sourcing, CELB helped design the company's response. When Fair Trade campaigners targeted Starbucks, Justin helped Starbucks design its internal "Café Standards" as an alternative to the third-party verified certification system. When McDonald's was challenged on its agricultural product sourcing, CELB helped it design sourcing guidelines for some foods, such as the whitefish for fish sandwiches, a significant proportion of which now comes from MSC-certified sources.

"About half" of Justin's staff of 30 became fully engaged with Wal-Mart in 2005 and 2006. They were paid for their services first through Wal-Mart's contracts with BluSkye and then through direct, tax-deductible grants to Conservation International, for which, Justin insists, proper tracking of the use of the funds takes place.

In December 2004, CELB organized the first quiet meeting in Bentonville for the leaders of some of the largest environmental groups in the US. There was a flurry of back-channel activity among the activists, who wondered whether they should allow CI and Wal-Mart to separate environmental issues from the social issues around which the campaign was also being organized. Wal-Mart was defensive in that first meeting, as were the environmental NGO leaders. Insiders who attended the meeting reported that Wal-Mart was warned it couldn't "solve all its problems" by making some concessions on environmental sustainability issues; rather, Wal-Mart was told that full sustainability involved better relations with communities, as well as better conditions for workers in its stores and in its supply chains.

The career path that brought Justin Ward to his role in the transformation of Wal-Mart's sustainability practices began at the University of Colorado and continued to the University of Montana and finally the University of Minnesota, where he earned a master's degree from the Humphrey Institute of Public Affairs. He then spent 17 years at the Natural Resources Defense Council (NRDC), beginning with work on forestry and sustainable agriculture in the US Pacific Northwest, then international forestry work, including a three-year term on the board of the Forest Stewardship Council. Justin moved to CI in 2000, joining the then-new CELB and rising to vice-president for business practices within three years.

Justin insists that Wal-Mart's transformation is beginning to affect the very groups with which the company is engaging. By conducting store-wide sustainability analyses, Wal-Mart puts increasing pressure on environmental advocacy groups to "come up with solutions" that it can implement. The search for "sustainable shrimp" is an example. The environmental NGO community disagrees over what constitutes sustainably harvested shrimp. Netting wild shrimp is generally seen as damaging to the estuaries where they are found. Shrimp aquaculture is roundly condemned because it often leads to destruction of coastal mangrove forests; the farmed shrimp are highly susceptible to viral infections that force companies to abandon the shrimp farms after the ecological damage has been done; and the farms produce runoff of chemicals and food waste that damage the estuaries which are critical to fish breeding. Wal-Mart is "pushing the envelope," seeing whether the industry-led Global Aquaculture Alliance can come up with standards and practices that would lessen the damage and the risk of criticism.

From Justin's perspective, the Wal-Mart work confirms that NGO commitments to help Wal-Mart design its new sustainability goals represent time and energy well spent. But the extent to which NGOs engage depends on their own internal cultures and their level of comfort with the possibility that they may be co-opted. A number of environmental NGOs are planning to establish permanent offices in Bentonville, he notes, with the expectation that they will continue to contribute to the environmental transformation of Wal-Mart. Others, such as Environmental Defense, have been unwilling to take corporate funding for their work.

bring together leading representatives of national environmental organizations to seek advice on what the company needed to do to "improve their environmental impacts." The meeting was tense, according to some of the participants, because the environmental leaders were conscious that Wal-Mart might try to "peel off" the environmental complaints in order to lessen pressure on its social policies, such as wages and benefits.

Wal-Mart's response to the environmental challenges tapped deeply into its competitive internal corporate culture. It set up more than 14 "sustainability networks," which were structured along the lines of its corporate management units and led by the vice-presidents of each unit.[43] The vice-presidents were named "network captains," and they were each challenged to come up with a variety of short-term and medium-term responses: three "quick wins" in terms of public relations moves on sustainability; two "innovation projects" that might take somewhat longer to work out; and one "big game changer" that might fundamentally change corporate practices worldwide. This was a whole new vein of activity for their buyers (or "merchandisers" as they are called within Wal-Mart), and it was added on top of their normal duties and included in their annual performance reviews. Environmental campaigners who were subsequently invited to Bentonville watched competitive "show and tell" presentations by the network captains in each of the major Wal-Mart buying areas.

The single most embarrassing moment for Wal-Mart in the first year of the campaign was Wal-Mart Watch's release of an internal memo to the Wal-Mart board of directors from Susan Chambers, the company's senior vice-president for benefits, that provided revealing insights into the company's attitudes toward its employees. As reported in the *New York Times,* the memo proposed numerous ways to restrain spending on health care and other benefits while attempting to minimize damage to Wal-Mart's reputation. Among the comments in the memo:

- It admitted that the company's "critics are correct in some of their observations"; specifically the company's "[health] coverage is expensive for low-income families, and Wal-Mart has a significant percentage of associates [employees] and their children on public assistance."
- It acknowledged that Wal-Mart's own records indicate that nearly half (46 percent) the children of employees were not covered by health insurance.
- It argued that Wal-Mart should seek younger employees because those with more years of service cost more, but were no more productive.
- It argued that Wal-Mart should discourage unhealthy job applicants by ensuring that "all jobs…include some physical activity," such as making cashiers gather carts from the parking lot.
- It proposed that Wal-Mart require insured employees to pay more for their spouses' coverage and that the company cut contributions to employee pensions from 4 percent of salaries to 3 percent.[44]

The negative publicity that followed the release of the memo effectively redirected media attention from some of the most important counterattacks that Wal-Mart launched in anticipation of a widely announced "Higher Expectations Week," the high-point of the 2005 campaign against Wal-Mart (see next section).

On October 24, 2005, one day before the revelation of the internal memo, Wal-Mart announced that it would improve its health benefits package slightly by offering a cheaper entry-level plan, with benefits costing as little as $11 per month, but with a $1,000 deductible, which was judged very high for workers earning only about $17,500 per year.[45] More importantly, on October 25, Lee Scott announced a wide range of policy changes designed to counter the image conveyed by the company's environmental critics. These will be discussed in more detail later in the chapter, but briefly, the new policies, crafted in consultation with Conservation International and other major environmental groups, proposed reducing energy use in Wal-Mart stores, doubling the fuel efficiency of its fleet of trucks, greatly reducing the use of packaging, and pressuring its thousands of suppliers to follow the same path.[46] This was a high point in the Wal-Mart counterattack, but it was completely overshadowed in national media by outrage over Wal-Mart's attempts to reduce the benefits of its workers who earn, on average, so little.

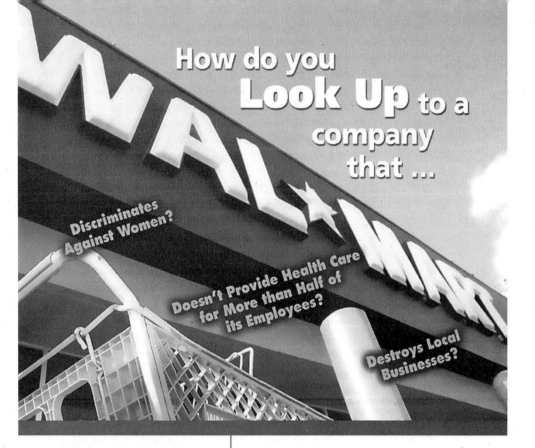

How do you **Look Up** to a company that ...

Discriminates Against Women?

Doesn't Provide Health Care for More than Half of its Employees?

Destroys Local Businesses?

Higher Expectations Week
A National Week of Action
NOVEMBER 13-19, 2005

Local Events

Monday 11/14   7:00 p.m.   Iowa City Public Library —
                             123 South Linn St.
                             (Iowa City)

Legislative Town Hall Meeting with Sen. Joe Bolkcom. Other speakers will include Sarah Swisher from Iowa for Health Care and Andrew Grossman, Executive Director of Wal-Mart Watch.

Tuesday 11/15   7:00 p.m.   Waterloo Center for
                              the Arts —
                              225 Commercial St.
                              (Waterloo)

Panel discussion on "Higher Expectations for Iowa's Working Families." Guests include David Osterberg, Executive Director of Iowa Policy Project, Jonna Higgins, Executive Director of 1000 Friends of Iowa and Jim Jontz, President Emeritus of Americans for Democratic Action.

Wednesday 11/16   8:00 p.m.   CSPS Theater —
                                1103 3rd St. SE
                                (Cedar Rapids)

Screening of the new documentary film "Wal-Mart: The High Cost of Low Price."

For more information on local events, call 1-877-557-2981.

ANNOUNCING

Higher Expectations Week
A National Week of Action

From November 13th-19th, over 400 organizations across the country — from small business owners to environmentalists to women's groups — are coming together to stand up to Wal-Mart.

Wal-Mart Watch is sponsoring over 1,000 public events in all 50 states, including town hall meetings with elected officials, sermons by religious leaders, and premiere screenings of the new documentary film, "Wal-Mart: The High Cost of Low Price."

Wal-Mart Watch wants your ideas, participation, and commitment to set higher standards for the world's largest company. As Wal-Mart founder Sam Walton once said, "High expectations are the key to everything". We agree.

Learn more at www.walmartwatch.com.

 WAL·MART**WATCH**

"Perhaps no other group is scrutinizing the company more thoroughly than Wal-Mart Watch."
— *Arkansas Democrat Gazette, 6/5/05*

This is your week to fight back!

Higher Expectations Week

Much of the early campaign activity focused on a week of coordinated actions from November 13 to 19. More than 400 groups across the country planned several hundred actions. Dubbed Higher Expectations Week, it coincided with the launch of *Wal-Mart: The High Cost of Low Price*, a feature-length movie by director Robert Greenwald about Wal-Mart and its practices. *Business Week* called it "bitingly satirical."[47] Although Wal-Mart promptly put up a website with selected bad reviews of Greenwald's earlier films, a typical review in the major media was more like the one by *Los Angeles Times* reviewer Kenneth Turan, which read, in part:

> "Wal-Mart: The High Cost of Low Price" is an engrossing, muckraking documentary about the retail giant that's been called "the world's largest, richest and probably meanest corporation." But if you're expecting an angry diatribe, you're going to be disappointed.
>
> Instead, the predominant feeling coming off the screen in the latest film from director Robert Greenwald ("Outfoxed: Rupert Murdoch's War on Journalism," "Uncovered: The War on Iraq") is a kind of baffled disenchantment and sadness. That's because Greenwald has shrewdly chosen not to go with classic talking head types like economists, academics and journalists. Instead he talked to current and former Wal-Mart employees, including several with a dozen or more years with the company. The story they tell is not a happy one.
>
> For these were people who had bought completely into the Wal-Mart mythology, the lure of working for a strong organization that offered opportunities for advancement and cared enough about its employees to call them associates. Realizing that the company they worked for was not the Wal-Mart of their dreams was often a shattering experience, a coming to terms with a god that failed.[48]

AdAge.com cited the filmmaker's innovative distribution methods — he used church groups and a 30-second web-based commercial, still available on You Tube.com, that was downloaded more than 100,000 times.[49]

> The nontraditional distribution model, which includes an online viral strategy, shows evidence of working already. A spot circulating on the Web, "The Gospel According to Sam Walton," stars James Cromwell, from HBO's Six Feet Under and former president of the Screen Actors Guild, along with Frances Fisher, who starred in Titanic. Set on a serene front-porch in the country, a couple asks why they haven't seen their neighbors — who recently got jobs at the new Wal-Mart — at church in awhile. "Do you think they still pray?" the wife asks. "Only for their shifts to end," the husband responds.[50]

Higher Expectations Week did, indeed, include hundreds of actions across the US. The Greenwald film was distributed "virally" through churches, colleges, community organizations, and an estimated 7,000 "house parties" of supporters who invited neighbors and friends to see it. In Philadelphia, the Ruckus Society specialized in projecting large-scale campaign posters onto the walls of buildings, including some Wal-Mart stores. Some of the slogans posted were "Wal-Mart 2-for-1 Discrimination (Gender and Race)," "Wal-Mart Clearance — Healthcare Benefits," and "Wal-Mart Never Respects Communities — Never!" A host of other activities were recorded, including the following:

- The Raging Grannies, an informal association of older women who sing satirical songs set to familiar tunes, campaigned at three Wal-Marts in Tucson; the story was picked up by several local television stations.
- Less than 30 miles from Wal-Mart's corporate headquarters, a screening of the Greenwald film played to a packed house at the Omni Center for Peace and Justice in Fayetteville, Arkansas.
- Author Barbara Ehrenreich spoke to residents of Charlottesville, VA, about her experience working at Wal-Mart, as chronicled in her bestselling book *Nickel and Dimed.*
- State Representative Joe Bolkom hosted a town-hall meeting in Cedar Rapids, IA, that was broadcast live to viewers across the state.[51]

There was extensive coverage of Higher Expectations Week events in newspapers across the US and abroad, including the following:

- *Newsday,* November 21: "What began many years ago as a low murmur of discussion has grown into a full-throated debate. It's a question that is engaging activists, economists, legislators and even the company around which the controversy swirls: Is Wal-Mart good for America?"
- *Denver Post* editorial, November 19: "Wal-Mart needs to treat employees better, rather than create an illusion it does. The Walton heirs, four of America's top 10 billionaires, can afford that instead of shifting expenses to the taxpayers."
- *Los Angeles Times,* November 21: "Like a noxious smell to which nobody wants to draw attention, there was a curiously unremarked subtext to the third-quarter earnings release from Wal-Mart Stores last week. Most news reports quoted its executives sounding upbeat about the coming Christmas season. But none saw fit to mention that investors haven't made a dime from this company's shares over the last five years."
- *Miami Herald,* November 12: "Wal-Mart, the world's largest retailer and the recent target of lawsuits, journalistic exposes, and grass-roots campaigns against its employment practices, is facing its most powerful moral opponent yet: faith-based groups."
- *London Daily Telegraph,* November 16: "Wal-Mart Watch, meanwhile, which campaigns to 'reveal the harmful impact of Wal-Mart on U.S. families,' is touring churches, synagogues, and mosques and sermonising on its alleged evils. Last weekend the multi-denominational drive saw more than 150 leaders address their congregations on the subject of Wal-Mart from a religious perspective."

- *Lansing State Journal,* November 18: "Clementine Mthethwa of Swaziland shivered in the bitter cold Thursday afternoon on the sidewalk outside the Wal-Mart store in Okemos. The 40-year-old factory worker from southern Africa makes sport shirts that are bought by Wal-Mart Stores Inc. and sold in its stores. She said she makes a penny for every five shirts she puts together. That earns her about $35 a month in U.S. currency. 'They should give people better wages,' Mthethwa said."
- WKOW-ABC (Madison, WI), November 16: "Wal-Mart Watch declared this week it's time for everyone to hold the company accountable for their poor business practices. An anti Wal-Mart documentary kicked off the new campaign against the retail giant. Rep. Terese Berceau says, 'When we've got a company that made $10 billion dollars last year they sure could be helping out by paying for health insurance cost for their employees.'"
- KOLD-CBS (Tucson, AZ), November 13: "And after seeing the film, Vincent Pawlowski believes change is on the way. 'I think it will change things, and I certainly hope it does. I'd like to see Wal-Mart become a better corporation and a better corporate citizen.'" [52]

In December, Wake-Up Wal-Mart organized three nights of candlelight vigils in front of Wal-Mart stores. The vigils were led by religious and civil rights leaders who challenged Wal-Mart's "morally bankrupt policies." This action was linked to a hard-hitting TV ad entitled "Should people of faith shop at Wal-Mart?" The ad commented on Wal-Mart's convictions for child-labor violations, noted that 600,000 of its employees had no company-provided health care benefits, referred to the class-action suits by women, and then asked, "If these are Wal-Mart's values, should people of faith shop at Wal-Mart?" [53] Other ads with a similar tone were placed in many TV markets.

The Campaign Continues

As 2006 began, the predictions of Salon.com feature writer Liza Featherstone seemed more and more prescient. At the end of the first summer of the campaign, she had written: "What's…unusual about this campaign is that it's successfully engaging policy and politicians. At the state and local level, the anti-Wal-Mart forces are working to pass legislation obligating Wal-Mart to reimburse governments for the costs it inflicts on taxpayers — in Medicaid, county programs for the poor, public emergency room costs — by declining to provide workers adequate healthcare." [54]

More evidence of Wal-Mart's dependence on state-subsidized health coverage emerged in two confidential Washington state government reports that were distributed to legislators and leaked to the press. According to the *Seattle Times,* 3,100 Wal-Mart employees in Washington state benefited from state-subsidized health care in 2004, nearly double the total for any other company.[55] "I think taxpayers should be outraged," one legislator observed to the newspaper. "They are subsidizing one of the wealthiest corporations in the world."

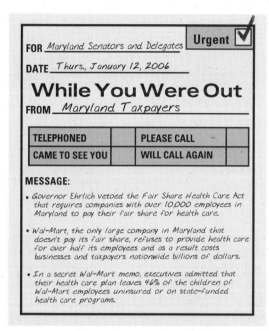

Figure 12.3. While You Were Out. Credit: WalMartWatch.com.

The state of Maryland introduced and passed a landmark Fair Share Health Care Fund Act in January 2006, with the strong support of a broad array of civil society organizations, including unions, and despite vigorous lobbying against the bill by Wal-Mart. The act required Maryland companies with more than 10,000 employees to spend at least 8 percent of their payroll on employee health benefits or make a contribution to the state insurance program for the poor. Wal-Mart was the only company with that many employees in Maryland. Maryland's Republican governor, Robert Ehrlich, who had received generous campaign financing from Wal-Mart, vetoed the bill, but the legislature overturned the veto after further clever campaigning by Wal-Mart Watch and others, including the ad shown in Figure 12.3.

A National Day of Action to "Help Cure the Wal-Mart Health Care Crisis" was organized in more than 35 US cities on April 26, 2006. Both Wake-Up Wal-Mart and the key unions of the Change to Win labor federation were co-sponsors, an important bridging of the divide that had split unions in earlier efforts. The rallies emphasized the high costs for local taxpayers because Wal-Mart fails to provide affordable health care to its workers.[56]

One of the cleverest invocations of moral authority against Wal-Mart was launched on May 23 when Wal-Mart Watch offered Wal-Mart "A Handshake with Sam," a reference to Wal-Mart founder Sam Walton. The "agreement proposed in good faith to Wal-Mart" was displayed in a full-page ad in the *New York Times*. It began by quoting Walton from his personal autobiography: "I am absolutely convinced that the only way we can improve one another's quality of life, which is something very real to those of us who grew up in the Depression, is through what we call free enterprise — practiced correctly and morally." [57] The ad then proposed that Wal-Mart reform its practices in seven key areas, each of which was given moral authority by additional quotes from the Walton autobiography, as shown in Figure 12.4.

RESULTS

Wal-Mart has responded to the many dimensions of the campaign with commitments to significant changes on many levels. Frankly, the results involved far more commitments than anyone had anticipated when the campaign began. Yet there are important areas where little or no progress was made.

The following two lists highlight the main outcomes of the campaign over the first 18 months, from February 2005 to August 2006. They include both positive consequences (new policies that may transform Wal-Mart) and negative consequences for Wal-Mart that may pressure the company to make additional change or may further restrict Wal-Mart's ability to function as it wishes.

Wal-Mart Responses to the Campaign

The following are a number of Wal-Mart's dramatic new commitments to change its social and environmental practices, announced as the campaign unfolded.

- **Wilderness protection to offset on-site environmental destruction.** In April 2005, just as the campaign was getting off the ground, Wal-Mart announced its first response to environmental critics by creating an Acres for America project in collaboration with the National Fish and Wildlife Foundation. Under this program it would offset every acre that it developed for stores and distribution centers by preserving an acre of critical wildlife habitat. The $35 million it committed to cover the next 10 years of its growth represented 3.4 percent of its 2005 profits, but a much smaller share of its profits over the next ten years.[58]

- **Immediate change in public attitudes toward Wal-Mart.** By July 2005, barely three months after the launch of the campaign, Wal-Mart Watch reported a significant change in the attitudes of people across the country about Wal-Mart. A poll taken just before the launch of the campaign, in March 2005, found that 59 percent of respondents, 18 and older, across the country had a "favorable" opinion of Wal-Mart; only 31 percent had an unfavorable opinion. By early July, a repeat poll found that those who were favorable to Wal-Mart had fallen to 50 percent; those unfavorable had risen to 36 percent, a 14-point net-negative shift.[59]

Figure 12.4. A Handshake with Sam: The Moral Responsibilities of Wal-Mart

Moral Principle	Sam Walton Quote	Proposed Action*
1. Protect human dignity.	"If you want people in the stores to take care of the customers, you have to be sure that you are taking care of the people in the stores."	Wal-Mart should work aggressively to see that employees are never mistreated…and that they are justly compensated so that they don't have to rely on public assistance.
2. Ensure quality and affordable health care coverage.	"You can't create a team spirit when the situation is so one-sided, when managements gets so much and workers get so little of the pie."	Wal-Mart should ensure that all employees have quality affordable health insurance and should promote full-time employment.
3. Use market power to improve supplier conditions and wages.	"We still want to drive a hard bargain, but now we need to guard against abusing our power."	Wal-Mart should ensure that the merchandise in its stores is produced under safe and humane conditions.
4. Enable and embrace self-sufficiency.	"Maybe the most important way in which we at Wal-Mart believe in giving something back is through our commitment to using the power of this enormous enterprise as a force for change."	Wal-Mart should pay a family-sustaining wage that ensures that federal, state, and local taxpayers are not forced to spend billions of dollars on public assistance for Wal-Mart employees.
5. Buy local first.	"For Wal-Mart to maintain its position in the hearts of our customers, we have to study more ways we can give something back to our communities."	Wal-Mart should commit to "Buy local first" in each country in which it operates, purchasing both agricultural and manufactured goods from family-owned farms and firms.
6. Keep it clean.	"I'd like to believe that as Wal-Mart continues to thrive and grow, it can come to live up to what someone once called us: the Lighthouse of the Ozarks."	Every step in Wal-Mart's supply chain should demonstrate sound environmental stewardship, and it should enforce this policy with all of its suppliers, both foreign and domestic.
7. Prove worthy of trust.	"As long as we're managing our company well, as long as we take care of our people and our customers, keep our eyes on those fundamentals, we are going to be successful. Of course it takes an observing, discerning person to judge those fundamentals for himself."	Wal-Mart, as the world's largest company and as a global institution in a position of great responsibility and trust, should be open and transparent in its dealings with the public, the news media, and its own employees, documenting and publicizing its progress toward fulfilling these moral principles.

Source: "An Agreement Proposed in Good Faith to Wal-Mart," *New York Times,* May 23, 2006.
*These "proposed actions" have been paraphrased from the original for the sake of space.

- **Increased truck fleet fuel efficiency.** In its October 2005 environmental commitments, Wal-Mart pledged to increase the fuel efficiency of its fleet of trucks by 25 percent within three years and to double it within ten years. While recognizing that this could save Wal-Mart more than $300 million per year by 2015, Lee Scott also recognized that if Wal-Mart demands this increased fuel efficiency from manufacturers, it will create conditions for changing truck efficiency "everywhere in the world." [60]
- **Reduced greenhouse gas production.** In the same October 2005 announcements, Wal-Mart committed to investing $500 million per year in technologies and innovations that would reduce greenhouse gases produced by all its existing facilities by 20 percent within seven years; designing new prototype facilities that would produce 25 to 30 percent less greenhouse gas within four years; and sharing all the technology that it develops. [61]
- **Reduced waste and packaging.** Those October 2005 announcements included a commitment to reduce solid waste from US facilities by 25 percent within three years; to work with suppliers to reduce packaging, increase product package recycling, and increase the use of post-consumer recycled materials; and specifically to replace PVC packaging with more sustainable and recyclable packaging within two years. Lee Scott noted that by reducing excessive packaging in just one Kid Connection toy product, Wal-Mart would use 497 fewer containers for shipment, save freight of more than $2.4 million per year, save more than 3,800 trees, and use a thousand barrels less oil. [62]
- **Increased use of organic cotton.** The October 2005 announcements included a commitment to sell additional organic cotton apparel in order to eliminate the toxic pesticides used widely in commercial cotton. In 2006, Wal-Mart announced that it would use 6,800 tons of organic cotton in the production of its apparel, more than the total global production of the product in 2000, according to *Fortune Magazine*. And it has committed to continue buying those quantities of organic cotton for at least five years, to give producers some assurance as they convert to organic production. [63]
- **Increased energy efficiency of stores.** The October 2005 energy and environment announcements included a commitment to reduce by 30 percent the amount of energy used in its stores. Building on advice from the Rocky Mountain Institute, Wal-Mart intends to use solar panels for energy and shredded tires for mulch; to heat with used cooking oil and motor oil; and to focus on energy reduction from mature trees and wind turbines. [64] It committed to using super-efficient light-emitting diodes in dairy cases. [65]
- **Initial changes in health care benefits.** In October 2005, in clear response to the overwhelming criticism of its health care benefits, Wal-Mart announced that it would offer a new lower-entry-cost health care plan, with minimum monthly payments as low as $25 for single employees and $65 for families. (The $11 per month premium, emphasized in Wal-Mart publicity, would be available in only a few geographic areas.) Comments from health insurance specialists cited by the *New York Times* suggested that "the lower premiums

were likely to attract more employees and reduce the ranks of the uninsured." But they also noted that the $1,000 deductible on the plan would be difficult for Wal-Mart employees, especially older workers who need to visit doctors more often. The plan, as announced, encouraged preventive care by allowing employees to visit a doctor three times in a year before they would have to begin to pay the deductible. Wal-Mart also announced the creation of a "health savings accounts," a Bush administration plan for setting aside pre-tax contributions to cover health care needs.

- **Call for an increase in the minimum wage...and then failure to act.** Lee Scott argued, in the famous October speech "Leadership for the 21st Century," that "the U.S. minimum wage of $5.15 an hour has not been raised in nearly a decade and we believe it is out of date with the times." And, he added, "we simply believe it is time for Congress to take a responsible look at the minimum wage and other legislation that may help working families." [66] In July 2006, the next occasion when Congress came close to modifying the minimum wage, Wal-Mart's top Washington lobbyist, Lee Culpepper, admitted to *Roll Call,* the Capitol Hill newspaper, that the company, in the midst of all its other lobbying activities, had done nothing to pressure Congress to raise the minimum wage.[67]

- **New fund to add diversity among suppliers.** Also in October 2005, Wal-Mart announced that it would set up a $25 million private equity fund to support the addition of businesses owned by women and members of minority groups to its supply chain. Wal-Mart denied that there was any link between the fund and the long-standing class-action sex-discrimination suit by 1.6 million women (the largest such suit ever filed in the US) or the July 2005 reports that African-American truck drivers were seeking class-action status for a suit claiming that they were denied promotions because of race.[68]

- **Commitment to purchasing certified seafood.** In February 2006, Wal-Mart committed to purchasing "all its wild-caught seafood from fisheries that, like Alaska's salmon fishery, have been certified as sustainable by an independent nonprofit called the Marine Stewardship Council." [69] In his October 2005 speech on environmental issues, Lee Scott had also committed to third-party certification of all shrimp farms supplying Wal-Mart in the US according to social and environmental best-practice standards, but he did not specify what certification might be used.

- **More improvements in health benefits.** In February 2006, responding to criticisms of the small October 2005 changes in health care benefits, Wal-Mart announced that it would, for the first time, allow part-time employees to enroll their children in the health insurance plan, and it promised to reduce the time that part-time employees would have to work in order to become eligible for insurance...but did not specify what the reduction would be. Previously, part-time employees had to wait two years to become eligible for insurance. The insurance still maintained high deductibles — $1,000 per individual and $3,000 per family — that kicked in after three ordinary doctor visits and three generic prescriptions per year, and total insurance was limited to $25,000 per year.[70]

- **Reversing course, agrees to sell Plan B contraceptive.** Wal-Mart had been the only major pharmacy chain that refused to sell the "morning after" pill, which can prevent pregnancy if taken within 72 hours of intercourse. Vocal criticism from such groups as the Planned Parenthood Federation of American and NARAL Pro-Choice America, who argued that the company was denying women access to a federally approved emergency contraceptive, combined with a successful lawsuit by three women in Massachusetts and the threat of similar suits in New York state and Connecticut. In March 2006, Wal-Mart announced that it would begin carrying Plan B in its 3,700 US pharmacies by the end of the month.[71]

- **Stops selling guns in one-third of its stores.** Denying that it had anything to do with gun-control advocates, in April 2006 Wal-Mart stopped selling guns in a third of its stores. Representatives argued that they were simply responding to differences across regions in the demand for guns. The National Rifle Association indicated that it was concerned people in rural areas might no longer have access to guns. A spokesman for the National Shooting Sports Foundation said that the change in Wal-Mart policy would be "a boon for mom-and-pop hunting stores" that had lost business to Wal-Mart.[72]

- **Offers assistance to local competitors.** Reeling from the complaints of critics over the damaging impacts its stores have on local businesses, Wal-Mart offered in April 2006 to provide financial grants, training, and even free advertising in Wal-Mart stores to help competing businesses survive. "We see we can be better for communities than we have been in the past if we are willing to stretch ourselves and our resources," Lee Scott told reporters.[73] Scott also acknowledged that the program was not completely altruistic, for Wal-Mart was planning to open 50 stores in urban neighborhoods in the next two years and was hoping to lessen resistance by offering help to the hardware stores, dress shops, and bakeries with which they would be competing.

- **CEO's tone changes.** Later in April, Wal-Mart held its second press conference. The *New York Times* reporter who had been following the year of change at the company noted, especially, how the "feisty, and at times defiant" tone of the CEO, Lee Scott, had changed. "Mr. Scott," he wrote, "called Wal-Mart a company 'in transformation' and offered what a year ago would have seemed an unthinkably long list of changes under way at the company.... Mr. Scott's message of change — he used the word 'transformation' five times in his speech — coincides with the one-year anniversary of the formation of two union-backed groups, Wal-Mart Watch and Wake-Up Wal-Mart, which helped turn the company into a social, political, and economic issue."[74]

- **Increased sales of certified organic foods.** In May 2006, Wal-Mart announced it would dramatically increase its sales of foods that met the USDA organic standard. Although, according to one report, it made this move to "help modernize its image and broaden its appeal to urban and other upscale consumers," the commitment was also seen as legitimizing the organic market, showing that was is no longer just a niche market. Wal-Mart indicated that it intended to sell its organic produce and processed foods at no more than 10 percent above the price of conventional products, well below the 20 to 30 percent premium charged in other stores. Some activists raised concerns that the move might mean significant increases in imports of certified organic products from places like China, where the inspection processes may be less rigorous; others expressed concerns about the impetus this would give to large industrial organic farms, to the detriment of the small, local organic producers. It was expected that Wal-Mart would soon become the largest vendor of certified organic products (surpassing Whole Foods Markets), having already become the largest vendor of organic milk in the US.[75]

- **Private-label Fair Trade certified coffee in Sam's Clubs.** In one of the first changes that recognizes concerns about the social conditions for producers of its products, Wal-Mart's Sam's Club stores began to sell a private-label coffee certified under Fair Trade rules by TransFair USA. The coffee, sold to Wal-Mart by Bom Dia Coffee Company of Brazil, was purchased from small-farmer cooperatives at prices well above world commercial prices. According to one farmer, quoted in the *Washington Post,* his co-op's profits have since doubled. But Wal-Mart found that it could pay the Fair Trade price, have the coffee roasted and packaged in Brazil, and still undercut the price it had been paying to Procter & Gamble for a comparable coffee. As a result, Wal-Mart was considering introducing the coffee into all its namesake stores. The *Washington Post* report suggested that it would be "a test of how deep its makeover will really go."[76]

- **New Environmental Health and Wellness Program.** Also in June 2006, Wal-Mart announced the creation of a new program to teach its 1.3 million employees in the US "how to take better care of themselves and the environment." Tentatively called the Environmental Health and Wellness Program, it was seen by reporters as an opportunity for Wal-Mart to potentially reduce its "health care spending on a work force that has higher rates of heart disease and diabetes than the general public." Illustrating its new willingness to reach out to its critics, Wal-Mart hired Adam Werbach, former president of Sierra Club, as a consultant for this program. Werbach had once written that Wal-Mart was like "a virus, infecting and destroying American culture."[77]

- **Leadership on developing standards for responsible mining.** In June 2006, Wal-Mart senior management responded to the campaign, and to its internal "sustainability networks," by participating with representatives of mining companies, mining advocacy NGOs (such as Earthworks and Mining Watch Canada), and retail jewelry companies (including Tiffany and the Council for Responsible Jewelry Practices) in what was billed as the Vancouver Dialogue (see Chapter 8). What emerged was the Initiative for Responsible Mining Assurance (IRMA), which began to develop standards for responsible

mining of gold and silver. The retail companies, including Wal-Mart, asked
for rapid agreement and implementation of the standards so that certified
gold and silver products would be available within two years. A Wal-Mart
representative took a leadership position within IRMA.[78]

- **Higher starting wages.** In August 2006, Wal-Mart announced that it would
raise starting pay rates for employees in about one-third of its US stores and
that it would then be paying full-time employees an average of $10.11 per
hour. (Observers compared this unfavorably with the $17.00 per hour paid by
its competitor, Costco Wholesale Group.) Wal-Mart further lessened the potential positive impact of the slightly higher starting wages by announcing
that it was going to cap the wages of some employees to encourage them to
seek promotions and other career advancement. Some media pointed out
that capping wages in certain positions could be seen as a response to concerns raised in Susan Chambers' October 2005 memo on benefits — for example, that they needed to find ways to replace older workers with younger
workers whose salaries and benefits were significantly lower.[79]

New Restrictions on the Wal-Mart Model

The national and international attention raised by the Wal-Mart campaign led to
further consequences that challenged the model, reduced Wal-Mart's ability to
expand, and generated greater negative publicity for the company.

- **New study challenges Wal-Mart profits, prices, and wages.** In October 2005,
in an effort to counterattack the burgeoning campaign against it, Wal-Mart
released a report by a hired consultant, Global Insight, which claimed that
Wal-Mart saved American consumers $263 billion per year. A report released
in June 2006 by the nonprofit Economic Policy Institute (EPI) re-analyzed
the data used by Global Insight and carried the research several steps farther.
EPI concluded that Global Insight's results failed the most rudimentary statistical testing, that there was new and robust evidence that Wal-Mart's entry
into local labor markets reduced the pay of workers in competing stores, and
that Wal-Mart could clearly pay higher wages and benefits for its workers
without having to reduce its profits or raise its prices significantly.[80]

- **Canadian government rejects rationale for closing unionized Quebec store.**
In September 2005, the Quebec provincial labor board rejected Wal-Mart
Canada's contention that it closed the unionized store in Jonquière for economic reasons in February 2005. The board ruled that Wal-Mart's dismissal
of the workers was illegal under Quebec law, that the workers could be eligible for compensation, and that Wal-Mart might be fined. The Jonquière store
was the first in North America to be recognized as a bargaining agent; Wal-
Mart's response was to close the store. Canadian organizers commented that
this ruling should make Wal-Mart think twice about closing another store
and that it should make employees less afraid of signing a union card.[81]

- **"Sweetheart" labor inspection deal revealed and cancelled.** In November
2005, the Inspector General of the US Department of Labor strongly criti-

cized his own department's officials for a "sweetheart deal" that they had made with Wal-Mart, effectively promising 15-day advance notice before labor investigators inspected its stores for child labor violations. Wal-Mart and labor department officials reached this agreement as part of the settlement for labor department charges that found Wal-Mart at fault for 85 child labor violations, involving employees in three states. The children were operating dangerous machinery, including chainsaws and cardboard baling machines. The agreement also allowed Wal-Mart to avoid fines for future inspections. If, despite the 15-day advance notice, it were still found in violation of the law, it would not be fined if it remedied the violations within 10 days of the inspection. The Inspector General's report was requested by Congressman George Miller, a Democrat from California, after word of the agreement leaked. It appeared that the labor department had done a special favor for a powerful friend of President Bush and an important contributor to the Republican Party.[82] The agreement was cancelled by the labor department in January 2005.[83]

- **Wal-Mart fined $172 million for failing to permit meal breaks.** Just before Christmas 2005, a California jury found Wal-Mart guilty of violating the state law that says a worker must be given at least 30 minutes for a meal break for every five hours worked. The class-action suit on behalf of Wal-Mart's 116,000 workers in California alleged that Wal-Mart had violated state law on meal breaks more than 8 million times between 2001 and 2005. Although Wal-Mart insisted that the decision affected only California, the winning law firm indicated that similar suits were pending in about 40 other states.[84]

- **Maryland passes big-box wage and benefits legislation that applies only to Wal-Mart.** As mentioned earlier in this chapter, the Maryland state legislature passed the Fair Share Health Care Fund Act in January 2006. The law required Maryland employers with 10,000 or more workers to spend at least 8 percent of their payrolls on health insurance or else make contributions of the difference into a state Medicaid fund. Wal-Mart was the only company to which the law would apply. The law was ultimately struck down by a federal judge in July 2006 on the grounds that regulations on health care benefits were pre-empted by the federal Employee Retirement Income Security Act (ERISA). But proponents of the law believe that similar legislation under consideration in other states, as well as the 2006 Massachusetts state law that requires all businesses to contribute in similar fashion, are likely to escape federal court rejection.

- **Major New York City project excludes another Wal-Mart.** In early February 2006, a $400-million redevelopment project was approved by the city council for the South Bronx. It will "transform a stretch of crumbling buildings in the shadow of Yankee Stadium into a shiny complex of brand-name stores, restaurants, and a waterfront park." Reflecting the level of antipathy toward Wal-Mart among elected officials and community groups in New York City, the developer specifically agreed that it would not lease space to Wal-Mart, "in deference to concerns among council members and community groups about the company's labor practices."[85] The first attempt to locate a Wal-Mart store in New York City was blocked in February 2005. On that occasion, barely two weeks after a development company had announced its intentions to include a Wal-Mart in a major Queens shopping complex, the developer announced that it had decided not to include Wal-Mart because of city council and community opposition. Small-business advocates were among the most vocal opponents; Rego Park, the city council member representing the district where the project was planned, warned Wal-Mart that to win approval it would have to "improve its wages, health benefits and pensions and end its vehement stance against unions."[86]

- **Wal-Mart found to have lied in its FDIC testimony in support of banking application.** A May 2006 Reuters story detailed how Wal-Mart representatives wrongly described some of the leases held by small community banks located in its stores. In an effort to convince the Federal Deposit Insurance Corporation (FDIC) that its application to open an industrial loan company would not replace the 1,200 small banks presently in its stores, Wal-Mart representatives argued that the leases held by those banks could only be cancelled by the banks themselves. But Reuters found leases where the decision to renew was subject to an agreement by both the bank and Wal-Mart.[87]

- **Norwegian pension fund drops Wal-Mart stock.** In early June 2006, the Norwegian government pension fund, the third-largest pension fund in the world, dropped $430 million in Wal-Mart shares from its holdings. The fund managers cited Wal-Mart for "serious and systematic" labor violations in several countries. Wal-Mart shares immediately dropped in value. This put Wal-Mart in the same category as companies that build nuclear weapons and land mines, seven of which had been dropped from the pension fund in January 2005.[88]

- **FDIC places six-month moratorium on ILC-type applications, including Wal-Mart's.** After six months of hearings on Wal-Mart's application to open an industrial loan company, the FDIC voted in July 2006 to put a moratorium on *all* applications of this sort because "some ILC business models have raised questions about the risks of ILCs to the deposit insurance fund." The FDIC wanted to determine whether "statutory or regulatory changes and revised standards and procedures" were needed to protect the fund.[89] News articles earlier in the year had reported that questions asked by regulators in hearings on Wal-Mart's request for approval of the creation of a bank suggested that any approval "would come with strict limits on the banking activities allowed."[90] Just four days before the FDIC decision was announced, Bloomberg.com reported that a coalition of 32 groups, including the American Bankers Association, had sent a letter to every member of Congress urging them to step in before federal regulators made their decision on Wal-Mart's pending application.[91]

- **Chicago passes big-box minimum wage increase, with benefits.** In July 2006 the City of Chicago passed an ordinance that required big-box retailers to pay wages of at least $10 per hour, plus at least $3 per hour in benefits, by 2010 for all employees who work more than ten hours per week. Though the *New York Times* editorialized that the law faced a stiff court review, it also called attention, one more time, to the fact that Wal-Mart's "meager health benefits often leave public hospitals and government programs for the poor paying the bill instead."[92] The *Chicago Sun-Times* called the legislation, passed by a veto-proof margin of 35 to 14, a "stunning defeat for Wal-Mart," which had threatened to cancel plans for as many as 20 new stores in the Chicago area.[93]

- **Merrill Lynch downgrades rating of Wal-Mart.** In July 2006, the key Merrill Lynch analyst watching Wal-Mart share value downgraded her recommendation from "buy" to "neutral" because of weaker sales and lower profit margins. Dow Jones' *MarketWatch,* reported that her note to clients was entitled "Bentonville: We have a problem." As Wal-Mart shares continued to fall, dropping 2.2 percent on July 13 alone, the analyst also noted that Wal-Mart's niche — low-income consumers — was particularly hard-hit by current economic conditions.[94]

- **Forced to leave Germany and Korea, with billion-dollar losses.** In early August 2006, Wal-Mart announced that it was leaving the German market, with billion-dollar losses, after being defeated by local discount retailers. It sold its 85 German stores to Metro AG, the country's biggest retailer. In May, Wal-Mart had announced its departure from Korean markets and sold its 16 stores there. The business press attributed the failures to customers who were less enamored of rock-bottom prices and to difficulties dealing with employee expectations in conditions where unions and nationally mandated benefits programs are stronger.[95]

- **First earnings drop in ten years.** Wal-Mart announced that its net income had dropped 26 percent in the fiscal second quarter of 2006, after it had pulled out of Korea and Germany. This was "a humbling slip for a company obsessed with growth," according to the *New York Times.* One security analyst noted that "this has been a worst-case scenario for Wal-Mart."[96]

- **Wal-Mart shares fall almost continuously during the campaign.** As illustrated by Figure 12.5, Wal-Mart's share value has fallen almost continuously since coordinated campaigns were launched in April 2005. The tide of negative publicity and concerns reported in the financial press has been associated with a drop in share value of more than 25 percent, beginning almost exactly at the start of the campaign, in March 2005, and extending through July 2006. The total value lost by Wal-Mart's shareholders over that period is in excess of US$55 billion.

REFLECTIONS

This first year of the campaign to transform Wal-Mart was extraordinarily successful despite some of its internal problems, such as tensions between the two major unions and difficulties coordinating the unions and civil society advocacy groups working to transform Wal-Mart. With the exception of the six demands set out by Wake-Up Wal-Mart fairly early in the campaign, there wasn't a clear set of broader demands that might have given Wal-Mart a sense of where it had to go in order to change the tenor of the campaign or reduce the pressure on its practices. The campaign has moved Wal-Mart to use existing certification systems (e.g., the Marine Stewardship Council, Fair Trade Certified, Certified Organic, and the emerging Initiative for Responsible Mining Assurance) for some of the products it sells, including seafood, apparel, gold and silver, and many other food products. By the middle of 2006 it had not made similar moves on such questions as sourcing its wood and paper products and packaging, toxics in cosmetics and children's toys, and many other areas, though its internal "sustainability networks" were known to be seeking solutions in many of those areas.

Wal-Mart succeeded in separating its harshest environmental critics from the campaigners on labor and other social issues by engaging with them as the broader campaign developed and by contracting with Conservation International to manage its relationships with major environmental groups. Yet the fundamental issues of wages and benefits, especially health care benefits, remained a lightning rod for almost universal public criticism that Wal-Mart still has to address. There was evidence in late summer 2006 that Wal-Mart was beginning to rethink its relationship with labor unions. This came in the form of suggestions that Wal-Mart might work more closely with unions to push for universal health care reforms, as well as in news that Wal-Mart had agreed to, and was going to cooperate with, the unionization of all its stores in China.[97] Reporters were quick to point out, however, that the official government-sanctioned unions in China, required by Chinese law, do not historically have bargaining power over wages and working conditions.

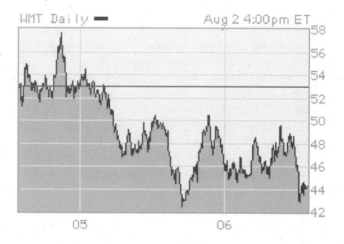

Figure 12.5. Wal-Mart Share Value, August 2004 to July 2006. Credit: CNN/Money.com.

If the initial transformation of Wal-Mart is to produce serious long-term re-sults, it is necessary to generalize the demands placed on Wal-Mart by the 2005–06 campaigns into a set of standards for ethical corporate practices by all large-scale retailers, including other big-box stores. Rather than attempting to develop massive new sets of standards, product by product, for those retailers, it might be enough simply to create pressure for, and verify compliance with, the existing and evolving best-practice standards in each commodity area. Standards for lo-cal social and environmental impacts would also be needed, but the bases for those standards are appearing in the demands of the myriad local groups that oppose the establishment of Wal-Mart stores in their neighborhoods.

Many of the voluntary concessions Wal-Mart has made to date have focused on "sustainability" issues. Amory Lovins of the Rocky Mountain Institute has shown the company that it can actually *save* money by being more sustainable, specifically through increased energy efficiency, truck fleet fuel efficiency, and re-duction of waste. Wal-Mart's pioneering efforts in this area may have the clout to transform much broader portions of the economy, especially if the scale of its purchases brings the cost per unit of solar power, more efficient engines, and re-cyclable packaging down significantly. In these areas, minimal monitoring will be needed. But for areas where political pressure is all that moves Wal-Mart — as in the case of higher standardized health care benefits — it may be more appro-priate to seek uniform federal legislation under ERISA rather than battling, state by state, court by court, to eliminate the subsidies provided by government.

Continuous monitoring will be needed in the arenas where Wal-Mart has promised voluntary compliance with standards well above legislative mini-mums. In its promised moves toward stocking sustainably harvested wood and paper products, eliminating PVCs in packaging, expanding Fair Trade products on store shelves, increasing MSC-certified seafood purchases, improving its monitoring of the working conditions of its suppliers, and supporting local competing businesses and increased diversity among local suppliers, Wal-Mart will need to adopt the practices of companies that have been targeted in the past — most importantly, transparent reporting on continuous improvements — to avoid the risk of new brand-damaging complaints by those who brought the de-mands originally.

13

Struggles on the Frontier:
Are There Limits to the "Certification Revolution"?

The certification revolution has shown remarkable success in creating the conditions that help transform corporate practices toward greater social and environmental accountability. But are there limits to the ability of certification systems to produce these results?

In this loosely referenced and more speculative final chapter, I will offer a number of reflections on this intersection of ethical business campaigns, certification systems, and the transformation of corporate social responsibility into certified corporate accountability. We will examine the proliferation of the concepts, as well as the risk of consumer and business confusion created by that proliferation. We will look again at the tensions between private voluntary certification and local, national, and international regulation. We will focus on the growing pains of the major certification systems and their struggles for financial viability. And we will discuss the tensions that develop within broad stakeholder coalitions as the years go by, and how the perhaps inevitable attempts to ratchet up standards create wedges that threaten to destroy the coalitions.

WHAT DO YOU DO WITH CAMPAIGNS THAT SEEM TO GO NOWHERE?

What happens when companies appear to resist the pressure from market campaigns successfully? Some campaigns have taken many years, though targeted companies are responding more quickly, and many respond, after the launching of a campaign, without being targeted explicitly. For example, the ForestEthics campaign against Victoria's Secret, highlighted in Chapter 1 (and featured in the *Wall Street Journal* even before it began), took more than two years to reach an agreement. ForestEthics fought to have Victoria's Secret increase the recycled and/or FSC-certified content of the paper on which its 395 million catalogs were printed each year. Limited Brands, the parent company, appeared to pay little or no attention to the campaign, yet it spurred significant responses from companies not targeted.

The campaign was launched in October 2004, and campaigners followed the Victoria's Secret marketing campaign Angels Across America, staging protests wherever it appeared. ForestEthics then orchestrated an escalating campaign of actions throughout 2005, including a Day of Action in April 2005 that involved 225 different locations, call-ins, and local letters of protest. ForestEthics was in dialogue with the company, but the discussions yielded no significant concessions. Mainstream media picked up the campaign in the fall of 2006 as protest actions occurred every week. When activists from Catalogs Without Clearcuts chained themselves to a Victoria's Secret store in New York City, the action was covered by CBS, ABC, WPIX radio, the *New York Times*, the *Village Voice*, and other media in the tri-state area. Figure 13.1 illustrates the tone of the final results.

On December 6, Limited Brands announced a "landmark agreement with ForestEthics on environmental stewardship."[1] The company, which also owns Bath & Body Works, C.O. Bigelow, the White Barn Candle Company, and the apparel lines Express, Henri Bendel, and The Limited, agreed to the following terms:

- It would work with its primary paper supplier to eliminate all pulp supplied from the boreal forest in Alberta's Rocky Mountain foothills and the inland temperate rainforest of British Columbia.
- It would ensure its catalogs were either 10 percent post-consumer-waste recycled paper or at least 10 percent FSC content by 2007.
- It would establish a corporate preference for FSC certification — referred to on its website as "the only credible certification for sustainable logging." (Limited Brands has, in fact, convinced one of its principal suppliers to shift four of its mills to FSC.)
- It would institute a program to reduce its overall catalog paper consumption.
- It would commit to continual improvement on environmental attributes of catalog paper and paper use. Its progress will be audited by an independent third party and made public.
- It made a commitment to phase out any paper from other "endangered forests."
- It committed to spend one million dollars on research and advocacy to protect endangered forests and ensure its leadership in the catalog industry.

Limited Brands didn't maintain its "leadership in the catalog industry" for long. In fact, Williams-Sonoma, Inc., the parent company of major home-furnishing retailers Williams-Sonoma, Pottery Barn, and West Elm, announced shortly before the Victoria's Secret breakthrough that it would immediately begin to use more than 95 percent FSC-certified paper in all of its catalogs.[2]

Not long after that Tiffany & Co., one of the companies with the highest proportion of its capitalized value in its brand (as we saw in Chapter 1), published its first sustainability report. The report quietly announced that Tiffany & Co. would seek to obtain at least 90 percent of the paper it uses in all its packaging materials and catalogs from FSC-certified sources.[3]

In a similar manner, the campaign to demand greater accountability from Mitsubishi began in 1994, as noted in Profile 3.2 of Michael Marx. It took almost eight years to produce key results. But on November 11, 2002, at a conference in

Figure 13.1. ForestEthics graphics from its Victoria's Secret campaign. Source: ForestEthics, with permission.

Tokyo organized by Forest Trends, the chairman of Mitsubishi Corporation, Minoru Makihara, announced that his company would seek third-party independent certification for all its forest operations — and FSC certification is what it would seek.[4] "This is more than a simple statement of principle," Makihara said. He noted that they were seeking FSC certification of Alberta Pacific Forest Industries, with 5.6 million hectares (15 million acres) in Alberta, Canada. That certification became, in 2006, the single largest forest management certification anywhere in the world.

It would be wrong to suggest that campaigns have never failed, but it has been relatively rare for a major branded company to resist completely the pressure on its brand reputation from a well-designed and well-organized campaign. It is also important to recognize that successful market campaigners are smart enough to create sets of demands that may appear infeasible at first, but that become more feasible as the pressure rises. And when others in the industry show that it is possible to live with, and even to benefit from, participation in the certification system toward which they are being pushed, it is more difficult for the targeted company to hold out.

IS THERE A RISK THAT THE CONCEPT OF CERTIFICATION WILL BE DILUTED?

These days we can find certification of one sort or another everywhere we look. There are certified pre-owned cars and trucks, Microsoft-certified systems engineers, certified fraud examiners, beer judge certification, certified Angus beef. The Bridgestone-Firestone tire plant in Illinois that was primarily responsible for the production of tires that cost the company a $600-million recall and replacement was ISO certified. A Google search for "certification" yields 299 million occurrences.

The key concept in all these certification systems is that some person, some product, or some service is certified to a specific set of standards. But just what those standards might be is a completely open question. If businesses and consumers are satisfied with any claim to certification, the concept may become diluted to the point of uselessness.

But the more important point is that anyone focusing on certification has to ask: Certified to what standards? How? By whom? And endorsed by whom?

So long as the leading certification systems for social and environmental accountability are required to demonstrate what their standards are, what independent third party certifies those standards, and who recognizes, supports, and endorses them, the field of competitive certification systems will remain lively and useful.

ARE THERE MARKET STRUCTURES WHERE THE CERTIFICATION REVOLUTION IS LESS LIKELY TO BE EFFECTIVE?

We have seen certification function especially well in market structures where there is a certain level of concentration, recognized industry leaders, and strong branding of companies, whether at the manufacturing level or the retail level. What happens in market structures that are diffuse and unbranded? The apparel manufacturing industry is a theoretical example, though production concentration is growing rapidly among giant Korean and Chinese firms.

The answer might be that the fulcrum in supply-chain leverage remains the final retailer of the products. The great open markets of the developing countries illustrate the largest outlets for completely unbranded (or fraudulently branded!) products from faceless manufacturers. As retail concentration takes place in those countries — and the tendency is apparent everywhere — there will be more opportunity to put pressure on the sourcing practices of companies selling into those markets. This implies that the "market for virtue" may remain much stronger in the higher-income markets, and the effectiveness of ethical business pressure will continue to be greater there.

The market for diamonds offers an interesting example. Although DeBeers and its associates account for the largest share of diamonds sold in luxury markets, the flow of diamonds from Brazil and West Africa — outside the branded channels, through Lebanese merchants, and into Internet-based final markets — is a severe challenge to traceability and other forms of accountability.[5] It is precisely because of this perceived weakness in the global supply chain, and the risks it poses for responsible firms, that the Kimberley Process for diamonds was created, and it is why some diamond companies are pursuing the notion of "Fair Trade" diamonds.

Provenance, a term made popular in the wine trade that refers to origin and chain of ownership, is now a quality dimension of products that retailers ignore at their own risk.

HOW CRITICAL IS CONSUMER CONSCIOUSNESS AND DIRECT CONSUMER DEMAND?

The cost of campaigns to build consumer preferences is almost always outside the range of market campaigners or those who are building social and environmental certification systems. One of the strongest and most interesting lessons learned in recent years is that certification systems have become most important in business-to-business (B2B) relationships, rather than in business-to-consumer (B2C) transactions. Yes, if consumers are not interested in purchasing a certified product or in paying a slightly higher price to cover the costs of improved social and environmental practices, there will be less demand for social and environmental accountability on the part of retailers. But the impact seems to be felt most strongly within supply-chain relationships. The retailer cannot afford to risk the publicly damaging criticism of unethical or inappropriate sourcing practices, so the retailer puts pressure on the manufacturer to make certain that the product meets prevailing (and continuously changing) social and environmental mores. One piece of evidence of this pressure is the rapid increase in the use of ethical seals for the private-label own-brand products of companies such as Marks & Spencer, Tesco, Costco, and Wal-Mart.

Differences in consumer consciousness of ethical sourcing, manifest in the differences between consumers in the Nordic countries or the UK and those in the US, or in differences between regions in the US, are reflected in areas where certification is relatively more powerful and less powerful. Consumer consciousness of environmental characteristics of products in the Nordic countries, where the Nordic Swan is recognized by the vast majority of shoppers, was generated by multi-million-euro government-backed education campaigns. For that reason, the Nordic Swan seal is available on a huge range of products.

College towns across the US seem to have the highest availability of Certified Fair Trade coffee, and not solely because United Students for Fair Trade has organized on more than 500 campuses. Notions of ethical consumption are just one way that the current college and university generation is responding to the social and environmental dilemmas they see around them in our rapidly globalizing world.

However, the appearance of ever-greater quantities of FSC-certified wood in Home Depot and Lowe's stores in the US is not a response to hordes of consumers asking for FSC. If you doubt it, just ask the sales associates; you'll find that it is still rare for a salesperson to have any notion of what the FSC represents. The Home Depot commitment represents both a corporate commitment to improved environmental practices in the sourcing of forest products, and a business leadership market need, now that most of its competitors have committed publicly to increasing their purchases and sales of FSC products.

HOW DOES THIS NEW FORM OF MARKET-BASED GOVERNANCE INTERACT WITH TRADITIONAL MODES OF REGULATION?

The question of how this new form of market-based governance interacts with traditional regulation feeds a rapidly expanding vein of academic research worldwide. It is one of the key topics at academic conferences on corporate social responsibility. And the jury is still out. But certain tendencies, which I'll summarize loosely, are becoming apparent.

As we noted at the start of the book, advocacy-based certification systems fill a governance need beyond what local and national regulation can achieve, especially under the current rules of the World Trade Organization. If no nation can block the importation of products solely on the basis of the conditions under which they are made (the so-called process and production methods rules), voluntary international standard setting may be the only vehicle available for reducing unethical and irresponsible production practices in global trade.

Yet even at the national level, businesses are increasingly willing to work within voluntary processes, even in the unruly arena of engagement with social and environmental advocacy groups, if it forestalls the imposition of more rigid, more onerous, or more costly government regulations. Conversely, companies that participate in certification systems, raising their social or environmental practices, demonstrate that higher standards are economically possible in the regulatory structure; and they then have an incentive to see regulatory standards raised, rather than find themselves undercut by less responsible competitors.

Most social and environmental advocacy groups would prefer to see the standards negotiated with industry in the process of creating certification systems converted into firm regulations. The burden of enforcement is then shifted to the government, rather than remaining on the shoulders of the NGOs. But in the context of pro-business local and national governments that are disinclined to create higher regulatory standards, or to enforce those that exist, market-led, private, voluntary standard setting is the best alternative available.

WHO WATCHES THE WATCHERS, CERTIFIES THE CERTIFIERS?

If this de facto governance role continues to shift toward these private systems, what accountability do they themselves have? The first answer is that it depends on the legitimacy of the certification effort. Is it a serious effort to transform corporate practices or is it an effort to enshrine the status quo and deflect attention? Certification systems that seek broad-based civil society credibility have begun to create mechanisms for ensuring their own accountability.

The International Social and Environmental Accreditation and Labelling Alliance (ISEAL) is, in its own words, an association of leading voluntary international standard-setting and conformity-assessment organizations that focus on social and environmental issues.[6] ISEAL has developed and is implementing an international code of good practice for setting social and environmental standards; most, but not all, of ISEAL's members have made their standard-setting processes compliant with the code.[7] The ISEAL code of good practice specifies a wide range of internal and external accountability mechanisms, covering stakeholder procedures for developing standards; balance among interested parties; review and modification of standards; and effectiveness, relevance and international harmonization of standards. All very dry stuff, admittedly. But only a few of the many organizations focused on setting standards for social and environmental issues worldwide have met even the limited standards proposed by ISEAL, and that reduces their credibility significantly. At the end of 2006, ISEAL members included Fairtrade Labelling Organizations International, Social Accountability International, Forest Stewardship Council, Marine Stewardship Council, Marine Aquarium Council, the International Federation of Organic Agriculture Movements, Rainforest Alliance, the Institute for Agriculture and Trade Policy, and a half dozen other associate and affiliate members.

HOW DO CERTIFICATION SYSTEMS BECOME FINANCIALLY SUSTAINABLE?

This is, in many ways, the main challenge facing the certification revolution. Most of the major certification systems we have studied in this book were started with funding from European governments and US private foundations that recognized the powerful influence they could wield over the transformation of corporate practices worldwide. That doesn't mean the early-investing governments and foundations were sure of strong social investment returns. What it reflects, however, is an NGO logic that suggests that "companies will not appreciate the value that we offer until our system is completely functioning. But they won't invest to get the system set up." I believe the certification organizations underestimate the importance of their approval to the industry they wish to transform — which is a logical conclusion from the feedback they receive.

It is true that fifteen years ago it took unusual prescience and perspicacity on the part of company executives to recognize that a proposed certification system could validate their corporate responsibility and provide third-party confirmation of their accountability. But the ground is shifting, and this recognition is coming sooner and more frequently than in the past.

We have seen the variation in financial models used by social and environmental certification systems. The FSC supports itself through significant donations from foundations and government agencies, together with a tax on certified operations that is collected by the certification bodies. There is reason to believe, based on discussions with executives of companies fully engaged with FSC certification, that FSC still fails to capture anywhere near the amount of value-added that it creates for its certified companies. The timidity with which it raises its fees reflects the competition between the FSC and its copycat schemes. However, the growing global consensus that FSC certification provides the only truly reliable, NGO-proof evidence of corporate accountability in the forest products sector opens new opportunities for the organization to capture a larger part of the value it adds. With those resources, the FSC global network will be able to function at even higher levels of efficiency and effectiveness.

From its inception, the certified Fair Trade movement found creative ways to charge labeling fees on final products to the companies participating in its system. A more significant part of its operating expenses are now covered by fees from licensed firms, based on volumes of Fair Trade products sold. For that reason, many of its national labeling initiatives have been able to generate high levels of social capital returns for the modest sums invested by foundations.

As the efficacy of the certification revolution becomes clearer, more companies appear willing to invest in the creation of certification systems. For example, jewelry companies recognized the magnitude of the risk to their industry if they did not find ways to transform contemporary mining practices. Rather than waiting till their products fell out of favor with younger, more ethically conscious consumers, jewelry retailers sought out NGOs, such as Earthworks, to help develop social and environmental standards, and a certification system, for responsible mining This was not initially a product of market campaign activities, but it has been accelerated by them. This is also an industry where the market impact of a small premium covering certification costs that confirm more responsible sourcing is not difficult to bear.

Future certification systems should find even easier roads toward financial sustainability, but only if they recognize the magnitude of the benefits they provide for the companies that engage with them.

CAN NONPROFIT ORGANIZATIONS LEARN TO FUNCTION AT THE SPEED OF BUSINESS?

All the certification systems we have discussed are nonprofit organizations, providing beneficial services to both civil society and corporations that probably go beyond what can be internalized by for-profit organizations. But the gap between the needs of business and the traditional cultures of nonprofit organizations is a fundamental challenge for the world of social and environmental certification.

Just a few years ago, I spoke with environmental NGO leaders in Europe who felt that environmental processes should be run primarily by volunteer staff rather than paid staff. When asked whether certification costs should be covered by licensing fees for the labels used by companies, their response was a resounding "No!" If companies were paying certification systems for the labels they received, these "commercial transactions" would eliminate the independence of the certification organization, lessen its credibility, convert it into a simple extension of the corporate world, and undermine its mission. That view still appears with striking frequency.

Nonprofit organizations have honed themselves on consultative processes, consensus decision making, extended debate, and slow, careful decision making. The corporate world thrives on — and requires — quick, clear, and definitive decision making. How can these two worlds interact? This is the question faced by all the leading social and environmental certification systems.

The answer is to develop new modes of interaction between nonprofits and companies. What is needed are nonprofits organized along the lines that business schools would recommend for for-profit businesses, with product-specific staff and client-specific assignments designed to maximize the social benefits of the program by expanding corporate engagement. Imagine companies seeking the services of an NGO to "solve" their supply-chain accountability problems. In such a system, NGOs need to be able to respond quickly to the huge variety of company inquiries, expectations, and recommendations. And they must work to avoid the consternation that results if companies cannot get a useful response from the certification organization in a timely manner. That's the reality of much of the certification revolution world today, and a continuing challenge. Some organizations seem capable of rising to this challenge, but not all.

CAN THE ADVOCACY NGO COMMUNITY REMAIN COMMITTED TO CERTIFICATION AS ITS SUCCESS GROWS?

What does the advocacy NGO community do when a controversial corporation, like Wal-Mart or McDonald's, begins to embrace what it has been advocating? Does this mean the end of the legitimacy of the certification system? Or should it be classified as a success because large and powerful corporations have agreed to transform *some* of their practices in the direction desired. Fair Trade coffee in Wal-Mart doesn't fix the company's mistreatment of its retail labor force or the displacement of its sourcing to sweatshops in China, nor does its presence in McDonald's eliminate the concerns over obesity stemming from the "super-sized" menu. Can Chiquita, the banana company associated with the United Fruit Company's involvement in exploitation and counter-revolution in Central America, ever become an accepted player in Fair Trade bananas?

Does the embrace of Fair Trade and other sustainability criteria for some products sold by these companies invalidate the benefits that certification may produce? The advocacy community supporting market campaigns and certification systems is divided on this question. But it's a division replete with mixed feelings. If McDonald's purchase of Fair Trade coffee significantly raises the incomes of tens of thousands of small-scale coffee farmers, this is an important benefit. However, some would want McDonald's to do much better for its local suppliers of garden vegetables, including tomatoes, before allowing the global corporation to bask in the partial and limited ethical accountability of Fair Trade. If Wal-Mart's (and Sam's Club's) embrace of Fair Trade for some products makes the Wal-Mart model more acceptable to some consumers and public officials, does that offset the local problems of traffic congestion, runoff, waste, and labor practices? Or is it simply "fair-washing" a corporate image?

Even more broadly, can the certification revolution move beyond the condemnation of those who believe that it is little more than "window dressing" in a conflict that has much deeper roots? Can it find a place in the process of transforming the corporate-led model of globalization into something that re-establishes the primacy of civil society over the juggernaut of corporate wealth and power? Civil society is undeniably finding new power in this model. Whether it is enough power to realign the power relations so that incorporation is once again recognized as a privilege extended to investors, rather than a right, remains to be seen.

CAN THE CERTIFICATION REVOLUTION AVOID DISCRIMINATING AGAINST THE GLOBAL SOUTH?

The certification revolution has been centered in the global North for logical reasons. It is in the global North that the highly branded corporations and the consumers with enough buying power to permit an ethical edge tend to be located. Can this process provide equitable benefits in both North and South?

There are those who believe that the creation of social and environmental standards in the North represents just the latest wave of discriminatory trade rules that reduce the competitiveness of production in the South. The FSC was initially created to provide verification of the sustainability of forest products sourced from tropical regions, as we noted. But the largest amount of FSC forest certification has taken place in the temperate forests of the global North, especially if we include the countries in transition from the former Soviet Union. Certification of tropical forests and their products as they are shipped into northern markets remains an underdeveloped component of forest certification, whether under FSC or under any of the other forest certification systems.

Fair Trade certification, on the other hand, has been deliberately limited to products produced in the global South, with special emphasis on those products sold in northern markets. Advocacy groups wanting Fair Trade certification for apparel produced under fairly paid conditions, distinct from sweatshops, in the US have been told that those products don't qualify for Fair Trade certification under the present definitions. So the bias in Fair Trade is toward products produced in the global South.

Ironically, the FSC has consistently maintained the most balanced North-South governance process, with the FSC-South (equivalent to the global South plus the transition countries) given equal representation in all decision making within the system. Fair Trade has been governed principally by the representatives of the labeling initiatives in the global North, with minority representation of producers in the global South. This is a source of major tension. Whether sustainable tourism certification emerges as a system with equitable North-South governance remains to be seen. Emerging principles for certification of the recycling of toxics seek to favor the global South by banning the shipment of toxic wastes to sites in the South, where conditions are presently among the most dangerous in the world. But they don't appear to permit certification of appropriate processes and conditions in the South as an alternative solution.

The complexity of these results, I suspect, further reflects the ambivalence among the advocacy NGOs, primarily in the North, who are the critical drivers of these processes. They seek to take responsibility for the social and environmental conditions created by consumption in their countries. They want to assure responsible solutions for the social and environmental dilemmas created by that consumption. They find that they have considerably more influence over corporations serving markets in the North, because of brand-driven corporate accountability. But, with the possible exception of the FSC, there has not been adequate engagement with civil society in the global South to design processes that meet the needs of both South and North in the process of transforming corporate practices worldwide.

In the end, these challenges do not come close to undermining the following amazing achievements of the past 15 years:

- Advocacy NGOs that have learned to find the corporate soft spot.
- Corporations that have recognized their vulnerability and have sought strong ethical solutions.
- Valiant nonprofit certification systems that have evolved to fill the need for independent third-party verification of the best contemporary corporate accountability.

All three groups are the heroes of the certification revolution.

Notes

CHAPTER 1

1. Some of this analysis appeared in an article I wrote in 2001, "Can Advocacy-Led Certification Systems Transform Global Corporate Practices? Evidence, and Some Theory" (PERI Paper DPE-01-07, September 2001), which was published on-line by the Political Economy Research Institute at the University of Massachusetts, Amherst. It was available in July 2006 at umass.edu/peri/pdfs/WP21.pdf.
2. "Banks Accept Environmental Rules: Citicorp, Barclays, Others to Shun Projects that Harm Environment and Livelihoods," *Wall Street Journal*, June 4, 2003.
3. Michael Shellenberger and the Ethical Business Campaigns Network, *Race to the Top: A Report on Ethical Business Campaigns*, accessed at businessethicsnetwork.org/knowledge.php on January 10, 2006 (no longer available online).
4. Lester Brown, "Crossing the Threshold: Early Signs of an Environmental Awakening," *World Watch Magazine*, March/April 1999.
5. See Colin Bates, *How to Build Your Total Brand*, accessed at buildingbrands.com on September 24, 2005.
6. Ibid.
7. *The Economist* has compiled and published a useful collection of articles from some 15 authors under the title *Brands and Branding* (London: Profile Books, 2003); this reference comes from Chapter 1, "What Is a Brand?" by Tom Blackett.
8. Ibid.
9. Ibid.
10. Robert Berner and David Kiley, "The Best Global Brands," *Business Week* special report, August 1, 2005.
11. Alan Cowell, "Coke Recalls Bottled Water Newly Introduced to Britain," *New York Times*, March 20, 2005.
12. Naomi Klein, *No Logo: Taking Aim at the Brand Bullies* (New York: Picador, 1999).
13. Robin Knight, "Gaining Street Cred: A fast-selling anticapitalist screed may lack perspective, but it explains why the mobs are angry," *Time Europe*, January 22, 2000.
14. Shellenberger and the Ethical Business Campaigns Network, *Race to the Top*.
15. Much of the information in this profile comes from a classic business school case study produced by Richard M. Locke, the Alvin J. Siteman Professor of Entrepreneurship and Political Science at MIT. Locke has had unparalleled access to NIKE internal data. The case study is "The Promise and Perils of Globalization: The Case of Nike," in *Management: Inventing and Delivering Its Future*, ed. Thomas A. Kochan and Richard Schmalensee (Cambridge, MA: MIT Press, 2003).
16. Anita Chan, "Boot Camp at the Shoe Factory: Where Taiwanese Bosses Drill Chinese Workers to Make Sneakers for American Joggers," *Washington Post*, November 3, 1996.
17. Locke, "Promise and Perils of Globalization."
18. Stephen Glass, "The Young and The Feckless," *The New Republic*, September 15, 1997.
19. Steven Greenhouse, "Nike Shoe Plant in Vietnam Is Called Unsafe for Workers," *New York Times*, November 8, 1997.
20. Timothy Egan, "The Swoon of the Swoosh," *New York Times*, September 13, 1998.
21. For more information on Underwriters Laboratories, see the organization's website at ul.com.
22. Consumers Union, the US affiliate of Consumers International, for example, downgrades any eco-labeling system in which representatives of corporations have played any role in standard-setting (see eco-labels.org). This is a logical extension of the Consumers Union's long and distinguished history of testing products against independent

298

technical standards, but it is, unfortunately, a bit shortsighted in the new world of certification systems for transformation of corporate social and environmental practices.

23. This profile draws heavily on excellent research undertaken by Ellen Hawes, a Yale graduate student.

24. This is according to personal communications with several members of the original board, who preferred anonymity in their reflections ten years later.

25. Harold Gilliam, "'Green Seal' of Approval," *San Francisco Chronicle*, June 10, 1990.

26. "SDA Protests Green Seal Standards," *Chemical Week*, December 16, 1992.

27. Judann Dagnoli, "Whose Job Is It to Define 'Green'?" *Advertising Age*, February 4, 1991.

28. Members of the Consumers Choice Council included Green Seal, the Institute for Agriculture and Trade Policy, the Center for International Environmental Law, the Sierra Club, and the National Wildlife Federation.

29. Abhijit Banerjee and Barry D. Solomon, "Eco-labeling for Energy Efficiency and Sustainability: A Meta-Evaluation of US Programs," *Energy Policy*, January 2003.

30. Christy Fisher, "Green Seal Tries to Take Root," *Advertising Age*, April 18, 1994.

31. Interview with Arthur Weissman on October 10, 2006.

32. Benjamin Cashore, Graeme Auld, and Deanna Newsom, *Governing Through Markets: Forest Certification and the Emergence of Non-State Authority* (New Haven, CT: Yale University Press, 2004).

33. This section is loosely based on a lengthy paper by Benjamin Cashore and Steven Bernstein, "Can Non-State Global Governance Be Legitimate? A Theoretical Framework" (presented at a joint IDDRI, CIRAD, and Sciences Po research unit conference, in conjunction with the Association Française de Sociologie, Montpellier, France, June 7–9, 2006).

34. The only public version of Cauley's results was offered in a June 2006 conference call for advocacy organizations, organized by the Business Ethics Network.

CHAPTER 2

1. From the website of the Centre for Business Relationships, Accountability, Sustainability, and Society, Cardiff University, brass.cf.ac.uk/history_L3.pdf, accessed on December 12, 2005.

2. Ibid.

3. Michael Hopkins, *A Planetary Bargain: Corporate Social Responsibility Comes of Age* (London: Macmillan, 2005).

4. Milton Friedman, "The Social Responsibility of Business Is to Increase Its Profits," *New York Times Magazine*, September 13, 1970.

5. Ibid.

6. David Vogel, *The Market for Virtue: The Potential and Limits of Corporate Social Responsibility* (Washington DC: Brookings Institution Press, 2005).

7. "Campaigners Welcome Law that Makes Companies More Accountable," *Independent Catholic News*, November 16, 2006.

8. Deborah Doane, "The Myth of CSR: The Problem with Assuming that Companies Can Do Well While Also Doing Good Is that Markets Don't Really Work that Way," *Stanford Social Innovation Review*, Fall 2005.

9. Michael E. Porter and Mark R. Kramer, "Strategy and Society: The Link Between Competitive Advantage and Corporate Social Responsibility," *Harvard Business Review*, December 2006, pp. 78–92.

10. Ibid., p. 83.

11. Ibid.

12. John Mackey, "Putting Customers Ahead of Investors," part of "Rethinking the Social Responsibility of Business," *Reasononline*, reason.com/news/printer/32239.html, October 2005, accessed on December 11, 2006.

13. Tobias Buck, "More Companies Reveal Social Policies," *Financial Times*, June 15, 2005, p. 8.

14. "Calvert Issues Corporate Responsibility Ratings on 100 Largest Companies," *CSRwire:*

The Newswire of Corporate Social Responsibility, February 6, 2006, csrwire.com, accessed on February 10, 2006.

15. See, for example, the Business and Human Rights Resource Centre website, business humanrights.org, where weekly updates list these charges, along with corporate responses to them.

16. Although the *Universal Declaration of Human Rights* was approved by the UN General Assembly in 1948 without dissenting votes, it is not a legally binding document. Legally binding covenants based on the *Universal Declaration* have been brought forward over the years, but the US has given only conditional and restricted ratification to a covenant on political and civil rights. It has not ratified the covenant on social, economic, and cultural rights. The US and Somalia are the only countries that have not ratified the international convention on the rights of the child. (In order to end the wholesale recruiting and training of child soldiers, this convention stipulates that no child under 18 may be recruited for military duty, but the US consistently recruits 17-year-olds.) The US has not ratified the convention on the elimination of all forms of discrimination against women nor any of the international labor conventions guaranteeing rights to organize and to engage in collective bargaining. See Joe Stork, "Human Rights and U.S. Policy," *Foreign Policy in Focus,* March 1999, fpif.org/briefs/vol4/v4no8hrts.html, accessed on December 8, 2006.

17. See the "Brief Description" under the "About Us" tab on the B&HCR website, business humanrights.org, accessed on December 6, 2006.

18. See "Statement by Linda Buckley, Vice President, Media Relations, Tiffany & Co.," March 2005, reports-and-materials.org/Tiffany-Linda-Buckley-statement-Mar-2005.doc, accessed on December 6, 2006.

19. See "Tiffany & Co. to Continue Moratorium on Purchase of Gemstones Mined in Burma," March 4, 2005, reports-and-materials.org/Tiffany-Burma-gems-statement-4-Mar-2005.pdf, accessed on December 6, 2006.

20. Business & Human Rights Resource Center, "New Website Spotlights Human Rights Impact of 2000 Companies: Launched Today In Davos By Mary Robinson," press release, January 28, 2005, accessed at reports-and-materials.org/Press-release-Resource-Centre-launch-28-Jan-2005.doc on October 20, 2006.

21. Christopher Avery et al., "Why All Companies Should Address Human Rights — (and How the Business & Human Rights Centre Can Help)," in *The ICCA Handbook on Corporate Social Responsibility,* ed. Judith Hennigfeld, Manfred Pohl, and Nick Tolhurst (London: Wiley UK, 2006). Available at cca-institute.org/pdf/avery_business%26humanrights.pdf, accessed on December 6, 2006.

22. *The Compact Oxford Dictionary of the English Language,* 2nd edition (CITY: Oxford University Press, 2004).

23. See the Responsible Care website (chemicalguide.com) for a discussion of its origins. Also see Ronie Garcia-Johnson, *Exporting Environmentalism: U.S. Multinational Chemical Corporations in Brazil and Mexico* (Cambridge MA: The MIT Press, 2000).

24. Porter and Kramer, "Strategy and Society."

25. Linda Grant, "And the Brand Played On," *Guardian,* August 12, 2006.

26. "Marks & Spencer Lays Off 4,390 staff," *Guardian Unlimited,* March 29, 2001.

27. Ed Williams, "CSR—A Changing Fashion or an Instrument for Fashioning Change" (paper presented at BITC Conference, Hong Kong, 24 February 2004. Available at bitc.org.uk/resources/viewpoint/edwihk.html, accessed on August 20, 2006).

28. Marks & Spencer, "Marks & Spencer Extends Fairtrade Offer," press release, June 20, 2005.

29. Anthony Fletcher, "Marks & Spencer Dives into Ethical Consumer Market," *Foodnavigator.com,* October 3, 2006.

30. Share value from Marks & Spencer historical prices at the Yahoo! Finance website, finance.yahoo.com, accessed on December 15, 2006.

31. Padraig O'Hannelly, "M&S Bucks the Trend," *Fool.co.uk*, April 4, 2006, fool.co.uk/news/comment/2006/c060411f.htm, accessed on February 18, 2007.

32. Marc Gunther, "Bleeding Heart Businesses: Corporate America Finds Profit in Tilting to the Left," *Washington Post*, November 14, 2004.

33. Marc Gunther, "The Rapid Rise of 'Moral Liability,'" *Business Ethics*, Winter 2005. A similar article by the same author, "Corporate America's Hidden Risks: Major Headaches Threaten Companies that Ignore Their 'Moral Liability,'" was later published in the online version of *Fortune Magazine*, June 28, 2006, money.cnn.com/2006/06/28/news/companies/pluggedin.fortune/index.htm, accessed on August 21, 2006.

34. Geoff Lye and Francesca Miller, "The Changing Landscape of Liability: A Director's Guide to Trends in Corporate Environmental, Social and Economic Liability" (London: SustainAbility, 2004). Available at sustainability.com/downloads_public/insight_reports/liability.pdf, and last accessed on October 10, 2006.

35. Ibid., p. 04.

36. Ibid., p. 07

37. Andrew Savitz, "Expecting Corporate Kindness," *Boston Globe*, July 25, 2006. Savitz is the author, with Karl Weber, of *The Triple Bottom Line: How the Best Run Companies Are Achieving Economic, Social and Environmental Success — and How You Can Too* (San Francisco: Jossey-Bass/Wiley, 2006).

38. Simon Zadek, "The Logic of Collaborative Governance: Corporate Responsibility, Accountability and the Social Contract" (Working Paper #3, Corporate Social Responsibility Initiative, Center for Business and Government, John F. Kennedy School, Harvard University, January 2005).

39. Simon Zadek, *The Civil Corporation: The New Economy of Corporate Citizenship* (London: Earthscan, 2001).

40. Peter Barnes, *Capitalism 3.0: A Guide to Reclaiming the Commons* (San Francisco: Berrett-Koehler Publishers, 2006).

41. Ibid., p. 50.

CHAPTER 3

1. Many of the ideas presented in this chapter derive from joint presentations that Michael Marx, CEO of Corporate Ethics International, and I have made on the subject of "The Evolving Nature and Importance of Markets Campaigns." I acknowledge my debt to him for many of these ideas, but they evolved in our joint talks in such a way that it is difficult to separate his contributions from mine. So I'll give him credit for all the good ideas, and I'll take responsibility for those that may seem dumb.

2. See the World Trade Organization explanation of the ruling at wto.org/English/tratop_e/envir_e/edis04_e.htm, accessed on July 26, 2006.

3. Anthony Ramirez, "'Epic Debate' Led to Heinz Tuna Plan," *New York Times*, April 16, 1990.

4. Kim Foltz, "Advertising Agency with a Cause," *New York Times*, May 21, 1990.

5. Philip Shabecoff, "3 Companies to Stop Selling Tuna Netted with Dolphins," *New York Times*, April 13, 1990.

6. Barry Meier, "Tuna Company Protests Accusations About Dolphins," *New York Times*, December 6, 1990.

7. For more information on the dolphin campaign, see the section of the Earth Island website on the International Marine Mammal Project, earthisland.org/immp, and click on the "Dolphins" link. Accessed on September 16, 2006.

8. Gary Gereffi, Ronie Garcia-Johnson, and Erika Sasser, "The NGO-Industrial Complex," *Foreign Policy*, July-August 2001, pp. 56–65.

9. Michael Shellenberger and the Ethical Business Campaigns Network, *Race to the Top: A Report on Ethical Business Campaigns*, 2004, accessed at businessethicsnetwork.org/report.pdf on July 10, 2006 (no longer available online).

10. This profile is based largely on a personal interview with Michael Brune, July 27, 2006.

11. Marc Gunther, "The Mosquito in the Tent: A Pesky Environmental Group Called the Rainforest Action Network Is Getting under the Skin of Corporate America," *Fortune,* March 31, 2004, available at money.cnn.com/magazines/fortune/fortune_archive/2004/05/31/370717/index.htm.

12. Jim Doyle, "S.F nonprofit a lean, green, fighting machine," *San Francisco Chronicle*, December 17, 2004.

13. Edelman, "Annual Edelman Trust Barometer — 2006," published as a special supplement to *PRWeek*, January 2006. Also available at edelman.com/image/insights/content/FullSupplement_final.pdf, accessed on September 15, 2006.

14. Ann M. Florini, ed., *The Third Force: The Rise of Transnational Civil Society* (Tokyo/Washington DC: Japan Center for International Exchange/Carnegie Endowment for International Peace, 2000).

15. Ann M. Florini and P.J. Simmons, "What the World Needs Now?," Chapter 1 in Florini, *The Third Force*, p. 4.

16. Ann M. Florini, "Lessons Learned," Chapter 8 in Florini, *The Third Force*, p. 211.

17. Ibid., p. 235.

CHAPTER 4

1. One of the best sources of information on the early history of the Forest Stewardship Council is a set of unpublished notes developed by Dr. Timothy Synnott, the first executive director of the FSC, who served from 1993 until 2000 and then continued as director of forest policy at the FSC for several years. Entitled "Some Notes on the Early Years of the FSC," and dated November 1995, they can be found on the FSC website at fsc.org/keepout/en/content_areas/45/2/files/FSC_FoundingNotes.doc.

2. Gerald Urquhart, Walter Chomentowski, David Skole, and Chris Barber, "Tropical Deforestation: The Rate of Deforestation," at NASA's Earth Observatory website, earthobservatory.nasa.gov/Library/Deforestation/deforestation_2.html, accessed on July 10, 2006.

3. Urquhart et al., "Tropical Deforestation: Deforestation and Global Processes," earthobservatory.nasa.gov/Library/Deforestation/deforestation_3.html, accessed on July 10, 2006.

4. Synnott, "Some Notes," p. 5.

5. D. Poore, P. Burgess, J. Palmer, S. Rietbergen, and T. Synnott, *No Timber Without Trees: Sustainability in the Tropical Forest* (London: Earthscan, 1989).

6. For a timeline, see "Forest Conservation through the Decades" at the World Wildlife Fund website, panda.org/about_wwf/what_we_do/forests/about_forests/timeline_forest_conservation/index.cfm, accessed on July 10, 2006.

7. I.L. Eastin, A. Addae-Mensah, and J. de-Graft Yartey, "Tropical Timber Boycotts: Strategic Implications for the Ghanaian Timber Industry" FAO Forest Department, *Unasylva* 43, no. 170(1992). Available at fao.org/docrep/u6850e/u6850e08.htm, accessed on July 10, 2006.

8. The timeline mentioned in note 6 includes information on these early efforts.

9. Synnott, "Some notes," p. 8.

10. Ibid., p. 9.

11. Ecological Trading Company, "Monitoring and Verification Mechanisms," unpublished paper, 2005, cited in Synnott, "Some notes," p. 10.

12. I had the privilege of participating as an individual member from the Social Chamber, carrying the proxies of a dozen others.

13. Synnott, "Some notes," p. 28.

14. Ibid.

15. Drawn from interviews in Oaxaca, Mexico, in August 2006.

16. This decision is discussed thoroughly on the Rainforest Alliance website: Richard Z. Donovan, "A Perspective on the Perum Perhutani Certification Suspension," August

2001, accessed at rainforest-alliance.org/news/2001/perhutani-perspective.html on July 20, 2006.

17. Lester Brown, "Crossing the Threshold," *World Watch*, March/April 1999.
18. There is a description of the alliance on the World Bank website, worldbank.org/html /extdr/thematic.htm under "Agriculture and Rural Development." Select "Forests and Forestry" and then "Partnerships," which has a link to the WB/WWF Alliance, accessed on August 21, 2006.
19. See M. Read, *Truth or Trickery? An Assessment of Claims of 'Sustainability' Applied to Tropical Wood Products and Timbers Retailed in the UK, July 1990–January 1991* (WWF, 1991) No longer available on WWF web resources.
20. RAN is unusual among advocacy NGOs in that it chronicles its successes on its website. This description of the campaign against Home Depot builds on RAN's own description, corroborated by a number of independent newspaper accounts. See ran.org/what _we_do/old_growth/history, accessed on July 20, 2006.
21. "Home Depot Joins Old-Growth Boycott," *San Francisco Examiner*, May 8, 1997.
22. James R. Hagerty, "Home Depot Vows to Change Policy on 'Sensitive' Wood Use," *Wall Street Journal*, August 27, 1999.
23. Editorial, *Vancouver Sun*, May 5, 2000.
24. Greenpeace, "Greenpeace Blockade of Ship in Long Beach Continues," press release, October 21, 1998.
25. Greenpeace, "Major Wood Supplier to U.S. Shut Down by Protesters," press release, September 5, 2000.
26. Greenpeace, "Illegal Logging Exposed in the Amazon, Greenpeace tows log raft to Brazilian environment agency officials," press release, May 18, 2000.
27. Greenpeace, "Brazil Announces End to Illegal Mahogany Trade, Greenpeace Investigations in Amazon Lead to Historic Decision by Brazilian Government," press release, December 5, 2001.
28. All data have been provided by the FSC International Center in response to specific requests.
29. Current data on the number of chain-of-custody certificates and the amount of certified forest is available at the "What's New?" section of the FSC website, fsc.org/en/whats_new /fsc_certificates.
30. Lincoln Quevedo, "Forest Certification in Bolivia," in *Confronting Sustainability: Forest Certification in Developing and Transitioning Countries*, ed. Benjamin Cashore, Fred Gale, Errol Meidinger, and Deanna Newsom (New Haven, CT: Yale School of Forestry and Environmental Studies Report Number 8, 2006).
31. Maria Tysiachniouk, "Forest Certification in Russia," in *Confronting Sustainability,* ed. Cashore et al.
32. Peter May, "Forest Certification in Brazil," in *Confronting Sustainability, ed.* Cashore, et al.
33. Based on an interview with Roberto Waack on November 10, 2006, in Bonn, Germany, at the first meeting of the FSC international board of directors that he attended after being elected.
34. The most complete analysis of the growth of certification in Canada can be found in Benjamin Cashore et al., *Governing Through Markets: Forest Certification and the Emergence of Non-State Authority* (New Haven, CT: Yale University Press, 2004).
35. Quoted in a presentation by Dr. Zhu Chunquan of WWF, "WWF China Promotes Responsible Forest Management with All Your Support" (speech to China State Forest Administration, March 28, 2006, organized by FSC in collaboration with WWF China.).
36. Personal communication with a high-ranking official in the AF&PA in 1999, who has asked to remain anonymous.
37. For more on the forest management principles of the Collins Companies, see collins wood.com.
38. Personal communication with Roger Dower, CEO of FSC-US, November 2006.

39. Ibid.

40. Personal communication with a Swedish forest company executive who asked for anonymity for competitive reasons.

41. Much of the material from the consultation on plantations is still available at the FSC website, fsc.org/plantations.

42. The final report is available at fsc.org/plantations under "Resources."

43. This profile is based on interviews in Bonn and by phone in November 2006.

44. See "Natural Quality and Sustainability: Certified Wood" on the Columbia Forest Products website, columbiaforestproducts.com/products/prodcert.aspx, accessed on August 12, 2006.

45. See "Forestry Programme: Responsible Sourcing…Certified Management," on tetra pak.com. This information was supplemented by discussions in November 2006 with Mario Abreu, director of Forestry and Recycling.

46. See "Social and Environmental Responsibility Report 2005," on the IKEA website, ikea -group.ikea.com/corporate/PDF/SandEReport2005_August.pdf, pp. 2–3.

47. See "Timber" at the B&Q website,diy.com. Follow links from "Corporate: About Us" to "Social Responsibility" and choose "Timber." Accessed on November 20, 2006.

48. See "About" at the FSC-Watch website, fsc-watch.org, accessed on February 21, 2007.

CHAPTER 5

1. See Stephanie Barrientos and Catherine Dolan, "Transformation of Global Food: Opportunities and Challenges for Fair and Ethical Trade," in *Ethical Sourcing in the Global Food System,* ed. Stephanie Barrientos and Catherine Dolan (London: Earthscan, 2006).

2. See Peter Robbins, *Stolen Fruit: The Tropical Commodities Disaster* (London: Zed Books, 2003).

3. See European Commission, *Agricultural Commodity Chains, Dependence, and Poverty: A Proposal for an EU Action Plan* (Brussels: Author, 2004), cited in Fair Trade Advocacy Office, *Business Unusual: Successes and Challenges of Fair Trade* (Brussels: Author, August 2006).

4. Much of this chapter is drawn from my previous work on Fair Trade, including the following articles: Michael E. Conroy, "Transnational Social Movements Linking North and South: The Struggle for Fair Trade" (paper presented at the conference "Alternative Visions of Development: Rural Social Movements in Latin America," University of Florida at Gainesville, February 23–25, 2006); Ann Grodnik and Michael E. Conroy, "Fair Trade Coffee in the U.S.: Why Companies Join the Movement," Chapter 6 in *Fair Trade: The Challenges of Transforming Globalization,* ed. Laura T. Raynolds, Douglas L. Murray, and John Wilkinson (London and New York: Routledge Press, 2006); Stephanie Barrientos, Michael E. Conroy, and Elaine Jones, "Northern Social Movements and Fair Trade," Chapter 4 in *Fair Trade: The Challenges of Transforming Globalization.*

5. This speech was accessed at whitehouse.gov/infocus/economy on July 20, 2006; as is the case with a number of President Bush's speeches, it is no longer available at that site.

6. "Bush Calls on Congress to Boost U.S. Competitiveness (Update1)," reported on Bloom berg.com website, February 4, 2006, bloomberg.com/apps/news?pid=10000087&sid= a7mmW4HiXGKM&refer=top_world_news.

7. Katherine Turman, "Fair Trade's Front Man," *Mother Jones,* January/February 2004. Available at motherjones.com/arts/qa/2004/01/12_100.html.

8. The petition adheres closely to the ideas articulated in Oxfam's report *Rigged Rules and Double Standards: Trade, Globalization, and the Fight Against Poverty* (Oxford: Oxfam, 2002). Available online at maketradefair.com/assets/english/report_english.pdf.

9. Created by the evangelical Church of the Brethren in 1949, SERRV International continues to function as an independent nonprofit that sells about $6 million worth of handicrafts from some 30 countries each year, mostly through Internet sales. For more information, see its website at cob-net.org/serrv.htm.

10. Ten Thousand Villages, "Vision, Mission and Principles," tenthousandvillages.com/php /about.us/mission.principles.php.

11. Ten Thousand Villages, "Annual Report, April 1, 2005–March 31, 2006," available at ten thousandvillages.com/pdf/annlreprt0506_rs.pdf, accessed on August 21, 2006.

12. Gepa, "Fifty Years of Fair Trade: A Brief History of the Fair Trade Movement," December 2003, available at gepa3.de/download/gepa_Fair_Trade_history__en.pdf, accessed on December 10, 2006.

13. For more information about Gepa, visit the organization's website at gepa3.de/htdocs _en/profil/index.html, accessed on December 10, 2006.

14. See IFAT Mission Statement, accessed at ifat.org on March 30, 2007.

15. See the NEWS website at worldshops.org.

16. Quote from the Fair Trade Federation website, fairtradefederation.org/index.html.

17. Fair Trade Advocacy Office, *Business Unusual*, p. 10.

18. For an ongoing discussion of these concepts, see Manish Verma, "What Is Solidarity Economy?" at the Association for Women's Rights in Development website, awid.org/go .php?stid=811, accessed on December 10, 2006.

19. Max Havelaar was a fictional character in an 1860 Dutch novel that focused on the colonial trade policies of the Netherlands in the Dutch East Indies. The book illustrated the ways in which Dutch consumer wealth was built upon the suffering of the farmers and other natives of the East Indies. The book ultimately led the Dutch government to implement a somewhat more ethical set of development policies.

20. The member organizations are TransFair Austria, Max Havelaar Belgium, TransFair Canada, Max Havelaar France, Max Havelaar Denmark, TransFair Germany, Fairtrade Foundation UK, TransFair Italy, Fair Trade Mark Ireland, TransFair Japan, TransFair Minka Luxemburg, Fairtrade Labeling Australia and New Zealand, Stichting Max Havelaar Netherlands, Max Havelaar Norge, Reilun kaupan edistämisyhdistys ry. Finland, Föreningen för Rättvisemärkt Sweden, Max Havelaar Stiftung Switzerland, TransFair USA, and Comercio Justo Mexico.

21. For detailed information on the standards, see the relevant section on the FLO International website, fairtrade.net/sites/standards/general.html.

22. This profile is based on several interviews with Bob Stiller and on his presentation to my Yale seminar in November 2005.

23. M.B. Grover, "Hippie Redux," *Forbes*, December 9, 1991.

24. Luisa Kroll, "Java Man," *Forbes*, October 29, 2001.

25. See David Raths, "100 Best Corporate Citizens for 2006," *Business Ethics* 20, no. 1 (Spring 2006), available at business-ethics.com/whats_new/100best.html#Article, accessed on October 10, 2006.

26. See the section on "Impact" at the FLO website, fairtrade.net/sites/impact/facts.html.

27. The International Coffee Organization provides statistics on coffee prices and market share at its website, ico.org/coffee_prices.asp. The information cited here was from "ICO Indicator Prices: Monthly and Annual Averages, 2004 to 2006," accessed on July 18, 2006.

28. G. Dicum and N. Luttinger, *The Coffee Book: Anatomy of an Industry from Crop to the Last Drop* (New York: The New Press, 1999).

29. See Specialty Coffee Association of America, "What Is Specialty Coffee?" scaa.org/what _is_specialty_coffee.asp, accessed on September 10, 2006.

30. Specialty Coffee Association of America, "Specialty Coffee Retail in the USA 2005," scaa.org/pdfs/news/specialtycoffeeretail.pdf, accessed on December 10, 2006.

31. Daniele Giovannucci, "Sustainable Coffee Survey of the North American Specialty Coffee Industry," (a report published by the Specialty Coffee Association of America and North American Commission for Environmental Cooperation, 2001). Available at cec.org/files/PDF/ECONOMY/CoffeeSurvey_EN.pdf, accessed July 10, 2006.

32. In recent year, the falling value of the US dollar relative to the Euro and other currencies has meant a de facto decrease in the price received by farmers, but the FLO system has not yet dealt with this issue.

33. The US-based Equal Exchange is not connected to the UK-based organization with the same name, although they share many of the same principles as well as the name.

34. Theories of unequal exchange form part of political economy-based dependency and world systems theory challenges to neoclassical economic theories of modernization.

35. V. Berman and M. Rozyne, "Never Underestimate Hope: The Impact of Fair Trade on Coffee Farmers," (an Equal Exchange Research Report from about 1992).

36. The history of the early Global Exchange campaign against Starbucks is captured best in an article written by Deborah James, a long-time Global Exchange campaigner: "Justice and Java: Coffee in a Fair Trade Market, *NACLA Report*, September/October 2000.

37. See "Open Letter to Starbucks," April 5, 2000, on the Global Exchange website, globalexchange.org/campaigns/fairtrade/coffee/OpenLetterToStarbucks.html, accessed on August 21, 2006.

38. The Global Exchange press release is available online at globalexchange.org/campaigns/fairtrade/coffee/pr041000.html, accessed on August 26, 2006.

39. Personal communication, Sarah Ford, coordinator of the LWR Interfaith Fair Trade Coalition.

40. Based on numerous personal contacts with Paul Rice in recent years, as well as a specific interview for this profile on August 10, 2006.

41. Laura T. Raynolds and Michael A. Long, "Fair/Alternative Trade: Historical and Empirical Dimensions," Chapter 2 in *Fair Trade: The Challenges of Transforming Globalization*, ed. Laura T. Raynolds, Douglas L. Murray, and John Wilkinson (London and New York: Routledge Press, 2006).

42. Jean-Marie Krier, *Fair Trade in Europe 2005: Facts and Figures on Fair Trade in 25 European Countries* (published jointly by FLO, IFAT, NEWS!, and EFTA, February 2006).

43. Douglas Murray et al., *One Cup at a Time: Poverty Alleviation and Fair Trade Coffee in Latin America* (Boulder, CO: Colorado State University Fair Trade Research Group, March 2003). This summary report and an array of contributing reports are also available at colostate.edu/Depts/Sociology/FairTradeResearchGroup.

44. In my experience, workers at tea plantations in Sri Lanka, who were on the Fair Trade registry but who had not succeeded in selling into Fair Trade markets, complained most about not receiving the community benefits that nearby estates had received from the social premium, including new kerosene stoves for all families (to replace wood stoves) and new housing units for some.

45. Eric Arnould, Alejandro Plastina, and Dwayne Ball, "Market Disintermediation and Producer Value Capture: The Case of Fair Trade Coffee in Nicaragua, Peru, and Guatemala," White Paper 06-001 (Tucson, AZ: Terry J. Lundgren Center for Retailing, The University of Arizona, June 2006). Available from cals.arizona.edu/fcs/tlc/research/MarketDisintermediation_Arnould.pdf, accessed on December 10, 2006.

46. Personal interviews with Perry Odak, in July 2006, while traveling with him to inspect supply chains among Nicaraguan Fair Trade coffee suppliers.

47. Kirsten Olsen, "Making It to McDonald's: How Fair Trade Coffee Moved out of Its Niche and into the Most Mainstream Market of All," *Stanford Social Innovation Review,* Winter 2007.

CHAPTER 6

1. Ernst and Young LLP, *Measures that Matter* (a report prepared by Ernst and Young's Center for Business Innovation), 1997, accessed at corporatesunshine.org/measuresthatmatter.pdf on August 21, 2006.

2. At one point there were copious materials on the Safeguard Principles available on the IFC website, but they have since been removed. A good history of their development may be found in "Safeguard Policies: Framework for Improving Development Effectiveness," a World Bank paper available at lnweb18.worldbank.org/ESSD/sdvext.nsf/04ByDocName/SafeguardPoliciesFrameworkforImprovingDevelopmentEffectiveness-ADiscussionNote/$FILE/SafeguardsFrameworkPaper-100702.pdf.

3. See AIDEnvironment, *Funding Forest Destruction,* report for Greenpeace, March 2000, and "Campaign Case Study: Dutch Banks and Indonesian Palm Oil," *Focus on Finance Newsletter,* March 2001.

4. WWF, "Is Your Ice Cream Bad for Elephants?" press release, December 11, 2002, accessed at panda.org/news_facts/newsroom/features on March 3, 2006.

5. Peter Bosshard, *Power Finance: Financial Institutions in India's Hydropower Sector* (Delhi /Sassenberg, Germany/Berkeley, CA: South Asia Network on Dams, Rivers, and People/ Urgewald/International Rivers Network, 2002).

6. World Commission on Dams, *Dams and Development: A New Framework for Decision-Making* (London/Sterling, VA: Earthscan Publications, 2000).

7. Robert Goodland, "Ecuador: Oleoducto de Crudos Pesados (OCP) (Heavy Crude Oil Pipeline): Independent Compliance Assessment of OCP with the World Bank's Social and Environmental Policies," September 2002. Accessed at amazonwatch.org/amazon/ EC/ocp/reports/ocp_asses_report_0209.pdf, on January 5, 2006.

8. Amazon Watch, "Peru: Camisea Natural Gas Project," active campaign report, September 2003, accessed at amazonwatch.org/amazon/PE/camisea accessed on June 15, 2006.

9. Friends of the Earth, "Pressure Groups Target the Private Banks Behind Corporate Misdeeds," press release, January 27, 2003, accessed at foe.org/new/releases/0103wef.html on June 15, 2006.

10. "Collevecchio Declaration on Financial Institutions and Sustainability," available on the Friends of the Earth website, foe.org/camps/intl/declaration.html, accessed on June 15, 2006.

11. Karen Cook, "Will the Citi Ever Weep?" *Village Voice,* March 9, 2000.

12. RAN, "Demonstrations Target CITIGROUP in 50 Cities as Corporation Announces Record Earnings," press release, October 17, 2000, accessed at ran.org/media_center/ news_article/?uid=104.

13. Marc Gunther, "The Mosquito in the Tent: A Pesky Environmental Group Called the Rainforest Action Network Is Getting Under the Skin of Corporate America," *Fortune,* March 31, 2004, accessed at money.cnn.com/magazines/fortune/fortune_archive/2004 /05/31/370717/index.htm on August 26, 2006.

14. Description of Citigroup's New Environmental Initiatives on the RAN website, accessed at ran.org/what_we_do/global_finance/citigroup_victory on June 15, 2006.

15. "Citigroup New Environmental Initiatives," accessed on the RAN website, ran.org/file admin/materials/global_finance/CitiEnvPolicy.pdf, on June 15, 2006.

16. This and other inside information on the crafting of the Equator Principles came from interviews with IFC staff who requested anonymity because they were not authorized to discuss this history publicly.

17. "The Equator Principles: A Financial Industry Benchmark for Determining, Assessing and Managing Social and Environmental Risk in Project Financing," July 2006, accessed at equator-principles.com/documents/Equator_Principles.pdf on July 26, 2006.

18. "10 Global Banks Endorse Socially Responsible 'Equator Principles,'" Agence France Presse, June 5, 2003.

19. Michael M. Phillips and Mitchell Pacelle, "Banks Accept Environmental Rules: Citicorp, Barclays, Others to Shun Projects that Harm Environment and Livelihoods," *Wall Street Journal,* June 4, 2003.

20. "Loan Rules with an Eye on Nature," *International Herald Tribune,* June 5, 2003.

21. This profile is based on personal interviews conducted on July 27 and August 21, 2006.

22. Alison Leigh Cowan, "Taking Protest to a Corporate Chief's Street, 3 Activists Face Charges in Greenwich," *New York Times,* March 13, 2005.

23. JPMorgan Chase, "Public Environmental Policy Statement," accessed on the RAN website, ran.org/fileadmin/materials/global_finance/JPMCPolicy.pdf, on June 15, 2006.

24. Brief timeline of RAN's JPMorgan Chase campaign accessed on the RAN website, ran .org/what_we_do/global_finance/hist/jpmorgan_chase, on June 15, 2006.

25. Claudia H. Deutsch, "Goldman to Encourage Solutions to Environmental Issues," *New York Times,* November 22, 2005.

26. Goldman Sachs, "Goldman Sachs Environmental Policy Framework," accessed on the RAN website, ran.org/fileadmin/materials/global_finance/GoldmanSachsPolicy.pdf, on July 28, 2006.

27. "Hear What the Experts Have to Say on the Goldman Sachs Policy," accessed on the RAN website, ran.org/what_we_do/global_finance/goldman_sachs_victory/goldman_sachs_what_the_experts_say, on July 28, 2006.

28. For more information, see the BankTrack website, banktrack.org, accessed on January 15, 2006.

29. This profile is based largely on an interview conducted on September 6, 2006.

30. Peter Thai Larsen, "HSBC wins top accolade for sustainable banking," *Financial Times*, June 13, 2006, accessed at ft.com/businesslife/bankingawards on August 15, 2006.

31. BankTrack, "Principles, Profits, or Just PR? Triple P investments under the Equator Principles: An Anniversary Assessment," June 4, 2004, accessed at banktrack.org/doc/File/OurPublications/BankTrackpublications/04060.pdf on August 15, 2006.

32. Personal communication with Motoko Aizawa, IFC Social and Environmental Development Department, October 24, 2006.

33. See OECD, "Recommendation on Common Approaches on Environment and Officially Supported Export Credits," December 19, 2003, accessed at oecd.org/dataoecd/26/33/21684464.pdf on October 26, 2006.

34. BankTrack, "Equator Principles II: NGO comments on the proposed revision of the Equator Principles," April 26, 2006, accessed at banktrack.org on July 27, 2006.

35. "Frequently Asked Questions about the Equator Principles," at the Equator Principles website, equator-principles.com/faq.shtml, accessed on July 12, 2006.

36. BankTrack, "Equator Principles II," pp.5–6.

37. This profile is based on personal interviews that took place on August 22 and 25, 2006.

38. From the Sustainable Finance Ltd. website, sustainablefinance.co.uk/aboutus/contact.htm, accessed on August 22, 2006.

CHAPTER 7

1. UN World Tourism Organization, "International Tourism Receipts by Country of Destination," in *Tourism Market Trends, 2005 Edition — Annex*, accessed at world-tourism.org/frameset/frame_statistics.html on August 20, 2006.

2. Peter Kuhbach and Bradlee A. Herauf, "U.S. Travel and Tourism Satellite Accounts for 2002–2005," Bureau of Economic Analysis, June 2006. Available at bea.gov/bea/ARTICLES/2006/06June/0606_TTSA.pdf, accessed on August 20, 2006.

3. UN Conference on Trade and Development, "Report of the Expert Meeting on ICT and Tourism for Development," Document TD/B/COM.3/EM.25/3 (Geneva: Author, December 2005).

4. UN Environment Program, "Tourism's Three Main Impact Areas," accessed at uneptie.org/pc/tourism/sust-tourism/env-3main.htm on August 20,2006.

5. UN Environment Program, "Negative Socio-Cultural Impacts of Tourism," accessed at uneptie.org/pc/tourism/sust-tourism/soc-drawbacks.htm on August 20, 2006.

6. The term was coined by Tourism Concern, a UK advocacy organization that campaigns to reduce the social and environmental consequences of tourism. See its website, tourismconcern.org.uk/campaigns/ssss.html, accessed on October 10, 2006.

7. UN World Tourism Organization, "Global Code of Ethics for Tourism," 1999, accessed at gdrc.org/uem/eco-tour/principles.html on October 11, 2006.

8. See Tour Operators Initiative for Sustainable Development website, toinitiative.org, accessed on August 20, 2006.

9. Tour Operators Initiative, "Statement of Commitment to Sustainable Tourism Development," 2001, accessed at toinitiative.org/about/statement_of_commitment.htm on August 20, 2006.

10. See the Tourism Concern website at tourismconcern.org.uk.

11. See the "International Fair Trade in Tourism Network" of the Tourism Concern website, tourismconcern.org.uk/fair-trade/index.html, accessed on October 10, 2006.

12. Chris Beddoe, *Labour Standards, Social Responsibility, and Tourism* (London: Tourism Concern, 2004).

13. Tearfund, "Worlds Apart: A Call to Responsible Global Tourism," January 2002, accessed at tilz.tearfund.org/webdocs/Website/Campaigning/Policy%20and%20research/Worlds%20Apart%20tourism%20report.pdf on August 20, 2006.

14. Guyonne James, "CSR in Tourism — Tourism Concern," *CSR Asia Weekly*, July 26, 2006.

15. See counterpart.org/DNN/Default.aspx?tabid=65; the National Geographic Society is now branding sustainable tourism as "geotourism," but that term has engendered no acceptance in the field because it lacks the value attributes of "sustainable tourism."

16. Quoted on the Eco India website, accessed at ecoindia.com/sustainable-tourism.html on October 10, 2006.

17. Eric Weiner, "Ecotourism: Can It Protect the Planet?" *New York Times*, May 19, 1991.

18. Ibid.

19. This definition was crafted in 1991 by the International Ecotourism Society. It is cited in Martha Honey, ed., *Ecotourism and Certification: Setting Standards in Practice* (New York: Island Press, 2002), p.1.

20. Ibid.

21. Ibid.

22. Quebec Declaration on Ecotourism, at the World Ecotourism Summit website, world-tourism.org/sustainable/IYE/quebec/anglais/declaration.html, accessed on August 20, 2006.

23. Martha Honey, *Ecotourism and Sustainable Development: Who Owns Paradise?* (Washington DC: Island Press, 1999), p.24.

24. Anita Pleumarom, "Eco-Tourism: An Ecological and Economic Trap for Third World Countries" (paper presented in preparation for the 5th meeting of the Conference of Parties to the Convention on Biological Diversity, in June 1999).Accessed at twnside.org.sg/title/cbd.htm on September 17, 2006.

25. Rosaleen Duffy, *A Trip Too Far: Ecotourism, Politics and Exploitation* (London: Earthscan, 2002), pp. 156–57.

26. Ibid., pp. 158–59.

27. Martha Honey and Abigail Rome, *Protecting Paradise: Certification Programs for Sustainable Tourism and Ecotourism* (Washington DC: Institute for Policy Studies, October 2001).

28. See the Green Globe website at greenglobe21.com, accessed on September 16, 2006.

29. Published by Island Press of Washington, DC, in 1999.

30. Honey, *Ecotourism and Sustainable Development*, p. 394.

31. Honey and Rome, *Protecting Paradise*, p. 75.

32. Honey, ed., *Ecotourism and Certification*.

33. See the Certification for Sustainable Tourism website, turismo-sostenible.co.cr/EN/home.shtml, accessed on September 16, 2006.

34. Certification for Sustainable Tourism, "What CST Is All About," n.d., accessed at turismo-sostenible.co.cr/EN/sobreCST/about-cst.shtml on September 16, 2006.

35. This profile is based on interviews with Karen Lewis at Lapa Rios on September 14, 15, and 17, 2006.

36. "US State Department Corporate Excellence Award 2005" at the Lapa Rios website, accessed at laparios.com/articles/lapa_rios_state_dept_award_2005.htm on October 12, 2006.

37. See the Green Deal website at greendeal.org/home.html, accessed on September 16, 2006.

38. "Ecotourism Kenya's Eco-Rating Scheme," at the Ecotourism Kenya website, accessed at ecotourismkenya.org/ecotourism-kenya-ecorating-scheme.php on November 14, 2006.

39. "Sustainable Tourism: Sustainable Tourism Certification," Rainforest Alliance, n.d., accessed at rainforest-alliance.org/programs/tourism/certification/index.htm on October 10, 2006.

40. Sustainable Tourism Certification Network of the Americas, "Baseline Criteria," on the Rainforest Alliance website, accessed at rainforest-alliance.org/tourism/documents/baseline_criteria.pdf on October 10, 2006.

41. This profile is based on interviews that took place on August 25 and October 9, 2006.

42. Rainforest Alliance, "About Us: Our Mission," accessed at rainforest-alliance.org/about .cfm?id=mission on October 9, 2006.

43. Rainforest Alliance, "Sustainable Tourism: Introduction," accessed at rainforest-alliance .org/programs/tourism/index.html on October 9, 2006.

CHAPTER 8

1. Michael E. Conroy, "Can Advocacy-Led Certification Systems Transform Global Corporate Structures? Evidence and Some Theory" (Working Paper 21, Political Economy Research Institute, University of Massachusetts, September 2001; available online at umass .edu/peri/pdfs/WP21.pdf).

2. Amazon.com returns a list of 1,905 titles in response to the query "mining, problems."

3. These quotes are taken from MMSD Project, *Breaking New Ground: Mining, Minerals, and Sustainable Development* (London/Sterling VA: Earthscan Publications, 2002), prepared for the International Institute for Environment and Development and World Business Council for Sustainable Development. Accessed at iied.org/mmsd/finalreport /index.html on August 15, 2006.

4. See Project Underground's sign-on statement against the MMSD report, available at moles.org/ProjectUnderground/campaigns/mmsd0104.html, accessed on August 15, 2006.

5. I was a participant in the shaping of this vision statement, but I don't believe that it exists on the Internet at this point.

6. Michael Janofsky, "Get the Lead Out: Tiffany Recalls a Line of Chinaware," *New York Times,* February 19, 1993. This article was complemented by personal conversations with Michael Kowalski in February 2005.

7. 2005 data, according to Interbrand, Inc., published in *Business Week,* July 17, 2006.

8. The letter appeared in the *Washington Post* of March 24, 2004, on page A11.

9. The framework is available online at frameworkforresponsiblemining.org.

10. Earthworks and Oxfam, *Dirty Metals: Mining, Communities and the Environment* (Washington/Boston: Authors, 2004). Available online at nodirtygold.org/dirty_metals _report.cfm, accessed on August 10, 2006.

11. "US activist groups urge Valentine's boycott of gold," Forbes.com, February 11, 2004, accessed at forbes.com/home_asia/newswire/2004/02/11/rtr1257024.html on November 21, 2006.

12. "No Dirty Gold in the news" at the No Dirty Gold website, nodirtygold.org/NDGitn .cfm, accessed on August 10, 2006.

13. National Mining Association, "Modern Gold Mining Practices Contradict Critics," press release, February 11, 2004, accessed in the Newsroom 2004 archives at nma.org on March 20, 2006.

14. Personal communication with Payal Sampat.

15. You can see the No Dirty Gold information page from *Southern Brides* at southern bride.com/1/features/charity/charity3-903.cfm, accessed on August 15, 2006.

16. I had the opportunity to participate in a number of these meetings, contributing an "academic perspective" on the evolution of certification systems.

17. "What We Stand For: Council Mission Statement" at the Council for Responsible Jewellery Practices website, responsiblejewellery.com/what.html, accessed on August 11, 2006.

18. Confidential communication from a person who worked closely with the CRJP in its early days.

19. For strategic reasons, the No Dirty Gold campaign has chosen not to publish this set of principles as it continues to negotiate with more jewelry companies and chains to endorse it.

20. Jane Perlez and Kirk Johnson, "Behind Gold's Glitter: Torn Lands and Pointed Questions," *New York Times,* October 24, 2005.

21. Jane Perlez and Lowell Berman, "Tangled Strands in Fight over Peru Gold Mine," *New York Times,* October 25, 2005.

22. Kirk Johnson, "A Drier and Tainted Nevada May Be Legacy of a Gold Rush," *New York Times,* December 30, 2005.

23. Marta Miranda, David Chambers, and Catherine Coumans, *Framework for Responsible Mining: A Guide to Evolving Standards,* October 2005, available on the Center for Science in Public Participation website at frameworkforresponsiblemining.org/docs.html, accessed on September 15, 2006.

24. Commonwealth Scientific and Industrial Research Organisation (CSIRO), "Mining Certification Evaluation Project" accessed at minerals.csiro.au/sd/SD_MCEP.htm on October 10, 2006.

25. Mining Association of Canada, "Towards Sustainable Mining," May 2006, accessed at mining.ca/www/Towards_Sustaining_Mining/index.php on October 10, 2006.

26. The meetings were remarkably transparent, and widely circulated consensus summary notes included the names of all participants. These notes are now available at the website of the Initiative for Responsible Mining Assurance, responsiblemining.net.

27. IRMA, "Providing Assurance by Third-Party Verification of Sustainability Performance in the Mining Industry — A Discussion Paper" (report on the outcomes from meetings held in Vancouver on September 22–23, 2006, and in Washington DC on December 8–9, 2006), accessed at responsiblemining.net.

28. The full list of participants may be found at responsiblemining.net/participants.html, accessed on November 21, 2006.

29. Personal communication with Payal Sampat, November 2006.

30. This profile is based on personal communications with Payal Sampat.

CHAPTER 9

1. This chapter is drawn largely from an academic paper I wrote: Michael E. Conroy, "Certification Systems as Tools for Natural Asset Building," in *Reclaiming Nature: Environmental Justice and Ecological Restoration,* ed. James K. Boyce, Sunita Narain, and Elizabeth A. Stanton (London, New York, and Delhi: Anthem Press, 2006). It also draws from an older conference paper: E. Walter Coward, Jr., Melvin Oliver, and Michael E. Conroy, "Building Natural Assets: Re-thinking the Centers' Natural Resources Agenda and Its Links to Poverty Alleviation" (paper presented at the International Center for Tropical Agriculture conference "Assessing the Impact of Agricultural Research on Poverty Alleviation," in San Jose, Costa Rica, September 1999).

2. See Michael Sherraden, *Assets and the Poor: A New American Welfare Policy* (New York: M.E. Sharpe, 1991); and Melvin Oliver and Thomas Shapiro, *Black Wealth, White Wealth: A New Perspective on Racial Inequality* (New York: Routledge, 1997).

3. Coward et al., "Building Natural Assets," page 5.

4. Thomas M. Shapiro and Edward N. Wolff, eds., *Assets for the Poor: The Benefits of Spreading Asset Ownership* (New York: Russell Sage Foundation Press, 1991).

5. See James K. Boyce and Barry Shelley, *Natural Assets: Democratizing Environmental Ownership* (Washington DC: Island Press, 2003).

6. James K. Boyce, "From natural resources to natural assets." *New Solutions* 11:3 (2001): 267–88, page 268.

7. Ibid., page 269.

8. Peter Barnes, *Capitalism 3.0: A Guide to Reclaiming the Commons* (San Francisco: Berret-Koehler Publishers, Inc., 2006).

9. James K. Boyce and Manuel Pastor, *Building Natural Assets: New Strategies for Poverty Reduction and Environmental Protection* (Amherst, MA: Political Economy Research Institute, University of Massachusetts, 2001).

10. See, for example, Benjamin Cashore, et al., eds. *Confronting Sustainability: Forest Certification in Developing and Transitioning Countries* (New Haven, CT: Yale School of Forestry and Environmental Studies Publications, 2006).

11. Benjamin Cashore, "Legitimacy and the Privatization of Environmental Governance: How Non-State Market-Driven (NSMD) Governance Systems Gain Rule-Making Authority," *Governance: An International Journal of Policy, Administration, and Institutions* 15:4 (October 2002): 503–29, page 503.

12. Laura T. Raynolds, "Consumer-Producer Links in Fair Trade Coffee Networks," *Sociologia Ruralis* 42:4 (October 2002): 404–24, page 404.

13. Forest Stewardship Council, *FSC News and Notes,* various issues, available at fsc.org.

14. See the Sustainable Forestry Initiative's website at sfiprogram.org.

15. "About PEFC" on the Programme for the Endorsement of Forest Certification website, at pefc.org/internet/html/about_pefc.htm.

16. Richard Eba'a Atyi and Marcus Simula, *Forest Certification: Pending Challenges for Tropical Timber* (Yokahama: International Tropical Timber Organization, 2002).

17. Chris van Dam, "La Economía de la Certificación Forestal: ¿Desarrollo sostenible para quien?" (paper presented at the Congreso Iberoamericano de Desarollo y Medio Ambiente, "Desafios locales ante la globalización," in Quito, Ecuador, November 2002).

18. Ibid., page 4.

19. Data from "FSC Facts, 2/11/06," provided by the FSC International Center.

20. Augusta Molnar, *Forest Certification and Communities: Looking Forward to the Next Decade* (Washington DC: Forest Trends, 2003); also Mark Rickenbach, "Forest Certification of Small Ownerships: Some Practical Challenges," *Journal of Forestry* 100:6 (September 2002): 43–47.

21. Molnar, Forest Certification and Communities.

22. Based largely on David Barton Bray, "A Purépacha Community Conserves Its Forests While Creating Wealth," in *Sustainable Solutions: Building Assets for Empowerment and Sustainable Development* (New York: Ford Foundation, 2002); supplemented with material from Mexico's national environmental protection agency, SEMARNAT, at semarnat.gob.mx/regiones/nuevo-san-juan/modelo.shtml, accessed on July 5, 2006, and with personal communications with community enterprise managers in September 2005.

23. Bray, "A Purépacha Community," pp. 10–11.

24. Ibid.

25. Chandra L. Meek, *Sustainable for Whom? A Discussion Paper on Certification and Communities in the Boreal Region — Case Studies from Canada and Sweden* (Jokkmokk, Sweden: Taiga Rescue Network, 2001).

26. Ford Foundation, *Sustainable Solutions: Building Assets for Empowerment and Sustainable Development* (New York: Ford Foundation, 2002).

27. Chris van Dam, "…¿Desarrollo sostenible para quien?"

28. In 2005, coffee producers agreed to begin to pay a small levy on all coffee sold through certified Fair Trade in order to strengthen the certification and monitoring services of FLO and to protect the legitimacy of the certified Fair Trade system. The International Standards Organization's rules for certification systems require that, in order to avoid conflicts of interest, the accreditation of certifiers who conduct the monitoring and auditing be separate from the establishment of standards and criteria. Producer contributions for monitoring and auditing were a partial result of FLO changes to respond to those mandates.

29. Douglas Murray, Laura Raynolds, and Pete Taylor, *One Cup at a Time: Poverty Alleviation and Fair Trade Coffee in Latin America,* a report of the Colorado State University Fair Trade Research Group (Fort Collins, CO: Colorado State University, March 2003).

30. Anne Tallontire, "Challenges Facing Fair Trade: Which Way Now?" *Small Enterprise Development: An International Journal of Microfinance and Business Development* 13:3 (September 2002): 21.

31. Clement Boateng, "Ecotourism: A Panacea for Rural Poverty," *Ghanaian Chronicle,* October 2, 2006.

32. "Cultural and Eco-tourism Development in Mountainous Regions" in the Poverty and Human Rights section of UNESCO's website, portal.unesco.org/shs/en/ev.php-URL_ID=4951&URL_DO=DO_TOPIC&URL_SECTION=201.html.

33. Critical Ecosystem Partnership Fund, "CEPF and Poverty Alleviation: An Overview," November 2003, accessed at cepf.net/ImageCache/cepf/content/pdfs/cepf_2epoverty alleviation_2efinal_2epdf/v1/cepf.povertyalleviation.final.pdf on October 10, 2006.

34. Quebec Declaration on Ecotourism, May 22, 2002, accessed at the World Ecotourism Summit website, world-tourism.org/sustainable/IYE/quebec/anglais/declaration.html, on September 10, 2006.

35. Martha Honey, *Ecotourism and Sustainable Development: Who Owns Paradise?* (Washington DC: Island Press, 1999), pp.22–24.

36. The Mineral Policy Center's early work in support of local communities has evolved under its new structure. See the "community support" sections of Earthworks' website, including the work of its major program, the Oil and Gas Accountability Project (OGAP), earthworksaction.org.

37. Marta Miranda, David Chambers, and Catherine Coumans, *Framework for Responsible Mining: A Guide to Evolving Standards,* October 2005, available on the Center for Science in Public Participation website at frameworkforresponsiblemining.org/docs.html, accessed on September 15, 2006. These social problems are listed on pages 48 to 49.

38. For further information, see the Community Forestry Resource Center website at forestrycenter.org.

39. For more information, visit the Tropical Forest Trust website at tropicalforesttrust.com.

40. Fadzilah Majid Cooke, *The Challenge of Sustainable Forests* (Honolulu: University of Hawai'i Press, 1999).

CHAPTER 10

1. "What is the Mayor's Fitness Council Partner Certification Program?" on the City of Austin Mayor's Fitness Council website, accessed at ci.austin.tx.us/fitness/partner.htm on September 1, 2006.

2. Richard Ellis, *The Empty Ocean* (Washington DC: Island Press, 2003).

3. The Bridgespan Group, summary report (unpublished report prepared for the David and Lucile Packard Foundation, the Oak Foundation, and the Esmee Fairbairn Foundation, February 23, 2004).

4. "Sustainability" in *Environmental and Social Report,* 2005, accessed at the Unilever website, unilever.com/ourvalues/environmentandsociety/env_social_report/sustainability on August 18, 2006.

5. James Allen and James Root, "The New Brand Tax," *Wall Street Journal,* September 7, 2004.

6. "History of MSC," accessed at the Marine Stewardship Council website, msc.org/html /content_470.htm, on August 18, 2006.

7. "MSC Principles and Criteria for Sustainable Fishing," November 2002, accessed at the MSC website, msc.org/assets/docs/fishery_certification/MSCPrinciples&Criteria.doc, on June 10, 2006.

8. "Western Australian Rock Lobster," accessed at the MSC website, msc.org/html/content _1277.htm, on June 10, 2006.

9. Ibid.

10. Information on the hoki fishery comes from the New Zealand Seafood Industry Council website, seafood.co.nz/hoki, accessed on June 10, 2006.

11. Interpress Service, "Green Group to Appeal MSC Hoki Endorsement," reprinted on Wordcatch.com, March 20, 2001, accessed on June 10, 2006.

12. Brendan May, "MSC Fights Back over 'Greenwash' Claims," Worldcatch.com, March 21, 2001.

13. Personal communication with a technical staff person at an NGO based in Washington DC, who requested anonymity because he was not authorized to speak on behalf of his organization.

14. Rose Prince, "Catching On: The Marine Stewardship Council Logo Means Increased Sales for Fisherman," *Daily Express,* July 7, 2001.

15. Unilever, "Our Fish Sustainability Initiative," accessed at the MSC website, msc.org/html

/content_1277.htm, on June 10, 2006. The document is no longer available at that location or on Unilever's own website.

16. Alison Maillard, "The White Sustainable Fish That Got Away," *Financial Times*, July 12, 2004.

17. "Alaska Pollock Gets Green Light from Certifier," *Seafood Business*, July 2004.

18. Personal communication, August 16, 2006.

19. Scott Highleyman, Amy Mathew Amos, and Hank Cauley, "An Independent Assessment of the Marine Stewardship Council," Wildhavens, January 15, 2004.

20. The Bridgespan Group, summary report.

21. Reported, laconically, in "MSC Forced into Review," *Seafood International*, April 2004.

22. This profile is based on a personal interview with Rupert Howes on August 16, 2006.

23. A description of the campaign is on the National Environmental Trust website, net.org/marine/csb.

24. Personal communication from Rupert Howes, MSC executive director, August 16, 2006.

25. D. Agnew, C. Grieve, P. Orr, G. Parkes, and N. Barker, *Environmental Benefits Resulting from Certification against MSC's* Principles and Criteria for Sustainable Fishing (London: MRAG UK Ltd and Marine Stewardship Council, May 4, 2006).

26. Ibid., page 4.

27. Personal communication, August 21, 2006.

28. Unilever, "Our Fish Sustainability Initiative."

29. A minor exception was a small, oblique campaign by the Humane Society of the United States, focused on the Red Lobster restaurant chain to create a boycott of all seafood from Canada in an attempt to pressure Canadians to stop the annual hunting of baby seals in the Maritime provinces. See, community.hsus.org/campaign/redlobster, accessed on August 26, 2006. The campaign ended without tangible impact on Canadian seafood imports to the US.

30. Quoted on the Answers.com website at answers.com/topic/sweatshop#after_ad1, accessed on August 26, 2006. (Early back issues of Scribner's are available at Cornell University Library's "Making of America" collection at cdl.library.cornell.edu/moa/browse.journals/scri.1892.html, accessed April 3, 2007. This article is in the July 1892 issue.)

31. Paraphrased from Clean Clothes Campaign (Stichting Schone Kleren Overlet), *Annual Report 2005* (Amsterdam: Author, 2006); available at cleanclothes.org/ftp/annual2005.pdf, accessed on August 26, 2006.

32. Ibid, p. 8.

33. See the Codes of Conduct section on the Clean Clothes Campaign website, cleanclothes.org/codes/index.htm.

34. Clean Clothes Campaign, *Looking for a Quick Fix: How Weak Social Auditing Is Keeping Workers in Sweatshops* (Amsterdam: Author, 2005); available at cleanclothes.org/ftp/05-quick_fix.pdf, accessed on August 26, 2006.

35. Business Week Online, "Secrets, Lies, and Sweatshops," November 27, 2006, available at businessweek.com/magazine/toc/06_48/B4011magazine.htm.

36. Steven Greenhouse, "Duke to Adopt a Code to Prevent Apparel From Being Made in Sweatshops," *New York Times*, March 8, 1998.

37. Steven Greenhouse, "Two Protests by Students Over Wages for Workers," *New York Times*, January 31, 1999.

38. Steven Greenhouse, "Students Urge College to Join A New Anti-Sweatship Group," *New York Times*, October 20, 1999.

39. Leslie Kaufman and David Gonzalez, "Labor Standards Clash with Global Reality," *New York Times*, April 2, 2001.

40. Steven Greenhouse, "Anti-Sweatship Coalition Finds Itself at Odds on Factory Code," *New York Times*, July 3, 1998.

41. Ibid.

42. "Workplace Code of Conduct," accessed on the Fair Labor Association website, fairlabor.org/all/code/index.html, on August 15, 2006.

43. Steven Greenhouse, "Groups Reach Agreement for Curtailing Sweatshops," *New York Times,* November 5, 1998.

44. Steven Greenhouse, "17 Colleges Join Against Sweatshops," *New York Times,* March 16, 1999.

45. Rev. David M. Schilling, letter to the editor, *New York Times,* November 16, 1998.

46. Steven Greenhouse, "Student Critics Push Attacks on an Association Meant to Prevent Sweatshops," *New York Times,* April 26, 1999.

47. "National News Briefs: Penn Students End Sit-In," *New York Times,* February 18, 2000.

48. Steven Greenhouse, "Anti-Sweatshop Movement Is Achieving Gains Overseas," *New York Times,* January 26, 2000.

49. For information on this analysis, see Richard M. Locke, "The Promise and Perils of Globalization: The Case of Nike," in *Management: Inventing and Delivering Its Future,* ed. Thomas A. Kochan and Richard Schmalensee (Cambridge, MA: MIT Press, 2003), pp. 39–70.

50. Ibid., p. 41.

51. Richard M. Locke, Fei Qin, and Alberto Brause, "Does Monitoring Improve Labor Standards? Lessons from Nike" (MIT Sloan School Working Paper No. 4612-06, July 2006; provided by the author).

52. Ibid., p. 19.

53. Ibid., p. 33. The analysis also provided evidence that "other factors" could account for improved working conditions at some Nike suppliers. Significant improvements in working conditions seemed to correspond to "improving the ability of suppliers to better schedule their work and improve their quality and efficiency" more than they did to simple monitoring.

54. "Frequently Asked Questions" on the Worker Rights Consortium website, workers rights.org/about_faq.asp, accessed on August 15, 2006.

55. "Model Code of Conduct" on the WRC website, workersrights.org/coc.asp, accessed on August 15, 2006.

56. "Governance" on the WRC website, workersrights.org/govern.asp, accessed on August 15, 2006.

57. The WRC list is at workersrights.org/as.asp; the FLA list is at fairlabor.org/all/colleges /list.html.

58. Information on the WRC's Designated Suppliers Program was obtained through personal communication with Scott Nova, WRC executive director, August 15, 2006.

59. Worker Rights Consortium, "The Impact of Substantial Labor Cost Increases on Apparel Retail Prices" (working paper, November 10, 2005); accessed at workersrights.org/ Labor_Cost_Increases_and_Apparel_Retail_Prices.pdf on August 10, 2006.

60. Scott Jaschik, "Codes Don't Work," *Inside Higher Ed,* September 28, 2006, accessed at insidehighered.com/news/2006/09/28/wrc on September 30, 2006.

61. Ibid.

62. Drawn from an interview on August 20, 2006, and from memories of previous encounters.

63. Gary Cohen, "Environmental Health Market Campaigns" (an extraordinary private presentation made by Gary Cohen, executive director of the Environmental Health Fund, for a group of foundation representatives in San Francisco on October 5, 2005).

64. Ibid.

65. Kendra Mayfield, "E-Waste: Dark Side of the Digital Age," *Wired,* January 10, 2003, available at wired.com/news/technology/0,1282,57151,00.html.

66. Silicon Valley Toxics Coalition, *Poison PCs and Toxic TVs* (San Jose, CA: Author, 2005).

67. This profile is based on an interview that took place on August 30, 2006.

68. Judith Cummings, "Leaking Chemicals in California's 'Silicon Valley' Alarm Neighbors," *New York Times,* May 20, 1982.

69. Laurie J. Flynn, "Love in the Time of Benzene," *New York Times,* November 17, 2003.

70. Ibid., p. 2.

71. See "About the Convention" on the Basel Convention website, accessed at basel.int/convention/about.html on July 13, 2006.

72. "Country Status/Waste Trade Ban Agreements," a chart on the Basel Action Network website, ban.org/country_status/country_status_chart.html, accessed on July 12, 2006.

73. The Basel Action Network and Silicon Valley Toxics Coalition, Toxics Link (India), and SCOPE (Pakistan), *Exporting Harm: The High-Tech Trashing of Asia*, February 25, 2002; available at ban.org/E-waste/technotrashfinalcomp.pdf, accessed on September 2, 2006.

74. Ibid., p. 1.

75. "About the Campaign: Campaign Partners," accessed at the Computer TakeBack Campaign website, computertakeback.com/about/founders.cfm, on September 7, 2006.

76. Delaney Hall, "Dell Urged to Recycle Responsibly," *Daily Texan*, September 10, 2002, svtc.etoxics.org/site/PageNavigator/svtc_dailytexan_dellrecycling, accessed on October 25, 2006 (no longer available on the site).

77. Sheila Davis and Ted Smith, *Corporate Strategies for Electronics Recycling: A Tale of Two Systems* (San Francisco: SVTC, June 25, 2003).

78. Ibid., page 19. The problematic practices of UNICOR were later revealed in much greater detail in a subsequent report, *Toxic Sweatshops: How UNICOR Prison Recycling Harms Workers, Communities, the Environment, and the Recycling Industry* (a joint report of the Center for Environmental Health, Prison Activist Resource Center, Silicon Valley Toxics Coalition, and Computer TakeBack Campaign, October 2006; accessed at svtc.etoxics.org/site/PageServer?pagename=svtc_toxicsweatshop on October 27, 2006).

79. John Markoff, "2 PC Makers Given Credit and Blame in Recycling," *New York Times*, June 27, 2003.

80. Laurie J. Flynn, "Dell Stops Hiring Prisoners for Its Recycling Program," *New York Times*, July 4, 2003.

81. Computer TakeBack Campaign, "Coalition Calls Steve Jobs a "Mini-player" in Computer Recycling, Flies Banner Over Stanford Graduation Where Jobs Was Speaking," press release, June 12, 2005.

82. Ibid.

83. Basel Action Network, "Finally, A Responsible Way to Get Rid of that Old Computer!" press release, February 25, 2003, accessed at See ban.org/pledge/pledge_prfinal.pdf on August 20, 2006.

84. Basel Action Network, "Electronics Recycler's Pledge of True Stewardship," accessed at ban.org/pledge/electronics_recycler_pledge.pdf on August 20, 2006.

85. Basel Action Network, "E-Stewards — Responsible E-cyclers," a table at ban.org/pledge/Locations.html, accessed on August 20, 2006.

86. See the report card on the SVTC website under "Our Work — Sustainable Technology — Electronics Purchasing," accessed on September 10, 2005.

87. "How the Companies Line Up," from the Greenpeace website, greenpeace.org/international/campaigns/toxics/electronics/how-the-companies-line-up, accessed on September 10, 2006.

88. "I.C.R.T.: The International Campaign for Responsible Technology," on the SVTC website, svtc.etoxics.org/site/PageServer?pagename=svtc_int_campaign_responsible_tech, accessed on September 23, 2006.

89. International Association of Electronics Recyclers, "Why Obtain IAER Certification?" at the IAER website, iaer.org/communications/cer-benefits.htm, accessed on August 21, 2006.

CHAPTER 11

1. A conference on this theme was organized by the Consumer's Choice Council in Washington DC in 1996, but it appears there are no published results of those deliberations.

2. James Montgomery, "Gold Miner Calls for Regulation of 'Rogue' NGOs," *Financial Times*, January 25, 2007.

3. James Montgomery, "Transcript: Peter Munk interview," *FT.com,* January 26, 2007. Accessed at ft.com/home/us (search for "Peter Munk") on February 1, 2007.

4. See, for example, Marie Dolcini, "Forging Non-Traditional Alliances," in the Sierra Club's newsletter *The Planet,* January 1997.

5. This list would include the Bulyanhulu mine in Tanzania, where local opposition led to the death of more than 50 opponents of the mine; the proposed Lake Cowal operation in Australia, stalled because of activism by local Aboriginal groups; and the Goldstrike mine in the US, which faced local opposition to its toxic emissions.

6. Benjamin Cashore, Graeme Auld, and Deanna Newsom, "The United States' Race to Certify Sustainable Forestry: Non-State Environmental Governance and the Competition for Policy-Making Authority," *Business and Politics,* 5, no. 3, November 2003.

7. Bill Rockwell, "The SFI Standard 2005–2009: The Times, They Are A-Changin'" (presentation made to the Forest Leadership Conference, Toronto, Ontario, March 1, 2005). Available at forestleadership.com/IMG/pdf/Bill_Rockwell_FLC_2005.pdf, accessed on August 21, 2006.

8. All three comments were made at a meeting I attended at the research forest of a major AF&PA company; they occurred in the context of a presentation for potential clients, including a highly branded grocery company that was asking about certification.

9. According to one TNC staff member, who asked for anonymity, TNC manages 250,000 acres under five FSC group certifications. Its only SFI certificate applies to a tract of 20,000 acres, acquired from International Paper Company, where the condition of the acquisition was maintenance of its SFI certificate. The TNC board has established forest operating principles that include third-party independent certification under systems approved by the World Bank/WWF Alliance on forests, which, to date, only accepts FSC.

10. The major characteristics of the SFI program may be found on the AF&PA website, despite its protests that SFI is a fully independent program. See afandpa.org/Content/Nav igationMenu/Environment_and_Recycling/SFI/SFI.htm, accessed on January 14, 2007.

11. Information on the Sustainable Forestry Initiative board members is at sfiprogram .org/boardmembers.cfm, accessed on January 15, 2007.

12. See the Alliance for Credible Forest Certification website at dontbuysfi.com, accessed on January 15, 2007. The alliance is a confidential coalition of advocacy NGOs.

13. This information comes directly from PEFC's website, pefc.org/internet/html/about _pefc.htm, accessed on January 15, 2007.

14. WWF, "New Insights on Credible Certification in Europe," July 22, 2005, accessed at panda.org/about_wwf/what_we_do/forests/our_solutions/responsible_forestry/gftn /news/index.cfm?uNewsID=22050 on January 15, 2006.

15. Fern, *Behind the Logo: An Environmental and Social Assessment of Certification Schemes,* May 2001; accessed at fern.org/publication.html?id=156 on August 15, 2006.

16. Fern, *Footprints in the Forest: Current Practices and Future Challenges in Forest Certification,* February 2004; accessed at fern.org/publication.html?id=156 on August 15, 2006.

17. I repeat here, for the sake of transparency, what I mentioned in the Prologue: I presently serve on the board of directors of TransFair USA, so my comments may be taken as reflecting a vested interest.

18. Rainforest Alliance, *Sustainable Agriculture Standards with Indicators,* November 2005; accessed at rainforest-alliance.org/programs/agriculture/certified-crops/documents/st andards_indicators_2005.pdf on August 15, 2006.

19. Hal Weitzman, "Coffee with a Conscientious Kick," *Financial Times,* August 15, 2006.

20. Andrew Purvis, "Is Global Business Hijacking the Fairtrade Bandwagon?" "Observer Food Monthly," *Guardian Unlimited,* January 29, 2006, accessed at observer.guardian.co .uk/foodmonthly/story/0,,1694445,00.html on January 6, 2007.

21. Weitzman, "Coffee with a Conscientious Kick."

22. The Utz Kapeh website, utzcertified.org/index.php?pageID=114, provides information on the codes of conduct; accessed on January 7, 2007.

23. The website for the 4Cs project is sustainable-coffee.net/project/index.html, accessed on January 6, 2007.

24. Utz Certified embers are listed at sustainable-coffee.net/partners/index.html, accessed on January 6, 2007.

25. For more on this competitor to SVTC and its work, see iaer.org/communications/cert-news2.doc, accessed on January 6, 2007.

26. For information on this industry-led and very weak process, see cyanidecode.org, accessed on January 6, 2007.

CHAPTER 12

1. See Stacy Mitchell, *Big-Box Swindle: The True Cost of Mega-Retailers and the Fight for America's Independent Businesses* (Boston: Beacon Press, 2006).

2. Spring 2001 Planning Studio, Graduate School of Architecture, Preservation, and Planning at Columbia University, "big box retail," accessed at columbia.edu/itc/architecture/bass/newrochelle/extra/big_box.html# on May 20, 2006.

3. Ibid.

4. Wal-Mart, "Wal-Mart Continues RFID Expansion; More Than 1,000 Stores and Clubs to Use Technology by End of Year," press release, September 12, 2006.

5. See, for example, Charles Fishman, *The Wal-Mart Effect: How the World's Most Powerful Company Really Works — and How It's Transforming the American Economy* (New York: Penguin, 2006); Nelson Lichtenstein, ed., *Wal-Mart: The Face of Twenty-First-Century Capitalism* (New York: New Press, 2006); and John Dicker, *The United States of Wal-Mart* (New York: Penguin, 2005).

6. Dr. James Hoopes, "Growth Through Knowledge: Wal-Mart, High Technology, and the Ever Less Visible Hand of Management" (presentation to the "Wal-Mart: Template for 21st Century Capitalism?" conference, University of California at Santa Barbara, April 12, 2004.

7. Liza Featherstone, "Will Labor Take the Wal-Mart Challenge?" *The Nation*, June 28, 2004 (posted online on June 10, 2004); accessed at thenation.com/doc/20040628/feather stone. The article refers to a manager's handbook containing company policy and procedures for dealing with various management issues such as labor organizing.

8. Ibid.

9. Steven Greenhouse, "Altering of Worker Time Cards Spurs Growing Number of Suits," *New York Times*, April 4, 2004, p. 12.

10. Steven Greenhouse, "In-House Audit Says Wal-Mart Violated Labor Laws," *New York Times*, January, 13, 2004, p. 16.

11. Ibid.

12. Abigail Goldman and Nancy Cleeland, "An Empire Built on Bargains Remakes the Working World," *Los Angeles Times*, November 23, 2003, p. 9; accessed at latimes.com on June 14, 2006.

13. Ibid.

14. Steven Greenhouse, "Wal-Mart Faces Class Action Suit," *New York Times*, November 11, 2003.

15. Mike Rogoway, "Wal-Mart Suit Could Mean More Scrutiny of Retailers: The Class Action Highlights the Gender Gap in Pay, Promotion," *The Oregonian*, June 24, 2004, p. B1.

16. Pew Oceans Commission, *America's Living Oceans: Charting a Course for Sea Change* (Arlington, VA: Author, May 2003).

17. Sierra Club, *The Rap Sheet on Animal Factories: Convictions, Fines, Pollution Violations and Regulatory Records on America's Animal Factories* (Washington DC: Author, August 2002).

18. George Miller, "Everyday Low Wages: The Hidden Price We All Pay For Wal-Mart" (report by the Democratic staff of the Committee on Education and the Workforce, February 16, 2004); accessed on July 15, 2006, at mindfully.org/Industry/2004/Wal-Mart-Labor-Record16feb04.htm.

19. Philip Mattera and Anna Purinton, *Shopping for Subsidies: How Wal-Mart Uses Taxpayer Money to Finance Its Never-Ending Growth* (Washington DC: Good Jobs First, May 2004), pp. 14–17.

20. Ibid.

21. Emek Baskere, "Job Creation or Destruction? Labor-Market Effects of Wal-Mart Expansion," *Review of Economics and Statistics* 87, no. 1 (February 2005): 174–83; cited in Fishman, *The Wal-Mart Effect*, pp. 140–44.

22. Stephan Goetz and Hema Swaminathan, "Wal-Mart and County-Wide Poverty" (AERS Staff Paper 371, Department of Agricultural Economics and Rural Sociology, Pennsylvania State University, University Park, PA, 2004), available at cecd.aers.psu.edu/policy_research.htm; cited in Fishman, *The Wal-Mart Effect*, pp. 164–66.

23. Scott DeCarlo, ed., "Forbes Global 2000," March 31, 2005, accessed at forbes.com/2005/03/30/05f2000land.html on June 20, 2006.

24. Wal-Mart, *Vested Interest: Wal-Mart 2005 Annual Report,* available at walmartstores.com/Files/2005AnnualReport.pdf, accessed on June 20, 2006.

25. "Is Wal-Mart Too Powerful? Low prices are great. But Wal-Mart's dominance creates problems — for suppliers, workers, communities, and even American culture" (Cover Story) *Business Week,* October 6, 2003, p. 102.

26. According to Hoover's company profile of Wal-Mart, Report 11600 (2004), p. 1; current reports on Wal-Mart are available at hoovers.com/wal-mart/—ID11600—/free-co-fact sheet.xhtml?cm_ven=PAID&cm_cat=BUS&cm_pla=CO1&cm_ite=Wal-Mart_Stores_Inc.

27. Goldman and Cleeland, "An Empire Built on Bargains," p. 1.

28. Ann Zimmerman and Sally Beatty, "That Chic and Cheap Are Tough To Mix 'n Match," *Wall Street Journal,* July 2, 2004, p. B1.

29. Kris Hudson, "Wal-Mart Cuts Hit Suppliers," *Wall Street Journal,* April 28, 2006.

30. Ibid.

31. Madeline Janis-Aparicio, "The Wal-Mart Challenge" (report prepared for Service Employees International Union meeting on Wal-Mart, May 12, 2004). Janis-Aparicio estimates that Wal-Mart invested over $1 million in the Inglewood Initiative Campaign.

32. "The High Cost of Low Prices," *Business Week,* October 6, 2003, p. 168.

33. Jeanne Cummings, "Wal-Mart Opens for Business in Tough Market: Washington," *Wall Street Journal,* March 24, 2004, p. A1.

34. Ibid.

35. Adam Geller, "Unionizing Wal-Mart, *Washington Times,* October 16, 2004.

36. Ibid.

37. Steven Greenhouse, "Opponents of Wal-Mart to Coordinate Efforts," *New York Times,* April 3, 2005.

38. WakeUpWalMart.com, "WakeUpWal-Mart.com Reaches out to Wal-Mart CEO with 'Six Demands for Change,'" press release, September 12, 2005, accessed at ufcw.org/press_room/index.cfm?pressReleaseID=172 on June 15, 2006.

39. Steven Greenhouse, "Suit Says Wal-Mart Is Lax on Labor Abuses Overseas," *New York Times,* September 14, 2005.

40. Ibid.

41. The story of Conservation International's engagement is told, largely from its perspective, in the *Fortune* cover story by Marc Gunther, "The Green Machine," August 7, 2006.

42. This profile is based on extensive interviews with Justin Ward on August 29 and September 18, 2006.

43. The sustainability networks included Greenhouse Gases, Energy, Logistics, Operations, Packaging, Apparel/Textiles, Electronics, Food and Agriculture, Forest Products, Chemical-intensive Products, Jewelry, Seafood, China, and Alternative Fuels. This information is from a confidential interview with a Wal-Mart staff person who was not authorized to discuss this matter.

44. Steven Greenhouse and Michael Barbaro, "Wal-Mart Memo Suggests Ways to Cut Employee Benefits," *New York Times*, October 26, 2005.

45. Michael Barbaro, "Wal-Mart to Expand Health Plan for Workers," *New York Times*, October 24, 2005.

46. Michael Barbaro and Felicity Barringer, "Wal-Mart to Seek Savings in Energy," *New York Times*, October 25, 2005.

47. Aaron Bernstein, "A Stepped-Up Assault on Wal-Mart," *Business Week*, October 20, 2005.

48. Kenneth Turan, "'Wal-Mart: The High Cost of Low Price' — Former employees who once believed in the retail giant are the soul of an engrossing and saddening documentary," *Los Angeles Times*, November 4, 2005.

49. Robert Greenwald, "The Gospel According to Sam," a commercial for *Wal-Mart: The High Cost of Low Price*, September 26, 2005, accessed at walmartmovie.com/wmtv/2005/09/the_gospel_according_to_sam_walton.php on August 9, 2006.

50. Mya Frazier, "Anti-Wal-Mart Film Uses Churches for Distribution," *AdAge.com*, October 7, 2005.

51. Wal-Mart Watch, "Higher Expectations Week Exceeds Expectations," press release, November 21, 2005; accessed at walmartwatch.com/press/releases/higher_expectations_week_exceeds_expectations on July 22, 2006.

52. Ibid.

53. WakeUpWalMart.com, "Should People of Faith Shop at Wal-Mart?" online commercial at wakeupwalmart.com/video/faith.html, accessed on July 20, 2006.

54. Liza Featherstone, "Wal-Mart's PR War," Salon.com, August 2, 2005.

55. Ralph Thomas, "Over 3,100 Wal-Mart Workers Got State Health Aid," *Seattle Times*, January 24, 2006.

56. WakeUpWalMart.com, "WakeUpWalMart.com and Change to Win Hold Rallies in 35 Cities to "Change Wal-Mart for the Better," press release, April 26, 2006, accessed at wakeupwalmart.com/press/20060426.html on June 10, 2006.

57. This and the Walton quotes in Figure 12.4 come from Sam Walton and John Huey, *Sam Walton: Made in America* (New York: Doubleday, 1992).

58. National Fish and Wildlife Foundation/Wal-Mart, "Wal-Mart Pledges One Acre for Every Acre It Develops," press release, April 12, 2005, accessed at walmartfacts.com/media/legacydocs/april2005_acres_for_america.pdf on June 15, 2006.

59. Wal-Mart Watch, "New Poll Reveals Dramatic, Negative Shift in Public Opinion for Wal-Mart," walmartwatch.com/blog/archives/new_poll_reveals_dramatic_negative_shift_in_public_opinion_for_wal_mart/, accessed on July 28, 2006.

60. Lee Scott, "Twenty First Century Leadership" (presentation by Wal-Mart CEO on October 24, 2005), p. 6. Accessed at walmartstores.com/Files/21st%20Century%20Leadership.pdf on June 15, 2006.

61. Ibid., p. 8.

62. Ibid., p. 9.

63. Marc Gunther, "The Green Machine, *Fortune Magazine*, August 7, 2006.

64. Scott, "Twenty First Century Leadership," p. 7.

65. Gunther, "The Green Machine."

66. Scott, "Twenty First Century Leadership," pp. 13–14.

67. Tory Newmyer, "Critics: Wal-Mart Flip-Flopped," *Roll Call*, June 28, 2006.

68. Michael Barbaro, "Wal-Mart to Start Equity Fund to Help Diversify Its Suppliers," *New York Times*, October 19, 2005.

69. Gunther, "The Green Machine."

70. Michael Barbaro, "Wal-Mart to Expand Health Plan," *New York Times*, February 24, 2005.

71. Michael Barbaro, "In Reversal, Wal-Mart Will Sell Contraceptive," *New York Times*, March 4, 2006.

72. Associated Press, "Wal-Mart Will Stop Selling Guns in a Third of Its U.S. Stores," *New York Times*, April 15, 2006.

73. Michael Barbaro, "Wal-Mart Offers Aid to Rivals," *New York Times*, April 5, 2006.

74. Michael Barbaro, "Chief's Tone Reflects Change at Wal-Mart in the Last Year," *New York Times*, April 20, 2006.

75. Melanie Warner, "Wal-Mart Eyes Organic Foods, And Brand Names Get in Line," *New York Times*, May 12, 2006.

76. Ylan Q. Mui, "For Wal-Mart, Fair Trade May Be More Than a Hill of Beans," *Washington Post*, June 12, 2006.

77. Michael Barbaro, "Wal-Mart Effort on Health and Environment Is Seen," *New York Times*, June 22, 2006.

78. I participated in this meeting; see further discussion in Chapter 9.

79. "Wal-Mart Hikes Starting Pay Rates for Employees," *Earthtimes.org*, July 8, 2006, accessed at earthtimes.org/articles/show/8011.html on July 20, 2006.

80. Jared Bernstein, L. Josh Bivens, and Arindrajit Dube, "Wrestling with Wal-Mart: Trade-offs Between Profits, Prices, and Wages" (Washington DC: Economic Policy Institute Working Paper #276, June 15, 2006), accessed at epi.org/content.cfm/wp276 on July 15, 2006. An abbreviated summary of the results is also available at epi.org/content.cfm/ib223.

81. Ian Austen, "Quebec Rules Against Wal-Mart in Closing of Unionized Store," *New York Times*, September 20, 2005.

82. Steven Greenhouse, "Labor Dept. Rebuked Over Pact With Wal-Mart, *New York Times*, November 1, 2005.

83. "Inspection Pact Ends for Wal-Mart Stores," *New York Times*, January 19, 2006.

84. Lisa Alcalay Klug, "Jury Rules Wal-Mart Must Pay $172 Million Over Meal Breaks," *New York Times*, December 23, 2005.

85. Winnie Hu, "Developer Will Compensate Merchants Evicted from Bronx Market," *New York Times*, February 2, 2006.

86. Steven Greenhouse, Charles V. Bagli, and Colin Moynihan, "Developer Drops Plan for City's First Wal-Mart," *New York Times*, February 24, 2006.

87. "Wal-Mart testimony inaccurate on bank leases," Reuters, May 9, 2006.

88. Vivienne Walt, "Norway to Wal-Mart: We Don't Want Your Shares," *Fortune Magazine*, July 24, 2006, accessed at cnnmoney.com on July 30, 2006.

89. Federal Deposit Insurance Corporation, "FDIC Places Six-Month Moratorium on Industrial Loan Company Applications and Notices," press release, July 28, 2006, accessed at fdic.gov.news/press/2006/pr06073.html on August 8, 2006.

90. "Regulators Seen Leaning Toward Limits on a Wal-Mart Bank," Reuters, April 12, 2006.

91. "Banks Lobby to Block Wal-Mart's Application with FDIC (Update 2)," Bloomberg.com, July 24, 2006.

92. "Chicago's Message," *New York Times* editorial, July 28, 2006.

93. Fran Spielman, "Retailers Expected To Fight 'Living Wage' Bill," *Chicago Sun-Times*, July 26, 2006.

94. Angela Moore, "Wal-Mart Cut to Neutral on Sales, Economic Worries," *MarketWatch*, July 13, 2006, accessed at marketwatch.com/news/story.aspx on August 8, 2006.

95. Lauren Coleman-Lochner, "Wal-Mart, Retailers Stumble Overseas as U.S. Formulas Falter," Bloomberg.com, August 1, 2006; also "Japan Isn't Buying the Wal-Mart Idea," Business Week Online, February 28, 2006.

96. Michael Barbaro, "Wal-Mart Posts First Earnings Drop in 10 Years," *New York Times*, August 15, 2006.

97. David Barboza, "Wal-Mart Agrees to Unionization in China," *New York Times*, August 9, 2006.

CHAPTER 13

1. Limited Brands, "ForestEthics and Limited Brands (Victoria's Secret) Reach Landmark Agreement on Environmental Stewardship," press release, December 6, 2006, accessed at on January 21, 2007.

2. Peter Gorrie, "Victoria's Secret Going Green," *Toronto Star,* December 7, 2006.

3. Tiffany & Company, "Sustainability: Our Most Important Design," 2006, accessed at tiffany.com/local/en-us/PDF/TCO_sustainability.pdf on January 15, 2007.

4. Mitsubishi Corporation, "Mitsubishi Endorses Third Party Certification for Forest Product Operations," press release, November 11, 2002, accessed at mitsubishicorp-us .com/documents/PressReleasekatoomba02.pdf on December 10, 2006.

5. Tom Zoellner, *The Heartless Stone: A Journey Through the World of Diamonds, Deceit, and Desire* (New York: St. Martin's Press, 2006).

6. See the ISEAL Alliance website, isealalliance.org, accessed on December 10, 2006.

7. ISEAL Alliance, "Code of Good Practice," on the website (isealalliance.org) under "Resources," accessed on December 10, 2006.

Index

About the Author

DR. MICHAEL E. CONROY is a PhD economist who taught developmental economics for 25 years at the University of Texas in Austin. His specialties were Latin American Economics, Urban and Regional Economics, and the Economics of Sustainable Development.

Michael has spent 12 years in various philanthropic positions, first at the Ford Foundation and then at the Rockefeller Brothers Fund for the development of certification systems for improved social and environmental practices.

He actively supports several key organizations, including the following:
- the Forest Stewardship Council and TransfairUSA (the Fair Trade certifier for the U.S.), early development of the Sustainable Tourism Stewardship Council,
- improved corporate accountability (including the campaign to improve corporate practices at Wal-Mart), and
- participation in the early stages of the development of standards for the responsible sourcing of gold and silver.

Michael also spent three years of research and teaching at Yale University on the development of social and environmental certification systems and their impacts upon corporate accountability.

Michael is the author of numerous books and articles, including *A Cautionary Tale: U.S. Development Policy in Central America* (Lynn Rienner Publishers, 1995).

If you have enjoyed *Branded!* you might also enjoy other

BOOKS TO BUILD A NEW SOCIETY

Our books provide positive solutions for people
who want to make a difference. We specialize in:

Environment and Justice • Conscientious Commerce
Sustainable Living • Ecological Design and Planning
Natural Building & Appropriate Technology
Educational and Parenting Resources • Nonviolence
Progressive Leadership • Resistance and Community

New Society Publishers

ENVIRONMENTAL BENEFITS STATEMENT

New Society Publishers has chosen to produce this book on recycled paper
made with **100% post consumer waste**, processed chlorine free, and old
growth free.

For every 5,000 books printed, New Society saves the following resources:[1]

38	Trees
3,436	Pounds of Solid Waste
3,781	Gallons of Water
4,931	Kilowatt Hours of Electricity
6,246	Pounds of Greenhouse Gases
27	Pounds of HAPs, VOCs, and AOX Combined
9	Cubic Yards of Landfill Space

[1]Environmental benefits are calculated based on research done by the Environmental Defense
Fund and other members of the Paper Task Force who study the environmental impacts of the
paper industry.

For a full list of NSP's titles, please call **1-800-567-6772**
or check out our website at:

www.newsociety.com

NEW SOCIETY PUBLISHERS